CLAS
IN M

MW00323492

Classical Traditions in Modern Fantasy

EDITED BY
BRETT M. ROGERS
AND
BENJAMIN ELDON STEVENS

OXFORD
UNIVERSITY PRESS

OXFORD
UNIVERSITY PRESS

Oxford University Press is a department of the University of Oxford. It furthers
the University's objective of excellence in research, scholarship, and education
by publishing worldwide. Oxford is a registered trade mark of Oxford University
Press in the UK and certain other countries.

Published in the United States of America by Oxford University Press
198 Madison Avenue, New York, NY 10016, United States of America.

Library of Congress Cataloging-in-Publication Data
Names: Rogers, Brett M., editor. | Stevens, Benjamin Eldon, editor.
Title: Classical traditions in modern fantasy / edited by Brett M. Rogers and
Benjamin Eldon Stevens.
Description: New York : Oxford University Press, 2017.
Identifiers: LCCN 2016027926 | ISBN 9780190610067 (pbk.) |
ISBN 9780190610050 (hardback)
Subjects: LCSH: Fantasy fiction—Classical influences. | Fantasy
fiction—History and criticism.
Classification: LCC PN3435 .C49 2017 | DDC 809/.915—dc23
LC record available at https://lccn.loc.gov/2016027926

1 3 5 7 9 8 6 4 2

Paperback printed by Webcom, Inc., Canada
Hardback printed by Bridgeport National Bindery, Inc., United States of America

Contents

Preface

Classical Traditions in Modern Fantasy is the second book to come out of our interest in how science fiction and fantasy—so important in modern literature, film, and other media—are deeply linked to Greco-Roman antiquity. In our first edited volume, *Classical Traditions in Science Fiction*, we argued that to read ancient classics and to read science fiction require similar suspensions of disbelief: similar acceptance of what we described, after literary theorist Darko Suvin, as textual worlds that are empirically and epistemologically different from the world as readers and authors know it. The present volume takes a similar approach to classics and fantasy. Its general assumption, discussed at some length in the Introduction, is that the fantastic represents an even greater difference from the world at hand: not simply an empirical or epistemological difference but a more complex and profoundly metaphysical one, in which the unreal becomes real and the impossible possible. The collected chapters suggest that fantasy's alterity—its requirement of belief in metaphysically different worlds—is powered in part by the genre's engagement with Greco-Roman antiquity.

Each contributor makes that suggestion with regard to particular texts and modifies it in his or her own peculiar way; even as they cohere, the chapters therefore both merit and reward individual consideration. In selecting the chapters we were able to consider a wide range of research, beginning with papers presented at a panel we organized for the 2012 annual meeting of the Pacific Ancient and Modern Languages Association in Seattle and extending to a directed call for papers the following year. We are pleased and honored to be able to present so much of that work for publication here. Diverse as its chapters are, the present volume is only a portal to an entire world of rapidly burgeoning scholarly interest in the topic. Many such pioneering works are naturally discussed throughout. It is a pleasure to be in this company, and one of our greatest hopes for the volume is that it helps inspire others to conduct their own exploration of this endlessly fascinating field.

It should be clear that we have many people to thank for helping make this work possible. Above all we are grateful to the contributors for sharing their work and for their energy and generosity over the course of the project. Special thanks are due to the team at Oxford, including Stefan Vranka, Editor for Ancient History, Archaeology, and Classical Studies; Editorial Assistants Sarah Svendsen and John Veranes; and Design (for the cover); and to the copyeditors and compositors without whose work this volume simply would not exist. Thanks are also due to Kris Kinsey and Special Collections in the University of Washington Libraries for help in obtaining the cover image, as well as to Krista Moll and Daniel Sealth Hill for their good humor and technical skill in capturing Dulac's *Argo* in all of its fantastic splendor.

Rogers would like to thank those students at the University of Puget Sound who have shared with him their infectious enthusiasm in talking about modern fantasy or Harry Potter, his colleagues in the department of Classics for their encouragement and support of this implausible work, and the University of Puget Sound for supporting the later stages of this project with a research leave during fall 2015. His deepest gratitude is owed to Jennifer for patiently enduring yet another series of late nights while he was lost in a neverwhere of frumious editing. He would like to dedicate his work on this volume to his daughter Elinor, who truly is a θαῦμα ἰδέσθαι.

Stevens would like to thank the students in his courses on under-worlds and afterlives at Bryn Mawr College and Trinity University for their adventurous explorations of imaginary places, and the Bryn Mawr Traditions Committee for casting—or simply identifying?—him as Puck in the *Midsummer Night's Dream*-themed May Day celebration in 2015. His work on the volume is dedicated to The Imaginary Gardeners, in the hope that it confirms their feeling that fantastical experiences do indeed have "real toads in them," and to his nephew Asher, whose first-ever visit to a bookstore led—with literature-professor uncle in tow—to a lovely hardcopy of Tolkien.

Contributors

Sarah Annes Brown Anglia Ruskin University

Sasha-Mae Eccleston Pomona College

Cecilie Flugt Danish Academy in Rome

Marcus Folch Columbia University

Genevieve S. Gessert American Academy in Rome

Robinson Peter Krämer Rheinische Friedrich-Wilhelms-Universität Bonn

Ayelet Haimson Lushkov University of Texas at Austin

Elizabeth A. Manwell Kalamazoo College

Jennifer A. Rea University of Florida

Brett M. Rogers University of Puget Sound

Benjamin Eldon Stevens Trinity University

Antonia Syson Purdue University

Jesse Weiner Hamilton College

Jeffrey T. Winkle Calvin College

Introduction: Fantasies of Antiquity

Brett M. Rogers and Benjamin Eldon Stevens

A TALE OF TWO HORACES; OR, FANTASY AND DISUNITY OF FORM

Once upon a time, the first and second editions of Horace Walpole's novel *The Castle of Otranto* (1764 [*Otranto*]) included the title pages below (Figures 0.1 and 0.2).

Some of the differences between these two editions merit attention for scholars and fans of both classical antiquity and modern fantasy. To begin with, the first edition offers the simple subtitle "A Story," whereas the second edition is subtitled "A Gothic Story." The addition of the adjective "Gothic" asserts a generic affiliation. What precisely 'Gothic' meant at the time and has meant since is beyond our scope here, but for our purposes, it is important to note that Gothic fiction is one of the feeder genres, and more recently subgenres, of a larger category that emerged in the eighteenth century: what Joseph Addison in 1712 called "the fairy way of writing" and what we now call—by way of an ancient Greek term for the faculty of imagination—'modern fantasy' (MF).[1]

In the context of MF, the second crucial difference between the two editions of *Otranto* lies in the second edition's inclusion of a quotation—two

---

[1] On Gothic and horror fiction more broadly, see Roberts (2012). See also Addison in Sandner (2004: 21–23). On the many meanings of Greek φαντασία, including 'image,' 'apparition,' and (the creative faculty of) 'imagination,' see Liddell, Scott, and Jones (1925 s.v. φαντασία, esp. 2a–c).

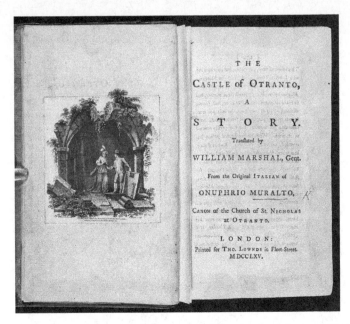

Figure 0.1 Title page to the first edition of *The Castle of Otranto* (1764). Credit: Public domain.

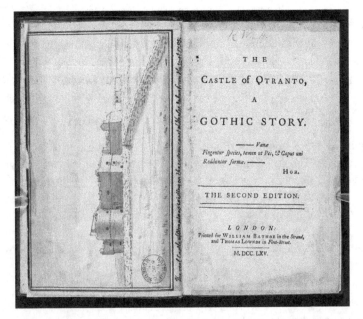

Figure 0.2 Title page to the second edition of *The Castle of Otranto* (1765), including quotation from Horace. Credit: Public domain.

partial lines and one full line of verse—attributed to "Hor." This refers to Quintus Horatius Flaccus, better known as Horace, a Roman poet of the first century BCE. The quotation derives from his *Ars Poetica* ("the Art of Poetry" [*AP*], c. 19 BCE), a treatise about which techniques work in poetry and which do not.[2] Enjoying the fact that one Horace is quoting another, we observe as well that the second edition of Walpole's novel asserts a link of some kind between MF and classical antiquity.[3] *Otranto* thus invites us to wonder about the nature and purpose of connections between the modern genre and materials drawn from the ancient world: it suggests that there is a case to be made for the study of classical traditions or classical receptions in MF.[4]

If a subtitle and a single quotation do not seem like much to go on, we can strengthen the case by looking more closely at what the modern Horace has quoted from his ancient Roman namesake: *vanae / fingentur species, tamen ut pes et caput uni / reddantur formae* ("empty appearances will be fashioned, but in such a way that foot and head are given to the same form"; *AP* 7–9).[5] In the *Ars Poetica*, Horace generally discusses what we might call 'unity of form.' In the quotation, from near the beginning of the poem, Horace is making the point that certain sorts of depiction or representation work well in the arts—not limited to poetry or writing, but including visual arts like painting—while others do not. At first glance, Walpole may seem to draw on that same aesthetic in *Otranto* by suggesting that certain "appearances" (*species*) will be depicted in a way that results in a "unified form" (*uni . . . formae*).

---

[2] For the *AP* see, e.g., Brink (2011) and Rudd (1990).

[3] Roberts (2012: 23–25) discusses the title page and reference to *AP*, but uses the third edition of *Otranto* (his Figure 1) and thus misses that the inclusion of the quotation dates to the second edition, which also includes Walpole's second preface offering a defense against critics. Roberts also does not observe that Walpole has changed Horace's Latin; see our discussion further, herein.

[4] 'Classical traditions' and 'classical receptions' offer different, if overlapping, images of how later authors and artists use ancient material: the study of 'traditions' focuses on something like a long-standing stream of thought flowing from antiquity; the study of 'receptions' emphasizes the complex and meaningful (mis)understandings of such material that are offered by later work. See recently, e.g., Grafton, Most, and Settis (2010), Hardwick and Stray (2008), Kallendorf (2007), Martindale and Thomas (2006), Hardwick (2003), and Highet (1949). In what follows, we also distinguish between 'classics,' meaning the ancient material itself, and 'Classics,' the modern field of study.

[5] The long history of translations of *AP* into English includes an influential version by Ben Jonson published in 1640, which renders our lines as follows: "shapes, like sick-mens dreames, are fain'd so vaine, / As neither head, nor foot, one forme retaine" (his lines 9–10); see Moul (2007).

But there is a wrinkle: Walpole has quoted—or at least the publishers, William Bathoe and Thomas Lownds, have printed—a version of Horace's lines that differs in crucial details from how they have been transmitted from antiquity and are usually printed by modern editors. Ancient Horace actually writes: *vanae / fingentur species, ut nec pes nec caput uni / reddatur formae.* The differences may seem slight—Horace's *ut nec . . . nec . . . reddatur* instead of Walpole's *tamen ut . . . et . . . reddantur*— but make for a significantly different meaning. As opposed to Walpole's meaning—"empty appearances will be fashioned, but in such a way that foot and head are given to the same form"—Horace's lines translate to "empty appearances will be fashioned, such that neither a foot nor a head is given to the same form."

In other words, what ancient Horace means here, and what distinguishes his point from Walpole's, is that a mishmash of forms makes for unsuccessful works of art. Horace's first example in the *Ars Poetica*, which comes from painting, is a particularly striking one for students of fantasy: "If a painter should wish to join a horse's neck to a human head and attach multicolored feathers to limbs brought together from every source . . ." (*humano capiti cervicem pictor equinam / iungere si velit et varias inducere plumas / undique collatis membris*; 1–3). For Horace, this is a hypothetical image of an unsuccessful work of art: a monstrosity marked by 'disunity of form.' Returned to their original context, these lines are thus not meant to suggest that *vanae species* can be brought into unity, but rather that such "empty appearances" cannot be brought into unity and therefore ought to be avoided in art.

Given both Horace's original words and their context, the version of Horace quoted by Walpole's second edition represents a seemingly conscious departure from the ideas expressed in the *Ars Poetica*.[6] The second edition of *Otranto* also included a new preface, in which Walpole defends his work against critics: in that context, it seems safe to call his departure deliberate and to identify it as part of a larger, unified defense. The Gothic genre, at least in works like *Otranto*, may therefore be read as imagining

---

[6] The manuscript tradition does not seem to show any variant readings for *ut nec pes nec caput*. *Fingentur*, the preferred reading for that verb here, is given thus in one branch of the tradition, while others give variants including *finguntur* (the present tense, "are fashioned") and *funguntur* (a misuse of a verb meaning 'to make use of'); see Brink (2011: 55, with discussion of the tradition at 1–51). In this context, the modifications in Walpole's quotation seem deliberate.

itself as having to do precisely with the sort of multiplicity or 'disunity of form' denigrated by Horace. It might not be too much to say that the Gothic, and by extension MF, represents a sort of artistic monstrosity— a celebration of 'disunity'—that an ancient reader of Horace's ilk would have disliked.

Such dislike would not have been due to surprise or lack of recognition; on the contrary, it seems rather that Horace anticipated the sort of thing Walpole got up to and, furthermore, would have had real ancient examples—not just his hypothetical painting—in mind. Nor was ancient Horace alone in his distaste for 'formal disunity,' as many other classical Greek and Roman authors show similar concerns about such disunity or hybridity. For example, the Roman poet Lucretius, writing a generation earlier than Horace, inveighs against the physical impossibility of hybrid creatures made from "discordant limbs" (*discordia membra*), like centaurs—half-human, half-horse—and the dog-like Scylla (*De rerum natura* [DRN] 5.878–898).[7] Lucretius has certain philosophical arguments in mind, but for our purposes, he may be regarded as following a long-standing tradition of criticizing hybridity as a particular example of a more general 'problem': the perception that the arts depict certain things implausibly or impossibly. One strain in that critical tradition is concerned with how poetry, especially epic poetry, portrays the gods and the supernatural. Thus Plato identifies "an ancient quarrel between philosophy and poetry" (παλαιὰ μέν τις διαφορὰ φιλοσοφίᾳ τε καὶ ποιητικῇ; *Republic* [*Rep.*] 607b5-6) in part for how the Homeric epics, the *Iliad* (*Il.*) and the *Odyssey* (*Od.*), show the gods engaging in unethical behavior. Although we should take the famously ironical Plato's statement with a grain of salt, in his view such depictions are artistically indecorous and ethically irresponsible because they are metaphysically impossible: gods, who by definition must be embodiments of good, are not able to act badly.[8] Similarly, later ancient readers report criticism of Virgil, the Roman successor to Homer, for what were perceived to be certain lapses

---

[7] On *discordia membra* in Lucretius and concerns about formal disunity in Mary Shelley's *Frankenstein*, see Weiner (2015: esp. 52–53). On ancient monsters and hybrids more generally, see, e.g., Felton (2012), Gilmore (2003), Atherton (1998), and duBois (1982).

[8] For this basic reason, Plato argues that imitative poetry would need to be excluded from a political state ideally configured to foster philosophy. For an emerging modern SF-*cum*-MF take on *Rep.*, see Jo Walton's *The Just City* (2014; with Stevens [2015b]) and *The Philosopher Kings* (2015).

of plausibility in his *Aeneid*, as for example when the Trojans' ships are saved from burning by being miraculously transformed into Nereids or sea-nymphs (9.77–122).[9]

There is thus no shortage of ancient examples of formal disunity or deeper metaphysical implausibility or impossibility, nor of readers who recognized—and could criticize—them as such already in Greco-Roman antiquity. But the reverse is also true: as Walpole reminds us in the preface to the second edition of *Otranto*, in which he claims to have composed the novel as "an attempt to blend the two kinds of romance, the ancient and the modern," the ancient world included other authors and audiences who seem to have enjoyed the implausible and the impossible. For example, in Plato's *Phaedrus*, Socrates criticizes and therefore points to the existence of people in classical Athens who devoted attention to understanding "multitudes of other impossible things and the extraordinary natures of portentous creatures" (ἄλλων ἀμηχάνων πλήθη τε καὶ ἀτοπίαι τερατολόγων τινῶν φύσεων; 229e1–2), such as chimaeras, gorgons, and pegasi. Socrates dismisses such attention as a poor use of time unless someone has the leisure (πολλῆς αὐτῷ σχολῆς; e3) to make sense of such stories in accordance with probability (κατὰ τὸ εἰκός; e2), and thus seems to divide audiences into two kinds: those who have time for 'the improbable' and those who (wisely?) prefer the 'probable.'[10]

We may therefore conclude that ancient readers who preferred 'formal unity' and 'the probable'—such as Horace, Lucretius, and Plato—formed only one among several kinds of readership in Greco-Roman antiquity. Another kind of reader, representing another tradition of reading, seems to have found aesthetic value or, at least, pleasure in works of art allowing formal disunity and the deeper metaphysical implausibilities or

---

[9] E.g., Servius mentions this scene, among others, as being objected to by readers "because it is worthy of condemnation when a poet invents the sort of thing that departs entirely from the truth" (*vituperabile enim est, poetam aliquid fingere, quod penitus a veritate discedat*; 3.46); Servius uses the same verb, *fingere*, as Horace does in *AP*. On the scene, see, e.g., Fantham (1990), Hardie (1987), and Hathaway (1968: 109–132); on the marvelous in Virgil, see further, e.g., Biow (1996: 13–36) and Williams (1967). Such criticism could yet be applied with a light touch: Servius acknowledges that "poets frequently vary fables" (*frequenter ... variant fabulas poetae*; 6.617); for Servius on 'poetic license,' see Zeeman (1996: esp. 162 and 171) and generally Kaster (1988: 169–197).

[10] Cf. Sandner (2004: 14–16) and Hume (1984). The notion that 'probability' (τὸ εἰκός) is important in poetic composition is found as early as Aristotle's *Poetics* 1451a12 and 1456a24–25; cf. 1454a24–26 (on 'plausibility' in character) and 1460b22–26 (on 'impossibilities' as a fault).

impossibilities such 'discordant limbs' can connote. For our purposes, what matters most is that this complex situation in antiquity is reflected in MF's equally complex manner of engagement with ancient sources. Having led us to this point, the value of a work like *Otranto* should be clear. Walpole's invocation of one particular, long-standing aesthetic tradition—his near-quotation of Horace's *Ars Poetica*—is deliberately playful enough to challenge that tradition's tastes and tenets by simultaneously invoking another ancient tradition (romance) whose standards and practices are quite different. In this way, an early example of the modern genre provides a first suggestion of the complex narrative constituting the reception of classical antiquity in MF.

DEFINING MODERN FANTASY: IMPOSSIBILITY AND CLASSICAL ANTIQUITY

Beyond provoking the ancient Horace's ire while delighting the modern Horace, our narrative brings us closer to a definition of fantasy that is, perhaps surprisingly, as applicable to certain ancient materials as it is to modern works like Walpole's novel and its successors. In *The Encyclopedia of Fantasy*, co-editor John Clute offers this definition: "A fantasy text is a self-coherent narrative. When set in this world, it tells a story which is impossible in the world as we perceive it . . .; when set in an otherworld, that otherworld will be impossible, though stories set there may be possible in its terms."[11] As we continue to investigate connections between MF and Greco-Roman classics, the most salient part of the definition here is the phrase "impossible in the world as we perceive it." Clute expands on that phrase as follows, under the subheading 'Perceive as impossible':

Before the beginning of the scientific revolution in Western Europe in the 16th century, most Western literature contained huge amounts of material 20th-century readers would think of as fantastical. It is, however, no simple matter to determine the degree to which early writers distinguished, before the rise of science, between what we would call fantastical and what we would call realistic. Nor is it possible with any certainty to determine how much various early writers perceived stories which adhered to possible

---

[11] Clute and Grant (1997: 338).

events and stories which did not as being different. There is no easy division between realism and the fantastical in writers before 1600 or so, and no genre of written literature, before about the early 19th century, seems to have been constituted so as deliberately to confront or contradict the "real." Though fantasy certainly existed for many centuries before, whenever stories were told which were understood by their authors (and readers) as being impossible, it is quite something else to suggest that the perceived impossibility of these stories was their point—that they stood as a counter-statement to a dominant worldview.

In this expanded definition, Clute summarizes a case for limiting the application of 'fantasy' as a description of a 'structure,' genre, or mode to materials dating from the 1600s (or early 1800s?) and later.[12] His main argument is that it is difficult to tell whether—and if so to what degree— works from "[b]efore the beginning of the scientific revolution" are "deliberately" or purposefully fantastic. Granted that "huge amounts of [such] material" would be thought of as 'fantastical,' for Clute it remains an open question whether it was therefore "their point" to stand "as a counter-statement to a dominant worldview" or to offer an alternative to realism in the arts.

It should be clear that any such open question is in fact answered by ancient examples like those discussed above. First, although it is indeed difficult to find evidence definitively proving that a given author or artist intended his or her work "deliberately to confront or contradict the 'real,'" there is plenty of evidence that is strongly suggestive of such intent, including the works of Apuleius, Lucian, Apollonius of Rhodes, and Homer (most notably, Odysseus' *apologoi* or so-called 'lying tales' in *Od.* 9–12). Second, and even more important, is the fact that we have examples already showing that "the perceived impossibility of [certain] stories" was recognized, and criticized as such, by at least some ancient readers (such as Plato's Socrates, discussed above). Taking these two points together, it is hard to see how the descriptive term 'fantasy' could meaningfully be denied to certain works of ancient literature. Readers

---

[12] The case for limiting 'fantasy' to the modern period is not made in the *Encyclopedia*: the entry for "History of fantasy" simply points to the entry for "Fantasy," where discussion of history is limited to the paragraph quoted in the text just above and to some comments on whether 'fantasy' as a critical term allows, but may not encourage, the inclusion of "much of 20th-century literature." Cf. the suggestive chronology in James and Mendlesohn (2012: xv–xxiv).

like Horace, Lucretius, Plato, and Servius—and by extension, authors like Homer, Virgil, Ovid, Lucian, and others—should indeed be considered "early writers [who] perceived stories which adhered to possible events and stories which did not as being different" from each other. This consideration gets us quite close to showing the 'deliberate' or 'conscious' practice in antiquity of a mode of fantasy in the precise sense of a mode of impossibility.

In other words, it is clear that 'fantasy' or 'the fantastical' not only existed prior to the scientific revolution or Gothic fiction but also was recognized as such—that is, recognized as representing a mode of impossibility or implausibility, in contradiction to reality or artistic realism. We may therefore say that the characteristic mode of MF's 'fiction' (a word derived from the same root as Horace's *fingentur*, 'to fashion or invent') is a departure from aesthetic standards promulgated by a select few classical readers (e.g., Plato, Aristotle, and Horace). Although the nature and manner of that departure remains to be explored much further, nonetheless this single example—Walpole's quotation of Horace—has already invited us to consider how MF is modern in part by being purposefully post-classical: MF is what it is in part because of its relationship to the classical tradition and its role as a site for classical receptions. Accepting this invitation, we may start to develop a theory for the study of classical traditions—and classical receptions—in modern fantasy.

THEORIZING RECEPTION: PROMETHEAN SCIENCE FICTION AND PROTEAN FANTASY

What might such a theory look like? In our previous collection, *Classical Traditions in Science Fiction*, we began developing a theory for the study of that subject by discussing a starting-point for modern science fiction (SF), Mary Shelley's *Frankenstein* (1818).[13] Discussing *Frankenstein* allowed us to note how closely linked SF is to ancient classics—how rich an area it is for classical receptions—thanks in part to Shelley's self-conscious nod to the classical tradition in the form of the novel's subtitle, "The Modern Prometheus." With that subtitle, Shelley intends for her aggressively modern scientist-antihero to be understood in relation to,

[13] Rogers and Stevens (2015: 1–6).

among other things, the Titan from ancient Greek myth who stole fire from the gods and gave it to humankind, leading to consequences for all, including introducing the artificial being—and first human woman— Pandora.[14] With fire understood as a symbol for technology, Shelley invites us to think of SF as a 'Promethean' genre or mode, interested in how 'technology'—in the broad, Heideggerian sense of any process that transforms unknown 'natural' materials into knowable 'cultural' products—helps define the human condition.[15] Since in some versions of the ancient myth Prometheus was not just a technology-giver but also a life-giver who provided humankind with its animating 'divine spark,' thinking of SF as a Promethean mode bears directly on the question of what it means to be human. From this perspective, *Frankenstein* exemplifies how SF, the genre perhaps most characteristic of the modern world, helps raise such urgent questions today in part by looking back to the philosophy, myth, literature, history, and art of the ancient Greek and Roman worlds.[16]

Constructing a parallel theory for the study of classical receptions in MF involves some complications that may, however, lead to a potentially illuminating image from classical antiquity.[17] First, if there is debate

---

[14] On Prometheus, see, e.g., Hesiod *Theogony* 507–616 and *Works and Days* 42–105 (both including accounts of Pandora's creation), Aeschylus *Prometheus Bound*, Plato *Protagoras* 320c–22a, Ovid *Metamorphoses* (1.76–88); see also Gantz (1993: i.152–66), Dougherty (2005), and Podlecki (2005).

[15] Cf. fire's connection to and identification as another god related to *technê*, Hephaestus (Lat. Vulcan), as in, e.g., *Il.* 2.426 and Aeschylus *Agamemnon* 280–316. For Heideggerian 'technology,' see his (1977 [1954]); cf. Barthes (1972 [1957]: 129) on how "myth today" obscures contingency by changing "history into nature."

[16] For *Frankenstein*'s classical receptions, see, e.g., Small (1973: 48–67), Dougherty (2005: 108–114), and Weiner (2015). On classical traditions in SF, see the essays in Rogers and Stevens (2015), Gloyn (2015), Bost-Fiévet and Provini (2014, esp. the editors' introductory chapters), and Brown (2008).

[17] We are not the first to borrow an image from classical antiquity in constructing a theory related to MF. Notably, Bloom (1982) borrows the notion of the *clinamen*, 'swerve,' from *DRN* as an "opening Lucretian swerve of a theory of literary fantasy," although his subsequent discussion develops instead, via Freudian psychoanalysis, the image of the Ovidian Narcissus in his reading of David Lindsay's *A Voyage to Arcturus* (1920). Indeed Lucretius' *clinamen* does not seem central to Bloom's theoretical model, and thus he does not refute Homer's Menelaus, who promises in his fantastic tale "not to speak in a swerving fashion" (οὐκ ἂν ἐγώ γε / ἄλλα παρὲξ εἴποιμι παρακλίδον; *Od.* 4.347–348). On the other hand, Bloom's formulation of 'fantasy' may have some interest for classical reception studies: "fantasy, as a belated version of romance, promises an absolute freedom from belatedness, from the anxieties of literary influence and origination, yet this promise is shadowed always by

surrounding *Frankenstein's* status as inaugurating SF, it is even more difficult to identify a corresponding starting-point for MF, whose roots and branches are if anything more varied.[18] This literary-historical difficulty is related to the question, discussed above, of how 'fantasy' is to be defined, with scholarship having reached no real consensus.[19] For example, the editors of *The Cambridge Companion to Fantasy Literature*, Edward James and Farah Mendlesohn, develop their working definition of MF by noting that, although "[t]he major theorists in the field ... all agree that fantasy is about the construction of the impossible whereas science fiction may be about the unlikely," "critics" as well as other readers "quickly depart" from each other.[20] In emphasizing "the construction of the impossible," James and Mendlesohn may be seen to draw on the definition offered by Clute in *The Encyclopedia of Fantasy*, discussed previously. To describe the situation, they follow Clute further by drawing on Brian Attebery's use of the mathematical concept of a 'fuzzy set': if MF is centered around "stories which share tropes of the completely impossible," it also includes "stories which include only a small number of tropes, or which construct those tropes in such a way as to leave doubt in the reader's mind as to whether what they have read is fantastical or not."[21] Given this sort of open-definitional discussion, it seems that fantasy studies may still be at a stage where each definition depends on the individual's preferred set of texts.[22]

---

a psychic over-determination in the form itself of fantasy, that puts the stance of freedom into severe question" (6). On fantasy and romance, see the chapters of Weiner and Lushkov (both this volume); on freedom, see Rea (this volume).

[18] *Otranto* is perhaps not a serious contender, although, as Roberts notes, "almost all scholars of the Gothic agree ... that it was this short novel ... which initiated the late eighteenth-century vogue for Gothic fiction" (2012: 23).

[19] This is not to say that SF has been defined to everyone's satisfaction; Clute (in Clute and Grant [1997: 338]) usefully contrasts MF's focus on "impossibility" with the idea that "sf tales are written and read on the presumption that they are possible—if perhaps not yet." We might add, "or not any longer," to account for and include tales that were intended to be SF but are now judged fantastical. See also Rogers and Stevens (2015: 5–11) with sources cited there.

[20] (2012: 1). The "theorists" named by James and Mendlesohn are Todorov (1973), Manlove (1975), Irwin (1976), Jackson (1981), and Hume (1984); to this list we would add Propp (1968 [1958]), Attebery (1992; cf. his 2014), Sandner (2004), and Mendlesohn (2008).

[21] James and Mendlesohn (2012: 1). Attebery describes fantasy as a fuzzy set at (1992: 12).

[22] For further discussion of this problem, see "Outline of the Volume" in this Introduction. See also Mendlesohn (2008: esp. xiii–xxv), who articulates the rhetorical strategies used in various works of modern fantasy.

Strikingly, however, this complicated situation affecting the study of MF includes a recurrent critical term derived from classical antiquity, a term that allows us to suggest a possible framework for theorizing classical traditions in MF that would be meaningfully parallel to 'Promethean' SF. For when it comes to characterizing the 'fuzziness' of the 'set' comprised by MF, more than one influential scholar has invoked the term 'protean.' Meaning 'metamorphic,' 'fluid,' or 'of no fixed form,' the term 'protean' derives from the ancient Greek figure of Proteus, an 'Old Man of the Sea' said to reveal truths to anyone who can wrestle him to a standstill—a near-impossibility since he continually changes his form (e.g., becoming animals) and substance (e.g., becoming fire or water).[23] The 'protean' qualities of MF may already be clear from the preceding discussion.

Moreover, although there is no single starting-point to MF that proclaims the genre's protean status—no inaugural text analogous to Shelley's *Frankenstein* and subtitled "The Modern Proteus"—the term recurs in scholarship. For example, Adam Roberts writes of "the *protean* force of the Gothic novel," a genre that we have seen identified as an important precursor to MF.[24] For Roberts, that quality is emblematized by 'monsters' like vampires, werewolves, and Stevenson's Mr. Hyde—that is, creatures who have the "*protean* ability to transform, to move from unexceptional 'human' behaviour to barbaric, violent, transgressive, and unfettered."[25] In a way similar to such fantastic monsters, the fantasy genre itself—or at least subgenres such as Gothic or horror—seems transformational, transgressive, indeed protean.

---

[23] Proteus first appears in literature in *Od.*, where he uses every "crafty trick" (δολίης... τέχνης; 4.455) to escape the hero Menelaus, including transformations into a bearded lion, serpent, leopard, massive boar, water, and a lofty tree (4.456–458); see also Gantz (1993: ii.575, 663–664), and esp. Baumbach (2013), for whom Proteus becomes symbolic of multivalent interpretations of the Homeric text itself. Note that in the passage from *Od.*, shape-shifting is considered a *technê*, offering an interesting parallel to Promethean SF. The term 'protean' also appears in SF criticism: e.g., Darko Suvin in his seminal study writes of his approach as being motivated by "the pleasing blend of protean formal-cum-substantial process identified by the ... metaphor of metamorphosis" (1979: xv). 'Protean' has also been applied to the study of classics; e.g., Kallendorf (2015).

[24] Roberts (2012: 31, emphasis added). Furthering the protean imagery in other terminology, Roberts suggests that the Gothic novel is thus "a *form* capable of being associated with supernatural excess, but one that proved easily capable of *assuming the shape* of mundane Victorian domestic fiction" (emphases added) .

[25] Ibid. (2012: 31, emphasis added).

These metamorphic qualities have seemed characteristic of MF more broadly, not limited to Gothic. For example, W. A. Senior identifies the same quality in a different subgenre, the quest fantasy: "[f]ar from a rigid formula, the quest fantasy is characterized by its *protean* quality, its ability to subsume and reflect varied purposes and narratives through the medium of Story."[26] Here Senior makes explicit what Roberts implies: the genre is felt to be just as protean, in terms of its structures and modes, as the creatures it represents are protean in their bodies and moods. This "protean quality"—or "force" or "ability"—in the stories is, then, repeatedly offered as the reason for the genre's resistance to definition. A final example serves to emphasize that this has been, and may productively be, applied to the genre as a whole. In an influential contribution to scholarship on MF, Rosemary Jackson, addressing the question of why MF has seemed to lack a coherent history, writes: "It seems appropriate that such a *protean* form has so successfully resisted generic classification."[27]

For these scholars and others, then, MF seems to be a profoundly protean form indeed. Not only does it routinely feature characters that change their shapes and moods, and rely on settings that cross impossible physical boundaries, but MF is also transgressive in itself, mixing narrative modes and making 'fuzzy' the metaphysical boundaries between what is real or possible and what is implausible, impossible, or, in a word, fantastic. We should acknowledge here that there is a risk of mistaking a fuzziness in analysis for the fuzziness of the thing being analyzed—mistaking our own failure to understand the genre for the genre's intrinsic resistance to being understood. In other words, and to resume the image of ancient Proteus, this would be the equivalent of failing to wrestle the genre to a standstill in fact, and believing that we have thus shown that it cannot be bested even in theory. The great potential value of the critical trope should nevertheless be clear: if MF is rightly identified as a protean mode, in parallel to SF as a Promethean one, its shape—or shape-shifting—and significance will be clarified by considering its close historical links to classical traditions and its continuing status as a rich site for classical receptions.

---

[26] Senior (2012: 199, emphasis added).

[27] Jackson (1981: 13, emphasis added), after Irwin (1976: x) and Rabkin (1976: 118). Jackson also engages in a bit of classical reception by briskly deriving the term 'fantastic' from Latin *phantasticus*, although she erroneously claims *phantasticus* derives from the (nonsensical) Greek term φανζαστικός (sic); compare n. 1 herein.

As a final illustration of this possibility, and by way of rounding out this Introduction, we note that thinking of MF as protean is a good description of—and possibly a historical justification for—the sort of 'disunity of form' we have seen mark Walpole's *Otranto* in deliberate contrast to the 'unity of form' advanced by the author of his epigraph, the ancient Roman Horace, in the *Ars Poetica*. It is perhaps no more than a coincidence, albeit a serendipitous one, that Walpole also helped bring to publication Erich Rudolf Raspe's *Critical Essay on Oil Painting* (1781), which featured Raspe's own motto derived from the programmatic opening lines of that most protean of Roman epic poems, Ovid's *Metamorphoses*: *In nova fert animus mutatas dicere formas* (*corpora*, continues Ovid: "My mind leads me to speak of forms changed into new [bodies]"; 1.1–2).[28] This may seem tangential, and its connection to MF tenuous.[29] But the links are suggestive, anticipating further developments still: for Raspe is doubtless better known as the author of *Baron Munchausen's Narratives of His Marvelous Travels and Campaigns in Russia* (1785), a fantastical and protean text if ever there was one. Thus in the wake of Walpole in the eighteenth century, there emerge still more forms changed into new fantasies, similarly animated by ancient notions of the impossible.

OUTLINE OF THE VOLUME

In the preceding sections of this Introduction, we have pointed to some ways in which the study of classical receptions in MF might proceed. Tracing links among texts, subgenres, and authors, and considering especially the possibility of MF being a protean mode, we have intended mainly to help articulate perennially open questions more precisely. The same intention guides this volume as a whole and is reflected in the selection of topics. Even as the chapters cover a wide range of texts representative of MF, all together they are deliberately less definitive than exploratory. What light do classical receptions shed on MF and vice

---

[28] Discussed in Carswell (1948: xxiv–xxv): "it was Walpole who saw it through the press, even though Raspe's name remained on the title page with his motto."

[29] To strengthen the connection, we could consider the role played by Ovid's poem, over centuries, as inspiration and sourcebook for countlessly many fantastical works of art; see, e.g., Brown (2002) and many of the essays in Gildenhard and Zissos (2013).

versa? What relationships do 'canonical' or well-known MF works have to antiquity, and do other, 'non-canonical' MF works have other types of relationships to ancient material? What could or should count as MF, and how might materials from classical antiquity help shape our approach to that question? By grappling with these and other, related topics in their own ways, the chapters collected herein offer not a single, unitary vision but a diverse range of approaches to the emerging study of classical traditions in modern fantasy.

The chapters are organized thematically. Like this Introduction, the chapters in Part I, "Classical Apparitions in (Pre-)Modern Fantasy," point to some of the fundamental ways ancient materials appear in—or haunt—the early stages of MF. Discussing examples of what we might call the prehistory of the genre or indeed 'pre-modern fantasy,' these four chapters emphasize that fantasy is indeed 'older than it may seem.' In particular, connections between Greco-Roman antiquity and MF are not limited to certain tropes, motifs, or images, but run deeply enough that similar theories of interpretation, similar ways of reading, are richly applicable to both areas. From this perspective, MF has not so much a linear history, including a simple classical tradition, as multiple histories that must be regarded as constituting complex 'fuzzy sets,' indeed, drawing on sources from a wide range of time-periods and types. Of course, a purpose of this volume is to justify a larger role for the ancient Greco-Roman world in particular.

That justification begins with fairly global questions about genre and reception through a focus on one of the most important current works in modern fantasy, George R. R. Martin's *A Song of Ice and Fire* (1996–). Anticipating many of the concerns in later chapters, Jesse Weiner ("Classical Epic and the Poetics of Modern Fantasy") draws particular attention to the ancient epic form by exploring some of the theoretical consequences of the common idea that modern high fantasy is 'epic in prose.' Detailing how *A Song of Ice and Fire* fits aesthetic guidelines developed in Aristotle's *Poetics*, Weiner argues that modern high fantasy—for many readers, the very paradigm of the modern genre—shares not only many of the superficial tropes of ancient heroic epic but also, and perhaps more importantly, some of its deeper aesthetic values. In the second chapter, Cecilie Flugt ("Theorizing Fantasy: Enchantment, Parody, and the Classical Tradition") shifts from ancient poetics to more recent theories of 'fantasy,' seeking to move beyond a traditional view of MF as having to do mainly with 'enchantment.' Recognizing how that slippery literary concept—and readers' experience—plays an important role, Flugt argues that modern works owe as much to ancient Greco-Roman examples of the parodic, such as Lucian's *True History* (second century CE), as they do to the enchanting or magical features of more commonly cited precursors such as medieval romances and Germanic fairy tales.

Next, Genevieve S. Gessert ("The Mirror Crack'd: Fractured Classicisms in The Pre-Raphaelites and Victorian Illustration") examines how Pre-Raphaelite artists and subsequent Victorian illustrators (especially Henry Justice Ford) incorporated the 'classical' into the development of what became MF's dominant visual style, seemingly 'medieval' but really a hybridization of the 'medieval' and the 'classical.' In asking how we look at periodization in the visual arts, Gessert affects how we understand MF narrative, since the illustrations she considers helped inspire such enormously influential authors as Tolkien and Lewis. In the final chapter of Part I, Robinson Peter Krämer ("Classical Antiquity and the Timeless Horrors of H. P. Lovecraft") reminds us of the importance of a closely related genre, horror, by surveying classical materials in Lovecraft, not only in his 'weird fiction' but also in documentary evidence regarding his life and education. Discussing Lovecraft's use of ancient languages, classical quotations, and repeated motifs, Krämer argues that such elements from Greek and Roman literature play a large role in establishing Lovecraft's trademark atmosphere of fantastically terrifying sublimity and timeless horror.

Several of the topics in the first four chapters—Weiner's focus on 'epic,' Flugt's interest in 'enchantment,' Gessert's examination of influential visual art, and Krämer's attention to a pioneering early author—combine to prepare us for the subjects of Part II, perhaps the two single most influential authors in MF: J. R. R. Tolkien and C. S. Lewis. Both were inspired by visual art like that found in Andrew Lang's *Fairy Book* series—Lewis famously attributes the original inspiration behind Narnia to his vision of a lone lamp-post in a snow-covered field, while Tolkien himself was a prolific illustrator of Middle-earth—and deeply interested in literary enchantments. Tolkien and Lewis have exerted a powerful influence on MF to this day and thus merit careful attention. In combination with authors like Lovecraft, they show—not only in their fictions but also in their own critical work and correspondence—that MF's deep connection to earlier periods is no accident, but is rather the result of deliberate cultivation. This fact should complicate any image of the genre as being simply 'modern.'

Building on the work of Part I, then, the chapters in Part II, "False Medievalism and Other Ancient Fantasies," examine an earlier period of particular importance to MF—namely, the medieval world, or, rather, visions of the medieval that are meaningful despite—or because of—not being historically accurate. These have been called 'false medievalism' after Lewis, who famously applied the phrase to MF's frequent dependence on an ahistorical, nineteenth-century Romantic image of chivalric Europe. For our purposes, the most important consequence of MF's emphasis on medievalism, whether true or false, has been to obscure the deep wellspring of Greco-Roman influences flowing through the genre, both on their own and in conjunction with the medieval. Suggesting ways of redressing that imbalance, the chapters in Part II examine several MF texts that feature a host of characters, icons, themes, and images that are 'other than they seem,' that readers often misperceive as simply medieval in origin, but in fact more complexly reflect even more ancient sources.

Benjamin Eldon Stevens ("Ancient Underworlds in J. R. R. Tolkien's *The Hobbit*") examines how Tolkien's novel revises the ancient motif of the journey into the underworld, focusing on Bilbo's encounters with Gollum and Smaug. Drawing on Tolkien's own statements about the effects produced by ancient and medieval literature, Stevens argues that *The Hobbit* consciously draws on—and departs from—ancient images of the underworld to emphasize themes of forgetting and thus achieve Tolkien's preferred melancholic "impression of depth." The next two chapters address the work of Tolkien's colleague, friend, and fellow Inkling, the likewise beloved and influential C. S. Lewis. Jeffrey T. Winkle ("C. S. Lewis's *The Voyage of the "Dawn Treader"* and Apuleius' *Metamorphoses*") examines the ancient narrative and philosophical traditions that provided thematic and theological foundations for Lewis's work. In comparing the many similarities between Apuleius' narrator Lucius (transformed into an ass) and Lewis's character Eustace Scrubb (transformed into a dragon), Winkle argues that both characters are 'Platonic sinners,' rendered and allowed to develop in accordance with neo-Platonic morality and imagery that bridges classical and medieval worlds. The final chapter of Part II maintains a focus on Lewis while offering the volume's most direct observation as to how MF's medievalism is complicated by the classical. Focusing on Lewis's retelling of the ancient myth of Cupid and

Psyche, Marcus Folch ("A Time for Fantasy: Retelling Apuleius in C. S. Lewis's *Till We Have Faces*") argues that Lewis himself problematizes the privileged position occupied by the medieval in MF's evocations of space and time by deliberately contrasting it to classical models. In Folch's reading, Lewis's imagined world changes from realistic to fantastic, becoming infused with supernatural presence, precisely when medieval structures are replaced by the classical.

Raising different versions of the question most central to this volume—"What, if anything, has the classical contributed to fantasy?"—the chapters in Parts I and II invite us not only to think diachronically, in terms of the influence of classical traditions on MF, but also to imagine how influence might flow in the reverse direction. How might the study of MF clarify our understanding of classical texts in their turn? Here is one of the highest potential values of classical reception studies, which serves to invite serious reconsiderations of ancient material in response to how that material has been 'strongly mistaken,' not in scholarship but in other literature and art. The chapters in the second half of the volume thus consider versions of that possibility by plunging more deeply into two notable estuaries for ancient classics and MF: in Part III, texts centering on children and monsters— that is, those whose bodies, changing in form and meaning, occupy humanity's imaginative margins and thus have the capacity to critique authority and subvert dominant ideology; and in Part IV, alternate histories, likewise suggesting critical readings of the world as we know it. These two protean aspects of the modern genre are richly suggestive of how much we might transform the shape of our own understanding of ancient materials as well.

MF has often been accused of being a form of 'children's literature,' and it is certainly true that MF often features children and fantastical creatures, whether as protagonists, helpers, or terrible forces to be overcome. Like much of recent scholarship, however, the chapters in Part III, "Children and (Other) Ancient Monsters" treat this aspect of MF rather as a source of interest and strength. Offering ways of understanding which particular roles ancient classics have played in relation to the genre's overlapping images of the young and the inhuman, these chapters contribute to the burgeoning argument that children's literature is not (only) for children: its sophisticated capacity to subvert authority is not limited to the present moment but should invite us to question both our relationship to traditions—including the classical tradition—and our capacity for inventive receptions.

In the first chapter, Sarah Annes Brown ("The Classical Pantheon in Children's Fantasy Literature") examines the relative absence of Greco-Roman mythology—as opposed to Norse and Celtic mythology—in MF by tracking perceptions of classical myth in children's literature. Surveying a wide range of examples—including E. Nesbit, Diana Wynne Jones, Rick Riordan, and Marie Phillips—Brown argues that children's literature and literature about children reveal a conspicuous preoccupation with and antipathy towards the authority of both the Greek gods and the classical tradition itself. An interest in authority also appears in Brett M. Rogers's chapter ("Orestes and the Half-Blood Prince: Ghosts of Aeschylus in the *Harry Potter* Series"). Exploring the unexpected quotation from *Libation Bearers* in *Deathly Hallows*, as well as a likely 'ghosting' of Aeschylus in *Half-Blood Prince*, Rogers argues that Rowling's depictions of Voldemort as a tyrant, and of schoolchildren responding to tyranny, draw on and revise Aeschylean ideas about education and kinship. The *Harry Potter* novels treat schools as objects of scrutiny and emphasize the processes of both learning and unlearning knowledge.

Similar questions about knowledge in fantastic literature are raised by Antonia Syson ("Filthy Harpies and Fictive Knowledge in Philip Pullman's *His Dark Materials* Trilogy"). Focusing on the harpies—their responses to Lyra's storytelling in *The Amber Spyglass* and their changing role throughout *His Dark Materials*—Syson argues that Pullman offers a critique of modern fantasy that destabilizes several binary oppositions. In their place, Pullman articulates two kinds of 'fictive knowledge,' one that expands knowledge and another that distorts experience. In the final chapter of Part III, Elizabeth Manwell ("Girls in Bears' Clothing in Greek Myth and Disney/Pixar's *Brave*") examines the nonconformist princess Merida and her mother, Elinor, within the larger context of fantastic tales about bear transformations, including Greek myths. Exploring how such tales could have been used to reinforce the mother–daughter relationship during a girl's transition into adulthood, Manwell suggests that the comparison with *Brave* may offer insight into ancient Greek rites like the Arkteia and Brauronia.

Offering a further variation on MF's fundamental theme of alterity—its capacity for suggesting changes both physical and metaphysical or epistemological—the chapters in Part IV, "(Post)Modern Fantasies of

Antiquity," focus on ways in which some of the genre's most transformative understandings of the (post)modern have been made possible by ancient materials. In subject matter, too, these three chapters cohere by making explicit a potential only implicit in the materials discussed earlier—namely, the potential for 'fantasy' to cover a much wider range of texts than generally considered, the crucial factor being an interest in 'impossibility' or 'unreality,' and the crucial result being an exposure of underlying ideology. The texts discussed in this part all realize that potential in various ways: although some are least likely to be recognized as MF, they nonetheless represent overlapping modes of 'unreality' in relation to the present world, in part by evoking similarly critical practices of classical reception. These chapters illustrate some of the ways in which, perhaps surprisingly, classical reception may help articulate meaningful challenges to traditional understandings of a genre like MF. Above all, they emphasize that 'modern fantasy' encompasses 'fantasies,' emphatically plural and diverse.

A first example of that potential for classically receptive 'fantasies' is explored by Sasha-Mae Eccleston ("Fantasies of Mimnermos in Anne Carson's "The Brainsex Paintings" (*Plainwater*)"). Like much of Carson's work, "The Brainsex Paintings" is *sui generis*, in its case combining loose translations of Mimnermos with an impossible, fictive interview with that archaic Greek poet. Eccleston argues that Carson uses such fantastic tropes to challenge the authoritative pose of traditional scholarship, rendering memory as obscure as fantasy. Jennifer A. Rea ("Aeneas' American New World in Jo Graham's *Black Ships*") emphasizes the potential political ramifications of classical reception in MF by examining how Graham's novel, a reimagining of Virgil's *Aeneid*, invites readers to question the prohibitively high price to be paid for the 'American dream.' *Black Ships* thus exemplifies the potential for classically receptive MF to raise urgent questions about contemporary 'fantasies' or cultural fictions about freedom—including the freedom to invent one's own destiny.

The final chapter of Part IV helps draw together many of the volume's threads by returning to the question—raised in the first chapter—of how critiques of 'traditional' MF are developed in the classical receptions performed by George R. R. Martin's *A Song of Ice and Fire*. Ayelet Haimson Lushkov ("Genre, Mimesis, and Virgilian Intertext in George R. R. Martin's *A Song of Ice and Fire*") examines how the relationship between Martin's Renly Baratheon and Loras Tyrell resonates with the Nisus and

Euryalus episode in Virgil's *Aeneid*. Exploring the various ways in which the two erotic pairs double one another and switch roles, Lushkov identifies a complex network of images and connections that belong to—and so invite critique of—the greater epic tradition.

The sorts of connections discussed by the preceding chapters are richly suggestive of possibilities for re-reading both the modern genre and its truly ancient—classical, not merely medieval—sources and antecedents. The chapters all together suggest how the ostensibly separate areas of Greco-Roman classics and MF are in fact closely linked, not only historically—in the form of relationships among particular works—but also metaphysically, with both areas involving what must seem, from the reader's perspective, to be 'impossibilities' or 'unrealities' of various kinds. From this perspective, both MF and the field of Classics—similarly inhabited by a vast bestiary of harpies and she-bears, trod upon by Psyche and even Proteus himself—are deeply connected by their commitments to 'disunity of form.'

As we hope to have suggested in the preceding outline, the chapters collected in this volume do more than cover a wide range of 'classical traditions in modern fantasy'—that is, they treat a great number and variety of sources from Greek and Roman antiquity, as well as more recent writing, televisual materials, and art emblematic of the genre. These essays also represent a wide range of approaches to this burgeoning area of scholarly activity. At the same time, we also recognize the limits to this collection, including the privileged place it offers, by accident of the chapters' topics, to a predominately Anglo-American imagining of MF (even if such a designation may itself be a 'fantasy' that occludes a complexly multifaceted and protean diversity). The collection is thus intended to be not so much comprehensive or definitive—as perhaps no collection or study could ever be—as exploratory and inviting, raising questions to which other readers may be inspired to find answers, and leaving open spaces that other scholars may seek to fill. In other words, we are all too keenly aware that this collection represents merely the "Once upon a time . . ." and that a long journey lies ahead, no "happily ever after" in sight. Nevertheless, and most importantly, it is our hope that the volume as a whole captures something of the protean nature, not only of the genre of fantasy, but also of its myriad images of the classical world. Full of unreal creatures and elements, hard to get one's hands—and head—around, always changing its forms, tones, and meanings: modern fantasy offers delight and the prospect of great insight into our ongoing relationship to what is real, what is possible, what is human. If only we, too, like the ancient Greek hero Menelaus, might succeed at wrestling that mythical, unerring 'Old Man of the Sea' and so learn the depths of our imagination.

Part I

Classical Apparitions
in (Pre-)Modern Fantasy

1

Classical Epic and the Poetics
of Modern Fantasy

Jesse Weiner

INTRODUCTION

The case studies in this volume testify to the depth, density, and complexity of the myriad links between modern fantasy (MF) and classical literature.[1] Although high fantasy in the strictest sense may be a modern literary phenomenon, the consummately mythological genre finds its roots in Homer, Aristophanes, Lucian, and other authors of Greek antiquity.[2] Famously, such foundational authors of MF as Tolkien and Lewis were philologists—scholars of language and literary traditions—and in

---

[1] I presented early versions of this essay at the October 2012 meeting of the Pacific Ancient and Modern Language Association in Seattle, and at Game of Thrones: Popular Culture and the Deep Past at Ohio State University in February 2014. In addition to the excellent feedback I received at both conferences, I am grateful for the comments, corrections, and suggestions I received from the editors and referees of this volume. This essay also benefited at an early stage from conversations with James I. Porter, Zina Giannopoulou, Kerry Mockler, and Michelle C. Neely.

[2] Fredericks (1978).

their wake it would be difficult to find a high fantasy novel that is not rich in classical intertextuality and allusion.

This chapter is intended to be not a specific case study but rather a broader exploration of the generic links between high fantasy and heroic epic, seen in part through the lens of ancient Greek aesthetics. I first trace the stylistic features, strategies, priorities, and preoccupations of contemporary high fantasy. I argue that high fantasy is, in many respects, modern-day epic in prose, since the genre closely fits Aristotle's aesthetic guidelines for authors of heroic epic poetry. The second portion of my chapter examines the divergent receptions of classical epic and MF (both by their respective cultures and in the modern canon) and attempts to explain what can only be described as a clash of aesthetics.

Amidst the summaries, teasers, and critical endorsements on the dust jackets and covers of high fantasy novels and series, from J. R. R. Tolkien's *The Lord of the Rings* to J. K. Rowling's *Harry Potter* series and George R. R. Martin's *A Song of Ice and Fire* (*SIF*), 'epic' is one of the most common words bandied about. For instance, *The Washington Post* calls *A Dance with Dragons* (the fifth book of *SIF*) "epic fantasy as it should be written," while *Time* magazine names the series "the great fantasy epic of our era."[3] Though I do not doubt that many critics use the word loosely, often as a substitute for 'high' or 'heroic' fantasy, they nevertheless tap MF's deep roots in epic poetry. All of the word's contemporary colloquial meanings ('long,' 'monumental,' 'heroic,' 'majestic') fit within the conventions and aims of classical epic. Fantasy shares many of its generic tropes as well as its broader aesthetic values with epic poetry.

For the sake of brevity and accessibility, I will ground my illustrations in *SIF*.[4] At one level, my choice of texts is somewhat arbitrary: given that my broader argument is at the level of generic tropes, almost any high fantasy series would have served. However, my argument engages with

---

[3] Other examples of 'epic' descriptions of *SIF* include: "Of those who work in the grand epic-fantasy tradition, Martin is by far the best."—*Time*; "George R. R. Martin continues to take epic fantasy to new levels. . . ."—*Locus*; ". . . Martin's epic advances his series with gritty characterizations, bold plot moves and plenty of action. . . ."—*St. Louis Post-Dispatch*; "A truly epic fantasy set in a world bedecked with 8,000 years of history. . . ."—*Publishers Weekly*; "It is perhaps the best of the epic fantasies."—Marion Zimmer Bradley. Clute and Grant (1997: 319, authored by Clute): "Unfortunately, the term [epic fantasy] has been increasingly used by publishers to describe heroic fantasies that extend over several volumes, and has thus lost its usefulness."

[4] On *SIF*, see further Lushkov (this volume).

'popular' literature, and *SIF* is, at the time of this writing, a worldwide phenomenon.

Prior to exploring the generic conventions of ancient epic poetry and their resonances in modern high fantasy literature, it seems prudent to define MF and to lay out in brief just what I mean by 'high' fantasy. First, I follow Brian Attebery's caution against overly rigid definitions of genre, and I suggest that fantasy is best understood—both on its own terms and in relation to other genres—as a 'fuzzy set.'[5] As Attebery also suggests, "fantasy is the most fictional of all modes."[6] Because fantasy points towards the unknown and unknowable, as David Sandner argues, its "strange encounters and wild possibilities" "bewilder the reader," and "the fundamental characteristic of the fantastic is displacement."[7] Despite its radical fictionality and strategies of estrangement, "a fantasy text is," as John Clute suggests, "a self-coherent narrative. When set in this world, it tells a story that is impossible in the world as we perceive it; when set in an otherworld, that otherworld will be impossible, though the stories set there may be possible in its terms."[8] Like this volume's editors in their Introduction, I distinguish fantasy from its speculative counterpart, science fiction (SF), by the nature of its impossibilities. Whereas the impossible fictions of SF are epistemological, fantasy's impossibilities are metaphysical.

For my purposes, there is no qualitative valuation of high fantasy over its opposite, low fantasy. Rather, 'high' and 'low' are technical, formal terms to classify and subcategorize the fantasy genre. I follow C. W. Sullivan (as well as Kenneth Zahorski and Robert Boyer) in defining high fantasy as fantastic literature marked by the creation of secondary worlds.[9] These secondary worlds may be entirely separate from our own primary world (e.g., Tolkien's Middle-earth, Martin's Westeros), they may be connected to our primary world through a

---

[5] Attebery (2014: 33). Sandner (2004: 7): "Modern fantastic literature is thus defined and delimited in relation to what has been characterized as the 'rise' of the realistic novel in the eighteenth century." On Attebery's and Sandner's definitions, see further this volume's Introduction.

[6] Attebery (1988: 86).

[7] Sandner (2004: 9).

[8] Clute and Grant (1997: 338, authored by Clute).

[9] Sullivan (1996: 300); Zahorski and Boyer (1982: 56). The term 'secondary world' is drawn from Tolkien (1965); see some additional discussion in Stevens (this volume).

portal (Lewis's Narnia), or they may exist as secondary worlds within our world, as long as they are created with their own structure and internal logic (Rowling's *Harry Potter* series). Low fantasy is distinguished from high fantasy, not by literary or aesthetic deficiency, but rather by eschewing the creation of secondary worlds to present the non-rational fantastic within our primary world (e.g., Neil Gaiman's and Terry Pratchett's *Good Omens*, Lynne Reid Bank's *The Indian in the Cupboard*, and the television series *Bewitched*).

While I focus on fantasy's formal and aesthetic links to Greco-Roman epic, I in no way suggest a simplistic intertextual model in which classical epic is the sole genealogical progenitor of high fantasy. In comparing high fantasy with classical epic, I do not deny the relevance of other literatures, both epic and not.[10] Many non-classical (and non-Western) cultures boast rich, autonomous epic and mythological traditions important to fantasy.[11] For example, the Sanskrit epic *Mahabharata* shares many of the generic features I trace in classical epic and MF, while fantasy is also influenced by the romantic novel, the Norse saga, and the fairy tale. It is worth noting, however, that all of those prose genres are themselves influenced by epic.[12] A feature shared between an ancient epic and a later epic may make its way into a MF text like *SIF* via an intermediary work, but it still represents an unconscious or unwitting reception of the ancient epic as well. All told, whether we view the influence of classical epic on fantasy as direct or as mediated through a number of heterogeneous strains, epic might emerge as both a mother and grandmother to fantasy.

[10] I here follow the caution with which Martin (2005: 9) introduces his study of the epic genre.

[11] See Clute and Grant (1997: 319, authored by Clute). Though Clute's epic genealogy begins with the *Epic of Gilgamesh* and is grounded in Western traditions, Clute and Grant (1997: 675, authored by Ashley) elsewhere acknowledge diverse influences upon fantasy ranging from East Asian to Native American and Aboriginal traditions. While classical epic is by no means the only tradition important to the development of MF, it is an essential one. In discussing the immense influence of Greek and Latin literature upon fantasy, Joe Bernstein argues that, although they did not invent fantasy, "the Greeks gave us fantasy"; Clute and Grant (1997: 433).

[12] On epic into prose sagas, see Saxby (1997: 147). While Tolkien fears reducing fairy tales to mere derivative recreations of past mythologies and literatures, he does grant these sources their place as part of a complex "web" or "soup" of story; Tolkien (1965: 20). Scholes (2003: 246): "For Lukács (1971: 61) the novel succeeds the epic as the proper narrative mode . . ."; see also Bakhtin (1981). Holzberg (1995: 33) acknowledges classical epic as a formal forerunner to the ancient romantic novel; see also the essays in Schmeling (1996).

HIGH FANTASY AND CLASSICAL EPIC:
SHARED CONVENTIONS

Let us begin with a brief look at generic tropes before broadening our focus to general aesthetic elements and values. Given that high fantasy is defined by the imaginative creation of secondary worlds, it is perhaps paradoxical that this creative emancipation from realism is accompanied by some rather formulaic generic structures and preoccupations.[13] As Brett M. Rogers observes of superhero narratives in comic books, writers of heroic high fantasy "exist in our world and have been conditioned by age-old storytelling traditions and specific ideas about how these traditions work."[14] As I will argue, these conventions are largely those of ancient epic.

Some of these shared conventions structure the plots of classical epic and high fantasy. In both genres, the origin or destiny of a land is often of central concern.[15] For instance, Virgil's *Aeneid* (*Aen.*) devotes space to depicting the fall of Troy, while its overarching teleological theme is the foundation of Rome and the rise of Augustus. In *SIF*, political power and the unity of the Seven Kingdoms are at constant issue. This political destiny is set against a larger Manichean struggle between good and evil, in which humanity is threatened by malevolent Others. Heroic quests also commonly structure the plots of both genres. In classical epic, Jason's quest for the Golden Fleece is the subject of the *Argonauticas* of Apollonius and Valerius Flaccus, while Homer's *Odyssey* and the *Aeneid* depict the rambling voyages of Odysseus and Aeneas in search of homelands. Bran Stark's journey to find the three-eyed crow and Brienne of Tarth's search for Sansa are two examples of heroic quests in *SIF*.[16]

---

[13] Bloom (1982: 6): "fantasy . . . promises an absolute freedom from . . . the anxieties of literary influence and organization, yet this promise is shadowed always by a psychic over-determination in the form itself of fantasy and puts the stance of freedom into severe question." Schlobin (1982: x) appears to suggest the opposite, but the ensuing discussion makes it plain that he refers to the fantastic, rather than high fantasy specifically.

[14] Rogers (2011: 73).

[15] Clute and Grant (1997: 310): "Any fantasy tale written to a large scale which deals with the founding or definitive and lasting defence of a land may fairly be called an epic fantasy."

[16] Timmerman (1983: 91–102) cites the quest as both a necessary element of fantasy and a point of congruence with ancient literatures. He distinguishes between quests and adventures, such that epic, rather than the romantic novel, appears to be the source for the trope of the quest. Ringel (2000: 163) also cites the quest as essential to high fantasy.

Others of these shared conventions are supernatural. For instance, magic and witchcraft feature prominently in both genres. In ancient epic, Homer's Circe and the Medeas of both Apollonius' *Argonautica* and Ovid's *Metamorphoses* (*Met.*) provide examples of powerful witches, while Mirri Maz Duur and Melisandre (the Red Priestess) fill similar roles in *SIF*. The reanimation of Catelyn Stark is also reminiscent of the corpse Erichtho revivifies in Lucan's *Bellum Civile* (*BC*). Classical epic and *SIF* also share world orders governed by fate. While fate and the divine apparatus may work differently from poem to poem, Homer, Virgil, and Apollonius each present worlds structured by predestination, and this predestination often reveals itself through riddling prophesies. In the *Argonautica*, Apollo warns Pelias that he will be undone by a man with one sandal, while in the *Aeneid*, the Harpies issue a famous curse that the Trojans will eat their tables; both prophecies come to pass. In the tradition of Tolkien, *SIF* presents a "Secondary World of epic fantasy," which, like those of classical epic, "is ruled by fate, its plots determined by prophets and oracles speaking in riddles."[17] The primacy of fate manifests itself in Jojen's dreams, in prophecies that the House Targaryen will return to power, and in prophecies that Azor Ahai is destined to rise again to battle the Others.

Still other conventions shared between epic and fantasy are ethical and cultural. These include cultures of hospitality, warfare, and political obligation. Both genres display thematic interests in communal meals and conventions of hospitality.[18] Greek and Roman epic features detailed scenes of feasting with a focus on guest–host relations (Greek *xenia*) and hospitality (e.g., Priam's visit to Achilles in *Il.*, Odysseus' receptions by the Phaeacians and Cyclops as well as Penelope's suitors on Ithaca in *Od.*, Apollonius' Argonauts with Phineus in the *Argonautica*, and Aeneas' reception by the Carthaginians in *Aen.*). *SIF* boasts numerous descriptive feast scenes. The 'Red Wedding' is a particularly infamous violation of guest–host relations. Martin's secondary world also features the civilizing custom that once a guest has eaten bread and salt, (s)he may not be harmed.

As for their principal leitmotifs and constructions of heroism, both classical epic and fantasy tend to be dominated by martial themes.

---

[17] Ringel (2000: 165).
[18] On feasts, wine, and guest–host relations as tropes in fantasy literature, see the essays in Westfahl (1996) as well as Slusser and Rabkin (1993).

Classical epic and modern high fantasy alike chronicle the heroic deeds of great warriors like Achilles, Odysseus, Jason, Aeneas, Aragorn, Aslan, and the ensemble cast of *SIF*, celebrating the life of warfare. Although Homer, Virgil, Tolkien, and Martin hardly present the hero's intense devotion to war as problem-free, they do single out the warrior's life as the central theme.[19] Also, private desires tend to be trumped by public moral obligations to duty, honor, and country, with political life "placed at the center of poetic concern."[20] In Virgil, Aeneas' political and religious *pietas* ('piety') demands that he abandon Dido, and, time and again, Martin's characters must make similar choices in *SIF*. When Rob Stark agrees to an unattractive political marriage out of necessity, his mother celebrates this decision as the moment he comes into his own as a true lord. When he later forsakes his political betrothal in favor of romantic love, that troubling inversion of epic values prompts his murder and unmakes his kingdom.[21] Because the origins and destinies of fantasy's secondary worlds are constantly at stake, thereby requiring this prioritization of public and political matters, Harold Bloom, John Dean, and others somewhat overstate their cases when arguing that fantasy is the direct descendent of romance.[22]

Still other shared tropes are temporal in nature, ranging from an obsessive concern with monumentalizing glory (Greek *kleos*) for posterity to nostalgia for an irretrievable bygone past. By its very title, *A Song of Ice and Fire* signals high fantasy's poetic filiations, in that ancient epic poetry sought to achieve immortality in culture through song; as in the *Iliad*, *Odyssey*, and *Aeneid*, so, too, in Martin's series there is value placed on the preservative power of poetry and the role of bards

[19] Cantor (2007: 375). Slusser and Rabkin (1993: 1) locate the origins of martial themes in speculative fiction with views of ancient warfare espoused by Homer and Virgil.

[20] See Cantor (2007: 375).

[21] Cf. Jon Snow's privileging of his duty to the Night's Watch over his personal romantic and political desires (Jon's abandonment of Ygritte is reminiscent of Aeneas abandoning Dido). Daenerys wrestles with the tension between public and private desire, agreeing to a political marriage to Hizdahr zo Loraq despite her strong preference for Daario Naharis.

[22] Bloom (1982) and Dean (1980). As Holzberg (1995: 33) observes, romance (at least the Greek romantic novels) inverts the public, political, and martial values of heroic epic. Most connections that Thompson (1982) draws between MF and the medieval romance can be applied to epic, despite the prevalence of medievalist settings in modern high fantasy.

in monumentalizing the *kleos* of heroes.[23] There are numerous internal bards and songs commemorating history and heroes, as well as many explicit statements of desire to be immortalized in song. The song called "Rains of Castamere" frequently resurfaces throughout the series. In the *Iliad*, Achilles is obsessed with being immortalized in song, while the *Odyssey* greatly reveres its bards. Numerous epics also make proclamations of poetic monumentality, suggesting that they themselves are vehicles for this process.[24]

Nostalgia for a bygone past is displayed in antiquity by Hesiod's descending Ages of Man in *Works and Days*, and Ovid revives the theme in *Metamorphoses*.[25] Material culture in Homeric epic is represented as being far richer than in historical Dark Age/archaic Greece, and figures later celebrated as demigods in cult appear in Homer as heroes. *SIF* repeatedly refers to 8,000 years of history and invokes an epic (and somewhat Roman) obsession with the 'good ol' days,' when kings and heroes were bigger and better and dragons were prevalent.

Finally, the secondary worlds of epic and fantasy must be both alien and familiar to their intended audiences. So it is that the landscapes, political structures, heroes, and values of fantasy worlds are both unfamiliar and bear a resemblance to our own frames of reference, and invented nomenclature in high fantasy frequently adapts familiar linguistic conventions.[26] Classicists know this narrative technique by another name: 'epic distancing.'[27] Epic accomplishes this through archaizing language, chariots (not used in historical archaic Greek warfare), talking rivers, monsters, and bronze weapons. Martin's secondary world and its names bear enough familiarity to our own to be understood, yet that world is alienating through its plants, magic, dragons, religions, and so forth. While each of these tropes is worthy of extended attention, this cursory survey of

---

[23] Sullivan (2000: 12) locates Tolkien's narrative mode in the ancient oral-formulaic tradition. For epic memory or glory and its opposites in Tolkien, see further Stevens (this volume).

[24] E.g., *Aen.* 9.446–449, *Met.* 15.871–879, *BC* 9.980–986.

[25] *Works and Days* 109–201, *Met.* 1.89–150.

[26] See Timmerman (1983: 113).

[27] See especially Morris (1986: 89). The techniques described by Morris pertain to both language and imagery and are as prevalent in fantasy as they are in epic. This distancing has an effect of archaizing and fantastic estrangement, and gives rise to an epic/fantasy "Heroic Age in which men were better in every way." Cf. Raaflaub (2005).

generic conventions points towards a profound relationship between ancient epic and contemporary high fantasy.

Though it would be reductive to suggest that all epic and high fantasy structure themselves through each of these organizing tropes, they nevertheless are integral to our understanding of their generic forms. As Hainsworth reminds us:

Form is indispensable to all sentimental genres. It signals to readers what it is that they hold in their hands. Epic poets who wished to be known as such invoked the Muse or her Christian equivalent; they found a role for God or gods; they were generous with marvels.[28]

Just as "not every poem incorporates all the details hallowed by Homer and Virgil," not every novel or series in the epic-fantasy tradition incorporates all the details hallowed by Tolkien, Lewis, and Martin. "But the more the formal characteristics are dispensed with, the harder it is to call a poem an epic," or a novel 'high fantasy.'[29]

AESTHETIC CONSIDERATIONS: ARISTOTLE'S *POETICS*

The generic tropes shared between ancient epic and high fantasy underscore broader aesthetic filiations, which become apparent when read through the lens of Aristotle's *Poetics* (*Poet.*).[30] These aesthetic similarities include the primacy of plot over character development and stylistic adornment, the depiction of heroic characters who are nevertheless profoundly human, simplicity of diction, and populist assumptions about the audience. The value of Aristotle's formalism and conceptions of genre lies in their reception in modernity. As Stephen Halliwell observes, Aristotle's treatise does not appear to have been widely known or read in classical antiquity.[31] Rather, the canonical status of the *Poetics* stems from its readers in the Renaissance and after. David Hopkins acknowledges as

---

[28] See Hainsworth (1991: 144). Cf. Feeney (1991).

[29] Hainsworth (1991: 144).

[30] Sandner (2004: 6): "The 'marvelous' is part of the epic machinery described by Aristotle."

[31] Halliwell (1999: 3–4). I use Halliwell's text of Aristotle throughout. Cf. Hutton (1982: 24–25).

common wisdom that the literary aesthetics and critical concepts of the Italian sixteenth century, the French seventeenth century, and the English Restoration were dominated by neoclassical literary theory, which was largely an "amalgam of Aristotle and Horace."[32] In the *Poetics*, Aristotle specifies that epic should be lengthy (1449b), given that it is unburdened by the practical restrictions of dramatic performance, and should also portray moral and/or fatal events involving good and serious characters. High fantasy tends to be a sprawling genre, and, like epic's, a great many of its defining works take the form of multi-book cycles and series. *SIF* is presently incomplete, and its five (out of an anticipated seven) books total nearly 5,000 pages.

Aristotle divides epic and poetry into constituent elements, which he discusses in hierarchical sequence according to their importance.[33] Tragedy contains six elements (*Poet.* 1450a), four of which are common to epic (1459b). Aristotle argues that these aesthetic judgements pertain to epic as well as tragedy. Therefore, epic is above all else a plot-driven genre, since "the most important of these [formal elements] is the arrangement of actions" and "plot, therefore, is the first principle, or even the soul, of tragedy [and epic], while character is second."[34]

Without action, there can be no epic (or tragedy), though an epic poem could well exist without other, more minor elements. After plot comes character, followed by thought. Content is therefore privileged over artistic adornment, and stylistic features such as poetic language, elaborate diction, and rhetorical ornamentation are less important to epic poetry than are plot and character. Aristotle argues "it is necessary

---

[32] See Hopkins (2010: 37–54, 39). Hopkins's summary of Aristotelian neoclassicism's importance follows Vickers (1974–1981). Specific to the reception of Shakespeare, Hopkins argues for a Longinian (as opposed to Aristotelian) turn. Nevertheless, Hopkins acknowledges Aristotle's predominant influence during the period and quotes (48) from John Dryden's preface to *The State of Innocence* (1677), which names Aristotle "the greatest Critique amongst the Greeks." Hutton (1982: 25) notes numerous resonances of *Poet.* in the aesthetic theory of Horace (*Ars Poetica*). For Horace and fantasy, see further the Introduction to this volume.

[33] Rogers's (2011: 75) overview of formal approaches to hero myths originates with Aristotle: "Aristotle examined the elements of Greek epic and drama, positing in the *Poetics* that every story should both prioritize action (i.e. the arrangement of incidents) over character (1450a15–b4) and contain a three-act structure: a beginning, a middle, and an end (1450b21–34)."

[34] *Poet.* 1450a: μέγιστον δὲ τούτων ἐστὶν ἡ τῶν πραγμάτων σύστασις. . . . ἀρχὴ μὲν οὖν καὶ οἷον ψυχὴ ὁ μῦθος τῆς τραγῳδίας, δεύτερον δὲ τὰ ἤθη. Translations are my own.

to be more a maker of stories than a maker of meters, since he is a poet through imitation, and he imitates actions."[35] Formal and aesthetic analyses of high fantasy tend to emphasize the absolute primacy of story, the development of heroic characters, and the subordination of stylized language and rhetorical adornment. If this already sounds a little like Aristotelian guidelines for epic and tragedy, John Timmerman's analysis of the genre further underscores an Aristotelian turn. Timmerman's study of high fantasy is among the most systematic treatments of the genre's formulae and aesthetics, following Aristotle's schema (though the *Poetics* is conspicuously not named). Story and heroic characters top Timmerman's list of essential traits for the construction of fantasy, and Timmerman describes plot in terms that are downright Aristotelian:

It seems obvious that fantasy relies upon a compelling, well-paced story.... In its traditional sense, story requires a narrative plot line, the unfolding of events, the development of characters into living beings who think about actions, who do act, and whose actions have effects. A story moves from a beginning, through a middle, to an end, and in the process emotionally or psychologically moves the reader.[36]

These lines appear to recall Aristotle's definition of 'plot,' which states, "the whole [plot] is that which has a beginning, middle, and end."[37] Timmerman emphasizes that "a good story has always been the foremost aim of fantasists," and above all else, fantasy literature is a genre of page-turners.[38] Likewise, heroes in high fantasy are constructed, according to Timmerman, much like those of ideal Aristotelian epic. If "story is to

---

[35] *Poet.* 1451b: τὸν ποιητὴν μᾶλλον τῶν μύθων εἶναι δεῖ ποιητὴν ἢ τῶν μέτρων, ὅσῳ ποιητής κατὰ τὴν μίμησίν ἐστιν, μιμεῖται δὲ τὰς πράξεις.

[36] Timmerman (1983: 5). These arguments develop Timmerman (1978). I do not mean to be polemical when I point out Timmerman's failure to connect explicitly his formal analysis of high fantasy with Aristotelian aesthetics. The late John Timmerman was not a classicist, and his book (which I largely agree with) belongs to an innovative first generation of work to treat speculative fiction as worthy of serious scholarly attention.

[37] *Poet.* 1450b: ὅλον δέ ἐστιν τὸ ἔχον ἀρχὴν καὶ μέσον καὶ τελευτήν.

[38] Timmerman (1983: 5). See also Attebery (1988: 86): "Fantastic tales generally emphasize story over verbal texture and depth of characterization." In writing about Greek literature and its value for SF, Asimov (1961: 11) suggests that the stories themselves, more than any particular poetic genius, are what give Homer's epics their enduring greatness.

bear relevance," this relevance "must arise through characters living the story immediately."[39] They should be mortal, naïve, of remarkable birth, a repository of value, and, above all, imperfect and all too aware of their mortality.[40] Aristotle also specifies that characters teach morality by their choices. "Since the mimesis is of action, and actions are done by people acting, it is necessary that these people be of a certain kind in character and thought, for it is on account of these qualities that we judge the actions."[41]

Characters should be good and of noble or divine birth, yet like other men (Achilles being the prime example; *Poet.* 1452b).[42] Aristotle stresses the need for naïveté not only in tragic character, but also in epic in order to induce *anagnorisis* ('recognition,' 1459b). Though these characters thus deconstructed appear flat and formulaic, this, too, is tied to the subordination of character to plot. Ursula K. Le Guin, one of high fantasy's great authors, avers (using Virginia Woolf's 1923 essay, "Mr. Bennett and Mrs. Brown") that fantasy has no room for the sort of fully developed complex characters who might overshadow story:

> If any field of literature has no, can have no Mrs. Browns in it, it is fantasy—straight fantasy, the modern descendant of folktale, fairy tale, and myth. These genres deal with archetypes, not with characters. The very essence of Elfland is that Mrs. Brown can't get there—not unless she is changed, changed utterly, into an old mad witch, or a fair young princess, or a loathely Worm.[43]

At the core both of the Aristotelian primacy of plot and character in epic and tragedy and of the centrality of these elements to high fantasy are populist assumptions about the goals of these genres. Whether there

---

[39] Timmerman (1983: 29).

[40] Ibid. (44–48).

[41] *Poet.* 1449b: ἐπεὶ δὲ πράξεώς ἐστι μίμησις, πράττεται δὲ ὑπὸ τινῶν πραττόντων, οὓς ἀνάγκη ποιούς τινας εἶναι κατά τε τὸ ἦθος καὶ τὴν διάνοιαν (διὰ γὰρ τούτων καὶ τὰς πράξεις εἶναί φαμεν ποιάς τινας).

[42] In *Poet.*, the noble birth of the hero is largely implicit though examples, but Aristotle also specifies that slaves do not have the stuff of epic and tragic heroes.

[43] Le Guin (1979: 106–107); Woolf (1928). Le Guin makes a partial exception, suggesting that Tolkien offers a "primitive version of Mrs. Brown," if one reads Frodo, Sam, Gollum, Sméagol, and Bilbo as one composite character. To anticipate my argument below, Le Guin avers that Mrs. Browns must find their way into SF for the genre to realize the form of the novel as high art, though she makes no such appeal for fantasy. In his essay "Odysseus' Scar," Auerbach (1953) reads Homeric characters as flat and underdeveloped.

is a didactic moral function to reading epic and fantasy (as Aristotle and Timmerman would have it), or an entertainment value to narrative modes of storytelling, or, more likely, both, Aristotle and contemporary writers on fantasy prize accessibility and envision a broad readership. Content is therefore privileged over artistic adornment, and stylistic features such as poetic language, elaborate diction, and rhetorical ornamentation are less important to epic poetry and high fantasy. Exceedingly dense and difficult descriptive verse and prose are to be avoided. Aristotle suggests that the epic poet keep such adornments to a minimum, arguing that the place for elaborate diction is in the less vital passages, because where character and thought are to be revealed, too brilliant a diction will obscure them. "It is necessary to place elaborate speech in the idle portions and not in the moral and thought revealing parts, since too brilliant diction obscures character and thoughts."[44] C. S. Lewis celebrates the formal and aesthetic preeminence of story and the devaluation of language in fantasy: "I fell in love with the Form [of fantasy] itself; its brevity, its severe restraints on description, its flexible traditionalism, its inflexible hostility to all analysis, digression, reflections, and 'gas.' "[45]

Thus modern high fantasy incorporates to an impressive degree many of the *topoi*, outlooks, and techniques of heroic epic, and its broader aesthetic aims mirror those put forth by Aristotle. Furthermore, these Aristotelian ethics are governed by similar conceptions of the intended audience.

DIVERGENT RECEPTIONS: A CLASH OF AESTHETICS

And yet I feel a discomfort with the Harry Potter mania, and I hope that my discontent is not merely a highbrow snobbery, or a nostalgia for a more literate fantasy to beguile (shall we say) intelligent children of all ages. Can more than 35 million book buyers, and their offspring, be wrong? Yes, they have been, and will continue to be for as long as they persevere with Potter.

Harold Bloom, *Wall Street Journal*, July 11, 2000

---

[44] *Poet*, 1460b: τῇ δὲ λέξει δεῖ διαπονεῖν ἐν τοῖς ἀργοῖς μέρεσιν καὶ μήτε ἠθικοῖς μήτε διανοητικοῖς· ἀποκρύπτει γὰρ πάλιν ἡ λίαν λαμπρὰ λέξις τά τε ἤθη καὶ τὰς διανοίας.

[45] Lewis (1966: 36). Timmerman (1983: 5): "story is always the central pole about which aesthetic excellences such as internal richness, complication, imagery, and harmony may revolve."

If high fantasy is, in contemporary English literature, something akin to, perhaps even an inheritance of, Greek epic, an obvious question arises: How do we account for the radical divergences in their receptions? If high fantasy has so much in common with epic poetry that is still canonized as essential reading, why is fantasy so often treated as 'low' literature? For the Greeks (excepting the neoterics), epic poetry occupied the penthouse suite in the hierarchy of genres, and the places of Homer and Hesiod in the canon were sacrosanct.[46] Aristotle, for instance, names epic and tragedy as the highest poetic genres, and, while he argues for the slight superiority of tragedy, he nevertheless acknowledges this as the minority view (*Poet.* 1461b–1462b).[47] Ovid introduces his *Amores*, however glibly, with an apologetic explanation for why he has chosen to write poetry of a genre baser than epic: "I was preparing to put forth arms and violent war with weighty meter, with material fit for the style, the lower line was equal: Cupid is said to have laughed and stolen one foot."[48] The premise of Ovid's playful defense of amatory verse is a cultural understanding that, both in form and content, epic occupies a position of generic superiority.

High fantasy, however, meets with more ambivalent receptions today. Attebery bemoans "the fact that those who don't or can't read fantasy consider themselves superior to it"; that fantasy's detractors assign "aesthetic defect" to the genre; and that "the tremendous popularity of fantasy texts only tends to make those color-blind people more resentful."[49] Fantasy series routinely top lists of best sellers, yet often they are critically maligned and stigmatized as base in genre (*à la* Bloom's critique of Rowling quoted here). When they are acclaimed, this praise frequently takes the form of rather backhanded compliments. For instance, the

---

[46] 'Neoteric' refers to an avant-garde movement in Hellenistic poetry (revived in the late Roman Republic), which turned away from epic poetics. Callimachus, a prominent neoteric poet, famously disparages epic in the prologue to his *Aetia*: "big book, big mistake" (μέγα βιβλίον μέγα κακόν). Cantor (2007: 375) describes as "traditional" the "concept of epic and tragedy as the supreme genres and the pinnacle of literary achievement."

[47] As Scholes observes in his foreword to Todorov's *The Fantastic* (1975: viii), "Aristotle's generic study became the basis for a most invidious kind of generic ranking."

[48] 1.1.1–4: *arma gravi numero violentaque bella parabam / edere, materia conveniente modis, / par erat inferior versus: risisse Cupido / dicitur atque unum surripuisse pedem.* The joke is that epic poetry is written in hexameter (six feet), while elegiac poetry is written in pentameter (five feet).

[49] Attebery (2014: 1).

Chicago Tribune calls *SIF* "a fantasy series for hip, smart people, even those who don't read fantasy," while *Booklist* offers that "Martin's command of English and of characterization and setting remains equal to the task of the fantasy megasaga." Noting "keen and complex human characters and the convincing force of their surroundings," *Locus* holds "Martin's first fantasy epic well above the norms of the genre." Likewise, the *Milwaukee Journal Sentinel* offers:

> With his introduction of characters who aren't as black and white as those typical of the genre, Martin has brought depth and believability to the usually cartoonish fantasy genre. . . . Martin's *SIF* series is that rare, once-in-a-generation work of fiction that manages to entertain readers while elevating an entire genre to fine literature.

Each of these pieces of apologetic praise for Martin's series can perhaps be paraphrased: "*SIF* is pretty darn good—for fantasy." Tolkien, Lewis, Rowling, and Martin may habitually be credited with writing classics of the fantasy genre, but, no matter how many books they sell, their novels are rarely listed among the classics of English literature. In many ways, the bipolar reception of contemporary fantasy has more in common with the afterlives of ancient Greek novels, in that the views of a critical elite are manifestly at odds with a popular audience.[50] The second half of my chapter attempts to account for this clash of aesthetics. The question is, I believe, both important and complex, and my preliminary attempts to answer it will inevitably lack the nuance they deserve. I suggest that the critical rejection of high fantasy as high art lies in the dialectics of modernism: in short, the critical reception of high fantasy has been doomed by modernism's aesthetic shift away from Aristotle's formalism.

When viewed in comparison with classical epic, the reception of high fantasy provides a brilliant illustration of modernist aesthetics and what has been called the 'Great Divide' between popular and high art in its various formulations. The eighteenth and nineteenth centuries experienced a newfound interest in the idea of fine art and renewed attempts to codify its principles.[51] Simultaneously, 'popular literature' arose or, more

---

[50] For one important discussion of popular acclaim preceding critical acclaim, see Kermode (1985).

[51] See especially Batteux (1747). Kristeller (1990) draws upon Batteux to argue that the separation of wholly autonomous fine art occurred in the eighteenth century. Porter's

accurately, resurfaced, in no small part in the form of the novel. At its outset, Victor Neuburg's celebratory history unabashedly defines popular literature as "what the unsophisticated reader has chosen to read for pleasure."[52] Thus, a tension between Charles Batteux's beaux arts and unsophisticated entertainment literature had already surfaced when, with modernism's emergence, the likes of Theodor Adorno, Georg Lukács, and Clement Greenberg theorized about this gulf between the aesthetics of high culture and those of mass appeal with a new, perhaps unprecedented, vehemence and hostility towards the popular. Greenberg's famous essay "Avant-Garde and Kitsch" begins by articulating a vast qualitative chasm between innovative high art and kitsch—derivative popular art—which Greenberg viewed as the unfortunate by-product of industrialization, mass culture, and universal literacy:

One and the same civilization simultaneously produces two such different things as a poem by T. S. Eliot and a Tin Pan Alley song, or a painting by Braque and a *Saturday Evening Post* cover. All four are on the order of culture, and ostensibly, parts of the same culture and products of the same society. Here, however, their connection seems to end. A poem by Eliot and a poem by Eddie Guest—what perspective of culture is large enough to enable us to situate them in an enlightening relation to each other?[53]

The same evaluative chasm may be framed as an opposition between Aristotelianism and modernism. Aristotle's aesthetics are populist—he rejects overly dense and stylized language as obfuscating, because the goal of high literature should be to reach and educate as many people as possible. Aristotle argues that poetry arose in part from the pleasure of learning through representation, since "learning is most pleasing not only to philosophers, but also to others similarly."[54]

(2009) critique of Kristeller traces Batteux's separation of fine art back to classical antiquity. Auerbach (1993) has also shown that popular literature reaches back to ancient Greece and Rome.

[52] Neuburg (1976: 12). It is telling of this critical moment, and the tension between the legacy of modernism and the rise of postmodernism, that Neuburg complains that "the study of popular literature in England today is scarcely accepted as an academic activity."

[53] Greenberg (1939: 34).

[54] *Poet.* 1448b: μανθάνειν οὐ μόνον τοῖς φιλοσόφοις ἥδιστον ἀλλὰ καὶ τοῖς ἄλλοις ὁμοίως. In the following clause, Aristotle does qualify that philosophers will, however, participate in the ever so pleasant activity of learning more than common men.

Modernism, however, offered a new dialectic, one that rejected Aristotelian literary aesthetics, and with them, those of high fantasy. A hierarchical binary emerged, which is often called the 'Great Divide,' a "presumably necessary and insurmountable barrier separating high art from popular culture." In its various formulations, the Great Divide aesthetics of high literature deny high fantasy a place in its canon.[55] The aesthetic values of the Great Divide's adherents (consciously or not) banish high fantasy from the 'Literature' shelves at your local brick-and-mortar bookstore, relegating it to 'Popular' or 'Speculative' fiction.[56] To borrow from Robert Scholes's schema, 'avant-garde,' 'classic,' 'serious,' and 'representative' became valued as good, and were set against bad art, variously characterized as 'popular,' 'kitsch,' 'romantic,' 'light,' and 'entertaining.'[57]

The very accessibility of fantasy makes it 'kitsch,' according to Greenberg's aesthetics:

Where there is an avant-garde, generally we also find a rear-guard. True enough—simultaneously with the entrance of the avant-garde, a second new cultural phenomenon appeared in the industrial West: that thing to which the Germans give the wonderful name of *Kitsch*: popular, commercial art and literature with their chromeotypes, magazine covers, illustrations, ads, slick and pulp fiction, comics, Tin Pan Alley music, tap dancing, Hollywood movies, etc., etc. For some reason this gigantic apparition has always been taken for granted. It is time we looked into its whys and wherefores.... Kitsch is a product of the industrial revolution which urbanized the masses of Western Europe and America and established what is called universal literacy.[58]

---

[55] Kurt Vonnegut's (1974: 1) satirical assessment of the critical reception of SF (which is also grouped frequently under 'popular' and 'speculative' fiction) pithily articulates the Great Divide: "I learned from the reviewers that I was a science-fiction writer. I didn't know that . . . I have been a soreheaded occupant of a file drawer labeled 'science fiction' ever since, and I would like out, particularly since so many critics regularly mistake the drawer for a urinal." *À propos* to many critical indictments of fantasy, Vonnegut writes (3), "The people in the field [of SF literature] who can be charged fairly with tastelessness are 75 percent of the writers and 95 percent of the readers—or not so much tastelessness, really, as childishness." Vonnegut pejoratively describes popular SF as "comic books without pictures."

[56] Huyssen (1986: ix). On the tension between mass culture and modernism, with particular attention to the Frankfurt School, see also Jameson (1979).

[57] Scholes (2003: 254).

[58] Greenberg (1939).

For Lukács, fantasy's status as entertainment literature negates its potential to participate in the form of the high novel.[59] Its generic tropes and formulae, its privileging of plot and content over style, its teleologies spurn the avant-garde, as Greenberg asserts that "kitsch is mechanical and operates by formulas."[60]

Adorno, whom Andreas Huyssen names "the theorist par excellence of the Great Divide," similarly rejects genre and *topoi* as "artificial or conventional" obstacles to the production of high art:

> The conventional genres continued to be alluring even though they had lost their power. This was the price that had to be paid for progress. Conventional genres are like after-images of authority—a headache for art more than anything else. Art cannot take them seriously.[61]

For Adorno, the unfortunate survival of generic conventions and formulae is due in part to the endurance of Aristotle's authority from antiquity through the German idealism.[62] As such, the aesthetics of Adorno's modernism feature an explicit disavowal of Aristotle. Adorno argues "the Aristotelian notion of catharsis is an outmoded piece of mythology, hopelessly inadequate for understanding the impact that art does have."[63] It is the "concept of the new," the avant-garde, that "gives the art work the power of transcendence." Aristotelian catharsis, manufactured through aesthetic formulae and generic *topoi*, becomes outdating and misleading, since "under the aegis of Aristotle's authority, classicism for more than two thousand years had falsely viewed catharsis as a means to endow art with dignity."[64] Modernism differentiates serious literature from narrative pleasure, and Adorno's aesthetics reject not only the traditional importance of plot but also the cohesive unity Aristotle and scholars of high fantasy deem essential.[65]

---

[59] Lukács (1971). See also Scholes (2006: 5) and (2003: 246).

[60] Huyssen (1986: ix).

[61] Adorno (1984: 290–291). Huyssen quote from his (1986: ix).

[62] Ibid. (290): "The aesthetics of genres has survived the age of nominalism and was able to hold its ground during German idealist philosophy. One reason for this anachronism is undoubtedly the authority that Aristotle still had during that time."

[63] Ibid. (338).

[64] Ibid. (339).

[65] Ibid. (266): "Unity is brittle and unsubstantial if the forms and moments of works consist simply of topoi rather than emerging directly from the individual work. . . . Modernism

Importantly, Adorno in no way rejects fantasy and the fantastic per se.[66] On the contrary, he praises fantasy—not the genre but the fantastic at large:

Fantasy alone, today confined to the realm of the unconscious and proscribed from knowledge as childish, injudicious rudiment, can establish that relation between objects which is the irrevocable source of all judgement: should fantasy be driven out, judgement too, the real act of knowledge, is exorcised.[67]

To adapt Attebery's distinction, Adorno embraces the fantastic mode while leaving little room to appreciate the fantastic genre.[68] In considering these lines of Adorno's, Ben Watson has reflected upon the fact that "'fantasy' has since been applied to a genre of popular fiction" and he asks the question, "What would Adorno have to say about *Lord of the Rings*?" Watson approaches the query from the perspective of political economics and Marxism, and he excludes the genre of high fantasy from Adorno's admiration for 'fantasy':

When Adorno said that fantasy—unconscious, childish, unjudgemental— is a crucial component of knowledge, he was not only criticizing Stalinist Marxism and its reduction of social phenomena to instances of positive historical law. He was also criticizing the liberal notion of fantasy as a zone of irresponsibility quarantined from both lived desire and organized knowledge. According to this critique . . . J. R. R. Tolkien's tales of hobbits . . . are kitsch, because . . . they flatter the private existence of the solvent individual in a repressive environment. Adorno's idea of fantasy is the opposite of such dependable, niche-marketed products. He senses something fascistic in the commodification of wish-fulfillment.[69]

---

serves notice that it will no longer put up with universality, understood as unreflected immediacy."

[66] On the potential for fantasy to achieve high art, see ibid. (246–249).

[67] Adorno (1974: 122–123). This tension between fantasy and knowledge is developed throughout Adorno and Horkheimer (1997), particularly in the first excursus, "Odysseus or Myth and Enlightenment."

[68] Attebery (1992: 1–17).

[69] Watson (2002: 222). Similarly, Attebery (2014: 1) considers much commercial fantasy, what "discerning fans call 'extruded fantasy product,'" to be an obstacle to serious critical inquiry into fantastic literature.

Adorno would similarly disavow high fantasy on aesthetic as well as political grounds (not that the two are easily separated). Irrespective of Adorno's celebration of the fantastic, under his modernist aesthetics the genre of high fantasy becomes paradoxically unimaginative and unoriginal. High fantasy becomes kitsch.

Under the Great Divide, Aristotle's aesthetics, which privileged ancient epic in part because it *was* popular literature, thereby became displaced by new disdain for the popular. Aristotelian formalism and linguistic accessibility are differentiated from avant-garde, difficult, 'highbrow' literature.[70] We have seen that Lewis celebrates the absence of stylistic "gas" in fantasy, which, although democratizing, consigns the genre to mass culture from a modernist perspective. Paolo Coelho's recent controversial criticism of Joyce further reifies this distinction from the other side of the Divide, while offering a defense of 'popular' aesthetics. Coelho recently remarked, "one of the books that caused great harm was James Joyce's *Ulysses*, which is pure style. There is nothing there. Stripped down, *Ulysses* is a twit." Coelho offset his remarks on Joyce with a populist promotion of his own work as "modern because I make the difficult seem easy, and so I can communicate with the whole world."[71] We might make a rough classicizing comparison, then, between the popular, perhaps Aristotelian, tastes of fantasy fans, and the neoteric aesthetics of the academy and its modernist canon that reject long, formulaic, plot-driven narratives frequently accessible even to children.

CONCLUSIONS

Postmodern traditions have begun to challenge this Great Divide, as the slow but steady rise in scholarly work on fantasy and popular literature

---

[70] John Fiske (1991: 109): "The conventionality of plot lines, too, enables readers to write ahead, to predict what will happen and then to find pleasure. . . . Generic readers know the conventions and are thus situated in a far more democratic relationship with the text than are the readers of highbrow literature, with its authoritative authors. . . . There is no requirement, in the popular domain, for a text to be difficult, challenging, or complex. In fact, just the reverse is the case. The popular text must align itself with the tastes and concerns of its readers." In Fiske's formulation, the "difficult" and "highbrow" in art serve less as markers of quality than of social exclusion.

[71] Coelho's comments on Joyce are quoted in *The Guardian*, August 6, 2012.

over the past several decades testifies.[72] For instance, China Miéville has responded to cultural elitists "who would be happy to read an analysis of the novels of George Eliot or the films of Ken Loach, but who blench at *Buffy the Vampire Slayer*."[73] By way of a few closing remarks, I suggest that, by its very title, *Classical Traditions in Modern Fantasy*, this volume both calls attention to the Great Divide and suggests an attempt to bridge it. We find a dialectical juxtaposition of ancient with modern, tradition with invention, and, I think, an implicit tension between (1) the foundational canon of the Western academy and (2) popular fiction that has been widely excluded from this canon. More importantly, however, the chapters in this volume attempt to mediate between these aesthetic polarities, not only suggesting in a very post-modern way strains of influence of the classics in fantasy, but also making an appeal that each area warrants a place in the same critical discussions.

Finally, a question: Provided that we accept the generic and aesthetic links between epic and fantasy, does not the same aesthetic shift that denigrates high fantasy like Martin's *SIF* as 'popular' and 'base' equally demand that we reexamine the canonical reverence still afforded to works like Homeric and Virgilian epic? After all, the contexts of oral-formulaic composition and performance offer the opportunity to read the *Iliad* and *Odyssey* as the mass-produced entertainment literature of a culture industry. If we continue to place the *Iliad* and *Odyssey* on required high school reading lists and to structure core humanities curricula around these poems in universities—for the record, I think we should—are we not obligated to ask and articulate just what their particular values are? To adapt the *fin-de-siècle* art critic and theorist Alois Riegl's schema, do we read and revere classical epic for its historical value today?[74] Have these poems remained canonical primarily for their importance as watershed

---

[72] See especially Huyssen (1986). While Huyssen (viii) is correct that "belief in the Great Divide, with its aesthetic, moral, and political implications is still dominant in the academy" to some extent, the institutional separation between literary studies and mass culture research has at least partially collapsed in the past three decades. As Scholes (2003: 254) notes, Lukács believed it was possible to unite low entertainment literature with high representational art. On the different readings afforded by modernist and postmodern approaches to fantasy, see Attebery (1992: 36–50).

[73] Miéville (2002: 40–41).

[74] Riegl (1982).

moments in intellectual, cultural, and literary history? These are indeed reasons enough to study them. But do ancient epics like the *Iliad* and the *Odyssey* also retain something of their aesthetic, artistic value today? Divorced from their historical contexts and read synchronically, do they remain 'high' literature?

2

Theorizing Fantasy: Enchantment, Parody, and the Classical Tradition

Cecilie Flugt

The beginning of modern fantasy (MF) is usually seen as disconnected from the classical literature that was influential in the nineteenth century, and more often thought of as closely connected to fairy tales and folklore of the same period.[1] This chapter aims to shed light on how our perception of certain literary eras colors the way we look at MF's literary roots and the apparent break with Greco-Roman literary traditions. Both MF's seemingly closer association with folklore, especially the German Romantic movement, and its complementary disassociation from classical literature, result in part from two traditional approaches to defining the genre of MF. On one hand is a tradition that views the fantastic with special attention to the sense of wonder or the uncanny—a feeling of 'enchantment'—a text might produce in the reader.[2] On the other hand is a different tradition that favors particular formal features (such as certain

---

[1] I would like to thank the anonymous reviewers and the volume's editors for their insightful suggestions and comments.

[2] Cf. Mathews (1997: 1): "Most critics agree it is a type of fiction that evokes wonder, mystery, or magic—a sense of possibility beyond the ordinary, material, rationally predictable world in which we live."

collections of tropes), with a strong focus on the element of magic. The popularity of these two approaches, referring as they most commonly do to eighteenth- and nineteenth-century work with fairy tale and folklore, means that scholarship has generally overlooked MF's debts to the Greco-Roman literary tradition.

It is of course difficult to pinpoint the precise influences from previous traditions that produce a new one. In this chapter, however, I argue on the basis of several early modern fantastic texts that several stylistic elements crucial to MF belong primarily to the ancient literary mode of parody. The Greco-Roman tradition of parody may broadly be defined as a polemical imitation of the world—that is, of social practices that include the production of text itself.[3] An author may not only direct parody at earlier texts but also use it to integrate older texts into new contexts. In what follows, I examine parody of previous texts, focusing especially on how authors make new use of old texts to frame their own. In shifting our criteria from one set of features (magical or fantastic elements) to another (parodic elements), I seek to show how literary traditions that reach back to Greco-Roman antiquity bridge the gap between fantastic texts of the eighteenth and nineteenth centuries. This helps us complicate traditional understandings of the fantastic as a mode of wonder and enchantment, placing additional emphasis on the genre's continued self-conscious use of the parodic.

TRADITIONAL LITERARY HISTORIES OF EARLY FANTASY

It is difficult to define MF as a genre, which in turn makes it difficult to describe its literary history. The problem of definition is connected with the term 'fantasy.' The type of literature that we today call 'fantasy' was not compiled under this heading until the mid-1960s in Anglophone and German literary history and scholarship.[4] The relatively late definition

---

[3] Dentith (2000: 17).

[4] Fantastic literature was previously seen as part of the genres called 'the Gothic novel,' 'the ghost story,' and 'romance' in English, and *Schauerroman* and *Gespenstergeschichte* in German. In French literary history, fantastic literature had been so named since the nineteenth century, although the definition was very loose. Some scholars assume that the reason for the French recognition of the genre is that fantastic literature generally was held in higher regard in France than in other countries; see Durst (2007: 19).

and categorization of fantasy also mean that the inclusion of older texts into the genre has happened retrospectively.

In recent years, two distinct traditions have emerged within research on fantastic literature. The first has expanded the genre of the fantastic beyond a literary genre to become an aesthetic category, where the fantastic is rooted in feelings of wonder and alienation that a text may produce in the reader.[5] The other tradition treats fantastic texts as a literary genre whose texts share some tropes that, to a greater or lesser extent, denote the fantastic.[6] Such theories have typically been built on observations made from texts produced in the nineteenth and twentieth centuries, and the move towards a broader definition has proven fruitful in promoting a new way of talking about fantasy. This less strict approach has also meant, however, that certain elements in the literary tradition linking the beginning of MF with Greco-Roman literature have been overlooked.

The literary origin of MF is conventionally situated in the nineteenth century with the beginning of Romanticism, especially German Romanticism.[7] The early Romantic period was marked by a growing interest in fairy tales and folklore. The interest of German writers was partly sparked by a desire to identify a story tradition that was, in their view, originally or natively Germanic. The impetus to focus on a Germanic tradition was partly driven by the desire to build a national myth that could compare or compete with the Roman legacy.[8] There had already been a long tradition of fairy tales in France, but it was the German tradition of fairy tales that became popular around the world in the nineteenth century. Fairy tales or popular folk-tales were perceived as emblematic of the mind of the rustic *Volk* ('folk' or 'people') of Germany, and these tales soon gave rise to a new kind of literature: literary fairy tales or *Kunstmärchen*.[9] Some of the best-known German tales were collected by the Brothers Grimm from local informants. However, the informants were not typically from the 'folk' but actually belonged to a

---

[5] Durst (2007: 20).

[6] James and Mendlesohn (2012: 1).

[7] See Ashley (2010: vi) and Pringel (2002: 11). Both acknowledge that fantastic tales were popular before the nineteenth century but argue that this period was a defining moment in the creation of the genre of fantasy as we know it.

[8] Teverson (2013: 62–63).

[9] For an overview of research on fairy tales, see ibid.

higher social stratum than the brothers let on in their initial publication.[10] Furthermore, this new genre, which developed on the basis of collected oral tales, coincided with an increasing respect among intellectuals for 'imagination' in reaction to the professed rationality of the eighteenth-century Enlightenment era.

The fact that fairy tales were originally transmitted orally may be part of the reason why modern literary companions to fantasy tend to include examples of the Greco-Roman epic tradition—itself originally based in an oral tradition—as part of the genre's history, while passing over other, strictly literary, written traditions from antiquity. A focus on oral traditions as the point of origin for MF can be seen, for example, in *The Cambridge Companion to Fantasy Literature*, where the genealogy reaches back to narratives strongly connected with an oral tradition such as *Beowulf* (c. eighth–eleventh centuries CE) and *The Mabinogion* (c. 1100 CE?), and in *Fantasy, Myth and the Measure of Truth*, where the German Romantic fairy tale is seen as playing a crucial role in the development of fantasy as a genre.[11] There is a tendency to link fantasy with texts rooted in an oral tradition, specifically in the tradition of oral folktales that became popular at the beginning of the nineteenth century and that were believed to belong to a much older tradition than was actually the case.[12]

Such a focus on both MF's roots in the oral tradition and its magical elements has strengthened links between theories of fairy tales and fantasy, coming at the expense of consideration for other theoretical approaches and literary devices. This diminished attention to MF's more literary features might also be due to timing: myth theorists had for a time been interested in fairy tales and folklore as an expression of cultural rites, and, just as scholarly interest in the literary fairy tale began to gather momentum, there arose an interest in psychoanalysis; subsequently, theories about oral fairy tales have been linked to the ideas of Sigmund Freud and Carl Gustav Jung, in the latter of whose terms characters are seen as 'archetypes' representing a 'collective unconscious.' The perceived affiliation between fairy tales and MF that arose only later may also explain why much scholarship on MF has been rooted in theories

---

[10] Ibid. (64–65).
[11] James and Mendlesohn (2012: xv–xxiv) and Gray (2009: 4), respectively.
[12] Zipes (2012: 59).

inspired by psychoanalysis.[13] Moreover, the perceived oral nature of the fairy tale led to Romantic fairy tales being interpreted as emblematic of an unsophisticated and single-layered story-telling culture—of a simpler 'collective unconscious'—with an emphasis on *telling*.[14] This inheritance has been passed on to the literary fairy tales that were produced after the earlier collections of fairy tales were published. The literary fairy tales retained some oral markers but, as literary products, were nevertheless inherently full of artifice. Authors used the new genre's propensity for playing with literary devices to its fullest extent and drew on the tension between fiction and reality.

Furthermore, there has been a tendency to read fairy tales separately from their original socio-historical context, which has subsequently eliminated some of their complexity and many-layered meaning.[15] The apparent simplicity made fairy tales seem more 'intuitive' and in tune with a poetic *ingenium*—with 'untutored' genius and imagination—than their classical antecedents had been, which are often overtly artificial and full of learned allusions to other texts, perhaps reminding readers of long, tedious hours in the classroom.[16] This perception of simplicity also helped create the related perception that MF draws more heavily on Germanic folklore than on Greco-Roman myths. Finally, the perception of a closer link between fantasy and the German Romantics (rather than the Greco-Roman tradition) was reinforced by the idea that readers did not develop the capacity for using their imagination and understanding the fantastical until the nineteenth century.

PARODY AND THE FANTASTIC: LUCIAN AND THE EIGHTEENTH CENTURY

Even if Greco-Roman myths were not a significant source for early fantasy, there is evidence for intertextuality with and parody of the Greco-Roman classics in fantastic texts before the impact of German Romanticism in

---

[13] Durst (2007: 20–33).

[14] Dégh (1991: 71).

[15] Praet (2011: 43–44).

[16] On the ambiguous role of classical texts in fantastic representations of education, see Brown (this volume).

the nineteenth century. Authors of the eighteenth century were deeply influenced by classical literature, and in particular the longstanding story-type of the 'imaginary voyage' flourished: placing a voyage's narrator in a strange setting of the 'Other,' authors could consciously manipulate the tension between fiction and reality in order to parody elements of society safely. One of the primary ancient sources of inspiration for this kind of parody was the *True History* (a Greek text known better by its Latin title, *Verae Historiae* [*VH*]), written by the Syrian-Greek writer Lucian of Samosata (mid-to-late second century CE).[17] *VH* is about an adventurer and his fantastic journey: he sets off to explore unknown lands beyond the *oikoumenê* (the inhabited world) and, in the course of his voyage, sails to the moon and other lands inhabited by fantastic beings. In *VH*, Lucian also explicitly and indirectly parodies earlier Greek authors (such as Homer, Ctesias, Herodotus, and Plato) as well as certain aspects of his contemporary society.[18]

Apart from such social and literary parody, Lucian also exploits other unbelievable elements in his text in order to construct and to complicate his relationship with his reader. *VH* contains a short preamble by a narrator, who seems to be the same person as the intradiegetic narrator. In this preamble, he introduces the text as consisting of "things . . . which, in fact, do not exist at all and, in the nature of things, cannot exist" (περὶ ὧν . . . ἔτι δὲ μήτε ὅλως ὄντων μήτε τὴν ἀρχὴν γενέσθαι δυναμένων; *VH* 1.4).[19] The narrator then proceeds to tell us about his adventures as if

---

[17] Lucian is but one of the writers from this period who produced texts with fantastic elements. Another prominent example from the period is Apuleius, author of *Metamorphoses* (also known as *The Golden Ass*). Interestingly, both authors were set aside during the nineteenth century, even though their texts had been popular between 1500 and 1800. The reason for this might well be that both authors were non-Europeans: Lucian was born in Syria, and Apuleius came from North Africa. During the nineteenth century, with the rise of nation-states and a concomitant nationalism, attitudes towards non-European writers changed, with texts in question being removed from school curricula and the classical canon; see Richter (2005: 88). This change in status with respect to the canon might explain why some Greco-Roman fantastic texts have been omitted from genealogies of fantasy. For Lucian and the related genre of SF, see Keen (2015) and Fredericks (1976); on Apuleius and MF, see the chapters by Winkle and Folch (this volume).

[18] Examples of Lucian's allusions to and use of earlier literature can be found in *VH* 1.3, 1.7, 2.17, 2.21, and 2.20. See also Smith (2009: 81–83), who argues that parts of *VH* can be read as commentaries on the imperialist expansion and cultural imperialism that took place in Lucian's time.

[19] Translation: Harmon (2006: 253).

they were true and mentions that some of the facts might not be believed by the reader, thereby implying that he *should* be believed: "I am reluctant to tell you what sort of eyes they have, for fear that you may think me lying on the account of the incredibility of the story" (περὶ μέντοι τῶν ὀφθαλμῶν οἵους ἔχουσιν, ὀκνῶ μὲν εἰπεῖν, μή τίς με νομίσῃ ψεύδεσθαι διὰ τὸ ἄπιστον τοῦ λόγου; *VH* 1.25).[20] This obvious gap between the voices of the two different narrators must have produced a hesitation in the reader's mind about how to view the intradiegetic narrator's voice and his level of truthfulness.[21] Through the readings of Lucian's many works, we can get a glimpse of the sophistication expected from ancient readers. Indeed, if they were expected to be naïve readers—that is, readers who simply believed the surface meaning of the text—then it would be impossible to make sense of this tactic in the *VH*.

The trope of the imaginary voyage that serves as the frame for *VH* emerges again in later western European literature as a literary sub-genre. One of the earliest and most famous examples is *Utopia* (1516) by Sir Thomas More, who was well acquainted with the works of Lucian. In the next two centuries, we see a steady rise in the popularity of the imaginary journey, appearing in works by Frances Godwin, Cyrano de Bergerac, and Ralph Morris—to name but three notable authors. In the eighteenth century, this type of story reached its peak in popularity at the same time as the novel began to flourish, and thus the imaginary journey became a fruitful locus for experiments with regard to both literary aesthetics and the relationship between truth and fiction. Novels containing the motif of the fantastical journey were later labelled 'imaginary voyages' (also known as *voyages imaginaires* or 'extraordinary voyages').[22] Much like its Lucianic predecessor, the imaginary voyage in the eighteenth century usually contains a journey that explicitly or indirectly parodies earlier, often Greco-Roman, voyage narratives, as well as texts from various other genres. Such tales are narrated in the first person by the voyager or by a narrator who claims to have been in contact with the voyager himself. Thus the story is presented as 'true'; for many tales of imaginary voyages, such 'truthfulness' is further supported by the inclusion in the preface of a letter of recommendation or verification of the text's 'authenticity.'

[20] Translation: Harmon (2006: 279).
[21] Todorov (1975: 25).
[22] See further Gove (1961), as well as Nicolson (1948) and Aldiss (1976).

To consider two prominent examples from the eighteenth century, these parodic elements are found in both Jonathan Swift's *Gulliver's Travels* (1726) and Ludwig Holberg's *Niels Klim's Journey Under the Ground* (1741 [*Niels Klim*]).[23] In *Gulliver's Travels*, the narrator is shipwrecked, and Gulliver observes the customs of the strange beings he encounters, such as the Lilliputians and the talking horses. In *Niels Klim*, Niels falls through a cave into the earth, which turns out to be hollow with another planet at its center. Here he lives among walking intelligent trees and civilized monkeys. In addition to the incredible journey, both narrators offer a description of the societies they encounter. In this way, Swift and Holberg could satirize their own contemporary societies, holding mirrors up to the world: by placing the parody of society in a fictive world, these writers were less likely to risk the wrath of the authorities.

These texts show similarities to Lucian's *VH*, such as the preamble in which the author or narrator raises a question in the reader's mind about the truth of the following story and thereby its relationship to the real world. The ambiguity was strengthened by the lack of the actual author's name on the publication and corroborated further by the physical books themselves, which usually contained a picture of the narrator—not the author—on the frontispiece.[24] Taken together with the preface, these texts create the illusion of truth, even though the stories were incredible. In creating this illusion—which we know contemporary audiences could and did recognize—the author produced the same sense of hesitation for his reader as did Lucian in the introduction to *VH*. This hesitation can be seen as a tool with which the reader could be dislodged from his familiar way of thinking and made to reconsider his worldview in light of the questions raised by the text.

Furthermore, in both *Niels Klim* and *Gulliver's Travels*, the reader is addressed directly, as was the case in *VH*. In *Niels Klim*, the foreword seems to be written by the protagonist's descendants and is addressed to "the Courteous Reader."[25] In *Gulliver's Travels*, the preface contains a letter from the publisher to the reader, wherein the publisher states that he

---

[23] *Niels Klim* was originally published in Latin, which was not very common in this genre at the time, as most of the imaginary voyages were published in the vernacular; see Gove (1961).

[24] Barchas (2003: 27–28).

[25] Holberg (2004: 1–5).

knows Gulliver personally and writes of his own hopes for the text: "hoping they may be, at least for some time, a better Entertainment to our young Noblemen, than the common Scribbles of Politicks and Party."[26] Both stories emulate Lucian's preamble by addressing the reader, pointing directly to the tension between fantastic fiction and reality. Finally, both texts parody older texts and their contemporary societies.[27] The degree of similarity between Greco-Roman texts and texts from the seventeenth and eighteenth centuries is perhaps not surprising, but the level of sophistication with regard to the authors' use of tension between reality and fictionality is striking in light of how readers and genres from this period have generally been viewed—that is, as naïve readers, and as genres following strict generic rules that did not allow for an author's creativity.

FANTASY, PARODY, AND PROSE
IN THE NINETEENTH CENTURY

We turn now to the nineteenth century, the point, according to many critics, at which MF begins. As Richard Mathews observes (following the work of Ian Watt), "[f]antasy as a modern literary category all its own took shape through a dialectic with th[e] new literature of realism," such that MF appeared in the form of short stories and novels.[28] In the following discussion, we shall see several threads that nevertheless link the classically inspired eighteenth century to the fantastic texts of the nineteenth century. These connections are found in the texts' use of parody and in their allusions to previous literary models. We focus on two writers from the beginning and middle of the Romantic period, the German writer E. T. A. Hoffmann (1776–1822) and the Danish writer Hans Christian Andersen (1805–1875).

Many critics take Hoffmann's work as the starting point for MF, along with the works of Ludwig Tieck (1733–1853) and Novalis (1772–1801).[29]

---

[26] Swift (2008: 11).

[27] For further reading on Holberg's parody of contemporary practice and use of ancient texts in *Niels Klim*, see Kragelund (1970). For further reading on parody in *Gulliver's Travels*, see Suarez (2003: 112–127).

[28] Mathews (1997: 3).

[29] Wolfe (2012: 12–13).

Many of Hoffmann's stories possess elements of wild fantasy and the uncanny: these elements are typically taken as pointing to an opposition between the aesthetic traditions of the eighteenth century and a new view of art that emerges around the turn of the century. Hoffmann's interest in earlier aesthetic norms is apparent in his use of poetic traditions from antiquity in dialogue with the aesthetic theory of the Romantics to develop his own stories.[30]

When we look at Hoffmann's use of earlier literary models, we find that there are certain points of contact between some of his works and the sub-genre of the imaginary voyage. Such is the case of *Brambilla* (1820), which takes place in Rome during Carnival. The actor Giglio and his lover, the seamstress Giazinta, each meet a new, fairy-tale-like love interest until they realize that their new lovers are actually identical to their existing lovers. Hoffmann adds to this story the subtitle *a capriccio after Jacques Callot*.[31] The reason for this reference, the reader learns in the foreword, is that the author has seen a review of one of his other works that has been analyzed "with a serious and solemn air," which was not his intent in its composition. He therefore recommends that readers of *Brambilla* "who may be ready and willing to put gravity aside for a few hours . . . not forget the basis on which the whole affair rests, Callot's fantastic caricatures, and also to consider what a musician may demand of a capriccio."[32] This preface is strongly reminiscent both of the prefaces to the imaginary voyages from the previous century and of Lucian's preamble wherein the audience is instructed in how to receive the text.

Hoffmann also directly engages with his readers in *Master Flea* (1822): "Once upon a time—what author nowadays dare begin his tale in such a way? 'Old-fashioned! Boring!' cries the kind or rather unkind

---

[30] Geiger (2013: 18) Geiger outlines the readings of some of Hoffmann's writings, such as *Jacques Callot* (1813), *Elixiren des Teufels* (1816), and *Signor Formica* (1820), among others, as a discussion of the creation and reception of art.

[31] Jacques Callot (1592–1635) was a French printmaker, famous for depicting folk life and bizarre or grotesque scenes. The term *capriccio*, which is also used in music for a series of improvisations, was used by Callot to describe a series of loosely linked drawings. The pictures that inspired *Brambilla* depicted characters from the Italian tradition of *commedia dell'arte*.

[32] Hoffmann (2008: 119). His first collection of stories was also called *Fantasiestücke in Callots Manier*.

reader, who, as the Roman poet sagely advises, wishes to be brought immediately *medias in res*."[33] In this foreword we find not only a direct reference to the "old Roman poet" Horace (65–8 BCE) and his advice on how to write poetry in the *Ars Poetica*, but also a conversation with a reader wherein the narrator both emphasizes the artificiality of the situation and at the same time parodies the fairy tale. Hoffmann thereby creates a situation in which the reader is made acutely aware that he is reading an untruthful text but must at the same time 'believe' the author in order to engage with the text. Hoffmann thereby creates an unreliable narrator of the sort we also find in fantastical texts from the eighteenth century.

Moreover, Hoffmann's texts have traces of the same parodic impulse that we observed in *VH*, *Gulliver's Travels*, and *Niels Klim*. Parody is evident in Hoffmann's *Master Flea*, a story about Peregrinus Tyss, who becomes involved in a conflict between supernatural characters. Set in the period of the Napoleonic Wars, the story includes a character called Councillor Knarrpanti, who is a parody of a real historical person, the director of the Prussian military police, Karl Albert von Kamptz. The analogy between the fictional and the historical person was in fact so obvious to contemporary audiences that Hoffmann was accused of libel.[34] Again we find the same basic similarities between Hoffmann's texts and the previous texts we have explored, including: the direct address to the reader; the parody of or allusion to earlier texts; and the parody of contemporary society. Furthermore, we have indications that these stories were aimed at a classically educated readership: both *Brambilla* and *Master Flea* include references to classical authors or Latin quotes. In *Brambilla*, we find references to Circe (known from the *Odyssey*) and Gyges' ring (known from Plato's *Republic*), among others; and in *Master Flea*, we find references to Horace (discussed above) as well as the Greco-Jewish philosopher Philo of Alexandria (first-century CE).[35]

---

[33] Hoffmann (2008: 239). On Horace's *Ars Poetica* and fantasy, see further this volume's Introduction and the chapter by Weiner.

[34] Scullion and Treby (2013: 139), arguing that the lampoon of von Kamptz in *Master Flea* represents a 'collapsing' of the narrative that does not fit the fairy tale. Here it may be productive to see the lampoon not as a violation of the fairy-tale genre but rather as an inheritance from the tradition of parody that goes back to antiquity.

[35] Hoffmann (2008: 184, 215, 239, 325).

In later works of MF, explicit references to classical texts are usually absent. An example of this are the works of Hans Christian Andersen, the many celebrated fairy tales written during the middle of the nineteenth century, and that are often placed on the continuum between Romantic and realist literature. Andersen's works are a good example of fantastic literature at this time. Critics tend to focus on his creative power and distinct voice, which set him apart from other authors from this period. His ability and imagination as a writer have been linked with his humble upbringing and his connection with a rural, unsophisticated population. However, Andersen was in fact rather well educated, both in contemporary and classical literature. If we compare his tales with the previously examined stories, we do not find any of the traits discussed—e.g., direct address to the reader or explicit references to Greco-Roman authors—although some of his works can be read as critiques of the prevalent norms of contemporary society. Furthermore, parodies of historical persons can be found in Andersen's stories.[36] Andersen sometimes uses classical elements in stories, such as *The Dryad*, in which the tree nymph, borrowed from Greek myth, is taken from her native countryside into Paris and vanishes in the modern city. But more often his stories revolve around creatures from Nordic myths.

This shift away from Greco-Roman literary models is interesting, especially in connection with the intended readership for such fantastic tales. In the second part of the nineteenth century, literacy increased; however, at the same time, there was a sharper focus on education in one's national language and literature, which meant that an education in the Greco-Roman classics was reserved for only a select group in society.[37] It is possible that texts began to include fewer references to classical literature due to an awareness of a growing popular audience without classical education.[38] But even though explicit references to classical texts may have dwindled, parody remained an important tool with which authors could highlight the fantastic.

---

[36] Bredsdorff (2005: 4).

[37] Mollier and Cachin (2009: 303).

[38] Cf. Joshua Scodel's entry in Grafton, Most, and Settis (2010: 475), which gives a short overview of connections between literary imitation of Greco-Roman predecessors and the decline of readers' knowledge of classical literature.

(DIS)ENCHANTMENT IN READERS OF THE FANTASTIC

The Romantic era has traditionally been described as a period when poets rebelled against the strict formal criteria and rationalism of the Enlightenment, and when the role of the 'untutored' imagination was emphasized.[39] In contrast to eighteenth-century literature, which held in high regard the clarity of the classical period and strict definitions of genre, Romantic literature of the nineteenth century is conventionally distinguished as being inspired by the medieval period.[40] Critics perceived fantastic literature from the Enlightenment era as less imaginative for conforming to strict generic conventions, which had been inspired by the renewed interest in Greco-Roman texts about poetic composition (including Plato's *Republic*, Aristotle's *Poetics*, and Horace's *Ars Poetica*). Furthermore, as we have seen in the previous section, Enlightenment-era authors openly adopted the practice of mimesis or 'imitation'—that is, the conscious use of models and motifs from earlier literature (such as the 'imaginary voyage'). The Romantics perceived elements like mimesis as unimaginative, even though Enlightenment-era texts contained many fantastic (i.e., imaginative) elements. In rejecting the aesthetics of the Enlightenment, the Romantics also passed over the Greco-Roman literary tradition, instead giving pride of place to oral traditions (including epic) in fantasy's genealogy, since the oral tradition was perceived as more 'original' and 'creative' than the Greco-Roman tradition of literary—written—imitation.

In other words, the Romantics sought to create literature in which the subjectivity of the author manifests itself in many different forms. Here the novel played a significant role: two of the most significant German Romantics, Friedrich Schlegel (1772–1829) and the aforementioned Novalis, saw the novel as a form of poetry in which the poet could display the multiplicity of his experience manifested in formal unity. In this genre all other genres could be mixed, and through these different modes, a single unified mode could be produced.[41]

This Romantic view has profoundly but anachronistically influenced the way we think about 'imagination' and 'creativity' in relation to the

---

[39] Graver (2010: 73).
[40] Gray (2009: 14).
[41] Blackall (1983: 65).

literature and readership of the eighteenth and nineteenth centuries.[42] However, recent scholarship has raised the possibility that there was a 'Re-Enchantment,' questioning how imagination worked in the two time periods and whether we can even talk about a 'naïve' or 'sophisticated' reader—a reader who believed in a supernatural world or a reader who knew fiction when he saw it (i.e., what we might wish to think of as a modern reader). By using this theory of Re-Enchantment to re-read central texts from those two centuries, we gain new insights into the literary history of the fantastic and its relationship to Greco-Roman traditions.

The eighteenth century generally, and the Enlightenment era in particular, has been viewed as marked by an increasing secularization and skepticism towards superstition and fantasy. This view has led some scholars to propose a theory about the 'disenchantment' of the world as a consequence of the period's rising secularization. One of the most prominent advocates for this view of the Enlightenment was the German sociologist Max Weber (1864–1920), who coined the term 'disenchantment' (*Entzauberung*) in order to describe the modern state of mind.[43] Disenchantment, of course, implies an earlier 'Enchantment' that in turn implies a world in which the mythic and mystical play a prominent role and the reader cannot necessarily tell the difference between fiction and reality.

Until recently, two different ideas have dominated discussion of disenchantment: the binary model and the dialectical model. According to the binary model, the notion of enchantment was developed in opposition to disenchanted modernity and pressed into the cultural fringes— i.e., into popular culture—by the Western-European cultural elite of the seventeenth and eighteenth centuries. This cultural elite viewed enchantment as a sign of the naïve mind belonging to subordinate social groups, including colonized natives, women, and the lower classes. The modern rational human being could pretend to be enchanted by reading

---

[42] For an explanation of mimesis ('imitation') and the use of this concept in literary traditions, see Scodel's entry in Grafton, Most, and Settis (2010: 472–475). Lindenberger discusses the broad influence Romantic aesthetics on how we value literature (1990: 28).

[43] See Weber's 1917 lecture *Wissenschaft als Beruf* (in Mommsen [1992]), in which he defines 'disenchantment' as the loss of overarching meanings, magical orientations, and spiritual explanations that had characterized the traditional world, resulting from the ongoing 'modern' processes of rationalization, secularization, and bureaucratization. Cf. Saler (2012: 8).

fanciful novels, whereas this type of literature was viewed, for example, as dangerous to most women, who were seen as being at risk of becoming truly enchanted, uncritically believing whatever they read. In the binary model, modernity is therefore seen as a loss of enchantment and is viewed with both regret for the loss of wonder and hope of knowledge and progress. In the dialectical model, enchantment is a negative part of an oppressing modernity, exacerbated by the associations of modernity with rationality and of progress with liberty. In this model, modernity itself is 'enchanted' and can be revealed as oppressive only through disenchantment.[44] Modernity is thus viewed negatively, and enchantment is inhabited by modern individuals who think of themselves as free and in possession of reason, whereas they are actually only enchanted—that is, enslaved by the modern condition.

Within the last twenty years or so, scholars have begun to discuss 're-enchantment.' The reason for this shift lies partly in the recognition of new areas of study such as gender studies, postcolonial studies, and new media studies, in which the focus falls outside of the Western cultural elite.[45] Given these new areas of study, the two previous models have become insufficient for describing the relationship between modernity and enchantment. Modernity is now seen as being modulated by both disenchantment and enchantment in a symbiotic relationship. Due to both the reconsideration of what modernity entails and the recognition that enchantment and naïveté are not necessarily the same, scholars are reconsidering the whole question of enchantment and whether there has ever existed a world in which people truly 'believed' as it is understood in a modern sense.[46] Was there, for example, ever a larger group of readers who actually believed that Lucian's narrator was blown by a storm to the moon, that Gulliver conversed with horses, or that Niels Klim lived among walking, talking trees? This re-evaluation of enchantment and modernity makes it possible to re-examine the concept of fiction and how readers perceived the fantastic before 1800. It is thus possible to push back the timeline for when MF can be said to develop in literature. Looking at the examples considered herein, it is possible to trace literary traditions that transgress the literary borders generally established for

---

[44] Saler (2012: 9–11).
[45] Styers (2004: 20).
[46] Paige (2009: 179).

the history of MF. In particular, of course, there is much to be gained by continuing to explore the genre's historical connections to material and modes from Greco-Roman antiquity.

CONCLUSION

We have seen how the fantastic played a significant role in fictional literature before 1800. Here authors used elements of the fantastic in their imagined conversations with readers such that readers were dislocated from their familiar worldviews. From the nineteenth century onwards, fantastic texts have not made *explicit* use of Greco-Roman traditions, but ancient literary devices such as parody still play a role in the sophisticated interactions between author and reader, between truth and fiction. This seems to suggest that authors from the periods under consideration in this chapter were inspired by the literary traditions from previous centuries: even though the Greco-Roman material seldom exists explicitly in the texts, it nonetheless seems to play a large role alongside more frequently cited sources such as Germanic folktale or Norse myth. The choice of source material itself even seems to have been made in dialogue with Greco-Roman traditions. A new approach to the literary history of MF, based on new perceptions of modernity's refiguration of imagination and creativity, could prove fruitful in uncovering the genre's genealogy more precisely. With multiple points of origin not limited to medieval and early modern material but including Greco-Roman antiquity, such a genealogy could very well contribute to a view of MF's literary history as being not a series of binary oppositions or exclusions, but rather a series of confluences that incorporate both literary devices such as parody and effects such as (dis)enchantment.

3

The Mirror Crack'd: Fractured Classicisms in the Pre-Raphaelites and Victorian Illustration

Genevieve S. Gessert

> *However good in themselves, illustrations do little good to fairy-stories. The radical distinction between all art (including drama) that offers a visible presentation and true literature is that it imposes one visible form. . . .*
>
> —J. R. R. Tolkien[1]

> *One thing I am sure of. All my seven Narnian books, and my three science fiction books, began with seeing pictures in my head. At first they were not a story, just pictures. . . .*
>
> —C. S. Lewis[2]

Though J. R. R. Tolkien's "On Fairy Stories" has been consistently mined for its revelations of the author's theories on the creative (or sub-creative) process, that famous essay also treats the relationship between illustration

---

[1] Tolkien (1994: 185).
[2] Lewis (1966: 42).

and text, especially in explaining the format and boundaries of fantasy worlds. In the epigraph above, Tolkien seemingly rejects the significance of illustration, yet elsewhere in the essay he describes the formation of the fantasy world in visual terms. In a later footnote to the essay, Tolkien bemoans the modern tendency to print illustrations in fairy books as "conterminous with the page . . . altogether inappropriate for pictures that illustrate or are inspired by fairy stories. An enchanted forest requires a margin, even an elaborate border."[3] Tolkien was himself an accomplished artist and created the illustrations and maps for his most beloved works.[4] C. S. Lewis, for his part, cites in *Surprised by Joy* the effects that images had on his young psyche and the sensation of his connection with ideas that defy written description. Certain concepts for Lewis reside in the realm of the visual: raw feelings, defining characteristics, and, as described above, seminal images. Whether via rejection, qualification, or acceptance, both writers implicitly acknowledge the power of images in the creation of ideas in fantasy.

Tolkien originally delivered "On Fairy Stories" as a lecture in 1939, perhaps the most famous installment of the lecture series at St. Andrews University named for its native son, the anthropologist and anthologist Andrew Lang.

For Tolkien's generation, it was primarily Lang who made such figures and talismans as good fairies, wizards, dragons, goblins, magic trees, and magic rings common knowledge to readers from childhood on. Tolkien quarreled with much of what Lang had to say, but he was, as he described himself, one of the children Lang was addressing—and he listened.[5]

Tolkien often cited Lang as a catalyst for his interests in Northern sagas, and scholars have traced Tolkien's innovative descriptions of dragons and other fairy beings back to the pages of Lang's *Coloured Fairy Book* series.[6] Lewis's letters indicate that he also knew Lang's work well and read his works even into his early formative years at Oxford.[7] But Lang's work was seminal and popular not just for its textual content, which brought an

---

[3] Tolkien (1994: 188, note H).
[4] Hammond and Scull (1995).
[5] Berman (2007: 134).
[6] Ibid. (134) and White (2001: 121).
[7] Berman (2012: 119–20) and Zaleski and Zaleski (2015: 76).

international fairy narrative to English children for the first time, but also for its accompanying illustrations.

Tolkien and Lewis grew up in the heyday of the illustrated book, in a period when books frequently were purchased, collected, and popularized for their pictures rather more than for their texts. Both men recognized the influence that the books they read as children had had on their adult interests, and their intellectual relationship was in part based on their shared love of fairy stories.[8] However, as seminal as particular stories and poems were to these two budding scholar-authors, the illustrations that they encountered were arguably more profoundly inspirational in forming the visual and conceptual frameworks that would underpin their most famous works.[9] As Lewis described the genesis of his childhood interest in myth, he was inspired to 'Northernness' by an Arthur Rackham illustration.[10] Tolkien as a child owned many illustrated volumes of stories, including *The Red Fairy Book*, in which he first encountered Sigurd and his first image of a dragon.[11] Many of the qualities that Tolkien cites in "On Fairy Stories" as appropriate for the illustration of fairy stories are distinguishing characteristics of the illustrations in the *Coloured Fairy Book* series. Yet, surprisingly, while scholars of early modern fantasy have dissected Tolkien's and Lewis's letters and papers to reconstruct the precise literary, philosophical, and religious allusions contained in their work, little attention has been paid to the visual influences that were equally seminal in forming the framework of their created worlds.

This chapter traces the evolution of the style and content of late Victorian illustration, taking as its primary example the drawings of Henry Justice Ford, the main illustrator of Lang's *Coloured Fairy Book* series. While Ford lacks the name recognition of Randolph Caldecott, the outré content of Aubrey Beardsley, or the precious polychromy of Arthur Rackham, his illustrations were far more numerous and widely distributed. Furthermore, unlike those and many other more celebrated children's illustrators, in the *Coloured Fairy Books* Ford was re-illustrating

---

[8] Carpenter (1978) and James (2012: 67).

[9] Lewis (1984: 17) and Carpenter (1978: 22–23).

[10] Carpenter (1978: 5) and Zaleski and Zaleski (2015: 47).

[11] *The Red Fairy Book* has been reprinted in the new *Tolkien's Bookshelf* series, which seeks to reprint illustrated volumes as Tolkien would have read them.

well-known popular stories and nursery rhymes for a twelve-volume compendium that sought to forge narrative connections across time and place. Between 1889 and 1910, Ford produced close to 1,000 illustrations for Lang's wildly popular anthology, creating a universal aesthetic by which all fairy narratives could be visualized.[12] By tracing Ford's background and influences, which included both classical academic study and alignment with the Pre-Raphaelite artistic movement, we can come to understand his aesthetic framework for 'Faerie' that influenced future writers of fantasy, including Tolkien and Lewis.

The first part of this chapter charts the Pre-Raphaelites' varied (and largely overlooked) engagement with classical models, and the transition from such engagement into illustrated products designed for broad commercial consumption. The title "The Mirror Crack'd" is taken from Alfred Lord Tennyson's 1832 poem *The Lady of Shalott*, a work with special resonance for the Pre-Raphaelites as they balanced a multiplicity of past styles and influences to craft a new aesthetic philosophy for the Victorian Age.[13] This complex engagement is demonstrated in William Holman Hunt's final painting inspired by the poem from 1910, in which the classical references, namely the story of Ariadne and the Labors of Hercules, are arrayed around the central medievalized figure of the Lady like the reflective splinters of an ancient fractured mirror. The second half of this chapter traces the Pre-Raphaelite influence in the illustrations of Henry Justice Ford for the *Coloured Fairy Book* series and other Lang publications, analyzing the ways in which Ford's particular aesthetic uses a hybrid classical-medieval visualization to provide a cognitive framework for the comprehension of Lang's universal fairy narrative.

THE PRE-RAPHAELITES AND THE VICTORIAN CLASSICAL IMAGINATION

Late in the summer of 1848, Dante Gabriel Rossetti and his intellectual compatriot William Holman Hunt met in a "studio conclave" to discuss the formation of a new artistic brotherhood, the Pre-Raphaelite Brotherhood

---

[12] Hares-Stryker (2009: 60–64).
[13] Poulson (1996: 173–194).

(PRB). As Rossetti later wrote to his brother William, the primary goal of this meeting was the drafting of a list of 'Immortals,' a select group of artists, writers, and cultural figures ranked by their influence on and importance to the nascent movement. Each figure received between zero and four stars. Only three men received four or three stars: Jesus (4), the author of Job (3), and Shakespeare (3). Among the two-star figures were artists and writers who were particularly important to the PRB's rejection of the themes and styles of the high Renaissance after Raphael (Chaucer, Dante, Leonardo da Vinci, Fra Angelico) and who aligned with the PRB's admiration of English literary artistry (Thackeray, Keats, Shelley, Browning).[14] In Holman Hunt's later account, the Immortals list became the backbone of the manifesto of the PRB:

> We, the undersigned, declare that the following list of Immortals constitutes the whole of our Creed, and that there exists no other Immortality than what is centered in their names and in the names of their contemporaries, in whom this list is reflected.[15]

Though the first wave of Pre-Raphaelitism was to be short-lived, this meeting of two iconoclasts concentrated the debate among the creative intelligentsia of the Victorian era on two significant topics: the creation of a new artistic canon, and the modern scholar-artist's relationship with the past.

Scholarly analysis of the Immortals list has focused on the names that underscore the perceived dominant themes of movement. The PRB is commonly associated with its promotion of medieval art and pre-Raphael artists, and its supposed rejection of the classical subjects and styles favored by artists of the later Renaissance. Thus the fact is frequently overlooked that the list of heroes included two significant Greek figures, the poet Homer (two stars) and the artist Pheidias (none). While seemingly out of place in terms of the major PRB themes cited above, these two figures are essential for understanding the reception of the classical past established by the Creed. As the grandfather of classical epic, Homer provided the foundation and inspiration for writers on the list such as Dante (two stars) and Tennyson (one), the latter a

---

[14] For the full list of Immortals, see Appendix 2 of Prettejohn (2012a: 277–278).
[15] Quoted in ibid. (277).

contemporary hero of the PRB.[16] Pheidias at the time was associated with the most famous sculptures on British soil, the Parthenon Marbles (or "the Elgin Marbles") and the Parthenon building. The accomplishments of Pheidias and his contemporaries provided the aesthetic framework for the Immortal visual artists like Leonardo, Michelangelo, and Raphael, and casts of the Parthenon Marbles and other 'true' sculptures were the regulation training models for nineteenth-century draftsmen. But perhaps most important is the implied cyclical parallel across artistic ages, undoubtedly influenced by the German art historian and archaeologist Johann Winckelmann: no Hellenistic-era or Roman artists or writers are included in the list, just as the followers of Raphael are thoroughly rejected. The cycles of cultural production lie in parallel like archaeological strata, with the past fundamentally supporting but increasingly overwritten by the present. The PRB thus presented a faded and fragmented view of the classical, one that looked back to ancient Greece for its narrative and visual structures but masked its content with the trappings of the Christian medieval world.

Though the corpus of the PRB is vast, stretching from its origins in the mid–nineteenth century to the years before World War I, a few examples that engaged with classical precedents can illustrate how this emulative fragmentation played out. We begin with the most iconic example: Dante Gabriel Rossetti's highly recognizable pseudo-portraits of Alexa Wilding, Fanny Cornforth, and Jane Morris.[17] From the directly classical characters such as *Helen of Troy* (1863), *Penelope* (1869), *Pandora* (1871), and *Proserpine* (numerous examples in the 1870s) to the broadly allegorical *La Donna della Fiamma* (Figure 3.1) and *Silence* (both 1870), Rossetti used these images to create his own visual list of female Immortals, including both figures from the past and their modern representatives. While popularized as meditations on the fraught relationship between Rossetti and Mrs. Morris, these works also express Rossetti's complex engagement with classical precedents in creating his own artistic philosophy. The images make use of Rossetti's signature later style and design, broadly derived

---

[16] Armstrong (2012: 20–21) and Canevaro (2014).

[17] Prettejohn (2012b: 109–114). While some see these portraits as a demonstration of Rossetti's departure from Pre-Raphaelite tenets, they remain nonetheless the works arguably most identified with the PRB and grace the covers of numerous fiction and non-fiction books on the Brotherhood, including Prettejohn (2012a).

Figure 3.1 Dante Gabriel Charles Rossetti (1828-82), *La Donna della Fiamma* (1870). Pastel & pencil on paper. Manchester Art Gallery, UK/Bridgeman Image.

from medieval and early Renaissance portraits; these features, combined with a lush palette of greens and purples and with Mrs. Morris's distinctive physiognomy, make the images the most recognizable and lampooned of all Pre-Raphaelite artworks.[18] But the works were also supported by considerable research into classical sources, which Rossetti would often use to craft a poetic inscription on the image or a separately published poem.

[18] Even within Rossetti's own lifetime: see Matson (2010: 34, 47).

For example, the series of paintings depicting Mrs. Morris as Proserpine were as much a result of Rossetti's detailed research into the Eleusinian mysteries and Platonic philosophy as they were a mythological allegory for the Rossetti–Morris affair.[19] *Proserpine* was accompanied by a poem in archaic Italian that drew on contemporary classical scholarship by Lemprière and Müller as well as the poetry of Ovid and Swinburne. In addition, Rossetti is known to have sketched from classical statues, and possibly derived inspiration from newly discovered classical sculptures, such as the Knidos Demeter and Persephone, as they arrived at the British Museum throughout the Victorian period.[20]

Another Pre-Raphaelite artist also took inspiration from classical texts and artworks as he produced designs for private consumption that intertwined fine and applied arts. In the early 1870s, Edward Burne-Jones planned a series of paintings depicting the tale of Cupid and Psyche for the dining room of his patron George Howard at 1 Palace Green in London.[21] Burne-Jones was a prodigious painter and frequent collaborator with William Morris, the pioneer of the Arts and Crafts movement; both men were major figures in the commercialization of Pre-Raphaelitism in the later Victorian era.[22] The cycle of Cupid and Psyche images had originally been conceived as illustrations to accompany Morris's poetic series *The Earthly Paradise*, a Victorian retelling of classical tales in a medieval framework. Burne-Jones's initial works for *The Earthly Paradise* were primarily influenced by the woodcuts in Morris's copy of the *Hypneratomachia Polipholi*, a Renaissance book characterized by the melding of classical and medieval sources.[23] In transitioning the cycle to a domestic space, Burne-Jones drew upon a broader range of classical and medieval sources to create resonant visual associations both within the cycle and with external works; this broadening typifies the proliferation of the Pre-Raphaelite aesthetic in the applied arts, including later commercial book illustration.

---

[19] Bentley (2009).

[20] Surtees (1971: cat. no. 612) is a pen-and-ink drawing entitled in Rossetti's own hand 'From a Statue,' presumably drawn in 1878–1879. The image depicts an unknown classical sculpture, probably a Venus, completed with a head of Jane Morris. For inspiration from new discoveries, see Bentley (2009: 63).

[21] Wippermann (2009: 84–95). The story of Cupid and Psyche has inspired many works; e.g., Lewis's *Till We Have Faces*, on which see Folch (this volume).

[22] Wildman and Christian (1998: 5–23).

[23] Pieri (2012: 19).

Figure 3.2 West Wall, Cupid and Psyche Frieze by Sir Edward Burne-Jones. ca. 1898. No. 1 Palace Green, London. Scanned image from *The Studio* 15 (October 1898).

While the overall design of the Psyche cycle owes much to medieval spaces like the Scrovegni chapel in Padua, the composition of the individual panels and the decoration of the figures rely on classical models, in particular the Parthenon sculptures. In the panel entitled "Psyche Led to Be Sacrificed to the Monster" (Figure 3.2), the rhythmical arrangement, in which small groupings of similarly depicted figures alternate with isolated individuals, has its compositional origins in the east frieze of the Parthenon.[24] Though set against a mountainous backdrop in the distance, the figures process primarily in profile along a single ground-line. As with the Rossetti portraits described above, the figures in the Psyche cycle sport medievalized garments in the vivid Pre-Raphaelite palette, but rendered in the plasticity and elaboration common to classical sculptures. Significantly, the figure of Psyche is rendered throughout in diaphanous white drapery, creating a stronger visual association between Psyche and the unpainted casts and Greek originals that served as her models. Burne-Jones became increasingly unavailable as he began work on two other classically inspired painting cycles in 1875, the *Pygmalion* and *Perseus* series for which he is best known. In the end, the

[24] See also the 1895 painting *The Wedding of Psyche* in Wildman and Christian (1998: cat. no. 41).

Howard house paintings were eventually completed using Burne-Jones's cartoons by Walter Crane, an artist who would later make his name in the world of late Victorian illustration alongside Henry Justice Ford. Significantly, both Burne-Jones and Crane relied on ancient sculptures to craft the volume and drapery of their painted figures: Walter Crane kept a cast of a Greek frieze in his studio;[25] Burne-Jones owned casts of two of the Parthenon's pedimental figures,[26] and his sketchbooks include numerous sketches from both these casts and the originals in the British Museum.[27]

The final example is the work that inspired this chapter's title and represents the Pre-Raphaelite engagement with the classical at its final complexity: William Holman Hunt's *The Lady of Shalott*, executed in the final years of the artist's life (1886–1910) and in the last decades of Pre-Raphaelite influence. Hunt had explored this subject in several earlier drawings, including one for the 1857 Moxon edition of Tennyson (over which he and Rossetti had a "rather unseemly dispute").[28] The story of the tragic heroine, who leaves her weaving to gaze out of her window at a passing Sir Lancelot and thereby activates the curse that leads to her death, is generally interpreted as a metaphor for the artist's engagement with society.[29] Lilah Canevaro has recently suggested that Tennyson's poem may have had another element of attraction for the Pre-Raphaelites— namely, its resonance with the poetry of Homer, one of Rossetti's and Hunt's founding Immortals.[30] Other artists favored the romantic potential of the Lady's death scene.[31] Hunt, however, was obsessed with the moment of transition as the Lady's diverted attention leads to an internal fracturing of both her tapestry work and her carefully constructed world, as symbolized by the mirror in her chamber:

She left the web, she left the loom,
She made three paces through the room,

---

[25] Jenkyns (1980: 302).

[26] Hanson in Grafton, Most, and Settis (2010: 307, s.v. 'Elgin Marbles').

[27] Wildman and Christian (1998: 113–114 and 131–132) and Wippermann (2009: 92).

[28] Poulson (1996: 175).

[29] Ibid. (177) and Bronkhurst and Holman Hunt (2006: 271).

[30] Canevaro (2014: 213).

[31] For example, John William Waterhouse's *Lady of Shalott* (1888) in the Tate Britain. See Goldhill (2011: 29).

She saw the water-lily bloom,
    She saw the helmet and the plume,
    She looked down to Camelot.
Out flew the web and floated wide;
The mirror crack'd from side to side;
'The curse is come upon me,' cried
The Lady of Shalott.[32]

Hunt's 1910 painting relies on his earlier Moxon Tennyson drawing for its basic composition: the Lady, her hair loose and undulating over her head, is ensnared in her unraveling tapestry and framed by the circular mirror behind her, cracks spidering across its surface. The cracks in the mirror and the tangled threads of the destroyed tapestry are intertwined: the artist risks both her work and her relationship with reality in attempting to balance her attention between them. In the painting (Figure 3.3), the details of the setting and decoration, over which Hunt cogitated for twenty years, also represent Hunt's personal reflections on his movement's engagement with cultural antecedents.[33] If we can see the Lady as a metaphor for the artist, her chamber is the artist's studio, the room created to contain the instruments of inspiration and creation.[34] The wall decorations include scenes both medieval and classical in style, and Christian and pagan in content, reflected and refracted along with the images of reality in the cracked mirror. As a further parallel, most of these elements were either constructed as models in Hunt's studio or were antiquarian objects in his collection.[35] The image of the Lady as a weaver, an artisan as opposed to a fine artist, also reverberates with the Pre-Raphaelite tension between high and popular art, though ironically contained within a high-priced (and by this time old-fashioned) oil painting.

Despite the variation in their dates of production and the idiosyncrasies of the individual artists, a number of unifying ideas may be observed in these emblematic works. Firstly, the interrelationship of drawing and

[32] Tennyson, "The Lady of Shalott" (1832).

[33] Bronkhurst and Holman Hunt (2006: 271).

[34] An interesting parallel could be made with John Ballantyne's series of portraits of Victorian artists in their studios, including one of Hunt himself, painted in the 1860s; see ibid. (106, fig. 16).

[35] Ibid. (271–272).

Figure 3.3 William Holman Hunt (English, 1827–1910), *The Lady of Shalott* (ca. 1890–1905). Oil on canvas, 74 ⅛ × 57 ⅝ in. The Ella Gallup Sumner and Mary Catlin Sumner Collection Fund, 1961.470. Wadsworth Athenaeum Museum of Art, Hartford, Connecticut.

writing so key to the PRB philosophy is demonstrated throughout via an underlying literary text, an allusive attribute, or an epigraph. One of the concepts implicit in the list of Immortals was the equality of art media: the visual and literary arts were companions, not competitors. Thus the PRB operated under the idea that not only could texts comment on and analyze images, but also images could do the same for texts. As a result, a wider range of art media, including the decorative arts and print journalism, could be used to express cultural theories in both subtle and overt ways to a wider audience. Art and beauty became consumable commodities, made accessible both to the larger elite (via the atelier of Morris) and to the masses (via the printed page).

The outcome of this democratization of art production, increasing focus on popular media, and reconsideration of the canon effected by the first wave of PRB was a more nuanced engagement with the antique. In the early Victorian era, the approach to famous originals like the Elgin Marbles was cautious reverence, whereas the later Victorian PRB followers and the Aesthetes presented a range of possible contacts, from fractured quotation to sensuous enrapture. Greek revivalism, made emblematic in Alma-Tadema's 1868 painting *Phidias Showing the Frieze of the Parthenon to His Friends*, pervaded the arts at all levels of society to the point that it could be parodied by Walter Crane in his popular collection of nursery rhymes, *The Baby's Opera* (1877).[36] Thus the quotation or emulation of the classical in this varied sense became so ubiquitous that it in itself could be claimed as Victorian. Canevaro writes:

William Morris argued that if one worked from a source text, there must come a point when the authority was laid aside: "In this way it would be transfigured, filtered through the consciousness of the recipient and thus remade." It also does not mean that the poet (etc.) must lead us by the hand through every resonance and echo. Classical reception entails engagement with the ancient world—but it does not need a footnote.[37]

The late Victorian era, a period steeped in classical scholarship, in a variety of classical reception methodologies, and in aesthetic movements and counter-movements, was also characterized by dramatic developments in the technology of printing. This coincidence of cultural factors allowed commercial publishing to become a dominant medium of expression for writers and artists emerging from this cultural melting pot.

---

[36] A drawing of lady in Grecian dress, bending down to feed a gluttonous hog in a sty with a Greek-style pediment and columns, accompanies the poem: "There was a lady loved a swine / 'Honey!' said she; / 'Pig-hog, wilt thou be mine?' / 'Hunc!' said he"; Jenkyns (1980: 302, with plate V).

[37] Canevaro (2014: 212).

ANDREW LANG AND HENRY JUSTICE FORD

The more than two decades that Holman Hunt worked on his highly symbolic *Lady of Shalott* coincide almost precisely with the publication of the Victorian era's most influential illustrated volumes for both adults and children. The development of photo transfer engraving, which allowed an artist to adapt a drawing to different print formats easily, combined with a highly literate populace interested in consuming printed and illustrated media, encouraged an explosion of illustrated periodicals of all genres.[38] The late Victorian and Edwardian eras were the heyday of *Punch* and *The London Illustrated News* as well as many other short-lived and specialized publications. A variety of national initiatives were promulgated in the nineteenth century to increase children's literacy, resulting in a highly literate adult population during the Victorian era.[39] Furthermore, the general economic prosperity promoted reading for pleasure at all ages and social stations. These developments also promoted the gift book, a lavishly illustrated volume of classic stories typically published for the Christmas season, as a popular medium.[40]

Thus, by the end of the nineteenth century, commercial illustration was a lucrative profession for the large number of students being produced by art schools of the Victorian period. Some of Britain's most reputable and influential art schools were established in the Victorian period, including the Brighton School of Art (1858) and the Slade School of Art (1868, now part of the University College London). The South Kensington Museum (1852, later renamed the Victoria and Albert Museum) and the South Kensington Schools (renamed the Royal College of Art in 1896) were founded particularly for "the purpose of teaching instructors in art throughout the kingdom, as well as for the instruction of students in drawing, designing, and modeling, to be applied to the requirements of trade and manufacture."[41] These students were essentially charged with transferring the ideas and aesthetics of the high art movements into practical applications, including commercial illustration. Many well-known illustrators of the era, including Arthur Rackham, Edmund Dulac, and

---

[38] Peppin (1975: 7–8).
[39] Bratton (1981: 11–19).
[40] Wootton (1999: 111–114).
[41] Clement and Hutton (1897).

Kay Nielsen, made their names and livings from these popular publications, many of which are still in print. The Pre-Raphaelites' pioneering illustrations, such as the 1857 Moxon Tennyson, and application of their motifs and designs in Arts and Crafts products, made the Pre-Raphaelite style an attractive option—increasingly so as fairy stories returned to popularity following the publication of *The Blue Fairy Book*, the first installment of Lang's influential anthology.

Lang was born and educated in Scotland, studying at the University of Glasgow and St. Andrews before taking a First in Classics from Balliol College, Oxford, in 1868. Despite his contemporary influence and extensive bibliography, Lang is a notoriously difficult subject. He ordered his wife to destroy all of his papers and correspondence after his death; she complied with his request, complaining of the pain in her wrists for weeks after her lengthy shredding session.[42] Thus Roger Lancelyn Green's pocket-sized biography of Lang was written based on brief mentions in other men's papers and the remembrances of now-elderly childhood acquaintances. As with many ancient scholars and writers, Lang's theoretical underpinnings are derived solely from his published work, in this case the prefaces of the anthologies.[43]

Lang began the *Coloured Fairy Book* series without any anticipation of its success, and the editor's introductions to the first two volumes of the anthology are brief and factual, recounting the origins of the tales and voicing the expectation that the current volume would be the last.[44] However, beginning with *The Green Fairy Book* (1892), the third volume in the series, Lang began to write more effusively and defensively on his theories regarding Faerie and story-telling in general. One early task was to defend his series against learned critics, primarily the membership of the Folk Lore Society, which apparently objected to the inclusion of stories that could 'mislead' children.[45] Most of the prefaces attempted to make clear the authorship of the adapted tales included in each volume: Lang averred that not only was he not the author of any of them (though he had written some original fairy stories prior to *The Blue Fairy*

[42] Green (1962: 8).

[43] For a brief biography of Lang, see Green (1980).

[44] Except in the limited edition, large paper printing of 113 copies of *The Blue Fairy Book* for collectors, which included a special introduction by Lang; see Green (1962: 45).

[45] Preface to *The Yellow Fairy Book* (1894: ix–x).

Book), but that for the most part the stories had no authors, only transla-
tors. Lang employed members of his family as story collectors and trans-
lators, whose renditions he presumably edited to create a uniform style
consistent with the overall message of the collection:[46]

[A]ll people, black, white, brown, red, and yellow, are like each other when
they tell stories; for these are meant for children, who like the same sort of
thing, whether they go to school and wear clothes, or, on the other hand,
wear skins of beasts, or even nothing at all, and live on grubs and lizards and
hawks and crows and serpents, like the little Australian blacks.[47]

This sentiment of universal mythopoesis led him to collect stories
from all over the globe, meant to be understood as linked by their similarities rather than their differences.

As is characteristic of the era, there is a strong Western bias in Lang's
universal theory, which also saw the roots of prehistory in fairy-stories.[48]
Lang frequently implied that the works of classical literature embodied the origins for both narrative elements and moral content of stories: "Though they usually take the side of courage and kindness, and
the virtues in general, the old story-tellers admire successful cunning
as much as Homer does in the *Odyssey*. At least, if the cunning hero,
human or animal, is the weaker, like Odysseus, Brer Rabbit, and many
others. . . ."[49] Not only that, but in Greek mythology could be found the
roots of Faerie itself: "All the history of Greece till about 800 B.C. is a
string of the fairy tales, all about Theseus and Heracles and Oedipus and
Minos and Perseus is a *Cabinet des Fées*, a collection of fairy tales."[50] Thus
the universal narrative contained an implied hierarchy, deriving its structure and concepts from the classical past.

It was not just Lang's style and theory that unified the disparate tales
and explained their relationships; the illustrations were also instrumental
in demonstrating these ideas:

Mr. Ford, as usual, has drawn the monsters and mermaids, the princes and
giants, and the beautiful princesses, who, the Editor thinks, are, if possible,

---

[46] Green (1962: 50).
[47] Preface to *The Brown Fairy Book* (1904: viii).
[48] Silver (1999: 5). See also Talairach-Vielmas (2014).
[49] Preface to *The Orange Fairy Book* (1906: vi).
[50] Preface to *The Lilac Fairy Book* (1910: viii).

prettier than ever. Here, then, are fancies brought from all quarters: we see that black, white, and yellow peoples are fond of just the same kinds of adventures.[51]

Henry Justice Ford began his collaboration with Lang with *The Blue Fairy Book* in 1889, and with each subsequent volume, Lang increasingly relied on Ford's illustrations to provide the overall framework to the universal world of narrative he was compiling.[52]

Henry Justice Ford, though widely recognized as a significant figure in late Victorian illustration, has not been the subject of a scholarly catalog *raisonné*. All of Ford's original drawings and printing plates were destroyed in the Longman Publishing House during the Blitz, and very little was written about him during his lifetime. Ford was born into a large, scholarly, cricketing family in 1860, and following a boyhood spent in and around London, took a First Class and his degree in the Classical Tripos in 1883.[53] During this time, he presided over a lampooning intellectual club, the Dilettanti, whose members included Owen Seaman (later editor of *Punch*) and Lancelot Speed (Ford's future collaborator on the illustrations for *The Red Fairy Book*). Following his bachelor's degree, Ford was trained in drawing at the Slade School of Art and the Bushey School.

Including both classical scholarship and fine art, Ford's training and biography were typical of that of his contemporaries who made their living from the engraver's stylus in the late Victorian period. Training typically began with an introduction to artistic drawing through the copying (whether slavish or free) of works by Great Masters and/or classical sculptures. Among the latter were certainly the Elgin Marbles, which many Victorian artists used for sketch practice or major study, either the originals at the British Museum or one of the many casts produced during the period and distributed among the art schools and royal cast collections, including that of the Victoria and Albert (opened to the public in 1873). The Slade School, Ford's first art school, was particularly known

---

[51] Introduction to *The Pink Fairy Book* (1897: viii). See also the introductions to *The Yellow Fairy Book* (1894: x) and *The Olive Fairy Book* (1907: v).

[52] Perhaps not without resentment: in 1909 Lang wrote to his brother John about *The All Sorts of Stories Book* (also illustrated by Ford) that "The work is poorly paid because of the expensive illustrations"; Green (1962: 45).

[53] For Ford's full biography, see Hares-Stryker (2009).

for its reliance on classical casts, and this period also saw an explosion in the use of the galleries of the British Museum by artists. According to the Annual Parliamentary Returns, artists' recorded visits to the galleries grew exponentially in the later Victorian era: in 1864, 1,140 visits were recorded, while only 15 years later, the number had grown to 15,626. Drawing students were granted exclusive access to the galleries on particular days, and, by 1886, the Museum began to acquire casts of ancient works expressly for drawing, including the *Hermes* of Praxiteles and the *Venus de Milo*.[54]

Following his basic training in London, Ford spent three years under Hubert von Herkomer at the Bushey School, a progressive art school that emphasized drawing from life. Though lampooned for his exacting methods, Herkomer was remarkably successful at connecting his students with lucrative commissions and seemingly encouraged his students to develop a signature style for that purpose. Ford returned to London in 1887 having already illustrated his first children's book: *Aesop's Fables for Little Readers* by Mrs. Arthur Brookfield. Ford is frequently cited as a "friend of Edward Burne-Jones" during this period, but the extent of this friendship has recently been questioned.[55] Nevertheless, Ford was certainly an influential and sought-after figure on the social and cultural scene of London. He was a member of the exclusive Savile Club, alongside artistic celebrities like Robert Louis Stevenson, Rudyard Kipling, and W. B. Yeats (as well as his *Blue Fairy Book* collaborators G. P. Jacomb-Hood and Lang). In addition to his many commercial commissions, Ford was exhibiting his paintings and drawings on historical subjects regularly at Royal Academy exhibitions. He also enjoyed a close friendship with J. M. Barrie, playing on the *Peter Pan* author's notorious cricket team the Allahakbarries and designing the costume for Peter Pan when the play first opened in London in 1904.[56]

This remarkable period saw both the evolution of Ford's career as illustrator and the development of his style, based on Pre-Raphaelite qualities and drawing on his academic and artistic training that not only used the classical as framework (Slade) but also sought to employ the details of life

---

[54] Jenkins (1992: 31–39).
[55] Hares-Stryker (2009: 44).
[56] Ibid. (41, 47).

to create realism (Bushey). There is no surviving account of his opinion of or access to major works of Pre-Raphaelite artists, but the dissemination of their work in printed form (books and periodicals) and in the decorative arts during the last decades of the nineteenth century had made their aesthetic ubiquitous. The mark of the Pre-Raphaelite style and philosophy is visible in Ford's work, in which he adapts the Pre-Raphaelite fractured classicism to a new medium and purpose.[57]

The stories of the *Coloured Fairy Book* series are replete with female protagonists, from stereotypical princess in distress to powerful fairy queen, so Ford had many opportunities to present iconic female (and male) figures in the Pre-Raphaelite mold. For example, in *The Pink Fairy Book* (1897), the characters of "Catherine and her Destiny" are depicted in a single illustration (Figure 3.4) that displays the range and detail of Ford's mature style.[58] Destiny stands in the foreground, body frontal and face profile, rendered in a strong linear style with very little shading, despite the complexity of her garment's classicizing drapery. Slightly behind her, Catherine is seated, body and face frontal, in a patterned medieval style dress, her face half-shadowed with cross-hatching. Here Ford employs both style of dress and artistry to differentiate between human and supernatural figures, yet their overall aesthetic is uniform and continuous. Furthermore, as with most of his full-page illustrations, Ford provides a decorative frame and an epigraph to the illustration, here rendered as an unfurled scroll with a tiny illumination. Similar arrangements are used in the same volume in the Japanese tale "Uraschimataro and the Turtle," in the translation of Hans Christian Andersen's "The Snow Queen," and in the adaptation of the French "Princess Minon-Minette" (to name a few). Though the origins of the stories differ and the characters in each are varied in their details of dress and physiognomy, the unity of style and the logic of its application across the volume forge an implicit connection between these disparate narratives.

The realistic shaded style is applied in an even more pronounced way when villains or inhuman characters are featured. Trolls, giants, and

---

[57] Peppin (1975: 19). Cf. Green (1962: 51): "[Ford's] illustrations, with their touch of Pre-Raphaelitism to give grace and beauty to his accurate and forthright interpretations, are among the best and most suitable ever accorded to fairy tales."

[58] *The Pink Fairy Book* (1897: 169).

Figure 3.4 Henry Justice Ford, "Catherine and Her Destiny," black and white illustration from *The Pink Fairy Book* (1897) published by Longmans and Co. Public domain.

goblins, as well as fully human evil stepsisters and crones, receive heavy shading and roiling composition as they react violently in the face of human impassivity, as seen in the illustration "The Witch flies into a Rage" in "The White Dove" (Figure 3.5). In this image, the details of the scene are fully medievalizing, down to the pointed shoes and feathered cap of the hero, but the framework upon which these trappings are hung—the Praxitelean pose of the heroine, the human transcendence in the face of inhuman danger, and the clean lines of the human profiles—can be

Figure 3.5 Henry Justice Ford. "The Witch Flies into a Rage," black and white illustration from *The Pink Fairy Book* (1897) published by Longmans and Co. Public domain.

seen to align with classicizing norms of the period. Furthermore, this broader application of the classicizing style creates a visual hierarchy, in which humans lie somewhere between the supernatural (Destiny, Snow Queen, etc.) and the base (witches, goblins, etc.), with the possibility of being 'drawn' to either side.

The application of this drawing style has a remarkable effect within the context of a volume intended for children. The classicizing style does not individualize the characters, but leaves them as an idealized blank to be imbued with the qualities and features of one's own imaginings. This concept was undoubtedly familiar to any artist who learned his technique by sketching the Elgin Marbles at the British Museum, as Ford had, with its metopes of animalistic centaurs contrasted with the idealized Athenians of the frieze. The popularity of the classicizing style in the later Victorian era also aided in imbuing Ford's supernatural and human characters with a sense of familiarity and acceptance. Fairy stories were not considered *à la mode* at the time *The Blue Fairy Book* was published; the series itself brought on a revival of interest in the genre, to which Ford's illustrations were undoubtedly contributory.[59] Here the general effectiveness of the classical style in conveying idealization and legitimacy was combined with the cognitive power of the black-and-white line drawing, the cartoon. As has been observed in relation to sequential art, a medium in some ways derived from book illustrations:

When you look at a photo or realistic drawing of a face, you see it as the face of another. But when you enter the world of the cartoon, you see yourself. . . . The cartoon is a vacuum into which our identity and awareness are pulled, an empty shell that we inhabit which enables us to travel in another realm. We don't just observe the cartoon, we become it![60]

Children could not see themselves in the haggard dark features of the witch, but mirrored in the idealized visage of a princess, hero, or fairy.

Furthermore, in parallel with the application of style in Ford's illustrations, the combination of medieval and classical decorative elements makes a particular statement about the order of things. As seen both in the illustrations cited above and throughout the anthology, Ford tended to apply classical or classicizing drapery, composition, and details, particularly for the fairies, the supernatural creatures.[61] In contrast, the minutiae of the medieval context—whether European, Arabian, or Oriental— function differently, providing the distinct visual and tactile material for the creation of modern fantasy, which requires a grounding in temporal and physical reality. As Tolkien later expounded in "On Fairy Stories,"

---

[59] See Green (1980: 249–250), Lupack and Lupack (2008: 175–176), and Hares-Stryker (2009: 40).

[60] McCloud (1993: 36).

[61] See Menges (2010: 60, 68, and 79) for a few (of many) illustrative examples from the later *Fairy Books*.

"creative Fantasy is founded upon the hard recognition that things are so in the world as it appears under the sun; on a recognition of fact, but not a slavery to it."[62] The appearance of classical allusions applied to supernatural figures, in interaction with the medievalized humans, allowed the apprehensible cognitive relationship between past and present to forge the necessary connection between fantasy and reality. Fantasy is not a world separate from ours, but a contiguous one to be discovered, like the Cupid-like "Boy in the Valley" from "The Satin Surgeon" (Figure 3.6).[63] This classical–medieval pairing had been part of the collective consciousness since the mid–nineteenth century, and thus could be employed by Ford without qualification to make tangible Lang's vision of narrative. Lang recognized the cognitive importance of Ford's illustrations. Certain aspects of the stories, particularly the frightening ones that defied or prohibited description, were given over to Ford's able hands.[64]

Equally important was the fact that Ford was illustrating the traditional work of the collective, rather than original stories by a single creative mind. The *Coloured Fairy Books* were a comprehensive anthology of Faerie, collected to emphasize significant similarities across time and culture in the telling of stories—the vast majority of which were illustrated in a unified style with a defined organizational principle. The aesthetic hierarchy employed by Ford became the norm for the differentiation between gods and mortals in illustrations in collections of classical stories as well, as can be seen in Lang's *Tales of Troy and Greece* (1907, illustrated by Ford) and *The Children's Plutarch* (1910, illustrated by Walter Crane). The frontispiece of the latter, entitled "Numa and the Nymph" (Figure 3.7), connects the Roman nymph Egeria visually with Ford's heroines of Faerie.[65] The use of these recognizable symbols anchors and legitimizes the fairy world in the minds of Victorian children (and their parents), fracturing the symbols and reassembling them in a comprehensible juxtaposition, thus creating a suitable environment for the growth of fantasy.

---

[62] Tolkien (1994: 161–162).

[63] *The Olive Fairy Book* (1907: 206).

[64] For example, Lang singles out the Danish story "The Princess in the Chest" in the introduction to *The Pink Fairy Book* as "not be read to a very nervous child"; the undead princess is not described in the text, and the reader is instead referred to Ford's illustration (1897: 65) to understand her appearance (in which she is only seen from behind).

[65] Gould (1910: frontispiece).

THE BOY IN THE VALLEY

Figure 3.6 Henry Justice Ford, "The Boy in the Valley," color illustration from *The Olive Fairy Book* (1907) published by Longmans and Co. Public domain.

CONCLUSION: TOLKIEN AND BEYOND

This chapter has considered ways in which the nineteenth-century vision of the classical past, with its myriad streams in the artistic and intellectual movements of the era, provided the underpinnings of the seminal works of modern fantasy. This chain of influence was not lost on modern fantasy writers themselves. Tolkien recognized his affinity with the PRB, comparing it to his own early intellectual group, the Tea Club Barrovian

NUMA & THE NYMPH

Figure 3.7 Walter Crane, "Numa and the Nymph," frontispiece from *The Children's Plutarch* (1910) published by Harper and Brothers. Public domain.

Society.[66] Tolkien and Lewis were surrounded by Pre-Raphaelite visual works at Oxford, most notably at Tolkien's Exeter College, which had Edward Burne-Jones and William Morris among its alumni.[67] The Inklings all acknowledged their connections to this recent cultural past

[66] Carpenter (1978: 73).
[67] Zaleski and Zaleski (2015: 57, 61); for Tolkien's particular interest in Morris during his undergraduate days, see Carpenter (1978: 69–70).

that was at once conservative and revolutionary, recognized the impact that childhood texts and images had had upon their creative and intellectual explorations, and formed fantasy worlds whose details can be traced to those childhood influences.

As Lord Acton wrote in 1859, "Two great principles divide the world and contend for its mastery, antiquity and the middle ages. These are the two civilizations that have preceded us, the two elements of which ours is composed.... This is the great dualism that runs through our society."[68] Understanding the position of the classical in the Victorian era is essential for understanding the position of the classics in modern society: the dialectic between the classical and medieval in the formation of British identity forms a construct for understanding the world, either real or imagined. The placement of these two cultural frameworks in relation to notions of the specific and universal provided the essential framework for the development of fantasy, which both creates a plausible closed sphere with its own details and rules, and allows that sphere to be permeated with universal attributes that allow the reader or viewer to connect with the created world across time and space. This cognitive process has fundamental links to the complex siting of classical texts, artworks, and ideas within the re-appreciation of medievalism in Victorian-era England. Furthermore, it is not a coincidence that the development of the fantasy genre went hand-in-hand with technological advances in the printing of illustrations *and* the dominance of the classics in education, both academic and artistic. This chapter contends that this particular mixture of modernism and anachronism in the visual arts allowed Tolkien and Lewis—and many other significant fantasy writers who had been children during this era—to create (or sub-create) fantasy worlds reflecting their own realities.[69]

A cultural theory such as this requires some oversimplification in the context of an edited volume. This chapter has concentrated on only a handful of the influential figures and movements that characterized this polymath period. Left in the background are several contemporary

---

[68] Epigraph of the journal *Studies in Medievalism* (1979-).

[69] So Zaleski and Zaleski (2015: 207), writing about the popularity of *The Hobbit*: "It is this anachronism, this bridging of worlds—ours with the archaic past—that gives the story its power to enchant and to disturb." On *The Hobbit* and classical reception, see Stevens (this volume).

artistic movements and schools that also contributed to the depiction of classical themes and subjects, most notably the Aesthetic Movement associated with Oscar Wilde and Aubrey Beardsley and the Neo-Classical painting of Frederic Leighton, Lawrence Alma-Tadema, and others. Many of the artists treated here participated in other artistic movements directly or implicitly, and Victorian patrons, publishers, and scholars influenced multiple concurrent strains of interpretation via their patronage and analysis. But the frame that holds this magnificent tapestry together is the period's constant engagement with classical and medieval models, and the tracing of this particular thread, from the Pre-Raphaelites to Tolkien through Ford, I hope will begin to elucidate the whole composition.

ADDENDUM: THE COMET'S TAIL

The application of Pre-Raphaelite art as the aesthetic of fantasy has persisted far beyond the genesis of modern fantasy; significantly, it has also become a commonplace in the visualization of the classical world. The Pre-Raphaelite construction of the past still provides the visual framework for original works of cover art in both fantasy and classical publishing. In particular, following the re-popularization of fantasy in the late 1970s, cover artists of the major fantasy authors turned specifically to the Pre-Raphaelites and Ford for inspiration: see, for example, the covers by Michael Whelan (for Anne McCaffrey), Hannah Shapero (for Marion Zimmer Bradley), and Robert Gould (for Michael Moorcock). Shapero links the popularity of Pre-Raphaelite–inspired covers to the rise of "Celtomania" in the fantasy novels of the 1980s and 1990s,[70] but several of these artists also have backgrounds in both Classics and Pre-Raphaelite art.[71] Among many examples, Hannah Shapero's adaptation of *La Donna della Fiamma* for the cover of Marion Zimmer Bradley's *Sharra's Exile* (1981) underscores this continuous Pre-Raphaelite undercurrent in the

---

[70] Personal correspondence with H. Shapero, October 21, 2014.

[71] "Seeking to explore the possibilities of combining picture and word in visual narrative, Robert [Gould] and writer Eric Kimball formed the company, Two Man Horse. Together they created and published numerous works inspired by their love of Pre-Raphaelite art and philosophy." See http://www.imaginosis.com/about.html. Accessed December 19, 2015.

Figure 3.8 Cover image of Marion Zimmer Bradley's *Sharra's Exile* (1981) by Hannah Shapero, based on Dante Gabriel Rossetti's *La Donna della Fiamma* (Figure 1). Image provided by the artist.

visualization of fantasy and the adaptability of its aesthetic to new narratives and creations (Figure 3.8).

Looking to even more recent publications, contemporary book cover designer Howard David Johnson, who promotes himself as a Pre-Raphaelite illustrator, is very prolific in fantasy novels and classical scholarship. His designs grace such scholarly works as M. L. West's *The Epic Cycle* (Oxford 2013), as well as numerous fantasy and historical novels. Kinuko Craft also works within these publishing genres, most notably a series of book covers inspired by Pre-Raphaelite works for Patricia McKillip, including an adaptation of *The Lady of Shalott* for *The Tower at Stony Wood* (2000). Here, too, the environment is littered with classical images, primarily golden arms and armor intertwined in the weaver's undulating diaphanous garment. Significantly, in a 2012 interview, Craft indicated her desire to create cover art for Homer's *Iliad* and *Odyssey*.[72] Perhaps most notable are the numerous examples in which the same Pre-Raphaelite painting is used to illustrate different works, thereby cementing the interrelation of Pre-Raphaelitism, ancient classics, and fantasy: Rossetti's *Monna Vanna* (1866) on *Lady Audley's Secret* (Penguin Classics) and *Propertius: The Poems* (Oxford); the ubiquity of Frederick Sandys's 1868 painting *Medea* on books dealing with ancient magic or Euripides' play; and the general use of Burne-Jones's Perseus and Psyche cycles as cover emblems for a wide range of titles.[73]

Henry Justice Ford's influence is equally ubiquitous in fantasy illustration, though less recognized. The *Coloured Fairy Books* have never been out of print and were reissued in paperback by Dover in the 1960s. Tony DiTerlizzi (*Spiderwick Chronicles*) and Hannah Shapero cite direct influences, and many comic book illustrators, such as Charles Vess and P. Craig Russell, derive their style from Ford's.[74] However, the implicit influences of Ford's work on the development of modern fantasy have perhaps been more formative. Through his thousands of illustrations, Ford created a legitimizing frame and aesthetic for the visualization of fantasy via the combination of classical and medieval elements, rendered in black and white to allow the individualized entry into the fantasy world by the viewer. His images, which illustrated not a single author's work but a universal narrative, provided the compositional underpinnings for modern fantasy itself.

[72] [Anon.] (2012).

[73] For example: Apuleius' *The Golden Ass* (Oxford World Classics); A. S. Byatt's *Possession* (Vintage); and several titles in the Millennium Fantasy Masterworks series, including S. Tepper's *Beauty* and E. R. Eddison's *The Worm Ouroboros*. This last series makes heavy use of original and adapted Pre-Raphaelite works in its cover art.

[74] Known from DiTerlizzi (2011) and personal correspondence with H. Shapero, October 31, 2014.

4

Classical Antiquity and the Timeless Horrors of H. P. Lovecraft

Robinson Peter Krämer

" . . . his face was a mask of fear worthy of Greek tragedy."
—H. P. Lovecraft, "The Shadow over Innsmouth"

Howard Philips Lovecraft (1890–1937) is one of the most important writers of horror, fantasy, and supernatural fiction.[1] He is especially famous for his creation of the so-called Cthulhu Mythos and the invention of the mythical *Necronomicon*.[2] In his work, Lovecraft frequently uses motifs and terms referring to Nordic traditions and ancient Egypt, but even

---

[1] I would like to thank my friends Lukas Bohnenkämper and Raffaella Da Vela for their helpful comments on earlier drafts of this chapter. Special thanks go to the editors of this volume, Brett M. Rogers and Benjamin Eldon Stevens, for allowing me to participate in this great project, commenting on my chapter, and saving me from some linguistic infelicities. All remaining errors and inaccuracies are my own. All page numbers in reference to Lovecraft's works are to Lovecraft (2011).

[2] The term 'Cthulhu Mythos' was invented by August Derleth and is not unproblematic. See Mosig (1980 = Mosig 2011), Joshi and Schultz (2001: 50–55 s.v. 'Cthulhu Mythos'), Tierney (2001 = Tierney 2011), Joshi (2011), and Mackley (2013).

more to Greek and Roman antiquity.[3] Although motifs from classical antiquity appear commonly in Lovecraft's stories, detailed studies of his reception of Greek and Roman classics are still a desideratum.[4] Therefore, a study of this point of contact between classical antiquity and modern fantasy (MF) seems worthwhile.

In this chapter, I first analyze Lovecraft's passion for classical antiquity in his childhood, arguing that his interest in the Greeks and Romans leads directly to the beginning of his writings and world-view. Second, I examine some of his early tales in which classical antiquity serves as a setting: the first two examples take place in the Greek and Roman Mediterranean; a third tale contains motifs, objects, quotations, and complete plot patterns taken directly from ancient sources. My third section deals with references to Greek and Roman antiquity in the 'Cthulhu Mythos,' including the *Necronomicon* and the use of an 'ancient vocabulary' for metaphors. In addition, Lovecraft quotes, mentions, and uses various sources as Latin mottos at the beginning of his stories, as inscriptions and demonic evocations of hideous cults, and even as a parody of Biblical events. Finally, we will see that, by contrast, Lovecraft sometimes evokes an unimaginably ancient horror that frightens because of how it precedes human history and time, including classical antiquity.

CHILDHOOD AND JUVENILE WORKS

There is much evidence for Lovecraft's fascination with the Greeks and Romans from his early childhood. His fascination with classical antiquity resulted in two long-term effects that influenced his life: what we may call a pagan world-view and an interest in writing. The young Lovecraft mentions that he was strongly influenced by the ancient

[3] For Lovecraft's references to Nordic traditions, see Eckhardt (2011); for ancient Egypt, see Reinhardt (2008), Murray (2011), and Krueger (2014: 54–56).

[4] This topic has attracted attention, in some case studies and biographies: e.g., Wetzel (1980: 80–82), Joshi (2001: 20–24), Wetzel (2001), Joshi (2004: 22–26, 48–49), Jantschewski (2012), Walter (2012: 110–118).

Greeks and Romans: "The most poignant sensations of my existence are those of 1896 when I discovered the Hellenic world";[5] and "When I was six my philosophical evolution received its most aesthetically significant impulse—the dawn of Graeco-Roman thought."[6] From ages six to eight years old, Lovecraft was greatly influenced by classical antiquity. During this period, he read many eighteenth- and nineteenth-century translations of ancient authors, such as Homer, Hesiod, Virgil, Horace, Ovid, Phaedrus, Juvenal, and others.[7] As Lovecraft describes in his letters, he enjoyed visiting the museum of the Rhode Island School of Design as well as other classical art museums in Providence and Boston; he also began a collection of plaster casts of Greek sculptures. The young Lovecraft was completely enchanted by Greek and Roman culture.[8]

Lovecraft's fascination with classical antiquity had two important long-term effects on his life. First, he became a pagan and refused Christian religion throughout his life. From 1896 onward, Lovecraft believed he saw satyrs and dryads, his intense imagination causing something of a religious experience:

I have in literal truth built altars to Pan, Apollo, Diana, and Athena, and have watched for dryads and satyrs in the woods and fields at dusk. Once I firmly thought I beheld some of these sylvan creatures dancing under autumnal oaks; a kind of "religious experience" as true in its way as the subjective ecstasies of any Christian. If a Christian tell me he has felt the reality of his Jesus or Jahveh, I can reply that I have seen the hoofed Pan.[9]

Because of his pagan world-view and troubling provocations against Christianity, he was allowed to stop attending Sunday school at the First

---

[5] Wetzel (2001: 55), with additional references there.

[6] Lovecraft *Selected Letters* (*Letters*) i.299, no. 160 (to Edwin Baird, February 3, 1924).

[7] Lovecraft *Letters* iii.407–408, no. 495 (to August Derleth, September 9, 1931), with Joshi (2001: 20–22, 31) and (2004: 22). See below for additional emphasis by Lovecraft on classical antiquity in his essay "Supernatural Horror in Literature" (1973: 20, written November 1925–May 1927).

[8] Joshi (2001: 22–23) and (2004: 25), with additional references there.

[9] Joshi (2001: 23) and (2004: 25–26), with reference to Lovecraft's "A Confession of Unfaith" (probably written in 1921, first published in February 1922). See also Wetzel (2001: 54–55).

Baptist Church at the age of twelve.[10] Already as a child, Lovecraft seemed to condemn Christianity due to his pagan philosophy:

> I felt that one good Roman pagan was worth any six dozen of the cringing scum riff-raff who took up with a fanatical foreign belief, and was frankly sorry that the Syrian superstition was not stamped out.... When it came to the repressive measures of Marcus Aurelius and Diocletianus, I was in complete sympathy with the government and had not a shred of use for the Christian herd.[11]

Furthermore, Lovecraft confesses: "at seven I sported the adopted name of L. VALERIUS . MESSALA . & tortured imaginary Christians in amphitheatres. Probably what appeals to me in the Roman is the aesthetic of power."[12] Aside from his terrifying cruelty, it is remarkable that Lovecraft at that age invented a Roman pseudonym for himself. The pseudonym shows clearly the important role played by the young Lovecraft's fascination with classical antiquity. The only other pseudonym he used for himself during childhood is the Arabic name 'Abdul Alhazred,' which he chose in later years as the name of "the Mad Poet" and author of the *Necronomicon* (Al Azif, written c. 730 CE at Damascus), as an important part of his cosmos of terror.[13] As we can see from these

---

[10] "None of the answers of my pious preceptors would satisfy me, and my demands that they cease taking things for granted quite upset them. Close reasoning was something new in their little world of Semitic mythology. At last I saw that they were hopelessly bound to unfounded dogmata and traditions, and thenceforward ceased to treat them seriously. Sunday-School became to me simply a place wherein to have a little harmless fun spoofing the pious mossbacks. My mother observed this, and no longer sought to enforce my attendance" (Lovecraft *Letters* i.110–111, no. 64 [to Reinhardt Kleiner, March 7, 1920]). See Joshi (2004: 26).

[11] Lovecraft *Letters* iii.431–432, no. 507 (to Robert E. Howard, October 30, 1931). See Joshi (2004: 26).

[12] Lovecraft, *Letters* iii.313, no. 466 (to Frank Belknap Long, February 27, 1931). See Joshi (2004: 26).

[13] "At one time I formed a juvenile collection of Oriental pottery and objects d'art, announcing myself as a devout Mohammedan and assuming the pseudonym of 'Abdul Alhazred'—which you will recognise as the author of that mythical *Necronomicon* which I drag into various of my tales" (Lovecraft *Letters* i.299, no. 160 [to Edwin Baird, February 3, 1924]). For Abdul Alhazred and the origin of the *Necronomicon*, see "History of the *Necronomicon* 621–622" (written September 1927), Carter (2001: 122–134, no. 37), and Joshi and Schultz (2001: 186–188 s.v. 'Necronomicon').

pseudonyms, both the Arabian world and classical antiquity played important parts in Lovecraft's formation as a writer.

Indeed, the second long-term effect on Lovecraft's life caused by his interest in classical antiquity was his starting to write.[14] Lovecraft started writing poetry at the age of six, possibly slightly before his interest in the Greeks and Romans. But his fascination with classical antiquity stimulated him directly from the beginning and strongly affected the subject matter of his poetry. Unfortunately, his first attempts at writing have not survived, but his oldest preserved work happens to be on a classical subject: "The Poem of Ulysses; or, The Odyssey: Written for Young People" (1897).[15] The poem is remarkable not only because of its subject but also because Lovecraft wrote it within a month and succeeded in creating a synopsis of Homer's *Odyssey* in 88 verses. In the same period, he wrote similar summarizing works of Homer's *Iliad*, Apollonius of Rhodes' *Argonautica*, Virgil's *Aeneid*, Ovid's *Metamorphoses*, classical myth, and ancient Egyptian myth.[16]

Around 1898, at eight years old, Lovecraft began to learn Latin, reading and translating Latin texts.[17] In later letters he describes his deep passion for ancient history, Latin, and Greek:

Latin and Greek were my delight—although I had a long-standing feud with teachers of the former over pronunciation. My grandfather had previously taught me a great deal of Latin, using the traditional English pronunciation taught in his day, but at school I was expected to follow the "Roman method" which attempts to duplicate the actual pronunciation of the Romans. Instead of Caesar (Seezar) I was expected to say "Ky'sar." Cicero became Kikero, Scipio, Skeep'io, and so on. It got on my nerves. . . . At least, it was a consolation to reflect that this odd way brought me closer to immortal Rome itself! . . . Ancient history I ate up avidly; aided by some previous acquaintance with the subject, and by my abiding love of Rome.[18]

When Lovecraft was eleven years old, he wrote the book *Poemata Minora*, which "was dedicated 'To the Gods, Heroes, and Ideals of the

---

[14] Joshi (2001: 21–23) and (2004: 23–27).

[15] Joshi (2001: 21–22), Joshi and Schultz (2001: 133–134 s.v. 'Juvenile Works: Poetry'), and Joshi (2004: 23–25).

[16] See Joshi and Schultz (2001: 133–134 s.v. 'Juvenile Works: Poetry' and 'Juvenile Works: Science'), as well as Joshi (2004: 25).

[17] Joshi (2001: 31–32) and (2004: 39–40).

[18] Lovecraft *Letters* iv.172–173, no. 611 (to Robert E. Howard, March 25–29, 1933).

Ancients.'"[19] In 1902, he wrote a second volume with the same title. Both volumes deal exclusively with classical antiquity and paganism. The five poems of volume two are: "Ode to Selene or Diana," "To the Old Pagan Religion," "On the Ruin of Rome," "To Pan," and "On the Vanity of Human Ambition."[20] Finally, in 1905, he also wrote *A Manual of Roman Antiquities*, in which he intended to include biographies of great Romans; in the end, Lovecraft probably did not include these biographies, and the *Manual* has not survived.[21]

Lovecraft makes the importance of classical antiquity most plain in an essay on the history of horror titled "Supernatural Horror in Literature" (November 1925–May 1927). There he writes that the beginning of horror literature is found in ancient sources such "as the werewolf incident in Petronius, the gruesome passages in Apuleius, the brief but celebrated letter of Pliny the Younger to Sura, and the odd compilation *On Wonderful Events* by the Emperor Hadrian's Greek freedman, Phlegon" (20).[22] Classical antiquity therefore represents the historical origin of his beloved genre as well as a personal source of inspiration for his work. Lovecraft uses Greek and Roman antiquity in his stories in many ways: some take place in Greek and Roman sites; specific terms from Greek or Roman culture are used to create atmospheric effects in stories; and occasionally Lovecraft uses specific passages from ancient sources as metaphors or to give hints to the storyline. It is to examples of these usages that we now turn.

ANTIQUITY AS A SETTING IN TALES

As Lovecraft was fascinated by antiquity since early childhood, it is no wonder that some of his earlier stories take place in the Greek and Roman Mediterranean. A first example, "The Tree," is set in Syracuse during the fourth century BCE and may be inspired directly by an ancient anecdote. A second story, "The Very Old Folk," treats of a sinister hill tribe in the Roman province Hispania Citerior. My third example is the short novel

---

[19] Joshi (2001: 39) and (2004: 48, quoting from Lovecraft's "A Confession of Unfaith").
[20] Joshi and Schultz (2001: 133, s.v. 'Juvenile Works: Poetry').
[21] Ibid. (134, s.v. 'Juvenile Works: Science').
[22] We do not know when Lovecraft read the materials mentioned here.

The Dream-Quest of Unknown Kadath (*Dream-Quest*), which does not take place in Greek or Roman antiquity but offers many explicit adoptions of ancient motifs, characters, quotes, and storylines.

In "The Tree" (written in the spring of 1920), the Tyrant of Syracuse arranges a contest between Kalos and Musides, two sculptors and close friends, to build a statue of Tyché (Greek Τύχη) for the city. Both sculptors work on their statues, but Kalos falls ill and dies despite aid from Musides. Therefore Musides wins the contest, but afterwards he himself is killed, and his statue is destroyed at once by an olive tree growing out of the tomb of Kalos that falls upon the house of Musides. It becomes clear Musides has betrayed his close friend and poisoned him, such that Musides' death is an act of supernatural revenge by his dead victim—or more likely by fate (Τύχη; 84–87).[23]

One interesting parallel is offered by the ancient Greek story of Theogenes of Thasos. Dio Chrysostom (31.95–96) and Pausanias (6.11.5–6) relate that Theogenes was one of the strongest and most famous athletes in Greece at the beginning of the fifth century BCE. In his disciplines—boxing, *pankration* (a kind of wrestling) and *dolichos* (long footrace)—Theogenes won some 1,200 to 1,400 times, including three times in the Olympic games. After his death, a man envious of Theogenes' success whipped his statue in Thasos every night in order to humiliate the dead athlete. One night, however, the statue fell on the envious man and killed him.[24] As this story features striking parallels to Lovecraft's tale "The Tree," it is probable Lovecraft knew its ancient sources and used this material as an inspiration for his own story.

"The Very Old Folk" (written in November 1927) arose from a "Roman dream" Lovecraft had one Halloween night, inspired by a reading of Virgil's *Aeneid*.[25] Lovecraft described his dream in detail (with slight variations) in at least three letters of 1927, and later he intended to write a short story about it but never did so. Donald Wandrei, one of the recipients of the letters, allowed in the summer of 1940 the publication

[23] Joshi and Schultz (2001: 277–278, s.v. 'Tree, The').

[24] For Theogenes of Thasos, see Bentz and Mann (2001: 231, with n. 19) and Decker (2002) for additional references.

[25] Lovecraft *Letters* ii.188–197, no. 303 (to Bernard Austin Dwyer, Friday, November 1927). In fact Lovecraft declared that he frequently had such "Roman dreams" in his childhood: "Roman dreams were no uncommon features of my youth—I used to follow the Divine Julius all over Gallia as a Tribunus Militum o'nights" ("The Very Old Folk" 623).

of Lovecraft's text, giving it its title.[26] During the late Republic, in the Roman province of Hispania Citerior near the town Pompelo, there lives a strange, sinister hill tribe.[27] Every year before the Kalends of May and the Kalends of November—that is, Halloween—these hill people kidnap some villagers of Pompelo. But in the year of the story, no villager has been taken, and the very old folk of the hills are suspiciously inactive. Therefore, the provincial quaestor L. Caelius Rufus, concerned about a greater menace, argues in favor of defeating and suppressing the very old folk once and for all. He convinces both the military tribune and the legate of this plan, and a Roman cohort of soldiers is sent into the hills. In the hills, the horses suddenly start to scream, the air grows colder, and the torches die out. A nameless horror arises and the story ends with words uttered by the old proconsul P. Scribonius Libo: "An ancient evil— it is an ancient evil . . . it comes . . . it comes after all . . ." ("*Malitia vetus— malitia vetus est . . . venit . . . tandem venit . . .*").[28] There are no records of the fate of that cohort, but at least the town is saved and continues to exist under the modern name Pamplona.[29]

My third example is the short novel *The Dream-Quest of Unknown Kadath* (written October 1926–January 22, 1927).[30] The tale is part of the 'dreamland' stories, a cycle full of strange and bizarre landscapes, as well as exotic places and life forms. The protagonist of these stories is often Randolph W. Carter, with whom Lovecraft identified. In *Dream-Quest*, Carter searches for a "sunset city" in the "dreamland" and undergoes many quests before finally arriving home in Boston. There exist some striking parallels between *Dream-Quest* and Homer's *Odyssey*. In a letter, Lovecraft describes his short novel as an

---

[26] Lovecraft *Letters* ii.189, no. 303 (to Bernard Austin Dwyer, Friday, November 1927): "The recent one [dream] was undoubtedly the joint product of (a) my re-reading of the *Aeneid*, with my usual thrill at Anchises' prophecy of future Roman glory, and (b) the Hallowee'en season, as impressed upon me by the echoes of festivities held elsewhere in the neighbourhood."

[27] Cf. Pliny *Natural History* 3.24; see also Schulten (1952) and Barceló (2001). In antiquity, the Roman town, which had been founded by Pompey in the winter of 75/74 BCE, was called Pompelo or Pompaelo. Today its name is Pamplona in Navarra.

[28] "The Very Old Folk" 628.

[29] On "The Very Old Folk," see also Joshi and Schultz (2001: 286–287, s.v. 'Very Old Folk, The').

[30] On *Dream-Quest*, see also Smuda (1997: 60–68), Joshi and Schultz (2001: 70–75, s.v. 'Dream-Quest of Unknown Kadath, The'), and Schweitzer (2001: 84–86).

'odyssey': "I did a whole young novel . . . letting my imagination build cosmic Odysseys without restraint."[31] Like Odysseus, Carter undertakes a number of adventures during a dangerous journey through weird and mysterious places. Both protagonists have a desire to return home but can only arrive there crabwise.[32] Some of the episodes and other characters of *Dream-Quest* are similar to those of the *Odyssey* (*Od.*). For example Lovecraft's character Kuranes was a monarch in dreamland (= the underworld) but "would gladly have resigned forever the whole of his power and luxury and freedom for one blessed day as a simple boy in that pure and quiet England" (*Dream-Quest* 447). This declaration reminds us of the dead Achilles' statement to Odysseus in the underworld (*Od.* 11. 488–491):

Nay, seek not to speak soothingly to me of death, glorious Odysseus. I should choose, so I might live on earth, to serve as the hireling of another, of some portionless man whose livelihood was but small, rather than to be lord over all the dead that have perished.[33]

μὴ δή μοι θάνατόν γε παραύδα, φαίδιμ' Ὀδυσσεῦ.
βουλοίμην κ' ἐπάρουρος ἐὼν θητευέμεν ἄλλῳ,
ἀνδρὶ παρ' ἀκλήρῳ, ᾧ μὴ βίοτος πολὺς εἴη,   490
ἢ πᾶσιν νεκύεσσι καταφθιμένοισιν ἀνάσσειν.

The general function of Kuranes in *Dream-Quest* is similar to that of Teiresias, another figure encountered in the underworld in the *Odyssey*, since Kuranes gives Randolph Carter much information and anticipates the future plot line (*Dream-Quest* 447–449).[34]

As the monarch of dreamland, Kuranes is not allowed to return to "the waking world because his body was dead" (*Dream-Quest* 447).[35] As Wetzel suggests, we can conclude that at least some souls of the dead dwell in dreamland. Therefore, dreamland is some kind of Hades or afterworld similar to that in Greek myth. The connection between dream/

---

[31] Lovecraft *Letters* iii.192, no. 431 (to Clark Ashton Smith, October 17, 1930); see also Smuda (1997: 61–62).

[32] Smuda (1997: 64).

[33] Translation: A. T. Murray.

[34] See also Smuda (1997: 64). For Teiresias' foreshadowing prophecy, see *Od.* 11.90–151.

[35] Wetzel (1980: 84) and (2001: 57).

sleep and death in the dreamlands also evokes Greek myth: for example, in Hesiod's *Theogony* (211–212), the personifications of sleep (Hypnos) and death (Thanatos) are brothers and the sons of the night (Nyx). Another interesting parallel between Lovecraft's and Homer's underworlds is mentioned by Schweitzer.[36] In *Dream-Quest* (435), the "Gate of Deeper Slumber" functions as a gateway to dreamland, like the Gates of Horn and Ivory mentioned in Homer's *Odyssey* (19.562–569) and Virgil's *Aeneid* (6.893–898).[37] The parallel between both Gates as entries to the dreamland/underworld is striking. As Wetzel and Schweitzer suggest, it is probable that Lovecraft's concept of 'dreamland' derives from Greek and Roman myth.

There are also close parallels between *Dream-Quest*'s plot and Lucian of Samosata's *True History* (*Verae Historiae* [*VH*]), which some consider the earliest work of science fiction.[38] In *Dream-Quest*, Carter is sailing by ship through the Basalt Pillars of the West when suddenly the galley shoots into planetary space and lands on the moon (*Dream-Quest* 419):

It was dark when the galley passed betwixt the Basalt Pillars of the West and the sound of the ultimate cataract swelled portentous from ahead. . . . Then with a queer whistle and plunge the leap was taken, and Carter felt the terrors of nightmare as earth fell away and the great boat shot silent and comet-like into planetary space.

Likewise, Lucian and his company sail westwards, pass the Pillars of Hercules, and end up lifted by a vortex to the moon (*VH* 1.5, 9):

Then, after I moved from the Pillars of Hercules and traveled to the western ocean [Okeanos], I was sailing with a fair wind. . . . About midday, when the island was not visible any longer, suddenly a typhoon arrived, whirled the ship and raised it to a height of 300 stades; the wind did not let the ship drop down to the sea, but held it in the sky and steered the ship by falling into the sails and swelling the linen.[39]

[36] Schweitzer (2001: 85).
[37] For additional discussion of ancient underworlds inspiring MF, see Stevens (this volume).
[38] See, for example, Fredericks (1976), Georgiadou and Larmour (1998: esp. 44–48), and Keen (2015); for a connection between Lucian, the imaginary voyage, and the parodic in MF, see Flugt (this volume).
[39] My translation.

ὁρμηθεὶς γάρ ποτε ἀπὸ Ἡρακλείων στηλῶν καὶ ἀφεὶς εἰς τὸν ἑσπέριον ὠκεανὸν οὐρίῳ ἀνέμῳ τὸν πλοῦν ἐποιούμην … περὶ μεσημβρίαν δὲ οὐκέτι τῆς νήσου φαινομένης ἄφνω τυφὼν ἐπιγενόμενος καὶ περιδινήσας τὴν ναῦν καὶ μετεωρίσας ὅσον ἐπὶ σταδίους τριακοσίους οὐκέτι καθῆκεν εἰς τὸ πέλαγος, ἀλλ᾽ ἄνω μετέωρον ἐξηρτημένην ἄνεμος ἐμπεσὼν τοῖς ἱστίοις ἔφερεν κολπώσας τὴν ὀθόνην.

Lovecraft's Carter arrives later at the seaport Celephais and meets its king Kuranes, a former human being (*Dream-Quest* 430–431). In close parallel, in Lucian, soon after their arrival on the moon, the narrator and his companions meet its human king, Endymion. Other story elements are also taken from *VH*. Just as Lucian is involved in battles in outer space between mythical creatures and monsters (1.13–20), so too Carter participates in fights between ghouls, night-gaunts, gugs, and moon-beasts. Lucian describes in detail the horse-vultures (ἱππόγυποι) and horse-cranes (ἱππογέρανοι) who serve as mounts and part of the troops, as well as the giant spiders that take part in the battle. Lovecraft similarly describes Shantaks, fabulous and enormous hippocephalic birds that Carter rides during his ventures. Spiders appear as well: "There were scenes of old wars, wherein Leng's almost-humans fought with the bloated purple spiders of the neighbouring vales" (*Dream-Quest* 460). Lovecraft's *Dream-Quest* may not take place in antiquity, but the storyline draws deeply on Lucian's *VH*, while passages regarding the dreamland and Kuranes derive from Homer's *Odyssey* and Virgil's *Aeneid*.

ANCIENT LANGUAGES IN THE CTHULHU MYTHOS

After *Dream-Quest* (1927), Lovecraft's interest in dreamland stories and Dunsanian writings ended, while the Cthulhu Mythos became his most important (and most successful) literary subject.[40] The major works of the Cthulhu Mythos tend to use ancient Greek and Latin language in different ways, which we may divide into three groups:

1. Terminology, neologisms, and metaphors. Lovecraft's creation of the *Necronomicon*, his comparison of Dagon and Cthulhu with

---

[40] Schweitzer (2001: 86–87).

Polyphemus, and his use of an 'ancient vocabulary' for horrifying, infernal, or monumental impressions are part of this category.

2. Quotations of and references to ancient sources. Here we find Latin mottos at the beginning of stories, in the tradition of Gothic novels. These quotations create a creepy atmosphere and also give the reader hints to the storyline. Demonic evocations and ancient inscriptions offer credibility and atmosphere, while there are direct parallels between characters in the tales "The Tomb" and "The Dunwich Horror" and figures from classical antiquity and myth (e.g., Jervas Dudley is compared to both the hero Theseus and Palinurus from Virgil's *Aeneid*, while Wilbur Whateley and his twin brother are compared to Jesus Christ).

3. Indications of the great antiquity of horrors. Here we deal with an 'abysmal antiquity', which clearly does not give testimony of historicity but of an unimaginably great age of cosmic horrors. Lovecraft's 'Great Old Ones' and their evil terrors existed before humankind, including classical antiquity, and they will exist forever. This is one of Lovecraft's chief ways of suggesting that humankind is inescapably doomed.

Terminology, Neologisms, and Metaphors

In the first category of Lovecraft's usage of ancient languages, we may count recurrent terms, neologisms, and metaphors. The best and most famous example is Lovecraft's invention of the *Necronomicon*, the fictional book of occult secrets. The title of the book is in ancient Greek, although the title and version of the tome (as it appears in Lovecraft's stories) reportedly derive from the Byzantine translation by Theodorus Philetas in AD 950.[41] The title *Necronomicon* may have been influenced by Manilius' *Astronomicon*, which was well known to Lovecraft; the pseudo-Greek neologism is also similar to Lovecraft's pseudo-Egyptian invention 'Nyarlathotep'.[42] The invented transmission of the fictional *Necronomicon*

---

[41] "History of the *Necronomicon*" 621–622. See also Carter (2001: 122–123, no. 37) and Joshi and Schultz (2001: 187, s.v. '*Necronomicon*').

[42] See Carter (2001: 133). Wetzel translates the title as 'Book of the Names of the Dead' or 'Guide[book] to the regions of the Dead,' stating that Lovecraft never explained or translated the title *Necronomicon*; see Wetzel (1980: 81, referring to D. Susan) and

through Abdul Alhazred and Theodorus Philetas, as well as its Greek name, serve to create a false sense of credibility. The reception and assimilation of the *Necronomicon* in a vast array of modern media—as well as the fact that some people thought (and still think?) the mythical book is real—prove the success of Lovecraft's invention.

Beyond that invented name, Lovecraft also frequently uses descriptive language and metaphors that make substantial links to classical antiquity. Descriptions of dark and subterranean vaults, holes, or caves often refer to the underworld or an infernal aspect of it, such as "that unhallowed Erebus" ("The Festival" 266, probably written in October 1923), "in the Stygian grotto" (267), "gazing into the Stygian deeps where no light had yet penetrated" ("Dagon" 25, written in July 1917), "after that eldritch flight through stygian space" ("Under the Pyramids" 280), and "in this grisly Tartarus" ("The Rats in the Walls" 254, written in late August and/or early September 1923).[43] Frightening situations likewise contain expressions alluding to ancient Greek or Roman culture: weird worshippers jump and roar "in endless Bacchanal" ("The Call of Cthulhu" 36, written in August or September 1926); nightmarish creatures are described as "clawing Furies ... [that] tore Harpy-like at my spirit" ("Under the Pyramids" 280); and when old Zadok Allen is caught speaking with one protagonist about the terrible secrets of Innsmouth, "his face was a mask of fear worthy of Greek tragedy" ("The Shadow Over Innsmouth" 836, written in November/December 1931). We also find phrases such as "great Cyclopean cities of titan blocks," "some terrible Cyclopean vista of dark and dripping stone," and "a Cyclopean architectural background" to express monumental and terrifying architecture.[44]

(2001: 57), as well as Carter (2001: 123). However, Lovecraft does explain in a letter written in 1937 that the title of this cursed book came to him in a dream and derived from the ancient Greek words *nekros* (corpse), *nomos* (law), and *eikon* (image), and thus means 'Image of the Law of the Dead.' As Wetzel notes, Lovecraft is mistaken, as the term would derive from *nekros, nemo*, and *-ikon* and mean 'Examination/Classification of the Dead' (Lovecraft *Letters* v.418, no. 927 [to Harry O. Fischer, late February 1937]). See also Carter (2001: 133), as well as Joshi and Schultz (2001: 187, s.v. '*Necronomicon*'). For Nyarlathotep, see Wetzel (1980: 82–83), Joshi and Schultz (2001: 190–191, s.v. 'Nyarlathotep'), and Murray (2011).

[43] "Under the Pyramids" was ghostwritten for Harry Houdini in February 1924 and also published as "Imprisoned with the Pharaohs."

[44] All quotations here are taken from "The Call of Cthulhu" (357–359).

In all of these cases, Lovecraft uses a kind of ancient vocabulary, single expressions creating a peculiar atmosphere without referring to particular ancient sources. An interesting exception is the description of the Great Old Ones, Dagon and Cthulhu. In the short story "Dagon" (26), Lovecraft depicts the rise of the Old One with an image evoking the Cyclops Polyphemus from Homer's *Odyssey* (book 9):

Then suddenly I saw it. With only a slight churning to mark its rise to the surface, the thing slid into view above the dark waters. Vast, Polyphemus-like, and loathsome, it darted like a stupendous monster of nightmares to the monolith, about which it flung its gigantic scaly arms, the while it bowed its hideous head and gave vent to certain measured sounds. I think I went mad then.

Nine years later, Lovecraft applied the same image to the rise of Cthulhu from R'lyeh in an even more impressive way ("The Call of Cthulhu" 378):

[T]he titan Thing from the stars slavered and gibbered like Polypheme cursing the fleeing ship of Odysseus. Then, bolder than the storied Cyclops, great Cthulhu slid greasily into the water and began to pursue with vast wave-raising strokes of cosmic potency.

At first view this simile seems odd; in Homer's *Odyssey*, Polyphemus does not enter the sea. But the famous Cyclops appears also in Virgil's *Aeneid*, where he slips into the water while Aeneas and his frightened fellows flee from him (3.662–665):

Soon to the vast flood of the level brine
he came, and washed the flowing gore away
from that out-hollowed eye; he gnashed his teeth,
groaning, and deep into the watery way
stalked on, his tall bulk wet by scarce a wave.[45]   665

---

[45] Translation: T. C. Williams. Ovid and Theocritus mention episodes with Polyphemus, which should be taken into consideration as well. Ovid describes Polyphemus' fruitless courtship of Galatea in his *Metamorphoses* (13.735–897), one of the ancient sources that attends Lovecraft's first attempts in his writing career (see above) and was therefore probably well known to and esteemed by him. Theocritus (*Idyll* 11.60) describes Polyphemus' attempt to learn how to swim because of his desire for the nymph Galatea; this passage may have influenced Lovecraft's choice of the motif.

Postquam altos tetigit fluctus et ad aequora venit,
luminis effossi fluidum lavit inde cruorem,
dentibus infrendens gemitu, graditurque per aequor
iam medium, necdum fluctus latera ardua tinxit.   665

Lovecraft most likely had this particular passage in mind. Not only does the comparison of Dagon/Cthulhu with Polyphemus evoke the gigantic and intimidating appearance of the monster, but the terrified and frightened protagonists of "Dagon" and "The Call of Cthulhu" also recall how Aeneas and his companions flee in the *Aeneid*.

Quotations of and Allusions to Ancient Sources

Quotations of or allusions to ancient sources form the second category of ancient language usage in the works of Lovecraft. First, let us consider three short stories that feature direct quotations of Latin from ancient sources in their introduction: "The Tomb," "The Tree," and "The Festival."

A tale similar to those of Edgar Allen Poe, "The Tomb" (written June 1917) is reminiscent of Gothic novels of the late eighteenth and nineteenth centuries in its style and subject matter. The narrator, Jervas Dudley, discovers a deserted tomb belonging to an old and exalted family, the Hydes. After years of obsession with the tomb, Jervas experiences entering the tomb and sleeping in a coffin, eventually believing that he experiences the death of the last of the Hydes, who had been incinerated by lightning and thus never buried in the family tomb; this man Jervas believes to be named 'Jervas Hyde.' Jervas Dudley is eventually caught by his father (who claims his son never entered the tomb at all) and is locked up in an asylum. However, at the end of the tale, Jervas finds out that a plate on the coffin in which he believes he had been sleeping "bears the single word 'Jervas.' In that coffin and in that vault they have promised me I shall be buried" ("The Tomb" 22).

It is typical for Gothic tales to include a Latin quotation as an epigraph in order to create an intellectual and exciting, even scary, atmosphere; the desire to create such a generic affiliation may thus explain why Lovecraft includes at the beginning of "The Tomb" a quotation explicitly attributed to Virgil: "*Sedibus ut saltem placidis in morte quiescam*" ("that at least in death I may find a quiet resting-place!").[46] This line comes from

---

[46] Translation here and for the next quotation from Virgil: H. R. Fairclough.

a passage in the *Aeneid* (6.371), where Aeneas starts his descent into the Underworld. On his way, Aeneas meets his dead helmsman Palinurus, who had fallen from the ship during the voyage to Italy and drowned. As he has not been buried and cannot cross the River Styx, Palinurus asks Aeneas either to bury him or to take him across the Styx, "that at least in death [he] may find a quiet resting-place." However, the quotation also signals a clear link to the plot of "The Tomb," possibly suggesting that Jervas Dudley may be possessed by the spirit of Jervas Hyde, who fears never being buried. Such an interpretation is strengthened by the narrator's direct reference to Palinurus: "I would claim my heritage of death, even though my soul go seeking through the ages for another corporeal tenement to represent it on that vacant slab in the alcove of the vault. Jervas Hyde should never share the sad fate of Palinurus!" (21).

In "The Tree" (discussed above), Lovecraft also quotes Virgil in an epigraph, although this time without naming the ancient author: "*Fata viam invenient*" ("the Fates will find a way"). The quotation comes again from the *Aeneid* (3.395), belonging to Helenus' prophecy to Aeneas. Helenus tells Aeneas that Aeneas still has to endure many dangers and labors, but his destiny is predetermined and sure: if Aeneas trusts in the gods, "the Fates will find a way." The quotation in "The Tree" refers clearly to the murder of the character Kalos. Musides betrays his friend Kalos by poisoning him, but fate (Tyché) takes revenge on the sinner and punishes Musides in the shape of a statue of Tyché. Musides cannot escape punishment for his crime because 'fate will find a way' for the sake of justice.

The third short story, "The Festival," includes a Latin quotation, not from Virgil but, according to the epigraph, from Lactantius, a Christian author of Late Antiquity: "*Efficiunt Daemones, ut quae non sunt, sic tamen quasi sint, conspicienda hominibus exhibeant*" ("Demons work upon people so that they see things that do not exist as if they exist").[47] In fact, Lactantius never wrote such a sentence. Lovecraft may have taken this false quotation from the *Magnalia Christi Americana*, where the sentence is falsely cited as coming from Lactantius' *Divinae institutiones* (2.15).[48] The *Magnalia Christi Americana* was written in 1702 by Cotton Mather, who is perhaps best known for his participation in the Salem witch trials in 1692. As Wetzel points out, the same false citation

---

[47] My translation.
[48] Joshi and Schultz (2001: 93, s.v. 'Festival, The') and Walter (2012: 113–114, with n. 27 and reference to Joshi).

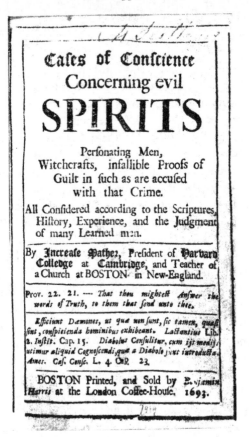

Figure 4.1 Pseudo-citation of Lactantius on the title page of *Cases of Conscience Concerning Evil Spirits* by Increase Mather in 1693. Public domain.

appears on the title page of *Cases of Conscience Concerning Evil Spirits*, written in 1693 by Increase Mather, Cotton's father (Figure 4.1). For his part, Lactantius seems to have written a somewhat similar expression in the *Divinae institutiones* in a section (2.14.10) immediately prior to the location of the false citation in *Magnalia Christi Americana*, and this may be the source for the Mathers' false citation.[49] In all probability, Lovecraft

[49] Walter (2012: 114, with nn. 28–30).

did not consult Lactantius, but rather cited the reference made by Cotton Mather, or more likely the front page of the tome written by Increase Mather, without checking its accuracy.

As for the story of "The Festival," the first-person narrator arrives at Kingsport at Christmas/Yuletide for a kind of gathering. The narrator and townspeople descend into the gigantic vaults under Kingsport, where they perform the Yule-rite and ride off on the backs of hybrid, winged creatures. The protagonist resists the Yule-rite, flings himself into the river, and wakes up in a hospital. There the narrator is told that he fell over a cliff, as evidenced by prints in the snow, and that his memories are wrong and the result of a psychosis. However, when he later reads the *Necronomicon*, the protagonist finds a description of the rites he witnessed.

As in "The Tomb," the Latin quotation in the epigraph of "The Festival" aligns the story with the tradition of the Gothic novel. In addition, the quotation foreshadows the protagonist's doubts about whether the things he has seen are indeed real or not. It is possible that Lovecraft used Lactantius intentionally since he was a Father of the Catholic church. The fact that such a figure as Lactantius pronounces judgement about demons and dark forces—in Latin, no less—lends an air of authority and credibility.[50]

These Latin quotations do (at least) three kinds of work in "The Tomb," "The Tree," and "The Festival." First, the quotations stylistically align these three tales with the tradition of Gothic novels. In connection to the romantic mood that is evoked through the Gothic genre, these quotations also produce a weird, even creepy, atmosphere. Second, the quotations of Virgil in "The Tomb" and "The Tree" demonstrate Lovecraft's knowledge of ancient sources, which lends credibility to his other evocations of the ancient past. Third, and perhaps most importantly, these Latin quotations offer hints about the content of the stories themselves; only readers who understand Latin and know the context for these quotations are able to decipher their hidden knowledge.

In addition to these direct quotations of Latin in the epigraphs, there are also several other indirect allusions to sources from classical antiquity in Lovecraft's stories. For example, in "The Tomb," an eleven-year-old

---

[50] Walter (2012: 111–114, 117–118).

Jervas Dudley stumbles "upon a worm-eaten translation of Plutarch's *Lives* in the book-filled attic" (16). He reads the passage in which Theseus is ready "to find his tokens of destiny whenever he should become old enough" to lift a great stone (16–17).[51] After reading the passage, Jervas starts comparing himself to Theseus, as he also has to wait to enter the tomb until he is able to open its gate. In this reference to Plutarch's *Lives*, Lovecraft not only creates an atmosphere of the 'ancient'—augmented by Jervas's references to his time spent among "ancient and little-known books"—but also offers a point of comparison between both characters, who are waiting to be ready for their fate (though, in Lovecraft's tale, that fate would mean Jervas's doom). Indeed, Jervas Dudley seems to mirror the young Lovecraft himself, insofar as both encountered classical antiquity at an early age and with decisive effects on their fates.

In "The Rats in the Wall," the main character finds Roman inscriptions that remind him of a passage of Catullus: "'P. GETAE. PROP ... TEMP ... DONA ...' and 'L. PRAEC ... VS ... PONTIFI ... ATYS ...' The reference to Atys made me shiver, for I had read Catullus and knew something of the hideous rites of the Eastern god, whose worship was so mixed with that of Cybele" (248).[52] This seemingly simple passage reveals much about Lovecraft's knowledge of classical antiquity. First, Lovecraft knew the strange and not very famous deities Attis and Cybele, and thus demonstrates his knowledge of ancient religion. Second, Attis appears only once in Catullus' poems (poem 63): Lovecraft must have read this poem as well as, probably, some modern literature on Attis. Third, Lovecraft refers to Attis as 'Atys,' which is a mistake from a modern scholarly perspective, but reflects the status of research during the nineteenth and early twentieth centuries: at that time, the mythical shepherd Attis and Atys, a son of Croesus mentioned by Herodotus (1.34–45), were considered identical.[53]

---

[51] Lovecraft is referring to Plutarch's *Life of Theseus* (3.4–5 and 6.2–3).

[52] Catullus writes only once about Attis; therefore, the protagonist in "The Rats in the Walls" must refer to Catullus 63. Attis and Cybele only appear a second time at the very end of the story. The protagonist is found insane and crouching over the half-eaten body of his friend stuttering: "Curse you, Thornton, I'll teach you to faint at what my family do! ... 'Sblood, thou stinkard, I'll learn ye how to gust ... wolde ye swynke me thilke wys? ... *Magna Mater! Magna Mater!* ... Atys ... *Dia ad aghaidh's ad aodaun ... agus bas dunarch ort! Dhonas 's dholas ort, agus leat-sa! ... Ungl ... ungl ... rrrlh ... chchch ...*" ("The Rats in the Walls" 255).

[53] On Attis and Atys, see Bremmer (2004: 536–540), with a detailed refutation of the equation of the two.

A similar example of explicitly foreign and weird rites appears in "The Horror at Red Hook" (323):

The writing was in red, and varied from Arabic to Greek, Roman, and Hebrew letters. Malone could not read much of it, but what he did decipher was portentous and cabbalistic enough. One frequently repeated motto was in a sort of Hebraised Hellenistic Greek, and suggested the most terrible daemon-evocations of the Alexandrian decadence:

"HEL * HELOYM * SOTHER * EMMANVEL * SABAOTH * AGLA *
TETRAGRAMMATON * AGYROS * OTHEOS * ISCHYROS * ATHANATOS * IEHOVA
* VA * ADONAI * SADAY * HOMOVSION * MESSIAS * ESCHEREHEYE."

Lovecraft did not invent this magical incantation but copied it from E. B. Tyler's article "Magic" in the ninth edition of the *Encyclopedia Britannica*, which Lovecraft owned. In a later letter, he tried to translate the inscription, committing several errors.[54] Tyler himself had copied the incantation from Georg Conrad Horst's 1821 tome *Zauber-Bibliothek oder von Zauberei, Theurgie und Mantik, Zauberern, Hexen und Hexenprocessen, Dämonen, Gespenstern, und Geistererscheinungen* (ii.90, seen in Figure 4.2). Whereas Lovecraft uses the spell as a demonic evocation, it seems to have in fact been an incantation for treasure hunting.[55]

In any case, the two occult references not only impress upon the reader Lovecraft's education in letters, but also assert a kind of authenticity through the use of ancient sources and documents. The most important aspect seems to be that in both cases we are confronted with 'exotic,' Eastern cults from antiquity. To this point, Lovecraft writes in his essay "Supernatural Horror in Literature" (17–18):

Cosmic terror appears as an ingredient of the earliest folklore of all races, and is crystallized in the most archaic ballads, chronicles and sacred writings. ... In the Orient, the weird tale tended to assume a gorgeous colouring and sprightliness which almost transmuted it into sheer phantasy. In the West, where the mystical Teuton had come down from his black boreal forest and the Celt remembered strange sacrifices in Druidic groves, it assumed a

---

[54] Joshi and Schultz (2001: 115, s.v. 'Horror at Red Hook, The') and Joshi (2004: 367).
[55] Harms and Gonce (2003: 95–96).

90

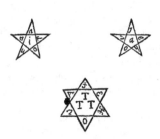

Nach diefem fchreite zu folgender und leßtern Befchwöß-
rung alfo:

     Im Rahmen Gottes deß Vatters ✠ deß Sohnes ✠ und
deß heiligen Geiftes ✠. Amen.

     Hel ✠ Heloym ✠ Sother✠Emmanuel✠Sabaoth ✠
Agla ✠ Tetragrammaton ✠ Agyros ✠ Otheos ✠ Ischyros ✠ Athanatos ✠ Jehova ✠ Va ✠ Adonai ✠ Saday ✠
Homousion ✠ Messias ✠ Eschereheye ✠
         unerfchaffener Vatter ✠
         unerfchaffener Sohn ✠
         unerfchaffener Heil. Geift ✠
         Jesus Christus fieget ✠
         Chriftus regieret ✠
         Chriftus herrfchet ✠
     Wenn dich nun fündige Seele. (NN. hier wende
dich zu der armen Seele und fpreche weiters) der
Teufel gebunden, oder fonft auf eine Arth dich ver-
fuchet und überwältiget, fo wird dich durch diefe Krafft
und durch fein Verdienft und große Barmherßigkeit

Figure 4.2 The magical incantation used in Lovecraft's "The Horror at Red Hook" derives from the *Zauber-Bibliothek oder von Zauberei, Theurgie und Mantik, Zauberern, Hexen und Hexenprocessen, Dämonen, Gespenstern, und Geistererscheinungen* (ii.90), written by Georg Conrad Horst in 1821. Public domain.

terrible intensity and convincing seriousness of atmosphere which doubled the force of its half-told, half-hinted horrors.

So, for one such example of "terrible intensity and convincing serious-ness," consider Lovecraft's use of Cybele, an ancient goddess worshipped by the Phrygians and Thracians in Asia Minor, and who later in antiquity was worshipped among the Greeks and Romans. The Greeks and

Romans themselves considered Cybele to be a strange deity with foreign origins, and this fact must have impressed Lovecraft as much as the ecstatic character of the goddess's rituals, which included the voluntary castration of cult members and perhaps the *taurobolium* (in which a cult member would stand in a pit and be covered by the blood of a bull sacrificed above him), although the veracity of this latter ritual is a subject of debate. Lovecraft was certainly as spellbound by Cybele and Attis as he was by the strange rituals of witches, of Germanic tribes in the black forest, and of Celts in Druidic groves. Through the exotic and secretive character of the cults of Cybele and Attis, Lovecraft evokes a hidden and hideous part of the earliest folklore, creating a sense of "cosmic terror." While official organizations, institutions, and even empires may exist, Lovecraft intimates that there also exist in the world hidden, dangerous cults serving truly ancient, cosmic forces.

A different approach to the citation of ancient literature can be seen in the story "The Dunwich Horror" (written in August 1928), which borrows a citation from the Bible. In a partly inhabited farmhouse outside Dunwich, Lavinia Whateley gives birth to a son whose father is unknown: the father turns out to be the god Yog-Sothoth. The boy, Wilbur, is a "dark, goatish-looking" child, and Lavinia delivers curious prophecies about his unusual powers and tremendous future. It is notable that the setting already seems similar to the Nativity of Jesus: the farmhouse is located just outside a small village, and the child is born (on Candlemas!) with unusual powers and no known father (and with a god as the real father). Later in the story, Wilbur dies trying to summon the Old Ones, and the danger he poses seems to have passed. But it turns out that in the farmhouse is a huge, deformed, and invisible monster that escapes from the farmhouse and kills several people. The story's protagonists manage to kill the monster on top of a hilltop, and the monster is revealed to be Wilbur's twin brother and another son of Yog-Sothoth, who is more similar to his divine father. As the twin dies, he shouts: "*Eh-ya-ya-ya-yahaah—e'yayayayaaaa . . . ngh'aaaaa . . . ngh'aaaa . . .* h'yuh . . . h'yuh . . . HELP! HELP! . . . *ff—ff—ff—*FATHER! FATHER! YOG-SOTHOTH! . . . " (666). These last words uttered by the powerful and monstrous child—or better, creature—of a Great Old One as he dies, strongly evoke Jesus' own last words as he dies upon on the cross: *Eloi, Eloi, lama sabachtani?* ("My God, my God, why have you forsaken me?" Psalm 22:1, Matthew 27:46, Mark 15:34). Thus Lovecraft uses these scenes at the beginning and end of the story to offer a dark parody of the Nativity and the Crucifixion of Jesus Christ, as well as parody of the source text. In this exceptional case, the function of such allusion is to create a destructive distortion of that most vital Christian subject.[56]

Indications of the Great Antiquity of Horrors

The third way Lovecraft uses ancient languages in his short stories is to indicate the great antiquity of his invented horrors. Lovecraft includes not only historic divinities in his stories but also ancient inscriptions (discussed above) recording the existence of ancient and cruel cults. In addition to the previously discussed example of Attis and Cybele in "The Rats in the Walls," Magna Mater also appears together with Hecate in "The Horror at Red Hook" ("Incubi and succubae howled praise to Hecate, and headless moon-calves bleated to the Magna Mater," 327). Lovecraft also refers to other divinities, such as Gorgo and Mormo ("who longest for blood and bringest terror to mortals, Gorgo, Mormo, thousand-faced moon," 323), as well as "Mother Hydra an' Father Dagon" ("The Shadow over Innsmouth" 834).[57] The narrator in "Dagon" seeks out an ethnologist in order to give warning of Dagon and his cults, which seem to have survived from antiquity into the present day (26): "Once I sought out a celebrated ethnologist, and amused him with peculiar questions regarding the ancient Philistine legend of Dagon, the Fish-God; but soon perceiving that he was hopelessly conventional, I did not press my inquiries."

Additionally, in some stories there are references to historical persons, cultures, and races. In "The Descendant" (written in early 1927), Lord Northam is the descendent of a "certain Cnaeus Gabinius Capito, military tribune in the Third Augustan Legion then stationed at Lindum in Roman Britain" (619). The same legion is also mentioned in "The Rats in the Walls": "Anchester had been the camp of the third Augustan legion, as many remains attest, and it was said that the temple of Cybele was

---

[56] See Joshi and Schultz (2001: 79–80, s.v. 'Dunwich Horror, The'), Houellebecq (2002: 106–107), and Burleson (2013: 106). The name 'Lavinia' may come from Virgil's *Aeneid*; for some discussions of Lavinia in MF, see Rea (2010) and her chapter in this volume.

[57] The 'Lovecraftian Dagon' is not a reception of Greek or Roman antiquity but derives from an ancient Philistine deity mentioned, e.g., twice in the Bible (Judges 16:23–24; 1 Samuel 5:1–7).

splendid and thronged with worshippers who performed nameless ceremonies at the bidding of a Phrygian priest" (242).

Besides such precise references to classical antiquity, Lovecraft has the narrator explain the great antiquity of horror in an imprecise, emotional way: "Those nightmare chasms choked with the pithecanthropoid, Celtic, Roman, and English bones of countless unhallowed centuries!" ("The Rats in the Walls" 254). There are also similar references to ancient Egypt and even prehistory.[58] In these cases, the precise culture or historical time period are less important than the feeling of antiquity, the great age of the horror. Thus the protagonist in "The Nameless City" refers generally to a diffuse antiquity: "Fear spoke from the age-worn stones of this hoary survivor of the deluge, this great-grandfather of the eldest pyramid; and a viewless aura repelled me and bade me retreat from antique and sinister secrets that no man should see, and no man else had ever dared to see" (141). Later he adds: "The antiquity of the spot was unwholesome" (142). In "The Shadow out of Time" (written between November 10, 1934, and February 22, 1935), even a mining engineer fears stones and stone formations because of their old age: "I have some knowledge of geology, and can tell you that these blocks are so ancient they frighten me" (976).[59] Additionally, in "The Call of Cthulhu," Inspector Legrasse finds a cult idol representing the Great Old One Cthulhu, which seems to possess an "air of genuinely abysmal antiquity . . . yet centuries and even thousands of years seemed recorded in its dim and greenish surface of unplaceable stone" (362).

All these references—the precise indications to legions, divinities, or cults, as well as the sentimental descriptions of 'abysmal antiquity'— attest not only to the historicity of past and present horror but also, and above all, to the very great age of the cosmic horrors. By presenting an unimaginably old antiquity, Lovecraft develops an impressive image of the eternity and inescapability of the described dangers. The Great Old Ones, the cosmic horrors, and the evil cults existed before the beginning of humankind, they exist now, and they will exist forever. Therefore, even

---

[58] "I saw the horror and unwholesome antiquity of Egypt" ("Under the Pyramids" 280); "some tribe whose last descendant had perished eras before the first ancestor of the Piltdown or Neanderthal Man was born" ("Dagon" 26).

[59] Cf. Price (2011: 125–126).

if humankind appears safe for the moment, doom and annihilation are its inescapable fate.

Lovecraft introduces his essay "Supernatural Horror in Literature" with the following statement: "The oldest and strongest emotion of mankind is fear, and the oldest and strongest fear is fear of the unknown" (12). Therefore, we may see Lovecraft's horror creations—extraterrestrial, most ancient, and unknown, even unimaginable—as attempts to represent humankind's strongest possible fears. Lovecraft thus manages to make a timeless, omnipresent horror out of even something as beloved as Christmas: "It was the Yuletide, that men call Christmas though they know in their hearts it is older than Bethlehem and Babylon, older than Memphis and mankind" ("The Festival" 262).[60]

CONCLUSION

Looking at the influence of classical culture on Lovecraft's work, we see that antiquity can serve very different purposes. Lovecraft did not insert classical antiquity in his tales in just one way, and indeed we do not find a specific order or system according to which he integrated Greek and Roman elements into his stories. Suggestive in this connection are the facts that Lovecraft had contact with classical antiquity from his early childhood onward and that he copied his sources in some cases without much attention or accuracy (e.g., the development of the term *Necronomicon*, the mis-citation of Lactantius in "The Festival," and the demonic incantation in "The Horror at Red Hook"). It is clear that Lovecraft had a vast knowledge of ancient sources, history, and myth, and that he applied this knowledge often and, in most cases, seemingly intentionally (e.g., especially the Latin quotations and the references to Cybele and Attis). But he often used ancient material seemingly without regard for ancient context and as it fitted the tale at hand. As for his sources, he tended to use Homer's *Odyssey* and Virgil's *Aeneid*, which, in the latter instance, might be due to his love of the power and glory of eternal Rome; in any case we have the impression that these ancient sources were his favorite and best known to him.

---

[60] See also Walter (2012: 114, with n. 31).

As I have argued, classical antiquity is not merely an important instrument and source of inspiration for Lovecraft's tales. More deeply, it defined his character and marked the beginning of his writings and his creation of cosmic horrors. If those horrors are famously, ineffably 'timeless,' still a great part of their effect is achieved through classical Greece and Rome. It is impossible to look at the weird, modern work of H. P. Lovecraft without also seeing classical antiquity.

Part II

False Medievalism and Other Ancient Fantasies

5

Ancient Underworlds in J. R. R. Tolkien's *The Hobbit*

Benjamin Eldon Stevens

The Hobbit begins "In a hole in the ground" (3).[1] Although that comfortable "hobbit-hole" is soon left far behind, J. R. R. Tolkien's beloved novel has much to do with holes in the ground, with places under the earth, and with yet other places and creatures that evoke such subterranean realms. In this chapter, I examine how *The Hobbit* is subterranean in a particular way, recalling and altering earlier depictions of underworlds as resting-places for the dead.[2] Ancient literature and myth abound in

---

[1] According to Tolkien, the story originated with that line; see letter 163 in Carpenter (1981 [*Letters*]). References to *The Hobbit* are to Tolkien (2012b). Published in 1937, the novel was revised by Tolkien in 1951 and 1966 and has been edited variously since; see Tolkien (1988: 321–328) and Rateliff (2007). As of 1951, Chapter V was rewritten to reflect *The Lord of the Rings* (Tolkien 2012a [*LR*]); see below, "Bilbo and Gollum." My chapter began as a keynote for the Hollins University Children's Literature program, summer 2014; thanks go to program director Amanda Cockrell for the invitation and to C. W. Sullivan III for comments. The chapter is dedicated to the spirited katabants in courses on underworlds at Bryn Mawr College and Trinity University. Golden boughs go to Eliana Chavkin, Ashleigh Gill, Sara Jo Powell, and Brett M. Rogers.

[2] Scholarship on Tolkien's underworlds has focused on *LR* and Virgil's *Aeneid*; see esp. Obertino (1993), cited by Drout (2007: 123) in *The J. R. R. Tolkien Encyclopedia* (*Encyclopedia*)

stories of living people journeying into just such deathly underworlds—
a type of journey called *katabasis* (the Greek for 'going below'; plural
katabaseis).[3] *The Hobbit*'s own underworlds represent a significant variation on that ancient theme by replacing the dead and their knowledge
of past and future—their memories and prophecies—with subterranean
or chthonic monsters that rather disorder knowing and embody forgetting. Given Tolkien's status as a foundational author and theorist of
modern fantasy (MF), such transformed underworlds are suggestive of
the genre's ancient roots—of its practices of classical reception.[4] In contrast to positing a simple 'classical tradition,' classical reception considers each moment of transmission as involving complex transformations,
resulting in a plurality of 'traditions.'[5] I therefore refer to 'ancient underworlds' in the plural. Although I note mainly ancient Greek and Roman
depictions, these form part of a larger set of materials underlying *The
Hobbit*, especially Old English and Norse stories, as well as Tolkien's own
invented mythology.

Although Tolkien disliked source criticism, nonetheless a multiplicity
of sources, with a diversity of meanings, is suggested in his scholarship
and correspondence.[6] Of special importance is his suggestion that a work
of literature may create

the illusion of surveying a past, pagan but noble and fraught with a deep
significance—a past that itself had depth and reached backward into a dark

---

entry 'Descent,' and Simonis (2014). Cf. Greenman (1992), Librán Moreno (2005), and
Reckford (1972); with Morse (1986: 10–14, 19) on the Dead Marshes, for which cf. Marian
Makins's 2015 talk, "Memories of (Roman) War in Tolkien's 'The Passages of the Marshes.'"

[3] See, e.g., Clark (1979). Contrast *nekyia*, a ritualistic summoning of the dead to the
world above; the paradigmatic example occurs in Homer's *Odyssey* 11—indeed that whole
book could be called 'the *Nekyia*' (e.g., Diodorus Siculus 4.39). By extension, the term could
describe historical events as 'hellish' (e.g., Cicero *Ad Atticum* 9.10). On *Odyssey* 11, see
further below, n. 16.

[4] On Tolkien's status, see James (2012), Shippey (2002: esp. 305–328), the entry 'Tolkien,
J(ohn) R(onald) R(euel)' in Clute and Grant (1997: 950–955, esp. 955, 'Aftermath'), and
Booker (2009). For his fantasy theory, see esp. Tolkien (1965) and correspondence on *LR*,
with, e.g., Shippey (2003: 49–54).

[5] See further this volume's Introduction. I do not adopt a particular theory of reception
but consider how Tolkien both engages with sources directly and may be read as resonating
with them, even if unconsciously.

[6] Tolkien (1984) collects several essays; cf. *Encyclopedia* entries 'Scholars of Medieval
Literature, Influence of' (594–598) and 'Oxford' (on 'Scholarship' 493–495).

antiquity of sorrow. This impression of depth is an effect and a justification of the use of episodes and allusions to old tales, mostly darker, more pagan, and desperate than the foreground.[7]

Here Tolkien describes a practice of reception—"the use of episodes and allusions to old tales"—in terms that evoke ancient underworlds: "a past that . . . had depth," "a dark antiquity of sorrow," "mostly darker, more pagan . . . than the foreground." Tolkien is writing to redeem the poetic value of the Old English epic *Beowulf* (c. eighth–eleventh centuries CE) but he describes the "impression of depth" as underlying "the similar effect of antiquity (and melancholy)" in a classical Latin epic, Virgil's *Aeneid* (19 BCE [*Aen.*]).[8] He explains further that "the real likeness [between the two epics] is deeper and due to certain qualities in the authors. . . . We have the great pagan on the threshold of the change of the world; and the great (if lesser) Christian just over the threshold of the great change in his time and place."[9] The "impression of depth" thus depends on how the *Aeneid* captures feelings caused by ineluctably passing time.

The feeling is such that Tolkien exclaims: "Alas for the lost lore, the annals and old poets *that Virgil knew*, and only used in the making of a new thing! . . . it is the poet himself who made antiquity so appealing."[10] For Tolkien, then, a great part of the interest of ancient poetic images of the past is their implication of yet larger, even older worlds that are all but lost.[11]

---

[7] Tolkien (1980: 26–27).

[8] Tolkien "was brought up in the Classics, and first discovered the sensation of literary pleasure in Homer" (*Encyclopedia*, s.v. 'Homer' 285). Other classical sources include Plato (Cox [1984]) and probably Ovid (Larsen [2011]). See Fisher (2011) and Caldecott and Honegger (2008).

[9] Tolkien (1980: 22–23). For 'threshold,' cf. Anzinger (2010) on turning-points in Tolkien and Virgil.

[10] Tolkien (1980: 27, emphasis added). Cf. Houghton (1990). Shippey suggestively describes Tolkien's conviction that "the power of philology . . . can resurrect from the dead a society long since vanished" (2003: 40; cf. 57); cf. Fisher (2010) and Gilliver, Marshall, and Weiner (2006). Tolkien writes that *LR* sprang from his desire "to create a situation in which a common greeting would be *elen síla lumenn' omentielmo*" (*Letters* 205) and so is "an essay in 'linguistic aesthetic'" (165). The Elvish phrase appears at *LR* 79, though Tolkien corrected the spelling of the final word to *omentielvo* after the first edition.

[11] Cf. Gilman (2012: 134); see also Shippey (2003), Petty (2002), Shippey (2002), and Carpenter (2000). Interpretations of Tolkien's reconstructions often incorporate his concept of 'eucatastrophe,' "a forceful expression of the esthetic fulfillment of hope" (*Encyclopedia* q.v., 177); see also Flieger (2002: esp. 11–31), Curry (1998: 112–138), *Letters* 89, and Manwell (this volume).

This feeling for lost worlds is especially present in underworldly episodes, in which the past represents death and forgetting—"a dark antiquity of sorrow" and "melancholy."[12] Thus it is significant that, to emphasize the depth of that feeling, Tolkien quotes a line from the *Aeneid*'s underworldly book 6: *multa putans sortemque animo miseratus iniquam* (332).[13] This describes Virgil's main character, Aeneas, "thinking about many things and, in his mind, pitying the unjust lot" of the dead, whom he sees gathered on the bank of the river Styx, filled with "longing for the farther shore" (*ripae ulterioris amore*; 314). Readers of Tolkien may hear in that last phrase an echo of the Elves' departure.[14] We consider this possible parallel, along with the most famous image from Virgil's scene, in this chapter's concluding section.

Here the quotation from Virgil serves as one example of how ancient underworlds help give the impression of a "past that . . . had depth" and that underlies *katabasis* in Tolkien's fictions. Virgil also provides a contrast in his focus on the dead: underworlds in Tolkien do not always involve the dead, and *The Hobbit*'s underworlds seem not to involve them at all.[15] Bilbo meets no ancestors (as, e.g., Aeneas meets his father Anchises in *Aen.* 6, or Odysseus his mother Anticleia in *Odyssey* [*Od.*] 11) and gains no certain knowledge of the future (as Aeneas does from his father, or Odysseus from the seer Teiresias).[16] Instead, he encounters visions of his own potentially darker path in the forms of chthonic monsters to whom he is uncannily similar. At a crucial point he catches not a heartening prophecy but a pitiable and horrifying "glimpse of endless unmarked days without light or hope of betterment" (*Hobbit* 81). With underworlds

[12] Senior (2000: 174) argues that Tolkien depicts a "sustained and grieved sense of loss." Yet his characters do not simply despair: e.g., Aragorn tells Arwen that "[i]n sorrow we must go, but not in despair" (*LR* 1038); cf. Shippey (2003: 154–160).

[13] Quoted at Tolkien (1980: 23).

[14] E.g., Galadriel's song: "*O Lórien! Too long I have dwelt upon this Hither Shore. . . . But if of ships I now should sing, what ship would come to me, / What ship would bear me ever back across so wide a Sea?*" (*LR* 363). Galadriel is "present and yet remote, a living vision of that which has already been left far behind by the flowing streams of Time" (364). Enchanting spaces produce a fleeting "feeling" of "a timeless land that did not fade or change or fall into forgetfulness" (342). Cf. the Elves, long-lived but not immortal; see also *Encyclopedia*, s.v. 'Elves' (150–152).

[15] *Hobbit* refers once to "the Necromancer" (129), but only in *LR* is he identified as the great enemy Sauron. Some *katabaseis* in *LR* feature encounters with the dead: see esp. the "Paths of the Dead" (756–787), with Obertino (1993).

[16] Whether Odysseus' *nekyia* involves—or leads to—*katabasis* is unclear; see Heubeck and Hoekstra (1989: 76 and 111 *ad* 568–627) and Clark (1979: 53–78).

thus inhabited by creatures that are not classical ghosts and that tend not to offer knowledge of the past, *The Hobbit's katabaseis* depart from what, in ancient epic, was an ordered system of memory and history.[17]

This departure from ancient *katabasis* may be linked to ambivalence in Tolkien's "impression of depth." Although an impression or a glimpse can be positive, evoking an "enchant[ing]" history or totality (*Hobbit* 198), it may also be negative, inducing a jealous lust for "magic" and other misleading falsehoods (16). For Tolkien, this is linked to a distinction between 'primary' and 'secondary worlds': between the world of fact, changes to which represent the will to power, and fictional worlds, whose mutability allows a positive "realization . . . of imagined wonder."[18] This makes epic center around a capacity to suggest truth via evocations of the lost pasts of secondary worlds: historical fictions are necessarily incomplete but they are not *mere* illusions, since they can inspire 'secondary belief.'[19]

That capacity is a motivating factor for Tolkien's more deeply ambivalent depictions of the underworld. Ancient depictions are not without their own ambivalences, including melancholy for lost time. Virgil thus asks whether Aeneas, having gone "there," can ever truly come "back again." His guide does not quite say "no" but emphasizes the difficulty (*Aen.* 6.128–131), and Aeneas exits oddly, via a gate reserved for "false dreams" (6.896–898).[20] But Aeneas *does* leave, and more importantly, like other ancient katabants he succeeded in finding ghosts, including ancestors, who remember the past and predict the future.[21] By contrast, Bilbo has no ancestral encounter and seems to receive no guidance.

---

[17] See further this chapter's concluding section.

[18] Tolkien (1965: 14). Enchantment "produces a Secondary World into which both designer and spectator can enter" (52); cf. Frodo in Lórien, "lost in wonder . . . as if . . . inside a song" (*LR* 341 and 342). Magic involves "an exercise of the will . . . to create changes in the 'Primary World'" (*Encyclopedia*, s.v. 'Enchantment,' 159–160); Sauron uses magic to reduce "the gap between the idea or desire and the result or effect" (*Letters* 155). See further *Encyclopedia*, s.v. 'Magic' (400–401). Cf. Curry (1999) and Bettelheim (2010), and, for a different approach to enchantment in fantasy, Flugt (this volume).

[19] See the entry 'Tolkien, J(ohn) R(onald) R(euel),' subsections 'The Secondary World' and 'Secondary Belief,' in Clute and Grant (1997: 951 and 952–953), as well as Saxton (2013) and Sandner (2000).

[20] See Horsfall (2013: 612–623), West (1990), Austin (1986: 274–78), and Otis (1959).

[21] For this ambivalence in *Aen.*, cf. Putnam (1995: esp. 152–171 and 286–315), Gransden (1984: 192–217), Johnson (1976: esp. 59–75 and 114–134), and Reckford (1972). Aeneas' heartening contacts are balanced by harrowing encounters with people he cannot save.

As we will see, he seems to lack a clear purpose at his most katabatic moments. Ambivalent as ancient underworlds are, then, *The Hobbit*'s paradoxes run deeper. This is embodied most of all in the creatures that take the place of the dead: Gollum and Smaug. Smaug sheds special light on Tolkien's receptions of ancient underworlds, not only representing the goal of the quest but also recalling the starting-point of Tolkien's turn to fantasy: he "desired dragons with a profound desire."[22] How meaningful, then, is Tolkien's image for the oblivion that comes with passing time: "the dragon of destruction."[23] In Tolkien's terms, we might say that a dragon or a dragonish being produces not only enchantment but also bewilderment. Such creatures are powerful symbols of the forgetting that haunts post-classical epic, taking the place where, classically, the dead and their memories and prophecies would go.[24]

In this chapter, I focus on Bilbo's encounters with Gollum and Smaug. I first consider how Tolkien sets such scenes, linking spaces below—tunnels and mountains' roots—to lost lore and forgetting. I then examine Bilbo's encounter with Gollum, which leads to a sympathetic vision of Gollum's life that comes in part from his embodying one of Bilbo's own *potential* paths; this is echoed in Bilbo's encounter with Smaug, which is contextualized by what Tolkien describes expressly as one of Bilbo's most significant *actual* experiences, "the bravest thing he ever did." Both chthonic monsters, Gollum (or Sméagol) and Smaug, are similar in several ways, including their names, their riddling, and their desire for gold. Most deeply, they are linked to forgetting: Gollum has displaced goblins from caverns and struggles to remember his past, while Smaug has taken the dwarves' ancestral hall, disrupting their history. These similarities resound in Bilbo as he travels below: stealing ill-gotten gold from each creature, he becomes like his former fellow hobbit, now adapted to darkness and divorced from normal time, and like the dragon whose hoard

---

[22] Tolkien (1965: 40–41). For 'desire' and fantasy, see Jackson (1981: 3) with Bould and Vint (2012: 102–103). For dragons and the "progressive potential of fantasy," see Baker (2012).

[23] Tolkien (1980: 27).

[24] Cf. Reckford (1972: 60): Tolkien "insistently evokes the power of time to ravish beauty, undo man's works, and carry into memory and song (or the Far West) all that we cherish and fight for in our brief lives." See also Obertino (1993: 161–164). For final journeys to the setting sun, see West (1997: 153–154) and cf. Lewis's *The Voyage of the "Dawn Treader"* (*DT*).

is a kind of reliquary and who is himself a relic of an evanescing age. I conclude by considering some ramifications of Tolkien's ancient underworlds for studying classical receptions in MF.

BILBO AND GOLLUM: "THE TUNNEL SEEMED TO HAVE NO END"

Bilbo's encounter with Gollum is katabatic, inviting us to consider how an underworldly quality is pervasive in *The Hobbit*'s design and extends into fundamental aspects of its characters. In the lead-up, Bilbo and the dwarves are escaping from the goblins: "Not for a long while did they stop, and by that time they must have been right down in the very mountain's heart" (62). Bilbo loses consciousness, and the story resumes in darkness.[25] He travels "down and down" along a tunnel that "seemed to have no end" (67). Tolkien prefaces this descent by describing the intrinsically katabatic quality of hobbits (66):

Hobbits are not quite like ordinary people; and after all if their holes are nice cheery places and properly aired, quite different from the tunnels of the goblins, still they are more used to tunnelling than we are, and they do not easily lose their sense of direction underground.

This suitability to life underground runs as deep as possible in a philological work like Tolkien's: he says (*LR* 1111) that the word 'hobbit,' "an invention" of his own, "might well be a worn-down form of *holbytla*, if that name had occurred in our own ancient language," i.e., in Old English: *Holbytla* is his translation into Old English of *kûd-dûkan*, used by the King of Rohan for "hole-dweller." Thus 'hobbit' already suggests a katabatic quality.[26]

---

[25] Darkness and loss of consciousness characterize other underworlds: e.g., in Homer's *Iliad* (*Il.*), Hades must not be exposed to the light (20.61–66); in *Od.*, the island where Odysseus encounters the dead is shrouded in darkness (11.15–19; cf. *DT*); the first circles in Dante's *Inferno* (*Inf.*) are dark, and the pilgrim repeatedly faints (4.151 and 5.141–142); and in Milton's *Paradise Lost* (*PL*), Hell is bathed in "flames" that produce "no light but rather darkness visible" (1.62–63). For darkness in Tolkien and Milton, see Sly (2000) on *LR*; for more general links, Duriez (1993).

[26] 'Holbytlan' is used by Théoden upon first meeting the Fellowship (*LR* 544): corrected to "hobbits," he remarks that their "tongue is strangely changed." Cf. Gillever, Marshall, and Weiner (2006: 142–152). The word 'hobbit' has been linked to 'rabbit'; see Shippey

This quality is linked to secret knowledge, "a fund of wisdom and wise sayings that men have mostly never heard or have forgotten long ago" (*Hobbit* 66). The centrality of this link in Tolkien's vision is evident in how hobbits and other creatures—including dwarves, goblins, and trolls—are well suited to underworlds.[27] When Bilbo first hears the dwarves' song, he "felt the love of beautiful things made by hands and by cunning and by magic moving through him, a fierce and a jealous love, the desire of the hearts of dwarves" (16). At that point, the dwarves, asked if they want light, insist that they "like the dark": "Dark for dark business!" "Dark business" means retrieving the dwarves' Arkenstone, but the song generalizes the point with reference to "the dwarves of yore" (14): "where no man delves / There lay they long, and many a song / Was sung unheard by men or elves" (15). Like the hobbits' suitability to spaces below, the dwarves' affinity for the dark underworld includes a link to secret knowledge. Here, then, is a clear example of a literal impression of depth in connection with "lost lore."

Such secret knowledge and desire for beautiful things, already ambivalent, is pushed farther into the negative by association with goblins. Goblins "can tunnel and mine as well as any but the most skilled dwarves" (*Hobbit* 59). The narrator denigrates them, saying that they can do so "when they take the trouble, though they are usually untidy and dirty." The crucial difference between dwarves and goblins here is that goblins "make no beautiful things, but they make many clever ones" (ibid.).[28] This distinction between 'beautiful' and 'clever' echoes the distinction, noted above, between wonderfully enchanting and dangerously magical. This is reflected in how the narrator describes the tunnels as constructed spaces. Ancient underworlds are frequently described on the model of architecture, but it is relatively rare for them to be described as built by human—or humanoid—hands.[29] By contrast, the underground places in *The Hobbit*

(2003: 67–70), *pace* Tolkien (*The Telegraph*, March 22, 1968). Cf. Lewis Carroll's Alice going "Down the Rabbit-Hole"—which "went straight on like a tunnel" before it "dipped suddenly down" (1)—and the "tunnels" linked to Gollum and Smaug, below.

[27] Trolls "must be underground before dawn, or they go back to the stuff of the mountains they are made of" (*Hobbit* 40); cf. *LR* 474 and the troll Alvíss in the *Poetic Edda*.

[28] Tolkien's narrator says further that "it is not unlikely that [goblins] invented some of the machines that have since troubled the world, especially the ingenious devices for killing large numbers of people."

[29] E.g., Homer refers to the 'gates' (*Od.* 14.156 = *Il.* 9.312) and the 'house of Hades' but does not describe them. In *Aen.*, the gates to Tartarus seem constructed (6.552–553) and the entrance to Elysium was built (by the Cyclopes, 6.630–632). Also constructed is Apollo's

(and in *The Lord of the Rings*) are emphatically 'cultural' spaces that have been built or shaped.[30] This emphasis on construction or materiality represents a departure from ancient underworlds, 'natural' or cosmological spaces intended for immaterial shades.[31] But still there is ethical judgement: it is in this physical space below that Bilbo discovers the most potent symbol of the danger caused by craft with earthly material: "a tiny ring of cold metal lying on the floor of the tunnel," the One Ring (*Hobbit* 65). This may be read in contrast to something like Aeneas' use of the golden bough (*Aen.* 6.201–211, 406–410, and 635–636): whereas Aeneas used the bough to access spaces reserved for bodiless shades, Bilbo discovers the golden ring in a physical space that is already below and uses it to dematerialize, becoming invisible and interacting with a less substantial world.[32] In an underworld lacking ghosts, it is the traveler himself who comes closest to fulfilling the ancient link between *katabasis* and encountering the dead. Bilbo is surrounded and infused by underworldliness: intrinsically suited to life in holes, he goes further, passing from view into an underground of darkness and invisibility and, by association, seeming at risk of embodying the oblivion that comes from passing time.[33]

---

temple inhabited by the katabatic Sibyl (6.14–33); see Putnam (1995: 73–99). Other places evoke underworlds: e.g., fiery Cacus' shadowy lair (*Aen.* 8.190–267), Carthage (book 4), and Troy (book 2); cf. Bruce (2012) for Gondolin echoing *Aen.*'s Troy. On the 'gates' and 'house of death' in classical and ancient Near Eastern sources, see West (1997: 156–162).

[30] For "archaeology" in Tolkien's "sense of history," see Sabo (2007), and cf. the *simbelmynë*—forget-me-nots—on the Rohirrim's funeral mounds in *LR*.

[31] The most haunting examples are when katabants attempt to embrace ghosts (*Od.* 11.206–208, *Aen.* 6.700–702). Aeneas' body causes Charon's skiff to swamp (6.413–414).

[32] Shippey (2000: 189–190) argues that the Ring's effect is not dematerialization, with Ringwraiths "defined by their shape (a twist, a coil, a ring) more than by their substance." Their "coiling" would link them to dragons; see below for Bilbo's and Gollum's similar changes. Cf. Shippey (2003: 148) for the coincidence (?) that the *Oxford English Dictionary*'s entry 'wraith' quotes from "Gavin Douglas . . . translator of Virgil's *Aeneid*," including (1b) "wraith or schaddo of Ene": "Tolkien worked on [the] 'w' entries in his youth." The Ring has been compared to Gyges' (Plato *Republic* [*Rep.*] 2.539c–360b); see *Encyclopedia*, s.v. 'Plato' (513–514), with De Armas (1994), Cox (1984), Morse (1980), and Nagy (2004: "superficial"); see also Flieger (1986). Cf. the Tarnhelm in Wagner's *Das Rheingold*, granting Alberich invisibility and metamorphosis into dragon and toad.

[33] Bilbo's brush with oblivion, beyond suggesting a psychological 'dematerialization' in parallel to Gollum's, could, like Frodo's experiences with the One Ring in *LR*, be compared to the oblivion that threatens to block homecoming in *Od.*: e.g., Odysseus' underworldly encounters in book 11 (he might have lingered if not spurred by Persephone), his men's consumption of the lethargic Lotus-flowers (book 9), his reluctance to leave Circe's island of Aiaia (book 10), and his risking shipwreck to hear the Sirens' song (book 12); for this idea I am grateful to Brett M. Rogers. For *Hobbit* and *Od.*, see n. 57.

Ancient underworldliness is heightened in Bilbo's encounter with the ghastly, not ghostly, Gollum. This first underworld in *The Hobbit* is deeper and more suffused with melancholy than even creatures like the goblins can withstand. Some of the underground spaces "go back in their beginnings to ages before the goblins, who only widened them and joined them up with passages, and the original owners are still there in odd corners, slinking and nosing about" (*Hobbit* 67–68).[34] Being a latecomer to the world below means having "a feeling that something unpleasant was lurking down there, down at the very roots of the mountain" (68): Gollum is thus even more chthonic than the goblins. But Gollum himself was not born to the world below but is only acclimated to it: he is, or was, a hobbit like Bilbo, and therefore more suited to life underground than human beings.[35] Living "deep down . . . by the dark water," he is "a small slimy creature . . . as dark as darkness," with eyes adapted to the darkness (ibid.) as well as "other senses that the darkness had sharpened" (81). Like all hobbits, Gollum is good at moving quietly, although his purposes are violent: "he took care [the goblins] never found him" so that he could "throttl[e] them from behind" (68). And he seems to have surpassed even ordinary hobbit sensitivity: when Bilbo, invisible thanks to the One Ring, "crept away from the wall more quietly than a mouse," Gollum heard him (81).

Gollum is thus emphatically chthonic. As a sort of guardian who blocks Bilbo's path, he resembles the watchdog Cerberus and Charon, ferryman of the dead. Like Cerberus in some ancient stories, Gollum is carnivorous and wishes to eat the katabant (*Hobbit* 70), as we are told he has eaten goblin (68).[36] Although he has an agency that Cerberus lacks, he is similar in blocking the way out. Gollum also "has a little boat," evoking Charon's skiff. Gollum lives on "a slimy island of rock in the middle of" a lake, partaking of his home's sliminess. To Bilbo, the nature of the

---

[34] Cf. Gandalf's statement that "far, far below the deepest delvings of the Dwarves, the world is gnawed by nameless things . . . [that] are older than [Sauron]" (*LR* 490).

[35] Gollum's backstory is not filled in until *LR*, but as noted above (n. 1), *Hobbit* was later revised to reflect it. See *Encyclopedia*, s.v. 'Hobbit, The' (278–279), and for the 1937 text, Tolkien (1988: 325–326); cf. Rateliff (2007: 153–197).

[36] In Hesiod, Cerberus welcomes visitors but eats escapees (*Theogony* [*Theog.*] 311 and 769–773); see Clark (1979: esp. 86–88) and Rohde (1950: 237, with n. 6). Gollum "liked meat too. Goblin he thought quite good, when he could get it" (*Hobbit* 68).

water is uncertain: "He did not know whether it was just a pool in the path, or the edge of an underground stream that crossed the passage, or the brink of a deep dark subterranean lake" (67). The water recalls other 'underground streams', bodies of water that defined the underworld in ancient myth. On the way down this can be the Acheron or the Styx, traversed by Charon in his skiff.[37] The Styx, sworn upon by the gods for unbreakable oaths, is also echoed in how "[t]he riddle-game" played by Bilbo and Gollum "was sacred and of immense antiquity, and even wicked creatures were afraid to cheat when they played it," since it is played "according to ancient laws" (75).[38]

Also recalled is the river Lethe, from which souls drink to forget their previous lives ahead of reincarnation to the world above.[39] This echoes the uncertainty surrounding the water: Bilbo's un-hobbitlike difficulty in finding his way is echoed in how Gollum has been changed, losing his memory. In response to Bilbo's second riddle, Gollum struggles to remember his past: he "brought up memories of ages and ages and ages before, when he lived with his grandmother in a hole by a river": "[h]e had been underground a long time, and was forgetting this sort of thing" (*Hobbit* 71). An effect of his long deprivation down below, Gollum's faded memory builds on how we are told that he played the riddle-game "with other funny creatures sitting in their holes in the long, long ago, before he lost all his friends and was driven away, alone, and crept down, down, into the dark under the mountains" (69). These descriptions are sharply pointed to forgetting and passing time. Not at all incidentally, then, the answer to Gollum's last, most difficult riddle is "time" (73–74).[40]

---

[37] E.g., Sappho 95.11–13, Aeschylus *Seven against Thebes* 856. Odysseus must cross the Ocean (*Od.* 10.508; 11.13–22 and 639); in Aristophanes' *Frogs* (*Ran.*), the water is a bottomless lake (137–138). Cf. the underground lake filled with corpses in J. K. Rowling's *Harry Potter and the Half-Blood Prince*; on Rowling see Rogers (this volume). For Charon, see *Lexicon Iconographicum Mythologiae Classicae* 3.1.210–216. On "crossing the water," see West (1997: 155–156).

[38] Bilbo cheats, posing a problem that is not a riddle; see nn. 45 and 57.

[39] For Lethe, see, e.g., *Aen.* 6.703–718, and cf. *Il.* 20.61–66, *Rep.* 621a, *Ran.* 186 ("plain of Lethe"; cf. Ecclesiastes 9:5), as well as West (1997: 160–161). Other lethargic comestibles in ancient literature include the Lotus-flowers (*Od.* 9.82–104) and the wine drugged by Helen (4.219–232); see Stevens (2014: 210–213).

[40] See Nelson (2008). Gollum's last riddle, based on the 'old age' riddle in *Solomon and Saturn II*, recalls *Beowulf*'s description of armor decaying with its dead wearers (2255–2260) and may evoke from Virgil's *Georgics* (*G.*) the image of long-buried armor (1.493–497).

Gollum thus embodies the "dark antiquity of sorrow" Tolkien builds into his reception of ancient underworlds. Forgetting his past and lacking knowledge of the future, he is an ambivalent figure, more sympathetic than a Charon or Cerberus but hardly willing to serve as guide. And yet he *is* a guide of sorts to Bilbo's future, embodying a path the younger hobbit might follow.[41] Gollum's dimly remembered prior life is similar to Bilbo's life in the Shire, and his descent is described in ways that echo the latter's *katabasis*. Gollum "crept down, down, into the dark" (*Hobbit* 69), and Bilbo has traveled "down and down.... It seemed like all the way to tomorrow and over it to the days beyond" (67).[42] This leads to sympathy: in a climactic passage, Gollum strikes Bilbo as "miserable, alone, lost. A sudden understanding, a pity mixed with horror, welled up in Bilbo's heart: a glimpse of endless, unmarked days without light or hope of betterment, hard stone, cold fish, sneaking and whispering" (81). At that point, Bilbo refrains from killing Gollum with his sword. We might think of Aeneas *not* refraining from killing his antagonist, Turnus (*Aen.* 12.919–952), or Achilles sparing Agamemnon thanks to Athena's intervention (*Il.* 1.188–222). Just as apposite would be a combination of Aeneas' pity for the dead with his thought to attack the bodiless beings just inside the underworld (*Aen.* 6.290–294).[43]

These comparisons emphasize that Bilbo, lacking a guide, has had to restrain himself. His pity proves consequential, for it is Gollum who will destroy the One Ring. Does Bilbo see, however dimly, that killing his double would doom himself?[44] It is tempting to call his feeling a sort of 'sympathy for the devil,' but the setting is less infernal than Limbo-like: Gollum's "endless unmarked days without light or hope" recall how Dante describes Limbo as brighter than the Inferno but blocked from heavenly light (*Inf.* 4.68–69 and 151) and its denizens as "living without

[41] Gollum will guide Frodo through underworlds; see Obertino (1993).

[42] Anderson annotates (Tolkien [1988: 81]) that "Tolkien's view of a mountain's roots is very dark" compared to MacDonald's in *The Princess and Curdie*; cf. *Encyclopedia*, s.v. 'Mountains' (441–442). For metals and jewels underground cf. Jules Verne's *Journey to the Center of the Earth* (e.g., chapter 18), with Stevens (2015a).

[43] Cf. Cervantes's *Quixote* "tilting at windmills" or Melville's Ahab pursuing the whale. Are all such monsters "dragons of destruction," symbolizing enchantment and forgetting?

[44] Later "[a] pang of fear and loss, like an echo of Gollum's misery, smote Bilbo" (83); cf. Obertino (1993: esp. 165–166). For Gollum as the hero of *LR*, see Nagy (2006) and Arthur (1991); cf. *Encyclopedia*, s.v. 'Heroes and Heroism' (269–271), Clark (2000) with Shippey (2003: 71 and 219), and *Letters* 163.

hope, in desire [of God]" (*sanza speme vivemo in disio*; 4.42). This situation elicits pity in the pilgrim and his guide. Is Bilbo's feeling for Gollum thus a Dantean pity, as if for a fellow 'sinner'? The pilgrim, Dante himself, is a poet; after the quest, Bilbo "took to writing poetry" (*Hobbit* 275).[45] And the object of pity, who describes his "living without hope, in desire"—echoed in Gollum's "endless, unmarked days without light or hope"—is none other than Virgil.[46]

BILBO AND SMAUG: "HE FOUGHT THE REAL BATTLE IN THE TUNNEL ALONE"

Bilbo's "glimpse" of Gollum's life is recalled in how Tolkien accounts for "[p]art of the attraction" of *The Lord of the Rings* as being "due to the *glimpses* of a large history in the background: an attraction like that of viewing far off an unvisited island, or seeing the towers of a distant city gleaming in a sunlit mist."[47] The glimpse is elaborated in the city's towers described as "gleaming," which echoes the sound and meaning of "glimpse." Tolkien continues by emphasizing the positive power of a glimpse by a negative contrast: "[t]o go there is to destroy the magic, unless new unattainable vistas are again revealed." The magic of a literary experience thus depends on partial views that come from distance.[48] Does this metaphorical accounting apply to literary journeys into ancient underworlds, and by extension to *katabaseis* themselves? As the katabant "goes there," does the magic get destroyed, or are "new unattainable vistas . . . again revealed"?

---

[45] In-world, *Hobbit* and *LR* are written by hobbits, who might be thought of as Muses as well as Homeric poets; Shippey (2003: 117). Compare the Muses' capacity to falsify (*Theog.* 27–28) with Bilbo's cheating Gollum and deceiving Smaug (herein, n. 57).

[46] Some denizens of Dante's Limbo were harrowed by Christ (i.e., taken to Paradise; *Inf.* 4.44–63), but of course Virgil will not be saved. Gollum likewise does not escape at this point. Frodo makes an inexact Christ-figure, as Shippey (2003: 204) observes, but *LR* has persuasively been interpreted as a Catholic epic: see *Letters* 142; *Encyclopedia*, s.v. 'Christian Readings of Tolkien,' 'Christianity,' and 'Catholicism, Roman' (99–101, 101–103, and 85–89); and Shippey (2003: 196–204): "The whole of Middle-earth, in a sense, is Limbo" (203). Cf. Bilbo's leap of faith "as if lifted by a new strength and resolve" (*Hobbit* 82).

[47] *Letters* 247, emphasis added.

[48] Cf. Grybauskas (2012). This positive literary 'magic' must be distinguished from dangerous 'magic' in Middle-earth.

These questions are important as Bilbo's second *katabasis*, into Smaug's hoard, is similar to the first in several ways. With an eye on how the dark post-hobbit is doubled in the "red-golden dragon," we will discover a sort of red herring: Smaug, the goal of the quest, is a secondary problem. To be sure, the dragon is "a vast danger" (*Hobbit* 197) and a meaningful symbol, and the encounter with him—the "Conversation with Smaug," as in Tolkien's own illustration (see Figure 5.1)—has a profound effect on Bilbo.[49]

But the descent's deepest meaning lies elsewhere: Bilbo "fought the real battle in the tunnel alone." With Bilbo already reflected in Gollum, and with Gollum doubled in Smaug, emphasis falls on the empty materiality of these tunnels or spaces below: lacking ghosts, and with monsters mirroring the hero, Tolkien's underworlds cause confusions of the past and passing time: they are inhabited by "dragons of destruction."

Like the encounter with Gollum "down at the very roots of the mountain" (*Hobbit* 68), Smaug's hoard is located in "the great bottommost cellar or dungeon-hall of the ancient dwarves right at the Mountain's root" (197). Bilbo's approach echoes that earlier descent as well as underworlds in Dante and Virgil (196):

The stars were coming out behind him in a pale sky barred with black when the hobbit crept through the enchanted door and stole into the Mountain. It was far easier going than he expected. This was no goblin entrance, or rough wood-elves' cave. It was a passage made by dwarves, at the height of their wealth and skill: straight as a ruler, smooth-floored and smooth-sided, going with a gentle never-varying slope direct—to some distant end in the blackness below. . . . Then the hobbit slipped on his ring, and warned by the echoes to take more than hobbit's care to make no sound, he crept noiselessly down, down, down into the dark.

"The stars . . . coming out behind" Bilbo, evidently at dusk, inverts Dante, whose pilgrim sees the stars of morning only after exiting the underworld (*Inf.* 34.139). Bilbo's journey into darkness is only

---

[49] As Bilbo is changed, Smaug, too, is affected: having first "shifted into other dreams of greed and violence," upon waking from "an uneasy dream" he notices "a breath of strange air in his cave," in parallel to Bilbo "gasping and taking pleasure in the feel of the fresh air again" (199); cf. Schlobin (2000). For Tolkien as "artist & illustrator," see Hammond and Scull (1995, with 136-139 on "Conversation with Smaug") and (2012).

Figure 5.1 J. R. R. Tolkien, "Conversation with Smaug" (1938). The Bodleian Libraries, The University of Oxford. MS. Tolkien Drawings 30.

beginning or begins repeatedly.[50] The next description highlights a similar difference: "It was far easier going than he expected" echoes a famous passage in Virgil, where the Sibyl tells Aeneas that "the way down into the underworld is easy." Ease of descent is overmatched by the difficulty of returning: "But to call your step back, and to fly out

[50] Does Bilbo see his quest as "a tour through darknesses" (Shippey [2003: 92])? *LR* enacts a cosmic "pattern ... in which stars and shadows are always at strife," recalling "Icarus or Prometheus" among other "familiar myths" (ibid. 112).

to the air above, this is the work, this is the labor." Only a few have succeeded (*Aen.* 6.126–131). Bilbo's own 'easy descent' thus makes us wonder whether he will, in some way, not return. Indeed, his descent is already different from Aeneas': whereas the Sibyl says "night and day the doorway of black Dis stands open," in *The Hobbit*, one daunting task was to open the hoard's enchanted door at all.[51]

These echoes and inversions of Dante and Virgil frame what follows. The descent is described in physical terms: the tunnel was "straight as a ruler, smooth-floored and smooth-sided, going with a gentle never-varying slope" (*Hobbit* 196). We noted above the significance of Tolkien's underworld spaces being built environments; that is sharpened here by contrasts among species: the tunnel and the hoard are dwarf spaces as opposed to goblin or wood-elf spaces. This tunnel is the "best" experienced by Bilbo, the space in which descent is easiest. And yet it is here, "in the tunnel alone," that Bilbo "fought the real battle," such that "[g]oing on from there was the bravest thing he ever did" (197). Tolkien's focus on the physical, including echoes of other ancient worlds, emphasizes that Bilbo's difficulties and implicit fears are *not* physical but psychological or even metaphysical.

Above all, Bilbo doubles Gollum. Gollum had "crept down, down, into the dark under the mountains" (*Hobbit* 69); and this resulted in what Bilbo perceived as a life of "endless unmarked days without light" (81). Bilbo has now "crept noiselessly down, down, down into the dark," on a path "to some distant end in the blackness" (196); his first movement, "through the enchanted door," is also "creeping." He is thus now following Gollum's path exactly, his second *katabasis* matching that earlier descent. Indeed, he has gone so far as to "sli[p] on the ring," learning from escaping Gollum but also as if in imitation of Gollum's goblin-hunting (76). He is further "warned by the echoes to take more than hobbit's care to make no sound": these literal echoes have figurative meanings as Bilbo becomes like Gollum, more than, or other than, merely hobbit. It is here that Tolkien says "[a]lready he was a very different hobbit from

---

[51] Cf. the contrast between Aeneas' golden bough and Bilbo's golden ring, discussed above. In *LR*, the entrance to Moria is similarly blocked by the Doors of Durin (294–300), while just outside a monster lives, like Gollum, in water: one of the "older and fouler things than Orcs" (301), as Gollum is older and fouler than the goblins that fear him. Obertino (1993) stresses Frodo's katabatic difficulties.

the one that had run out without a pocket handkerchief from Bag-End long ago" (196).

For Bilbo and Gollum to be so closely linked at this point, long after their encounter and on the doorstep of a different chthonic monster, suggests that such dark reflection is the true burden carried by *The Hobbit*'s *katabaseis*. This is emphasized in how Bilbo does *not* kill the dragon. No "sudden understanding" of Smaug is explicit, but perhaps it is not needed: this is not a dragon-slaying episode, and the traveler poses a different threat.[52] As he learns the role of thief, Bilbo becomes a kind of rival for Smaug's own theft of the hoard.[53] In reverse, Smaug represents a further version of the path walked by both hobbits: Smaug is a perfection of Gollum's habitual, and Bilbo's developing, creeping and stealing, occupying a farther point on a continuum of underworldliness, obliviation, deception, and greed.[54] This is deepened by additional similarities. Tolkien writes that the name 'Smaug' comes from the "Germanic verb *Smugan*, to squeeze through a hole."[55] This describes not only Smaug's motion but also Gollum's, who is originally named Sméagol.[56] But it also recalls how Bilbo is introduced as living "[i]n a hole" (*Hobbit* 3). Close by is a related Old English verb, *smeagan*, "to think out, reflect, scrutinize, look close into." Putting the meanings together, we might think

---

[52] *Pace* Stein (1968). For discussion of dragon-fighting heroes of 'Sigurd,' 'Thor,' and 'St. George' types, see Evans (2000: 28–29). Cf. Watkins (1995: 297–303) for the story-formula 'HERO SLAYS SERPENT'; for application to *Beowulf*, see Lionarons (1996). Is Smaug like the serpent guarding the golden fleece in Greek myth, and his slayer, Bard, like Jason? For Bilbo as 'trickster' see n. 57; I learned much from C. W. Sullivan III's expansion of his unpublished 2012 talk, "Tolkien and the Traditional Dragon Tale: An Examination of *The Hobbit*."

[53] Asked whether "the hobbit's stealing of the dragon's cup [is] based on the cup-stealing episode" at *Beowulf* 2211–2311, Tolkien responded that "*Beowulf* is among my most valued sources; though it was not consciously present" (*Letters* 25). The dragon that inspired Tolkien most is Fáfnir from *Völsunga Saga*; see Byock (2013). Fáfnir's hoard includes a magical ring, Andvaranaut, that makes gold and is cursed to "be the death of all who possess it" (18). On dragon-lore in Tolkien, see Evans (2000) and, more generally, Evans (1987) and Ogden (2013).

[54] After Shippey: "the strong sense of familiarity in [Smaug's] speech puts it back into the 'continuum of greed', makes it just dimly possible that dragon-motivations could . . . have some affinity with human ones" or hobbit ones (2003: 91). Cf. his 87: "maybe the dragon-curse is *itself* avarice" (italics original), followed by Evans (2000: 29).

[55] *Letters* 25. See Gilliver, Marshall, and Weiner (2006: 190–191).

[56] In 1954, Tolkien wrote that " 'Sméagol' was not . . . fully envisaged at first, but I believe his character was implicit" (*Letters* 156).

of 'insinuation': Smaug's and Sméagol's sinuous motions are matched by their cleverness, 'smuggling' ideas in.

This is borne out in their riddling: Gollum's is discussed above, while Tolkien says of Smaug both that "no dragon can resist the fascination of riddling talk" (*Hobbit* 205) and that his talk is therefore dangerous, with Bilbo "in grievous danger of coming under the dragon-spell" (206). The danger is compounded by Bilbo's ignorance: "Had he known more about dragons and their wily ways, he might have been more frightened" (203), and such heedlessness is "the effect that dragon-talk has on the inexperienced" (207)—enchantment verging on bewilderment. It is compounded further by his conscious dissimulations: pressed by Smaug for his identity, Bilbo replies in riddles, saying—truthfully but tellingly—that he comes "from under the hill" (204).[57] Finally, although Tolkien writes that Gollum "got his name" from "when he said *gollum* ... mak[ing] a horrible swallowing noise in his throat" (68–69), it may also recall Old Norse *gull* or *goll*, "gold, treasure, something precious."[58] It is as if Sméagol is materially like the One Ring he calls his "precious"; and of course "he always called *himself* 'my precious,'" too (69). "Precious, golden" Gollum thus anticipates and mirrors "red-golden" Smaug (198).[59]

In turn, Smaug represents an uncanny point on the continuum of greed, at once far from human form and yet uncomfortably suggestive of human vice. Gollum we have seen changed by desire for his precious gold. Other creatures are also taken in, especially the dwarves with their affinities for metals and jewels. And Bilbo is susceptible: in *The Lord of the Rings* he is poisoned by exposure to the Ring; but already in *The Hobbit* he shows signs of dragonish being. In connection with "golden"

---

[57] Bilbo echoes Sigurd responding to Fáfnir; cf. Shippey (2003: 86–93). Cf. Odysseus tricking Polyphemus (*Od.* 9.355–370). *Hobbit*'s Odysseanism would repay focused study; *Encyclopedia*, s.v. 'Homer' (285) is unhelpful. Peretti (2007) locates the roots of *LR*'s chapter "Mount Doom" (912–926) in the folktale motif of "the ogre blinded" (Aarne Thompson tale type 1137), of which Polyphemus is the earliest example; see Hansen (2002: 289–301). Cf. Niedbala (2006) on Odyssean and other qualities in Lewis's *The Silver Chair*.

[58] After Hieatt (1981).

[59] This recalls the "old superstition" that dragons are humans changed by avarice; Shippey (2003: 89). Although central to Tolkien's beloved *Völsunga Saga*, that superstition is not the origin of dragons in Middle-earth; see Evans (2000: esp. 28–29). But it is intriguing that the "father of dragons" in Tolkien, Glaurung, is "golden" (Tolkien [2001: 151]), while *Hobbit* mentions "Were-worms" (19), presumably humans who change into dragons. Cf. the transformation of Eustace in *DT*, discussed by Winkle (this volume).

Gollum and the metal armor of "red-golden" Smaug—"armoured above and below with iron scales and hard gems" (208)—we might think of Bilbo's *mithril* coat of "silver-steel." This item from the hoard causes him to "feel magnificent" but "expect" that he "look[s] rather absurd" (219). Although eventually he "kept his head more clear of the bewitchment of the hoard than the dwarves did" (219), his first response to the hoard is revealing (198):

> To say that Bilbo's breath was taken away is no description at all. There are no words left to express his staggerment.... Bilbo had heard tell and sing of dragon-hoards before, but the splendour, the lust, the glory of such treasure had never yet come home to him. His heart was filled and pierced with enchantment and with the desire of dwarves; and he gazed motionless, almost forgetting the frightful guardian, at the gold beyond price and count.

Thus the same character who will resist the hoard more than dwarves do at first cannot. It is telling that this happens at the goal of Bilbo's second *katabasis*, echoing the first. His "motionless gaze" here recalls his "glimpse of endless unmarked days" in the encounter with Gollum: at both moments, Bilbo's looking causes him to freeze, and his "heart" is the seat of an experience ("filled," "welled up").[60] The experience is so powerful that Bilbo "almost forget[s] the frightful guardian": such is the dragonish being's disordering of history that the present moment, too, is out of joint. Destruction of memory, "the dragon of destruction," is more dangerous than the real dragon.

Tolkien emphasizes this by stating outright that Bilbo's encounter with Smaug is not the most consequential moment of this *katabasis*. Prior to entering the hoard, Bilbo stopped in the tunnel. "Going on from there was the bravest thing he ever did. The tremendous things that happened afterwards were as nothing compared to it. He fought the real battle in the tunnel alone, before he ever saw the vast danger that lay in wait" (197). This is the climax of Bilbo's *katabasis*.[61] "The tremendous things that happened afterwards" must include not only encountering Smaug but also

---

[60] Cf. *Encyclopedia*, s.v. 'Gaze' (232–233), suggesting that "[d]ragons . . . have the power." This relates to their "watchful love of treasure," as Evans (2000: 31) notes, which for the philologist Tolkien recalls the etymology of 'dragon': **derk-*, 'to see'; cf. Evans (1987: 34–38).

[61] This downward journey is not identical to the encounter with Gollum—that was cold and dark, and this is hotter and growing brighter—but both are physical.

other events, like helping defend Esgaroth and brokering peace amongst
the victors. All of that is significant but less so than this moment, when
the traveler is already changed—into nothing so much as a reflection of
other travelers whose underworldly journeys have been more consequential and complete.

The greatest effect on Bilbo is therefore located not in any encounter with a chthonic monster but in the downward journey, the *katabasis*
itself. Like the "real battle," the true danger to Tolkien's katabant is to
be found in "the tunnel alone," where he is at risk not of encountering
a monster but of becoming one—or of being revealed as one.[62] In *The
Lord of the Rings*, Bilbo will seem even more like poisoned Gollum or
hoarding Smaug, and already he is "a very different hobbit" (*Hobbit* 196).
To be a different hobbit means being a different 'hole-dweller,' as if to
say a dweller in a different type of hole, perhaps of a sort disavowed at
the story's beginning. Bilbo's underworld journeys have taken him out
of his element—out of certain sorts of holes—and placed him, time and
again, in tunnels and at the roots of mountains. His journeys are thus
too underworldly: like many an ancient katabant, Bilbo has undertaken a
descent from which even he, a natural hole-dweller, cannot easily return.

"ALMOST YOU MAKE ME REGRET THAT I HAVE NOT SEEN THESE CAVES": TOWARDS A TOLKIENIAN THEORY OF UNDERWORLD JOURNEYS

Why does a traveler journey into the underworld? What does she lack,
or what has been lost, that may be found only there? Answers vary even
within a story and are filtered through the katabant's knowledge. In *The
Hobbit*, Bilbo is long unaware of the dwarves' purpose; he does not realize that the One Ring represents a "turning point"; he does not see how
his future is mirrored in Gollum and Smaug; he does not think seriously
of the dangers of interacting with the dragon; and more. This variation
is matched by other *katabaseis*, in which travelers seek to consult the
dead; seek their ancestors; seek to rescue someone untimely deceased;

---

[62] Cf. Lionarons (1996), identifying *Beowulf*'s variations on "the idea of the 'monstrous
double' . . . inherent in the dragon myth as a whole" (7).

must acquire a guardian creature or guarded person; hope to find the secret to immortality; embody immortality and harrow Hell; and more. As Tolkien knew, all of these reasons and others are found in a long tradition of underworld journeys. By drawing on, and departing from, that tradition, Tolkien—and perforce MF—engages in complex receptions of ancient material.[63]

I have focused on ancient underworlds in *The Hobbit* as a way of building on research on *The Lord of the Rings*.[64] Such research can be richly suggestive. In a footnote to his study of trees in Tolkien and Virgil, Kenneth J. Reckford suggests "that Virgil exercised a great indirect influence on Tolkien through the mediation of Tennyson," including the latter's *Idylls of the King* (1859–1885) and his poem on the nineteenth centenary of Virgil's death.[65] In Reckford's view, the *Idylls* must play a role in mediating a Virgilian vision of "the lonely, faithful, compassionate" king, with Tennyson's Arthur evoking Virgil's Aeneas and inspiring figures like Aragorn and Frodo. For Reckford, Frodo's "passing into the West as observed by Sam" recalls "the Passing of Arthur (and Bedivere's place in it)" in the *Idylls*, "which was itself probably influenced by the ending of *Aeneid* [book] II." Reckford concludes that "[w]ere it not for his upbeat ending, [Tennyson] would have come close to writing a Christian *Aeneid* in a minor key." We have already noted how Tolkien's stories have been considered Christian versions of classical epic.

We might go further, and return to questions about theory raised above, by considering how images from Tennyson's poem resonate with Tolkien. Especially resonant is Tennyson's description of Virgil as "majestic in thy sadness / at the doubtful doom of humankind; / Light among the vanish'd ages; / star that gildest yet this phantom shore; / Golden branch amid the shadows, / kings and realms that pass to rise no more" (23–28). These lines evoke Virgilian underworlds: the "Golden branch amid the shadows" recalls the golden bough in the dark forest (*latet arbore opaca; Aen.* 6.136) and its association with "shades," while the "phantom shore" evokes the banks of the rivers Styx and Lethe, thick with ghostly forms

---

[63] See, e.g., *Sir Orfeo*'s depiction of a sylvan faerie host (vv. 281–287). For *LR* and "the western narrative tradition," see Simonson (2008).

[64] The quotation beginning this section is from Legolas's response to Gimli's description of the Glittering Caves, or Aglarond (*LR* 535).

[65] Reckford (1972: 84 n. 17). On trees, cf. Flieger (2000).

(6.305–314 and 706–709). To these images from Virgil we could compare moments in Tolkien: when Bilbo finds the One Ring, its gold obscured by the tunnel's darkness; or when the entrance to Smaug's hoard is opened with a "gleam of light" and an "old thrush" gives "a sudden trill," as if in parallel to the doves that led Aeneas to the bough. These and other parallels only deepen our sense of classical receptions in Tolkien's ancient underworlds.

As we have seen, Tolkien anticipates this interpretive mode, emphasizing the value of "dark antiquities of sorrow" by quoting Virgil's description of Aeneas pitying the dead, who gather "in numbers like leaves falling in forests at the first frost of autumn" (*quam multa in silvis autumni frigore primo / lapsa cadunt folia; Aen.* 6.309–310).[66] That famous simile resounds in Tolkien. For example, at the end of *The Fellowship of the Ring*, Lórien seems "like a bright ship masted with enchanted trees, sailing on to forgotten shores, while [the members of the Fellowship] sat helpless upon the margin of the grey and leafless world" (367). Galadriel's parting song begins: "Ah! like gold fall the leaves in the wind, long years numberless as the wings of trees!" (*Ai! laurië lantar lassi súrinen, / yéni únótimë ve rámar aldaron!*; 368). Her earlier words to Samwise place additional emphasis on passing time: "catch a glimpse far off of Lórien, that you have seen only in our winter. For our spring and our summer are gone by, and they will never be seen on earth again save in memory" (366).[67] We note the characteristically Tolkienian interaction among "glimpse," "memory," and passing time: as the year grows darker, so does the past become more vividly a "dark antiquity of sorrow" and "melancholy."

Examples like these illustrate Tolkien's interest in how receptions of earlier material lead to new mythic creations. We have seen him exclaim: "Alas for the lost lore, the annals and the old poets that Virgil knew, and only used in the making of a new thing!" Tolkien deeply valued sources. "However," writes Tom Shippey, "he also meant everyone to realise that the 'new thing' was worth more than the 'lost lore.'"[68] The

---

[66] Cf. *Il.* 6.146–149, Apollonius of Rhodes *Argonautica* 4.216–217, *G.* 4.471–480, *Inf.* 3.112–116, and *PL.* 1.301–304.

[67] Galadriel's previous song includes: "O Lórien! The Winter comes, the bare and leafless Day; / The leaves are falling in the stream, the River flows away" (363); and Gimli asserts that "[m]emory is not what the heart desires" (369).

[68] Shippey (2003: 229). Cf. *Letters* 156, Curry (1998: 112–138), and the Introduction to this volume on Horace *Ars Poetica*.

value of the ancient is not simply its suggestion of antiquity, but how it allows new myths to achieve that impression of depth. Tolkien has found this by drawing on ancient authors; as it were, consulting them like ancestors. Thus an intriguing turn of phrase in a katabatic context, 'impression of depth' is also suggestive in connection with theory and so of other ways of looking into Tolkien's ancient underworlds. For example, Fredric Jameson writes of a "flatness or depthlessness" as being "perhaps the supreme formal feature of all postmodernisms."[69] The impression of depth could help account for a contrasting feature of fantasy: a feeling of belief in the fantasy world, as opposed to the cynicism that marks other modes. Paradoxically, fantasy's elevation of the imagined, fictional world over the real world would be what convinces, offering not a shallow displacement but a profounder shock of recognition.[70] Brian Attebery thus suggests that Tolkien, for all his self-conscious artistry, "is not a postmodernist."[71] Tolkien's stories do have elements that could be called postmodern, including maps that are printed ahead of the stories themselves, a literal "precession of simulacra" suggesting a Baudrillardian 'hyperreal.'[72]

But the material considered in this chapter suggests that, for Tolkien, such glimpses have meaning not in themselves but insofar as they are founded on a sense of the reality of ancient history. A mysterious golden ring or an unguessable hoard may bewilder, but bewilderment is a pale and superficial reflection of the deeper feeling—enchantment—that comes from the hint of historical provenance. It is because history, especially ancient history, is only partially known that a story like *The Hobbit* may be centered around forgetting: both the present fact of forgetting the past, and the certainty that oblivion will only deepen with passing time. The One Ring thus exerts a power because it symbolizes—enigmatically as a closed loop—its own making at a point so unrecoverably past as to be, for all practical purposes, outside of time.[73] Smaug's hoard symbolizes history so contested as to be desolated: the meanings of objects,

[69] Jameson (1984: 60).

[70] For 'displacement,' see Frye (1961); *pace* Todorov's 'hesitation' (1970: 29).

[71] Attebery (1992: 39). On Tolkien and postmodernism, see Flieger (2005) and (2002), Nagy (2005), and Curry (1998: 1–15).

[72] Baudrillard (1981). A famous example in Tolkien is the "cats of Queen Beruthiel," mentioned once (*LR* 303) and never explained. For *LR*'s "cartographic plot," see Shippey (2003: 94–134).

[73] Cf. how the Ring's destruction is linked to the fading of Lothlórien and the Elves.

and the memory of their bearers, are lost under material known merely as weight, "to an ounce" (*Hobbit* 199). In the context of such dragonish destruction, each item from the past—each object or word—matters in itself. As a result, Tolkien's fantasies are serious invitations to consider the (alternate) histories, the lost antiquities, evoked by those rare and precious relics.[74]

All of this helps us see more precisely how Tolkien's fictions, those foundational modern fantasies, are epic in an ancient mode. The avowed purpose of epic in antiquity was to preserve memory in the form of 'undying fame' (Greek *kleos aphthiton*): just a 'glimpse,' we might say, of what was, but a 'glorious' one.[75] Depending on a lost past, epic is ambivalent, pairing glory with melancholy.[76] Of course, this is the feeling Tolkien found in ancient poems and infused into his own writing. It takes a special place in worlds below: it takes the place formerly—classically—inhabited by the dead, with their capacities for memory and prophecy. *The Hobbit's katabaseis* cannot but reinforce the sense that, eventually, all memory will be lost to passing time.[77] And yet, as I hope to have shown, certain images persist: "down there, at the very roots" of Tolkien's influential version of modern fantasy, are truly ancient underworlds indeed.

[74] Cf. Shippey's comparison of Tolkien's work to "the horn . . . from the hoard of Scatha the Worm . . . a magic one, but only modestly so," showing "the limits of [Tolkien's] wishes and their non-correspondence with reality" (2003: 175)

[75] Greek *kleos* ('fame') and English 'glimpse' and 'glory' share a root: although *kleos* may emphasize auditory aspects (as in the related English 'loud'), while 'glimpse' is visual, these and other, related words share a basic meaning of 'standing out.' On ancient epic and modern (high) fantasy, see further Weiner (this volume).

[76] Cf. Reckford (1974: 86): "The point is not just moral, that bad creatures (or people) pollute the landscape. The sadness of time and change goes deeper"; and Brawley (2007). This is echoed in Galadriel's sympathy for the dwarves: "If our folk had been exiled long and far from Lothlórien, who of the Galadhrim . . . would pass nigh and would not wish to look upon their ancient home, though it had become an abode of dragons?" (*LR* 347).

[77] Cf. the contrast between Achilles' choice (a short, glorious life over a long, obscure one; *Il.* 9.410–416) and his dislike of the underworld (*Od.* 11.488–491); for the latter, see also Heubeck and Hoekstra (1989: 106 *ad* 11.488–503).

6

C. S. Lewis's *The Voyage of the "Dawn Treader"* and Apuleius' *Metamorphoses*

Jeffrey T. Winkle

In this chapter, I explore the observation that C. S. Lewis's 1952 novel *The Voyage of the "Dawn Treader"* (*DT*) is, more so than the other books in the Narnia series, "generally about the spiritual life."[1] The narrative arc of one of the principal non-Narnian characters—Eustace Scrubb—shows striking parallels with major narrative points and Platonic philosophical themes found in Apuleius' *Metamorphoses* (*Met.*), also known as *The Golden Ass*, written in the late second century CE.[2] Apuleius' narrator, Lucius, undergoes physical transformations from human to ass and back to human, and a spiritual transformation at the hands of the goddess Isis at the end of the novel. By reading Lucius' transformations alongside Eustace's similar metamorphoses, we may better understand the ancient narrative and philosophical traditions that give thematic and theological foundations to Lewis's novel, and even see Apuleius' *Metamorphoses* as a

---

[1] Harrisson (2010: n. 3). To eliminate any ambiguity between the (shortened) name of Lewis's novel and the (full) name of its titular ship, this chapter refers to the novel as '*DT*' and to the ship as '*Dawn Treader*.'

[2] I believe there are also strong parallels to Apuleius in Lucy's journey in *DT*, but space permits exploring only Eustace's arc, which I would argue is the most obviously Apuleian element in the novel.

direct inspiration for *DT*. Along the way, we will deepen our understanding of *DT*'s classical receptions via attention not only to Apuleius' novel but also to a number of other Platonic works whose allegories underpin Apuleian themes and, by extension, inform Lewis's novel as well.[3] Both Lucius and Eustace reveal themselves as 'Platonic sinners' whose inner darkness—displayed by lust and greed, respectively—is made manifest in outer, bestial transformations. Likewise, both characters require transcendent, divine intervention to return them to human form and—more important—to transform their souls.

For the reader's convenience, I offer short summaries of both novels. *DT* is the third published volume from Lewis's *Chronicles of Narnia* (1950–1956) and shows up as the fifth volume in the sequence of recent editions. The book centers around Prince Caspian's sea voyage on his ship, the *Dawn Treader*, in which he seeks to fulfill his coronation oath by finding out what happened to the seven lost lords of Narnia. The quest takes the crew—which includes Lucy and Edmund Pevensie as well as their disagreeable cousin Eustace—through many adventures on many strange islands culminating in their arrival in the "utter east," where lies the land of Aslan, a lion who has guided the Pevensie children in their previous adventures in Narnia.

The *Metamorphoses*, the one complete surviving Latin novel from antiquity, is a picaresque tale in 11 books that centers on a young man, Lucius, whose prurient interest in magic leads him unwittingly to turn himself into a donkey. In this form he has several comic and tragic misadventures until the final book where, in desperation, he prays for help from the goddess Isis. In response, the goddess changes him back into human form but also demands that he dedicate the remainder of his life to her cult. Since my discussion focuses on Platonic themes, we should note that Apuleius was a Middle Platonist—that is, he explicitly professes in his other writings to follow a version of the precepts expressed by the classical Athenian philosopher Plato (427–347 BCE).[4]

LEWIS AND APULEIUS

While it may be impossible to prove that Lewis deliberately patterned the transformations detailed below on elements in Apuleius' novel, there

---

[3] For Platonic elements in *Met.*, the best place to start is Schlam (1970).
[4] For Apuleius as a Middle Platonist, see Dillon (1977: 306–338).

can be no doubt regarding Lewis's comprehensive knowledge of both the *Metamorphoses* and Apuleius' other surviving Platonic writings. First of all we note that Lewis's 1956 novel *Till We Have Faces* (*TWHF*)—a work he himself described as his "best book"—is a reworking of the 'Cupid and Psyche' tale at the center of the *Metamorphoses*.[5] This myth clearly haunted Lewis from an early age.[6] Here, at age eighteen, he writes to a friend about some books he is having bound:

In a fit of extravagance I am getting two more done. One is an Apuleius: he as you know wrote the book in which the 'Cupid & Psyche' story occurs. I have found his complete works in the college library and their brooding magic no less than their occasional voluptuousness & ridiculous passages have made me feel that I must get a copy of my own.[7]

Elsewhere, Lewis grappled with daemonic and spiritual ideas expressed in the *Metamorphoses*, as well as in Apuleius' Middle Platonic tract *De Deo Socratis* (late second century CE).[8] All this I take to be solid ground for exploring narrative arcs and certain (middle Platonic) themes as specifically Apuleian where they crop up in Lewis's fiction.

While Lewis may not have had Apuleius' *Metamorphoses* at the forefront of his mind when crafting the respective transformation of Eustace in *DT* (though I think it likely), he clearly saw his own fictional writings not as emerging *ex nihilo* but rather as continuing a long chain of influences, firmly rooted in the themes, characters, plots, and patterns of ancient myths.[9] Thinking of such a chain, we might even view Apuleius'

---

[5] Kilby in Schakel (1977: 171).

[6] In the introduction to *TWHF*, Lewis writes of the book and himself: "This re-interpretation of an old story has lived in the author's mind, thickening and hardening with the years, ever since he was an undergraduate. That way, he could be said to have worked at it most of his life" (1). It is generally accepted that Lewis began work on what would become *TWHF* in 1922 but did not finish it until 1955; see Hooper (2004: iii.1668). On *TWHF* and Apuleius, see Schakel (1984); on its classical receptions, see Folch (this volume).

[7] From a letter to Arthur Greeves, dated May 13, 1917; see Hooper (2004: i.304–305).

[8] In a letter to his former student Alaistair Fowler, dated November 22, 1960, Lewis (1964: 40–44) considers various presentations of the goddess Venus in ancient literature, including a passage from *Met.* 9.2. Lewis explores Apuleius' use and interpretation of Platonic ideas regarding the various kinds of spirits and gods that inhabit the universe (as well as their respective places in it), particularly with an eye toward their influence on later medieval thought.

[9] In a letter written near the end of his life to one Francis Anderson, dated September 23, 1963, Lewis comments on questions regarding the possible influence of Tolkien on himself and vice versa: "The similarities between [Tolkien's] work and mine are due, I think . . . to

Metamorphoses as one of the first fantasy novels to emerge in the Western tradition, sharing as it does many aspects of the modern fantasy genre to which Lewis's *DT* belongs. On one hand, both the *Metamorphoses* and *DT* are rooted in the putative real world. On the other hand, each casts its characters out into a kind of alternate world (overlapping with and separate from the 'real' world), in which various kinds of fantastical creatures dwell and where the power of magic—to change, heal, and destroy—is present and palpable. Thus I suggest that Lewis's use of Apuleius, whether conscious or unconscious, is that of an author of fantasy going back to one of the genre's main sources. At the very least, I hope to show that an Apuleian interpretation of *DT* is a fruitful one, and one I imagine Lewis would certainly have approved.

A METAMORPHOSIS TO FIT THE CRIME

We begin with the character in *DT* most in need of transformation: Eustace Scrubb. We meet him on the first pages of the novel as the disagreeable cousin of Edmund and Lucy Pevensie, who are coming to stay at his house.[10] He is glad that his cousins are coming, not because he likes them (he does not), but rather because he likes "bossing and bullying" (4) and is looking forward to fresh targets. Even after Edmund, Lucy, and Eustace enter Narnia via a dreamlike encounter with the painting of a ship—actually the *Dawn Treader*—in Lucy's room in the Scrubb household, Eustace is a thorn in everyone's side with his constant complaining and know-it-all-ism, the risibility of which is underlined by his continuous inability to accept the reality of Narnia and to see things as they actually are.[11] As the *Dawn Treader* heads out into uncharted waters, Eustace quickly makes enemies of all on board: from Caspian he receives at best a kind of strained patience, while his clashes with the talking mouse Reepicheep culminate in physical hostilities.

---

common sources. We are both soaked in Norse mythology, Geo[rge] MacDonald's fairytales, Homer, Beowulf, and medieval romance"; see Hooper (2004: iii.1458).

[10] Note the novel's wonderful opening line: "There was a boy called Eustace Clarence Scrubb, and he almost deserved it" (3).

[11] A good deal of the early narrative is communicated through Eustace's peevish diary entries.

About a third of the way through the novel, the ship arrives at a seem-ingly deserted, mountainous island. As the crew comes ashore and begins the difficult work of repairing the ship and replenishing rations, Eustace decides to slip away. He quickly gets lost and finds himself in a remote valley where he stumbles upon the entrance to a cave. From a hiding place he espies an aged dragon that crawls out of the cave and dies while (apparently) trying to reach a pool in order to take a drink. A hard rain begins to fall and Eustace takes shelter in the dragon's cave, where he finds a great pile of treasure: "crowns ... coins, rings, bracelets, ingots, cups, plates, and gems" (87). He considers how much treasure he might be able to cart away and slips a bracelet on his arm (which only fits if worn above his elbow). He then falls asleep in the cave, later waking up only to discover that he has metamorphosed into a dragon and that the armlet is now stuck, painfully constricting his now much larger 'arm.'

There are many parallels between this metamorphosis of Eustace and that of Lucius in the *Metamorphoses*. Both protagonists are morally com-promised and change into beasts that serve as symbols for their particu-lar moral failings. But why does Lewis have Eustace change into a *dragon* specifically? Here we may see Lewis dipping back into ancient Greco-Roman source material and tapping into longstanding connections between the dragon/serpent and the pitfalls of avarice. In *The Discarded Image*, Lewis recognizes the ancient narrative foundations of later medi-eval legends (with which he was undoubtedly familiar) and comments on a dragon that appears in one of the short, moralizing tales of the first-century CE fabulist Phaedrus[12]:

But [Phaedrus'] dragon—a creature born under evil stars, *dis iratus natus,* and doomed to guard against others the treasure it cannot use itself—would seem to be the ancestor of all those dragons whom we think so Germanic when we meet them in Anglo-Saxon and Old Norse ... Beowulf's dragon and Wagner's dragon are unmistakably the dragon of Phaedrus.[13]

---

[12] Lewis (1964:147) cites this as Phaedrus 4.20. The Latin and facing English translation of this fable may be may be found as Phaedrus 4.21 in Perry (1965: 332–335).

[13] Lewis (1964: 147–148). The fable "The Fox and the Dragon" concerns a fox that stumbles upon a 'dragon' (*draco*) guarding his treasure hoard. The fox has no use for the treasure, and it becomes clear that neither does the dragon; the dragon is simply ill-starred and doomed by fate to act thusly. *Draco* in Latin means simply 'serpent,' and one ought not to imagine here, say, Tolkien's Smaug. Still, the *draco* in Latin literature often has sacred, uncanny associations and is commonly depicted as guarding treasure hordes. Lewis's

The greed here is not simply a desire for material gain but greed for its own sake. The wealth is hoarded because that is the fatal flaw and tragedy of this kind of creature. Eustace is certainly awash in solipsistic avarice. When he stumbles upon the dragon's hoard, he quickly calculates how he might use it toward selfish ends: "They don't have any tax here ... and you don't have to give treasure to the government. With some of this stuff I could have quite a decent time here—perhaps in Calormen.... I wonder how much I can carry?" (*DT* 87). Then, following his transformation, the narrator notes, Eustace "had turned into a dragon while he was asleep. Sleeping on a dragon's hoard with greedy, dragonish thoughts in his heart, he had become a dragon" (91).[14]

As the *Metamorphoses* begins, we meet the protagonist Lucius on his way into the heart of Thessaly. He is marked early on by a lusty nature and a deep desire to dabble in the dark magic for which north-central Greece was renowned in antiquity.[15] With tales of witchery swimming in his head, he quickly seduces Photis, the maid of a local witch named Pamphile, in order to use the girl as a way to gain access to the magic of her mistress (and satisfy his libido). Through Photis' machinations, Lucius eventually comes to spy upon Pamphile using a magic ointment (*unguedo*) to turn herself into a bird and fly away (3.21). Lucius desperately wishes to cast this spell upon himself, but when Photis (apparently) gives Lucius the wrong ointment; he smears it on his body and becomes not an owl but an ass.

As with Eustace becoming a dragon, Lucius' bestial form is fitting for his character and (possibly) for the narrative arc of the novel as a whole. Immediately reflective of Lucius' character are the long-held associations across many cultures of the ass with deviant sexuality, including excessive libido. Moritz has noted that a Sanskrit name for an ass, *gardabha*, probably means something like 'the lascivious beast.'[16] The priapic and lustful

---

connections are astute. See also Cicero *Philippics* 13.12, Propertius 4.8.3, Pliny *Natural History* 16.234, Valerius Flaccus 2.276, Tacitus *Annals* 11.11, and *Corpus Inscriptionum Latinarum* 6.143.

[14] Cf. Tolkien's similar use of the symbolism of the dragon in *The Hobbit*, with Evans (1987) and (2000) and Stevens (this volume).

[15] At *Met.* 2.1, Lucius describes Thessaly as *quo artis magicae nativa cantamina totius orbis consono ore celebrentur* ("the native land of those spells of the magic art which are unanimously praised throughout the entire world"). Translation here and throughout is from Hanson (1989).

[16] Moritz (1958: 16 n. 6).

nature of the ass was also a well-known theme in the classical world, and thus, as with Eustace, Lucius' aberrant longings are realized in a fitting form.[17] In addition, of special import to a Platonist like Apuleius would surely have been Plato's own associations of the ass with lower, baser workings of the soul. In a striking passage from Plato's fourth-century BCE dialogue *Phaedo* (*Phd.*), Socrates predicts that souls given over to sensual pursuits may be reincarnated as asses (81d–82a):

SOCRATES: And it is likely that those are not the souls of the good, but those of the base, which are compelled to flit about such places as a punishment for their former evil mode of life. And they flit about until through the desire of the corporeal which clings to them they are again imprisoned in a body. And they are likely to be imprisoned in natures which correspond to the practices of their former life.

CEBES: What natures do you mean, Socrates?

SOCRATES: I mean, for example, that those who have indulged in gluttony and violence and drunkenness, and have taken no pains to avoid them, are likely to pass into the bodies of asses and other beasts of that sort.

ΣΩ. καὶ οὔ τί γε τὰς τῶν ἀγαθῶν αὐτὰς εἶναι, ἀλλὰ τὰς τῶν φαύλων, αἳ περὶ τὰ τοιαῦτα ἀναγκάζονται πλανᾶσθαι δίκην τίνουσαι τῆς προτέρας τροφῆς κακῆς οὔσης. καὶ μέχρι γε τούτου πλανῶνται, ἕως ἂν τῇ τοῦ συνεπακολουθοῦντος, τοῦ σωματοειδοῦς, ἐπιθυμίᾳ πάλιν ἐνδεθῶσιν εἰς σῶμα· ἐνδοῦνται δέ, ὥσπερ εἰκός, εἰς τοιαῦτα ἤθη ὁποῖ᾽ ἄττ᾽ ἂν καὶ μεμελετηκυῖαι τύχωσιν ἐν τῷ βίῳ.

ΚΕ. τὰ ποῖα δὴ ταῦτα λέγεις, ὦ Σώκρατες;

ΣΩ. οἷον τοὺς μὲν γαστριμαργίας τε καὶ ὕβρεις καὶ φιλοποσίας μεμελετηκότας καὶ μὴ διηυλαβημένους εἰς τὰ τῶν ὄνων γένη καὶ τῶν τοιούτων θηρίων εἰκὸς ἐνδύεσθαι.[18]

Lucius' asinine form not only reflects his base nature but also marks him in Platonic terms as a kind of 'philosophical sinner,' attached particularly to the pleasures of food and sex. So, too, we may see Eustace's Phaedrean dragon form as underlining his own 'philosophical sin,' especially if we accept that Lewis here is drawing on an ancient Greco-Roman

---

[17] See van Mal-Maeder (1997: 108–109, and esp. n. 74) and Winkle (2013: 19).
[18] Greek text and English translation are from Fowler (1966), emphasis added.

source whose themes and morals merge with comparable Platonic allegory.

TABOOS AND UNCONTROLLED MAGIC

In both *DT* and the *Metamorphoses*, there are elements of taboo-breaking, of looking where one should not, of tempting powers that neither protagonist fully understands and that further underline their flawed characters. Lewis highlights Eustace's extreme ignorance and inability to recognize the magic in front of him as he lays eyes on the old dragon. As he watches the creature crawl out of the cave, the narrator informs us that Eustace "never said the word *Dragon* to himself. Nor would it have made things any better if he had. But perhaps if he had known something about dragons he would have been a little surprised at this dragon's behavior" (*DT* 84, Lewis's emphasis). When he soon thereafter takes refuge in the dragon's cave and greedily slips the bracelet on his arm, Eustace dabbles in a kind of magic beyond his knowledge and control. While Lewis never explicitly presents the armlet as the locus of the magic that transforms Eustace into a dragon—as, say, the ring of power effects invisibility in Tolkien's epic—the text does, I argue, push the reader in that direction.[19] The thing itself quickly comes to represent the dangers of such dabblings: the armlet painfully constricts Eustace's lizardly 'arm' as a constant reminder of his greed, poor choices, and sullied character. At the end of the episode, following Eustace's re-transformation, the crew strongly suspects that the armlet once belonged to the lost Lord Octesian and that the old, dead dragon that Eustace saw by the pool may have been Octesian himself, paying the final price for his own greed. Just before the crew sails from the island for good, the narrator mentions that, for Eustace (now changed back into human form), "the cure had begun" (112), which is immediately followed by Caspian tossing the armlet into the air where it catches on a rock face, far out of reach, a cautionary talisman for future adventurers.

[19] After Eustace slips on the arm ring, he falls asleep and wakes up in dragon form. There is no language explicitly asserting that the ring effects the transformation.

Anticipating Lewis, Apuleius draws a direct connection between, on one hand, the turpitude and ignorance of his protagonist and, on the other hand, the breaking of taboos and the practice of dark magic. Throughout the opening books, there is a strong correlation between the dangerous enchantments of Thessaly and illicit sex, from the lecherous witches Panthia and Meroë in a horrific tale told by one Aristomenes (*Met.* 1.3–19) to Lucius' entanglement with Photis in order to pry from her secrets about her mistress' magic. As Lewis does with Eustace, Apuleius paints Lucius as a too-gullible stranger in a strange land, surrounded by weird and uncanny things beyond his ken. As he enters Hypata, Lucius sees the world through a fevered, magical lens (2.1):

Nothing I looked at in that city seemed to me to be what it was; but I believed that absolutely everything had been transformed into another shape by some deadly mumbo-jumbo: the rocks I hit upon were petrified human beings, the birds I heard were feathered humans, the trees that surrounded the city wall were humans with leaves, and the liquid in the fountains had flowed from human bodies. Soon the statues and pictures would begin to walk, the walls to speak, the oxen and other animals of that sort to prophesy; and from the sky itself and the sun's orb there would suddenly come an oracle.

Nec fuit in illa civitate quod aspiciens id esse crederem quod esset, sed omnia prorsus ferali murmure in aliam effigiem translata, ut et lapides quos offenderem de homine duratos, et aves quas audirem indidem plumatas, et arbores quae pomerium ambirent similiter foliatas, et fontanos latices de corporibus humanis fluxos crederem; iam statuas et imagines incessuras, parietes locuturos, boves et id genus pecua dicturas praesagium, de ipso vero caelo et iubaris orbe subito venturum oraculum.

In such a place without boundaries, things can only go wrong for the naïve visitor. Indeed, magic is shown to be dangerous and chaotic even in experienced hands if each element of the spell is not precisely attended to: Photis substitutes goat hair in a love spell cast by her mistress Pamphile, which results in a bizarre animation of wineskins that 'attack' and then are 'killed' by a drunken Lucius after nightfall (2.32). It is no surprise, then, that when the inexperienced Lucius spies on Pamphile through the key-hole and tries to replicate her bird-transformation magic, he finds himself transformed into an ass. Like Eustace, Lucius thinks he understands the world in which he finds himself, but when he crosses the line from observation to physical participation, his gullible, greedy, lusty, and selfish interior is subsequently expressed externally.[20]

In terms of Platonic corollaries, the tales of Eustace and Lucius strikingly recall Plato's famous telling of "The Ring of Gyges" in the *Republic* (*Rep.*). In Plato's tale, Gyges, like Eustace, stumbles upon an underground cavern with mysterious things within (359d–e). The story goes that

he [Gyges] was a shepherd in the service of the ruler at that time of Lydia, and that after a great deluge of rain and an earthquake the ground opened and a chasm appeared in the place where he was pasturing; and they say that he saw and wondered and went down into the chasm; and the story goes that he beheld other marvels there and a hollow bronze horse with little doors, and that he peeped in and saw a corpse within, as it seemed, of more than mortal stature, and that there was nothing else but a gold ring on its hand, which he took off and went forth.

εἶναι μὲν γὰρ αὐτὸν ποιμένα θητεύοντα παρὰ τῷ τότε Λυδίας ἄρχοντι, ὄμβρου δὲ πολλοῦ γενομένου καὶ σεισμοῦ ῥαγῆναί τι τῆς γῆς καὶ γενέσθαι χάσμα κατὰ τὸν τόπον ᾗ ἔνεμεν. ἰδόντα δὲ καὶ θαυμάσαντα καταβῆναι καὶ ἰδεῖν ἄλλα τε δὴ ἃ μυθολογοῦσιν θαυμαστὰ καὶ ἵππον χαλκοῦν, κοῖλον, θυρίδας ἔχοντα, καθ᾽ ἃς ἐγκύψαντα ἰδεῖν ἐνόντα νεκρόν, ὡς φαίνεσθαι μείζω ἢ κατ᾽ ἄνθρωπον, τοῦτον δὲ ἄλλο μὲν οὐδέν, περὶ δὲ τῇ χειρὶ χρυσοῦν δακτύλιον ὄντα περιελόμενον ἐκβῆναι.[21]

Gyges discovers that he is invisible when he wears the ring and uses this newfound power to seduce the queen of Lydia, kill the king, and take the throne for himself. Socrates later argues that to abuse the power of the ring of Gyges is to be a slave to one's appetites, and that the truly rational man would not use the ring at all (612b).

The parallels with Eustace and the armlet are abundant: the dead man from whom Gyges takes the ring finds an echo in the lost, probably dead—and possibly dragonish—Lord Octesian, with both men serving as cautionary tales to the traveler. Eustace, a slave to his appetites, wears

---

[20] Many scholars have noted that the ass was commonly associated with the irrational, destructive force of the Hellenized Egyptian god Seth-Typhon, who, as a principle of disorder in the universe, acts as the antithesis of the goddess Isis, the very deity who saves Lucius in the final book and restores him to human form. As such, Lucius-as-ass anticipates the Isiac ending in a metaphorical sense. Lucius dabbles in an improper magic that can ultimately only be reversed by the true, pure magic of Isis. See Schlam (1992: 110–112).

[21] Greek text and English translation are from Shorey (1969).

the arm ring, and his subsequent dragon form makes his internal ugliness visible to all. Note, too, how the details surrounding Gyges' discovery of the ring resonate with a Platonic reading of Lucius-as-ass in Apuleuis' novel: Gyges finds the ring-bearing corpse inside the hollow of a bronze horse. Could the odd presence of the horse be Plato's way of expressing the bestial, corrupt nature of the unnamed man who succumbed to the power of the ring?[22]

At this point, the reader may wonder whether the works of Plato may be a better target than the *Metamorphoses* in the search for Lewis's classical source material for *DT*. I admit the possibility. However, given the rather skeletal nature of Plato's tales compared to Apuleius' fully fleshed out—and thoroughly Platonic—fable, and given Lewis's own published recognition of Apuleius' narrative as philosophical allegory, I still contend that any Platonism we may see in *DT* is best viewed through an Apuleian lens. When all the comparative details of character are considered, although Gyges is a good model for Eustace, Lucius is a better one.

RE-TRANSFORMATION AND SALVATION

After Eustace peers into his reflection in a pool of water and realizes that he is a dragon, his shock soon gives way to a kind of relief—he posits that in dragon form he himself "was a terror now and nothing in the world but a knight (and not all of those) would dare attack him" (*DT* 92). He also thrills at the discovery that he can fly. These feelings, however, soon are sublimated to Eustace's deep sorrow and regret for his past behavior (ibid.):

[Eustace] realized that he was a monster cut from the whole human race. An appalling loneliness came over him. He began to see that the others had not really been fiends at all. He began to wonder if he himself had been such a nice person as he had always supposed. He longed for their voices.

With this epiphany, Eustace breaks down in tears and flies off to seek his companions. The ship's crew is understandably wary of this strange

---

[22] See Ferrari (1985) for Platonic connections between equine imagery (black horse, ass) and debased, corrupt human behavior.

creature, but as Eustace weeps and attempts to communicate, they—and especially Lucy—take pity on the poor wounded creature. Eustace's companions soon guess that some enchantment is at work, and he thumps his tail and wails when someone asks, "You're not—not Eustace by any chance?" (82). Once identified, Eustace's character is transformed: he helps his companions by catching animals for food, lighting their fires, keeping them warm, and taking them for flights over and around the island. Still, Eustace despairs at his appearance and the seeming hopelessness of rejoining the expedition as a dragon.

Then one morning Eustace emerges from the woods reshaped into human form, although changed from his former self; Edmund is the first to see him but does not immediately recognize him. Eustace then relates to Edmund a dreamlike encounter in which the lion and savior-figure, Aslan, appears to him, bathed in moonlight, painfully tears off his scaly exterior layer by layer, washes him in water, and dresses him in new clothes.[23] Eustace is a new creature—not perfect, but certainly transformed, as the narrator assures us at the end of the episode (112):

It would be nice, and fairly nearly true, to say that "from that time forth Eustace was a different boy." To be strictly accurate, he began to be a different boy. He had relapses. There were still many days when he could be very tiresome. But most of those I shall not notice. The cure had begun.

Indeed, from this point on Eustace becomes a helpful, valued crew-member aboard the *Dawn Treader*, a change that carries over into his life back in England and also anticipates his heroism in later books in the Narnia series.[24]

There are many touch-points between Eustace's conversion and re-transformation that act as evidence that the *Metamorphoses* may have served as a kind of mythic and moral template for Lewis. Lucius, too, despite his horror at becoming an ass, soon discovers that being such has

---

[23] Edmund minimizes Eustace's previously bad behavior by mentioning his own failings detailed in *The Lion, the Witch and the Wardrobe*, saying to Eustace: "That's all right. . . . Between ourselves, you haven't been as bad as I was on my first trip to Narnia. *You were only an ass*, but I was a traitor" (*DT* 110, emphasis added).

[24] From the last page of the novel: ". . . everyone [back in England] soon started saying how Eustace had improved, and how 'You'd never know him for the same boy'" (*DT* 248). Eustace also appears in *The Silver Chair* (1953) and *The Last Battle* (1956).

its benefits: as an ass he can at times mingle unnoticed among human beings and is able to satisfy his deep curiosity by observing secret behaviors and eavesdropping on tale after salacious tale. However, by the time we reach the end of book 10, Lucius has reached a breaking point. There we find him in Corinth, still in asinine form and slated to perform in a perverse and histrionic public execution of a condemned girl by copulating with her before a voyeuristic crowd (*Met.* 10.23). Overwhelmed by anxiety and shame, Lucius snaps his tether and runs; in doing so, he at last breaks with his former, morally compromised self.

When he collapses on the nearby Cenchrean shore, he has hit rock bottom and is ready to meet the goddess. As book 11 opens, Lucius beholds the rising of the full moon and, overcome with a tangible sense of the numinous, he raises a prayer to the moon goddess who soon after reveals herself to Lucius in her true form—the goddess Isis. As with Eustace's first encounter with Aslan in a dream, so, too, does Isis appear to Lucius in a dreamlike vision (*Met.* 11.3). She lays claim to his loyalties and arranges for Lucius to eat some roses, the antidote to his bestial form, offered to him by a priest. Then, stripped of his asinine shape, he is presented naked before the dumbstruck crowd of Isis-worshippers. Like Eustace, Lucius, too, is whittled down to his core and then rebuilt, redressed in the garb of the cult.[25] From this point to the end of the novel, Lucius devotes himself wholly to the Isiac cult, abstaining from meat and taking a kind of vow of poverty. Still, as with Eustace, Lucius' conversion does not immediately effect a kind of perfection: in the last chapters, we find Lucius relapsing, frustrated and angry with the continual demands of the cult and the need for further mystical initiations (see below). But in the end we might say that, for Lucius as well, the "cure had begun." In the last lines of the novel, we see him back in society, advocating in the law courts, but hardly the same human being—both within and without—we met riding into Thessaly in the opening chapters.[26]

---

[25] In ancient (or at least late antique) Christian romances, it is a common narrative trope that a character's change of dress signals a change of spiritual identity: new clothes denote a new person; see Montiglio (2013: 222).

[26] The line of interpretation taken here assumes that we are to read Lucius' conversion and the behavior of the Isiac priests to be serious and genuine. This is quite controversial, with many scholars seeing Lucius in this final book as a dupe, taken advantage of by a duplicitous and avaricious cult. For this view, see Harrison (2000), Finkelpearl (2004), Montiglio (2013: Chapter 4), and especially Winkler (1985).

It is worth noting here that the rather Middle Platonic, syncretistic cosmology present at the end of the *Metamorphoses* dovetails nicely with—and may even provide an ancient foundation for—Michael Ward's provocative reading of *DT*, which links *DT*'s themes and narrative arc to medieval cosmological visions of the planet Sol.[27] In Ward's reading, Aslan is particularly marked by solar imagery, and the ultimate quest for the crew of the *Dawn Treader* is a spiritual one, as the crew make their way to the farthest east—that is, to the land of the sunrise that is synonymous with the land/heaven of Aslan himself. Here the crew experiences a kind of mystic "Solar Christophany," with Reepicheep even going over the falls into Aslan's heaven, never to return to Narnia.[28] Likewise, in Apuleius, the lunar Isis returns Lucius to his human form, but arguably her more important role is pointing him to a series of higher initiations after which he has an ineffable encounter with the solar Osiris in the last pages of the novel (*Met.* 11.30), suggesting that Lucius' story ends with an 'ultimate' experience of the highest level of deity.

Compare the experience of Eustace: his first encounter with Aslan is on the dragon's isle, in the moonlight—moonlight that seems to shine only on Aslan himself wherever he walks. Aslan restores Eustace to his human form, but this is not the end of Eustace's journey; this merely prepares him for a deeper, more metaphysical encounter with Aslan at the eastern edge of the world. Ward writes of Eustace's first encounter with Aslan: "[t]his emphasis on moonlight is appropriate for a Solar Christophany ... for moonlight is 'sunlight at second hand.'"[29] What Eustace first sees is only the reflected glory of Aslan, not the full solar epiphany he and the others encounter at the end of the story. In both novels, the lunar principle effects the physical re-metamorphosis and "begins

---

[27] In Middle Platonic works of the second century CE, including those of Apuleius himself, we see a move toward fusing Platonic ideas and cosmology with Greco-Roman and Egyptian cultic figures and ritual. For example, Plutarch (late first/early second centuries CE) connects Isis with the moon, identifying her as a kind of cosmic, Platonic intermediary reflective of and pointing to her consort Osiris, who is identified with the sun and the highest, most transcendent form of deity (*On Isis and Osiris* 372B–F). Many have seen here a direct influence on Apuleius' Platonic presentation of Isis and Osiris at the end of *Met.*; see Schlam (1992: 15–16).

[28] Ward (2008: 108–120).

[29] Ibid. (116).

the cure" but also directs the protagonist to a higher, more spiritual, more *solar* principle.

CONCLUSION

Given Lewis's own scholarly expertise as a medievalist, Ward and others have, for good reasons, looked primarily to medieval models for explaining influences and themes in Lewis's later fiction. Still, I hope that I have shown here that Lewis, who recognized the deep debt medieval myth owed to Greco-Roman antiquity, was reliant upon it and in particular upon Apuleius. At the very least, I take the above observations as an invitation to explore more deeply other Apuleian, Platonic, or more broadly classical connections to the Narnia fantasies. There is certainly more ground that could be covered with respect to parallels between Apuleius' *Metamorphoses* and Lewis's *The Voyage of the "Dawn Treader"* than the space of this chapter allows. But even our rather narrow scope here reveals a correspondence between the novels' respective protagonists that is too conspicuous to ignore: both Eustace and Lucius journey from greed and lust, through picaresque adventures, through dangerous and ignorant magical experimentation, through bestial metamorphosis, to divine intervention and re-transformation. In the end, we might say, you would hardly know them for the same boys.

7

A Time for Fantasy: Retelling Apuleius in C. S. Lewis's *Till We Have Faces*

Marcus Folch

DEFINING FANTASY: MEDIEVALISM, ALLEGORY, AND CHRONOTOPES

C. S. Lewis's wildly popular *Chronicles of Narnia* is now counted among the foundational works of modern fantasy (MF).[1] In it, the staples of the genre crystallize in a manner that reappears throughout the twentieth and twenty-first centuries: a journey of unlikely heroes from a 'primary' or natural to a 'secondary' or supernatural world; a disbelief in the secondary world, which is thematized in the text; a rejection of technologically advanced society; a nostalgia for a pre-modern, presumably simpler time; and a sharp boundary between good and evil.[2] Lewis's fantastic worlds also participate in a 'false medievalism,' Lewis's term for a Romantic notion of chivalric Europe, in which "the real interests of the Middle Ages—Christian mysticism, Aristotelian philosophy, and Courtly

---

[1] I wish to express special thanks to the editors of this volume, whose support, comments, and criticisms have improved this essay immeasurably.

[2] On 'primary' and 'secondary' worlds, see Tolkien (1966: 73).

Love—mean nothing," but which nevertheless serves as the genre's distinctive spatiotemporal coordinates.[3] Compare Philip Pullman's *His Dark Materials*, J. K. Rowling's *Harry Potter*, and George R. R. Martin's *A Song of Ice and Fire*: all favor a false medievalism as the normative ecology for fantastic literature. This is not to suggest that fantasy has always and only looked to the medieval and overlooked the classical; as a number of contributors to the present volume show, classical structures often subtend fantasy's medievalizing edifice. But it does raise the question of why the main currents of Anglo-American fantasy have flowed far and wide of the classical tradition. Are there qualities within (popular conceptions of) Greco-Roman literature and history that render both inadmissible for the kinds of generic ambitions that define fantasy? Are such qualities intrinsic to ancient narrative structures and literary forms? What, in short, has the classical contributed to fantasy, one of the most widely read genres in the English-speaking world?

One way to address such questions is to consider Lewis's final novel, *Till We Have Faces: A Myth Retold* (*TWHF*). Set in a fictional and remote Hellenizing kingdom in the Caucasus named 'Glome,' *TWHF* presents itself as a *correctio* to Apuleius' *Metamorphoses* (*Met.*), also known as *The Golden Ass*.[4] As the epilogue to the American edition reveals, Lewis believed Apuleius got the story at the center of the *Metamorphoses*, the tale of Cupid and Psyche, wrong; he characterizes Apuleius as the 'transmitter' of the myth, and the *Metamorphoses* as a "strange compound of picaresque novel, horror comic, mystagogue's tract, pornography, and stylistic experiment" (313).[5] *TWHF* is Lewis's final effort—there were two others—to represent the story "the way the thing must have been" (313).[6] The result is a recounting of Apuleius' myth from the perspective of Psyche's older sister, Orual.[7] In what Lewis regarded as the most important departure from *Metamorphoses*—in which Psyche's sisters

---

[3] On 'false medievalism,' see Lewis (1969: 219, 223).

[4] Lewis describes Glome in a letter, quoted in Schakel (2010: 283), as "a little barbarous state on the borders of the Hellenistic world with Greek culture just beginning to affect it."

[5] Unless otherwise indicated, all references to and quotations of Lewis are from the 1956 American edition of *TWHF*. For the differences between Lewis's and Apuleius' versions of the myth, see Kranz (1969), Schakel (1984: 61–68), and Myer (2004: 145–153).

[6] On Lewis's varied attempts to versify and dramatize the myth of Cupid and Psyche, see Hooper (1996: 246–247) and Schakel (2010: 281–283).

[7] *TWHF* contains no fewer than three retellings of the myth of Cupid and Psyche; see Donaldson (1991: 159–161).

see Cupid's palace before convincing her to gaze upon the god's forbidden body—in *TWHF*, the palace becomes definitively visible only after Psyche has betrayed her oath; prior to that point, its appearance has been fleeting, leaving Orual uncertain whether she has glimpsed God's house. The change, Lewis suggests, "brings with it a more ambivalent motive and a different character for [the] heroine and finally modifies the whole quality of the tale" (313). Orual's psychology is also significantly revised. Instead of envy (the sisters' motive in Apuleius), Orual's fierce love of Psyche and rational skepticism regarding the existence of anthropomorphic divinities lead her to persuade Psyche to expose the god—who is not (*pace* the hasty syncretism of publishers and commentators alike) Cupid, but a primal deity worshipped among the people of Glome as the nameless god of the Grey Mountain and, more ominously, the Shadow Brute, son of Ungit, a chthonic fertility goddess who demands human sacrifice. In Lewis's version, the jealous sisters do not die; Orual becomes the queen of her city. Aged, bitter, and on her deathbed, she records her accusations against the god who raptured her younger sister; *TWHF* is her exculpatory autobiography and unfinished indictment.[8] Her charges center on questions of epistemology and culpability—both Orual's and the gods': whether Orual is justified in having doubted the existence of the divine and having persuaded her sister to betray her lover; whether the gods, if they exist, are not hideous creatures who have mistreated Orual and Psyche by masking their identities and yet demanding worship; and whether Orual's efforts to protect her sister are not justified by her love.[9]

Released in 1956, *TWHF* was met with mixed reviews. One critic panned it as "pallid," another as "bothersome," a third—a Latin teacher—gave it a 'D' for "difficult and/or dull."[10] Outside Christian circles, in which Lewis has attained near-hagiographic status, *TWHF* has received little scholarly attention; it remains his least popular—and most unconventional—work.[11]

---

[8] Schakel (2010: 283) observes that the decision to cast Orual as an unreliable first-person narrator marks a departure from Lewis's customary usage; his earlier novels are told from the perspective of an invariably reliable and customarily male third person.

[9] For discussion of epistemology in *TWHF*, see Hoyler (1991).

[10] Tucker (1957: 94), de Mott (1957: 141), and Beall (1960: 10). On the reception of *TWHF*, see also Schakel (2010: 281, 290–291 n. 1).

[11] For book-length studies, see Schakel (1984) and Myers (2004). Donaldson's (1988) reading of *TWHF* in light of Ricoeur's theory of metaphor, though in many respects

Classicists have all but ignored it.[12] Yet, Lewis—who tried and failed to secure a lectureship in Classics at University College, Reading—regarded *TWHF* as his best book, an opinion shared by numerous modern commentators.[13] For those interested in classical reception, it presents a fascinating retelling of Apuleius' myth set at the crossroads of Greco-Roman antiquity and medievalizing fantasy.[14] On one hand, *TWHF* signals a formal and thematic membership in the genre of fantasy. The narrative occurs within a pre-technological past, and Orual—a woman, a virgin, and an ugly one at that—is the unlikeliest of unlikely heroes. Throughout her childhood and ascendancy as queen—events that, occurring after Psyche's banishment, represent Lewis's most extensive augmentation of Apuleius' myth—Orual shuttles between the primary, natural world and a secondary, supernatural realm in which gods interact and mate with humans. On the other hand, there is much that seems un-fantastic or anti-fantasy. Glome is unvarnished, brutish, and violent, its culture and people hardly idyllic. Evil and good inhere within the same persons and gods; no clear distinction is drawn between the two. Most strikingly, much of *TWHF* eschews the medievalizing spatiotemporal frame or, to use terminology from the literary theorist Mikhail Bakhtin, the 'chronotope' that characterizes Anglophone fantasy. As a result, it provides an exemplary context in which to examine the status of the classical in MF from one of the doyens of the genre.

This, of course, raises the well-nigh unanswerable question, What is fantasy? Instead of positing a universal definition of MF or identifying a single, essential feature that recurs in instantiations of the genre, I wish to invoke the notion of 'family resemblance,' a concept developed by the philosopher Ludwig Wittgenstein to account for internally heterogeneous but notionally interrelated phenomena such as games.[15] Games, Wittgenstein argues, are almost impossible to classify under a single definition. While any one class of games (e.g., board games) may resemble

---

unconvincing, is especially salubrious in its refusal to engage in the authorial idolatry that vitiates much secondary literature on Lewis. For helpful, if summary, analysis, see Hooper (1996: 243–263) and Adey (1998: 152–164). On the unconventional qualities of *TWHF*, see Manlove (1991: 272–276).

[12] A single footnote in Edwards (1992: 77 n. 1) is, to my knowledge, the only exception.
[13] For Lewis's early and abortive career as a classicist, see Montgomery (2000: 52–53).
[14] On *TWHF* as 'Romance,' see Haigh (1991: 194).
[15] See Wittgenstein (1958: §65–71).

each other on numerous levels, such correspondences may be shared only partially by games of a second class (e.g., card games); other classes of games (e.g., Olympic Games, the Roman *ludi*) will betray little resemblance to the first; while particular games drawn from separate classes may hardly resemble one another at all (e.g., solitaire and *venationes*). Fantasy is one such phenomenon: it may embrace such disparate and unrelated media as classical Athenian comedy and the twenty-first-century British novel, and it may be found in innumerable cultures around the world. When we analyze fantasy in all of its intricate variegation, we discover not an essence of the fantastic but in Wittgenstein's words, "a complicated network of similarities overlapping and crisscrossing: sometimes overall similarities, sometimes similarities of detail."[16]

If we treat fantasy as a Wittgensteinian family, individual members of the family may share certain features that appear in some but not all other members. This has the benefit of enabling analysis of features that appear especially salient or definitive within one class, while not glossing over the diversity and nuance that characterize the family as a whole. We may, for instance, follow the editors of this volume in emphasizing that MF, particularly in its Anglo-American manifestations, has often centered on and developed the capacity of storytelling to portray phenomena and events that exist impossibly and defy the metaphysical laws of the world as we know it. We may, furthermore, recognize that the recurrent fascination in MF with metaphysical alterity reveals something important about the culture(s) in which Anglo-American fantasy has evolved and remains current.[17] For the purposes of this essay, I focus on two resemblances that characterize Anglo-American fantasy, which are also overriding concerns in *TWHF*: the spatiotemporal setting that fantasy has often assumed in the twentieth and twenty-first centuries (namely 'false medievalism'), and the range of possible interpretive responses to phenomena that exist impossibly.

This essay develops two interlocking arguments. First, it contends that *TWHF* offers a reflexive commentary on the genre of fantasy, one that shows up the limitations of medievalism as a stylistic reservoir for

---

[16] Ibid. (§66).

[17] I have in mind a recent analysis suggesting that the Western fascination with fantasy—absent, for instance, from the world's largest film industry (India's)—represents an elaborate expression of Weberian disenchantment with capital; see Folch (2013).

fantastic literature. Not only does the text depart from MF by retelling an ancient myth anchored in ancient time, but the narration of Orual's life is also laden with classical structures and motifs. For example, the novel ends in tragic style: an oneiric vision in which Orual journeys to the underworld (*katabasis*). There she conducts an ecphrastic interpretation of her life, which she sees etched, in Virgilian fashion, on a temple frieze (cf. *Aeneid* 1.453-493). In what Aristotle would call an *anagnorisis*, she recognizes the role she has played in her own life; acknowledges that her love has been her 'tragic flaw' (*hamartia*); accepts the god's innocence and her guilt; and, in a sudden change of fortune (*peripeteia*), is ultimately forgiven and joins Psyche as one of the god's consorts. Time and space evolve in the course of Orual's autobiography, and the narrative moves in and out of a classical chronotope: Glome begins as a nascent, Hellenized city; it transforms over Orual's life into a medieval kingdom with her as its warrior queen; and in the end it returns to a classical chronotope. If one takes seriously Bakhtin's claim that "the chronotope in literature has an intrinsic generic significance"—that time and space define genre and generic distinctions—the interplay of chronotopes in *TWHF* may be read as an exploration of the spatiotemporal parameters of the genre to which the text claims affiliation—an exploration that ultimately problematizes the elevated position that medievalism enjoys in MF.[18]

Second, this essay argues that *TWHF* thematizes a specific hermeneutical activity: the reading of fantasy—in particular, of allegorical fantasy. This claim requires more theoretical discussion. On one hand, allegory is a deeply classical and medieval mode of literary exposition; and Lewis retains the allegorical qualities of the myth in Apuleius—so much so that orthodox interpreters often read Lewis's retelling of the *Metamorphoses* allegorically as a Christian parable of the soul's migration through rational atheism, revelation, repentance, forgiveness, and integration within the church.[19] On the other hand, many commentators believe that

---

[18] Bakhtin (1981: 84–85). For discussions of the applicability of Bakhtin to Greco-Roman literature, see the treatments by Branham and Nightingale in Branham (2002).

[19] On the origins of allegory in classical Greek literature, see, most recently, Struck (2004: 21–76).

For *TWHF* as Christian allegory, see Starr (1968), Schakel (1984: 6, *passim*; 2010: 286–87, 289–90), Hoyler (1991), Manlove (1991: 273), Adey (1998: 159), and Myers (2004: 45, 175–182). Pérez-Diez (2001: 329) adds a wrinkle to this doctrinal unanimity by insisting that *TWHF* may also be read as a retelling of the parable of the Prodigal Son and of Lewis's own conversion to Christianity.

allegory is antithetical to fantasy; Todorov, for instance, defines fantasy as the genre that resists allegorical interpretation.[20] Fantasy's distinguishing literary motif, its master signifier, Todorov insists, is triggered by the compresence of events that defy natural explanation:

In a world which is indeed our world, the one we know, a world without devils, sylphides, or vampires, there occurs an event which cannot be explained by the laws of this same familiar world. The person who experiences the event must opt for one of two possible solutions: either he is a victim of an illusion of the senses, of a product of the imagination—and the laws of the world then remain what they are; or else the event has indeed taken place, it is an integral part of reality—but then this reality is controlled by laws unknown to us.[21]

For Todorov, the sense of hesitation between natural and supernatural explanations defines fantasy. It obtains on two levels: such hesitation is experienced by characters in the narrative who are confronted by an interruption in the natural order of things; and it is made available to, even foisted upon, the reader. In fantasy, we are invited to share the characters' interpretive *aporia* ('state of doubt'). Both character and reader thus participate in the same hermeneutical activity—the reading of a narrative in which events are inexplicable according to laws of nature. In this respect, Todorov argues, reader experience is emplotted within fantastic narratives.

In contrast, in Todorov's view, allegory undermines fantasy's master trope; for where the *explanandum* may be dismissed as merely allegorical, there can be no hesitation between natural and supernatural explanation.[22] Once allegorical explanation is adduced to rationalize the story as a fanciful redescription of an otherwise natural historical event (e.g., that a woman was blown off a cliff), it ceases to be fantastic, 'marvelous,' or even 'uncanny.'[23] Such narratives are, instead, prosaic and unremarkable.

[20] Todorov (1973: 33).

[21] Ibid. (25).

[22] Ibid. (32): "There exist narratives which contain supernatural elements without the reader's ever questioning their nature, for he realizes that he is not to take them literally. If animals speak in a fable, doubt does not trouble the reader's mind: he knows that the words of the text are to be taken in another sense, which we call *allegorical*."

[23] Ibid. (25) classifies as 'uncanny' narratives in which the *explanandum* is ultimately shown to conform to natural laws, and 'marvelous' those that suspend those natural indefinitely. For allegorical readings as sophistry, see Plato *Phaedrus* 229b–230a.

Ostensibly unnatural events are shown upon allegorical interpretation to be signifiers—and therefore affirmations—of another law within the natural, primary world. Because mysterious *explananda* may be dismissed, not as aberrations from, but as symbols of the laws of the primary world, 'our world,' allegory dispels both the hesitation between natural and supernatural explanation and the moment of ambiguity that arises when the secondary world appears to rupture into the primary. Readers of allegory know, moreover, not to take ostensibly supernatural events literally; our perspective is therefore radically unlike that of the characters within a fantasy. This should not imply that allegory cannot employ fantastic motifs, but that fantasy itself loses its distinctive markers—the wavering between natural and supernatural explanation and the emplotting of the reader's experience of fantasy within fantastic narratives—when introduced into, and subsumed by, allegorical genres.

To be clear, Todorov's formulation of the fantastic cannot be applied *tout court* to all specimens of the genre, and, as this study argues, his insistence that fantasy is incommensurable with allegory is in need of revision.[24] Yet Todorov throws into relief a key narrative structure in *TWHF*; until the god appears to Orual unambiguously (approximately halfway through the novel), she oscillates between rational and supernatural accounts of the inexplicable phenomena troubling her world; she and, with her, the reader are made to waver between competing explanations of the natural world. The reader shares in Orual's interpretive uncertainty, and, in Todorov's terms, the genre of the text is 'fantastic' in the strictest sense. Yet, even once the gods have demonstrated their presence incontrovertibly, hesitation between explanations is not dispelled. Although the appearance of the god in *TWHF* renders naturalistic rationalization untenable, interpretive uncertainty continues to be emplotted within the text, but now, this essay argues, the kind of uncertainty thematized is allegorical. Through Orual's effort to make sense of herself, the god who steals her sister, and the curse he lays upon her, both she and the reader participate in the same hermeneutical activity: the reading of Orual's life as an allegory of Psyche's trials. In this respect, Lewis has refashioned Apuleian myth to make (Orual's and the reader's) hesitation between naturalistic and allegorical explanation its axial problem.

---

[24] To be fair, Todorov (1973: 166) acknowledges the limitations of his theory.

THE SETTING: ERÔS AND THE MAIDEN'S GAZE

I am old now and have not much to fear from the anger of the gods. I have no husband nor child, nor hardly a friend, through whom they can hurt me. My body, this lean carrion that still has to be washed and fed and have clothes hung about it daily with so many changes, they may kill as soon as they please. The succession is provided for. My crown passes to my nephew.

Being, for all these reasons, free from fear, I will write in this book what no one who has happiness would dare to write.[25]

So begins Lewis's retelling of the myth of Cupid and Psyche, and, just like the original, *TWHF* foregrounds questions of interpretation.[26] Orual's opening lines take classical antiquity as a coherent system of knowledge and mode of reading. The discourse of a happiness determined only upon death harkens to the dialogue on *eudaimonia* between Solon and Croesus (Herodotus 1.30–32), as though Orual recognizes herself as a Herodotean negative *exemplum*, whose lifelong misery inures her to divine punishment. Orual writes in Greek (3); indeed, the second sentence is not quite English; the awkward conjunctions ('no ... nor ... nor') recall the syntactic structure of Attic negation (*ouk ... oute ... oute*). Orual accuses the gods "as if [she] were making [her] complaint of him before a judge," hoping that a visitor from the 'Greeklands' will convey her narrative to Greece, wherein "there is great freedom of speech even about the gods themselves" (3–4). With the gesture toward dicastic rhetoric and 'freedom of speech' (*parrhê-sia*), classical motifs thicken, and the text's averred genre emerges: a composite of philosophical historiography, forensic oratory, autobiographical epistolary, and adventure novel—not unlike Apuleius' *Metamorphoses*—which assumes a specific readership: Greek, classically learned, free of speech and mind, and fearless before the sacred.

---

[25] Lewis (1956: 3).

[26] The story that spans *Met.* 4–6 figures as a *mise en abyme*, a microcosm of the work as a whole offering an embedded heuristic to decipher Lucius' exploits as a man cursed with overweening *curiositas* and *simplicitas*, an ass abused but given privileged access into the baser aspects of everyday Roman life, and a neophyte initiated into the cult of Isis; see Kennedy (1990: 12–17). In Lewis, by contrast, the myth is presented as self-contained, lacking a larger narrative setting in which to be contextualized.

Against the narrator's Hellenism stands Glome, a city of hard syllables and inelegant names.[27] We are told "Glome stands on the left hand of the river Shennit to a traveller who is from the south-east, not more than a day's journey above Ringal" (*TWHF* 4). The effect is to focalize geography through the gaze of a visitor from Greece (i.e., the south-east). But Hellenized focalization gives way to the perspective of a native, with geography redescribed in distances traveled by peasants: "The city is built about as far back from the river as a woman can walk in the third of an hour, for the Shennit overflows her banks in the spring. In summer there was then dry mud on each side of it, and reeds, and plenty of waterfowl" (4).[28] The same description would suit the Nile or Mesopotamian flood valleys prior to the invention of diversion dams, irrigation canals, and large-scale dredging. Glome's civilization yields to nature, lacking the instruments to master its rhythms and forces. The city is thus grounded in distinct temporal coordinates, a primeval time against which the classical appears modern and scientifically advanced.[29] The city's primitive geography and technological impotence before the natural world are, moreover, coeval with its primordial religion (4):

About as far beyond the ford of the Shennit as our city is on this side of it you come to the house of Ungit. And beyond the house of Ungit (going all the time east and north) you come quickly to the foothills of the Grey Mountain. The god of the Grey Mountain, who hates me, is the son of Ungit. He does not, however, live in the house of Ungit, but Ungit sits there alone. In the furthest recess of her house where she sits it is so dark that you cannot see her well, but in summer enough light may come down from the smoke-holes in the roof to show her a little. She is a black stone without head or hands or face, and a very strong goddess.

Glome's primitive geography is also more directly connected to the sacred, a correspondence captured in the resonance between the river

---

[27] Orual's father, e.g., is Trom.

[28] Emphasis ought to fall on imperfect—'there was then'—for the phenomena that Orual portrays will alter once she has become queen; the picture of Glome here provided marks the point of departure for her biography.

[29] Myers (2004: 204–209) classifies polytheism and religious temporality in *TWHF* according to Gilbert Murray's four (or five?) stages of Greek religion, but her classification is neither entirely convincing nor exhaustive; Myers' reminder that Lewis's conception of Greco-Roman paganism was influenced by the anthropology (new at the time) of Frazer and Harrison is nevertheless illuminating.

Shennit, whose overflowing regulates biological life, and Ungit, the 'strong goddess' whose masked, faceless form delineates the city's spiritual geography.[30] Movement through Glome is therefore both a journey in time and space, and also a metaphysical egress into divine presence.

TWHF thus maintains a set of polarities between a 'Greek' epistemology and hermeneutic, and an epichoric religious tradition, embedded within Glome's primal landscape. Orual's biography is formed in the dialectic between the two—a dialectic embodied in two characters: the Fox and the Priest, both of whom appear upon the untimely death of Orual's mother and the King's marriage to the woman who would bear Psyche, his last-ditch effort to secure a male heir to the throne. A philosophically minded Greek slave imported as a tutor for the King's much-anticipated son, the Fox (whose free name is Lysias) is clearly a Socratic figure. When Orual first sees him, his legs still bear the marks of iron fetters—a scene reminiscent of Plato's *Phaedo* (59e–60d [*Phd.*]), in which Socrates on the morning of his execution converses with his friends and rubs his limbs after having spent a night in shackles.[31] Equipped with a store of Stoic aphorisms and an Epicurean antipathy for poetry, the Fox nevertheless evinces an ingrained love of epic and lyric, at one point (*TWHF* 8–9) quoting Sapphic fragments and paraphrasing the *Homeric Hymn to Aphrodite* (*h. Aphr.*)—omitting the naughty bits.[32] The Fox thus introduces within Glome's barbaric culture the voice of Greek philosophy with its cosmopolitan aspirations and ambivalence toward poetic mimesis. He also represents a specific hermeneutic—an insistence on naturalistic explanation of apparently supernatural events—that will define one of the novel's interpretive poles.

At the other pole is the Priest, a shamanistic physician who also attends the wedding and is called to perform a Caesarean section on Psyche's mother. Orual describes him thus (*TWHF* 11):

I had a fear of the Priest which was quite different from my fear of my father. I think that what frightened me (in those early days) was the holiness of the smell that hung about him—a temple-smell of blood (mostly pigeons' blood,

---

[30] On names and cases in 'Glomish' (!), see Myers (2004: 188–191).

[31] The scene also has metatextual relevance: Socrates does in *Phd.* 59e–60d precisely what Lewis does in *TWHF*—namely, rewrites an ancient author.

[32] Among his favorite aphorisms: "No man can be an exile if he remembers that all the world is one city" and "Everything is as good or bad as your opinion makes it" (*TWHF* 7). On the Fox's Stoicism, see Schakel (1984: 13–14) and Myers (2004: 214–218).

but he had sacrificed men, too) and burnt fat and singed hair and wine and stale incense. It is the Ungit smell. Perhaps I was afraid of his clothes too; all the skins they were made of, and the dried bladders, and the great mask shaped like a bird's head which hung on his chest. It looked as if there were a bird growing out of his body.

The Priest's 'holiness'—his theriomorphic visage and sacral fetor—personifies the brutality of Glome's primal spatiotemporality; and he espouses sacred epistemology that, in contrast to the Fox's rationalism, resists reason and defies systematicity. In anticipation of the wedding, the King intimidates the Fox into teaching the palace girls—including Orual and her younger full sister Redival, a blonde wanton whose coy tittering and precocious prurience instantiate Aphrodite in her carnal, pandemic manifestation—to sing a Greek *epithalamion*. They perform atrociously, but it is their ignorance of the language that most humiliates the Fox. The Priest, who neither cares for nor understands the words, music, or artistic value, remains indifferent to the foci of ancient Greek literary and music theory: the mimetic content of the logos; the psychological influence of *rhythmoi* and *harmoniai*; and the ethics of aesthetic response. His concern is ritual propriety, and he asks merely whether the singers will wear veils (11). The King's answer to the Priest's query regarding veils—"Do you think I want my queen frightened out of her senses? Veils of course," the King says with a gesture to Orual, "And good thick ones too" (11)—is Orual's first moment of self-awareness; in this scene she learns that she is ugly. When the King threatens the Priest, demanding an explanation for the birth of a girl and repayment for his inefficacious sacrifices to Ungit, the Priest answers: "Ungit hears, King, even at this moment. . . . And Ungit will remember. You have already said enough to call down doom upon all your descendants" (15–16). In the Priest, then, Orual is confronted with the embodiment of a presence and a kind of knowledge that proceed without proposition or explanation, and are materialized in ritual.

By virtue of being analyzable within both rationalistic and sacred epistemologies, the birth of Psyche (or Istra, as she is also called) foregrounds the fraught nature of interpretation. On one hand, Orual describes Psyche in Aristotelian, teleological terms as "the most natural thing in the world. As the Fox delighted to say, she was 'according to nature'; what every woman, or even every thing, ought to have been and meant to be, but had missed by some trip of chance" (22). On the other, in Orual's eyes Psyche's beauty has an uncanny power to suffuse her surroundings; in her company unsightly phenomena are beautified, and she "made beauty all around her" (22). In literary analysis this is known as the 'pathetic fallacy,' but in the Greco-Roman tradition it is a sign of epiphany (22–23):

> I think the almonds and the cherries blossomed earlier in those years and the blossoms lasted longer; how they hung on in such winds I don't know, for I see the boughs always rocking and dancing against blue-and-white skies, and their shadows flowing water-like over all the hills and valleys of Psyche's body. I wanted to be a wife so that I could have been her real mother. I wanted to be a boy so that she could be in love with me. I wanted her to be my full sister instead of her half sister. I wanted her to be a slave so that I could set her free and make her rich.

Part of the point is that Orual perceives Psyche in the manner that the god who marries her sees her, and even as Ungit sees her; she is consistently drawn closer to the gods whom she accuses. The larger observation is that Greek has one word for the myriad passions Orual experiences: *erôs*.[33] It is telling in this respect that only through Orual's gaze does Lewis eroticize Psyche; she is otherwise an an-erotic aesthetic object; the customary response is to fail to notice her beauty and later to recollect it with reverence. It is never made clear whether the vitality that blossoms in the world upon Psyche's arrival ought to be understood as immanence or projection—as the presence of divine beauty instantiated in and emanating from Psyche's mortal beauty, or as Orual's extroversion of an internal, psychological state. Such lack of clarity may be the point; immanence and projection are not exclusive realities (or delusions). Epiphany often has a corresponding manifestation in the soul; gods are present in the ways people feel.

In Psyche one finds the first intimations of allegory. Orual regards her adolescence with Psyche as the happiest time of her life. She, the Fox,

---

[33] Cf. Aphrodite's power to make wolves, lions, bears, and leopards couple in *h. Aphr.* 69–74. On Donaldson's (1991: 159) reading, Orual experiences what Ricoeur refers to as "'configurational' time, or time understood as nonlinear signification," a distinction between 'profane' and 'sacred' time; that is, between time as it is experienced sequentially by temporally bounded humans and time as it is transcended by Psyche, who throughout her life is being prepared to enter an extra-temporal realm.

and Psyche study philosophy, nature, and music, uninterrupted by divine intervention. Meanwhile, Redival—an aphroditic figure, whose overt sexual allure is contrasted to Psyche's austere, aesthetic beauty (22)—is caught in a tussle with one of the King's guards. He is promptly castrated, and she forced to accompany her sisters. The allegorical layering is almost heavy-handed: Orual's childhood appears as an Edenic image of prelapsarian innocence, surrounded by de-eroticized beauty of character and body (Psyche) and of mind (the Fox), only to be interrupted by carnal desire (Redival). Equally compelling is a reading of Orual's childhood as an allegory of psychosexual development, of the progression from childhood purity, through competing forms of beauty, knowledge, and value, to the attainment of sexual maturity, and, according to Catholic theology, its natural end, marriage. If allegorical interpretation is right on this point, Redival and Psyche succeed precisely where Orual fails: in the processes of maturation and gendering, their journeys and identities consummated in marriage, mortal and divine, respectively.[34] Orual's is the story of female sexuality arrested in prepubescence, a defective, unmarriageable virginity that denies sexual submission and falls short of her *telos*; it is she who is not 'according to nature.'

On another level still, Psyche's beauty raises the fundamental question of the existence and definitive characteristics of the divine. As is often the case, God is first apprehended in transgression and fear. When the Fox sings a hymn of praise in honor of Psyche—"Prettier than Andromeda, prettier than Helen, prettier than Aphrodite herself"—the triadic priamel fills Orual with foreboding: "Speak words of better omen, Grandfather," she replies (23). Fox's retort—"It is your words that are ill omened. The divine nature is not like that. It has no envy" (24)—articulates the text's principal theological crux: whether the nature of the divine is depersonalized, rational, and apprehended by reason, or invidious and anthropopathic. A series of sacrilegious acts succeeds the Fox's encomium: expectant mothers offer Psyche gifts and kiss her hand in hopes of bearing beautiful children as well; Redival ridicules their gesture—"Did you not know our step-sister had become a goddess" (27); and divine vengeance appears to follow. Rebellion breaks out in Glome, which the

---

[34] As Hinz (1976: 906) observes, the marriage of Cupid and Psyche may also be understood in metaphorical terms as a hierogamy, the mythological conjunction of elemental forces (e.g., earth and sky, or beauty and the principle of combination).

King quells violently, only weakening his position. The city is stricken by plague, and Psyche must nurse the Fox, who has fallen ill. The restive people attribute his recovery to Psyche and demand that she touch and cure them as well (32–33). When the people leave votive offerings at the palace instead of the temple of Ungit, signs of divine retribution intensify: the river Shennit dries; livestock die; famine enters the city; and the people demand to be fed from the royal larders, turning against the King, whose infertility they perceive as a blight on the city (36). They soon shun and declare Psyche 'the Accursed,' who "made herself a goddess" (39).

Into this chaos of incident and interpretation—for no one can explain the famine's cause or its remedy—the Priest arrives, blinded, weakened by the plague. His reading is decisive: the 'Shadow Brute'—the god's bestial manifestation—he claims, has been spotted in the countryside, and Ungit demands the 'Great Offering' (54).[35] If the 'Accursed' (i.e., the victim) is male, he is to be called Ungit's husband; if female, her son's wife; in both cases, they are sacrificed on the Grey Mountain. Whereas Apuleius is careful to portray Psyche's father as coerced by an oracle to surrender his daughter, Lewis casts the myth as a retelling of Aeschylus' *Agamemnon*, an exploration of the psyche of a monarch eager to sacrifice his daughter for political gain (cf. *TWHF* 58). The King is relieved to learn that not he but Psyche is to be the victim (55); the sacrifice provides an opportunity to consolidate his reign. When the Fox contests the Priest's interpretation, he is exposed as weak and cowardly, a captive who cast aside his shield rather than fight to death in battle; his cowardice, the Priest insists, renders him incapable of understanding "holy things" (50). Orual offers herself as the sacrifice instead, but the King stands her before a mirror and says, "Ungit asked for the best in the land as her son's bride.... And you'd give him that" (62). Redival and her nurse are revealed as co-conspirators in Psyche's murder, having gossiped about and maligned her to the Priest. Psyche, however, is willing to be offered, having had a premonition throughout her life that she was meant to live on the Grey Mountain, to "be a great, great queen, married to the greatest king of all ... [who] will build [her] a castle of gold and amber up there on the very top" (23; cf. 74, 101). Her

---

[35] Once again masking appears as a physical signification of the sacred: the Priest, garbed in the skins of animals, is also accompanied by two temple girls, whose appearance is "strange under the sun, with their gilt paps and their huge flaxen wigs and their faces painted till they looked like wooden masks" (42). The description will be relevant once Orual chooses permanently to veil herself.

acquiescence confounds Orual, who experiences it as rejection (71). When Orual last sees her younger sister, she is dressed as a temple priestess and drugged, soon to be led to the Grey Mountain, chained to an ancient tree, abandoned, and declared 'Blessed.'

All succumb to an interpretation that accords with the Priest's primitive immanentism and from which an image of the gods as petty and cruel emerges. In Orual's words (80):

It is, in a way, admirable, this divine skill. It was not enough for the gods to kill [Psyche]; they must make her father the murderer. It was not enough to take her from me, they must take her from me three times over, tear out my heart three times. First her sentence; then her strange, cold talk last night; and now this painted and gilded horror to poison my last sight of her. Ungit had taken the most beautiful thing that was ever born and made it into an ugly doll.

This is Orual's perspective at the end of her life, but at the time of the sacrifice, it remains unclear whether the gods have indeed intervened. Rains begin the day after the sacrifice, the river flows again, birds return, and the lands recover. The King's domestic and international problems resolve of their own accord, and although he will not have another child, fecundity—agricultural and economic—is restored to Glome. All of this may be read as the rewards of expiation, the fruits of a fertility goddess appeased and imbuing the land with her characteristics. But the Fox dismisses it as "cursed chance," accidents of nature that "nourish the beliefs of barbarians" (85). It is not until long after Orual decides to bury Psyche and meets her and the god on the Grey Mountain that the Priest's interpretive model is indisputably confirmed. In the meantime, Orual and, with her, the reader must waver between rational and supernatural accounts of phenomena that appear to violate the laws of the natural world. The reader shares Orual's uncertainties, the unsettling journey from rational to supernatural explanation as the text migrates into the genre of fantasy.

THE TEMPTATION OF PSYCHE: CHRONOTOPIC SLIPPAGE AND THE ASSERTION OF THE MEDIEVAL

Orual's decision to visit and bury Psyche's sacrificed body is a crossroads in the narrative. It commences with an act of classical self-fashioning, as the protagonist stylizes herself as Antigone; and, as we noted above, it is fraught with fantastic hesitation as Orual attempts to make sense of the city's seemingly miraculous recovery following the sacrifice. Yet, once Psyche has departed, the novel's spatiotemporal anchors begin to dissolve; the classicizing properties of the narrative are interrupted by tropes of a different genre; and a chronotope familiar from medievalizing fantasy impinges upon the erstwhile Hellenizing Glome. Premonitions of chronotopic slippage first become evident in Orual's character. The King's captain at arms, Bardia, for whom Orual will conceive an unrequited love, gives her dueling lessons to carry through the pain of having lost Psyche, only to discover that swordsmanship is her true gift (*TWHF* 90–91). Even as Orual identifies herself as a tragic heroine, her metamorphosis into a medieval warrior queen has begun, a transformation that is dramatized in spatial terms as a journey from Glome to Psyche's burial site on the Grey Mountain. Along the way, Orual and Bardia encounter the house of Ungit (94):

Its fashion is thus: great, ancient stones, twice the height of a man and four times the thickness of a man, set upright in an egg-shaped ring. These are very ancient, and no one knows who set them up or brought them into that place, or how. In between the stones it is filled up with brick to make the wall complete. The roof is thatched with rushes and not level but somewhat domed, so that the whole thing is a roundish hump, most like a huge slug lying on the field. This is a holy shape, and the priests say it resembles, or (in a mystery) that it really is, the egg from which the whole world was hatched or the womb in which the whole world once lay. Every spring the Priest is shut into it and fights, or makes believe to fight, his way out through the western door; and this means that the new year is born. There was smoke going up from it as we passed, for the fire before Ungit is always alight.

The dimensions of the megalithic structure—the omphalos of Glome's brutish faith—correspond exactly to the Sarsen Circle of Stonehenge: grey silicate sandstones 4.1 meters (13 feet) high and 2.1 meters (6 feet, 11 inches) wide—that is, twice the height of a man and four times the thickness. Orual's journey from Glome to the Grey Mountain may therefore be read as representing in spatial terms a voyage into the neolithic past, in which the house of Ungit appears as a memorial of a religious substrate that predates Greco-Roman antiquity and is affiliated with Anglo-Saxon paganism.

Psyche's absence thus presages chronotopic and generic reloca-
tion, as the text begins to shed its classicism and acquire the pseudo-
medievalizing attributes of MF. Important for our purposes, the narrative
moves beyond the polarity between Hellenism and primitivism that has
heretofore defined the conceptual possibilities of Orual's city and biography. When Psyche's body is nowhere to be found, Orual strays into what
is known as "the secret valley of the god," a *locus amoenus* in which she
meets Psyche, hale, happy, and oblivious to her arboreal surroundings.
Here it suffices to note that Orual demands that Psyche return to Glome;
Psyche in turn is convinced that she stands amid the golden and amber
palace of the god to whom she is wed, and is horrified that her sister cannot see it. On the night of her visit, Orual is granted a fleeting glimpse of
the palace through the mists that rise from the valley, one that she insists
does not prove the god's existence (132):

There stood the palace, grey—as all things were grey in that hour and place—
but solid and motionless, wall within wall, pillar and arch and architrave,
acres of it, a labyrinthine beauty. As [Psyche] had said, it was like no house
ever seen in our land or age. Pinnacles and buttresses leaped up—no memories of mine, you would think, could help me to imagine them—unbelievably
tall and slender, pointed and prickly as if stone were shooting out into branch
and flower.

The god's temple is, of course, a Gothic cathedral, with its flying buttresses, pointed arches, rib vaults, and elaborate tracery.[36] Psyche and her
god inhabit a medieval topography—a figuration that is especially striking given that medievalism is also characteristic of both Ungit's temple
and the world that Orual fashions upon returning to Glome. The text,
in other words, offers competing visions of medievalism: Ungit's Anglo-
Saxon temple, Psyche's spiritual cathedral, and Orual's secular, chivalrous Glome. Insofar as medievalism—especially Orual's de-sacralized
variety—is also the popular signifier of fantasy as a literary genre, the
contrast lays the groundwork for a critical examination of the medievalizing chronotope in MF.

Psyche's temptation and transgression, in which Christological interpretations hit pay dirt, reveal *TWHF*'s indebtedness to another literary

---

[36] Cf. Medcalf (1991: 133).

tradition—the Christian Bible. As Orual attempts to convince her sister to return to Glome or expose her lover, discourses from the Pentateuch and New Testament are interwoven with *topoi* from Greco-Roman literature, and a 'Biblical' chronotope emerges, in which Orual is recast as the Tempter and Psyche's uncovering of her husband as Original Sin, and in which the valley is no generic *locus amoenus*, but a Garden of Eden (later, it is destroyed in Mosaic fashion by lighting, flood, and rain).[37] In *TWHF* the myth retold is not Cupid and Psyche but the Fall of Man— or, better still, Cupid and Psyche as the Fall of Man. Only when Orual threatens to take her own life does Psyche agree to her sister's demands (136–137, 165); but because she has not yielded to temptation, Psyche's lapse occurs without culpability; her disobedience is at the same time a Christ-like sacrifice for Orual's salvation. The result is a condensation of Greco-Roman, Anglo-Saxon, Hebraic, and Judeo-Christian time and space, in which Apuleius' Cupid and Psyche are repackaged as an allegory of Adam and Eve tempted by the Serpent (who in this case is Orual) and of Christ's sacrificing himself to redeem humanity (who is also Orual). The upshot is that *TWHF* accomplishes on an allegorical plain the central project of medieval Christian theology—the wedding of Greco-Roman, Judaic, and New Testament traditions.

ALLEGORY, THE MEDIEVAL CHRONOTOPE, AND PRESENCE

The god's epiphany and curse, which follow the destruction of the valley, foreclose fantastic hesitation as a legitimate interpretive posture. Yet, just as divine presence incontrovertibly nullifies the Fox's naturalist explanation, another interpretive *aporia* is emplotted in the narrative. The god appears to Orual undeniably divine, beautiful beyond comprehension, and, gazing on her with "passionless and measureless rejection" (*TWHF* 173), he damns her with Delphic ambiguity: "Now Psyche goes out into exile. Now she must hunger and thirst and tread hard roads. Those

---

[37] 'Biblical' is to be preferred over a less specifically Christian designation (e.g., Mosaic or Hebrew), because Lewis frames Hebraic myth through a decidedly Christian interpretation of the Pentateuch.

against whom I cannot fight must do their will upon her. You, woman, shall know yourself and your work. You also shall be Psyche" (174).

The god's curse introduces the interpretive problem that defines the remainder of the novel; for what does it mean that Orual shall know herself and her work, and also shall be Psyche? On one level, with the exception of the oneiric visions that trouble her final days, the remainder of Orual's biography is devoid of divine intervention, filled instead with events that obey the laws of nature. On another level, Orual is somehow Psyche, and vice versa: her life is to be understood as a fulfillment of the prophecy, deciphered by constant reference to the god's utterance. It is left to Orual and the reader to make sense of the correlation between the two sisters' lives, to conduct parallel forms of reading—to interpret Orual's life both as an autobiography of events that occur in the natural world and obey natural laws, and as an analogue to the myth of Cupid and Psyche. Because both character and reader must decode the significance of the god's words—because we share in the protagonist's efforts to make sense of the analogical relationship between her life and Psyche's trials—and because only at the end of Orual's life is she (and, with her, the reader) able retrospectively to reinterpret herself as Psyche, the reader's allegorical interpretation is thematized in the text. One form of hesitation resolves into another: the hesitation is no longer between naturalist and supernatural explanations. Rather, the question now is how to interpret Orual's life as allegory of Psyche's.[38] Let us call this 'allegorical hesitation,' the uncertainty presented when shuttling between a text's primary, overt interpretation (as an autobiography of Orual's ascendance in the natural world, 'our world') and its reinterpretation as an allegory (in this case, of Psyche's passion).

Within such an allegorical mode, the narrative finalizes its transformation into a medievalizing chronotope. Orual returns to Glome and begins permanently to wear a veil to hide her ugliness. Because her voice is mysteriously deep and mellifluous, it endows her with a preternatural power

---

[38] Todorov (1973: 25, cf. 42–57) would perhaps insist that Lewis does not undermine his construal of the fantastic, since, at the moment that the god appears, all hesitation is removed and the text ceases to be fantastic, becoming instead an instance of the 'marvelous,' the genre concerned with unnatural worlds. But our argument is that the principal hermeneutic operation thematized in *TWHF*—both in the first half as Orual wavers between natural and supernatural explanation, and later, once she has been cursed—remains the reading of allegory.

over the men who form her inner circle.[39] The King stumbles and suffers a mortal wound. His is a slow demise, crazed and afflicted, and he spends his waning days screaming whenever Orual approaches, "Take her away! Take away that one with the veil. Don't let her torture me. I know who she is. I know" (185). His cries point to the numerous strata of meaning that veiling has acquired in the narrative as a mechanism of concealment and also a symbol of divine immanence. In another sense, the King sees into the other world—a common motif in Greek literature—apprehending Orual in her allegorical role as both Psyche and the jealous, faceless goddess, Ungit.

The Priest, too, falls ill and is succeeded by a second priest, Arnom, a suave pragmatist, whose ascension makes way for a new theology and politics. He joins forces with Orual in exchange for property and revenue for the temple of Ungit, and has a new statue of Ungit—a white marble sculpture in the Hellenistic fashion, which the Fox finds risible—placed prominently in the temple. Later, he recasts Ungit as a metaphor signifying Nature's procreative cycle and as the Earth, the "womb and mother of all things" (270–271). There develops a divide between the superstitious laity and the learned priesthood, who banish mysticism from religious practice; as Orual says of Arnom, "there was no feeling that Ungit came into the room with him" (205). Instead, Glome's religion serves an ideological function; Orual's politics receives a sacred charter from Arnom's brand of rational deism.

The most substantive focus of chronotopic transformation is Orual herself. As her father dies in madness, she must seize control of a kingdom riven by elites vying for power at home and beset by two armies abroad, each led by princes who are rivals to their father's throne. One prince, Trunia, is routed in ambush, wounded, and escapes into Glome, where he is imprisoned by Orual. The other, Argan, invades to ferret out his brother and take advantage of Glome's internal instability. Because Glome is still blighted by months of famine and drought, and unequipped to repel either army, Orual challenges Argan to a duel. In a brilliant distillation of all Greek thought on ethics and gender, the Fox decries the arrangement as "[m]onstrous—against all custom—and

---

[39] On Orual's veil, see Schakel (2010: 287).

nature—and modesty" (197). Monomachy is not unknown in the ancient literary tradition, nor are female warriors, but Lewis goes to great lengths to erase Greco-Roman cultural references from the battle; the weapon of choice (long swords), armor (gilded broad shields, chain-mail hauberks, helmets with eye slits and without crests), and the ornate rituals leading up to the single combat, replete with cavalry and trumpeters, converge in a depiction of a knightly, chivalrous match (213–218).

Just as the medieval chronotope that defines modern Anglophone fantasy emerges as the narrative's primary spatiotemporal frame, the fraught nature of allegorical interpretation asserts itself. En route to the battle field, Orual attempts to divine her future, connecting her impending contest, which she hopes to lose, to Psyche's fate: "So Psyche had gone out that day to heal the people; and so she had gone out that other day to be offered to the Brute. Perhaps, thought I, this is what the god meant when he said You also shall be Psyche" (216). Yet, Orual is the better swordsman, and she does not lose. What she remembers most is the change that comes over Argan's face before she severs his femoral artery (219):

It was to me an utter astonishment. I did not understand it. I should now. I have since seen the faces of other men as they began to believe, "This is death." You will know it if you have seen it; life more alive than ever, a raging, tortured intensity of life.

In the celebrations that follow, the novel's chronotopic transformation is complete (223–224):

That night's banquet was the first I had ever been at and the last I ever sat through (we do not lie at table like Greeks but sit on chairs or benches).... "Faugh!" I thought. "What vile things men are!" They were all drunk by now (except the Fox, who had gone early), but their drinking had sickened me less than their eating. I had never seen men at their pleasures before: the gobbling, snatching, belching, hiccuping, the greasiness of it all, the bones thrown on the floor, the dogs quarreling under our feet.

The squalid feast and Fox's departure signal the novel's new time and space; formerly Hellenizing, Glome now has become a medieval kingdom, authorized by an anodyne, politically embedded Catholicism.

What are the qualities of this chronotope? Perhaps most strikingly, it is characterized by absence. It has been noted that Orual is permanently veiled. Even in battle—her crowning achievement—she refuses to go "bareface" (215, *TWHF*'s original title), but her visage is more dreadful still: "Trunia had started when he first saw me shrouded like a ghost; neither throat nor helmet to be seen, but two eye-holes in a white hummock; scarecrow or leper" (216). Her appearance is analogical for her psychology; as she ascends to power, Orual sunders herself, constructing a persona she calls 'The Queen,' whom she inhabits and through whom she functions, forcing her younger self, whom she refers to as 'Orual,' to die (211). The Fox, whom Orual liberates but to whom she refuses to reveal the events on the Mountain, perceives that secrets now lie between them (180). Bardia becomes ever more unattainable, viewing her as desexualized—"It's a thousand pities," he laments, "they didn't make you a man" (197); when he learns that his expectant wife is in labor, he recuses himself from Orual's victory feast. Virginal and sterile, Orual spends her life alone, sleeping in a spare wing of the castle, where she hears nightly the chains of an old well, creaking, a reminder of Psyche's cry as she was banished from her husband and god. The gods also cease to intervene in her life. Orual is, of course, cognizant of her isolation, but she appears unaware of its allegorical implications, oblivious to the fact that, just as Psyche has been expelled from her lover's bed to undergo exile, the Queen, too, endures estrangement from herself, her gods, and the men and women she holds dear. Orual's life as a medieval queen is shown to be void and loveless; and, with it, the chronotope that defines twentieth-century fantasy and is conventionally represented as the most fantastic—in which the boundaries between primary and secondary worlds are portrayed as most permeable—turns out to be the least. The medieval is exposed as a dystopic chronotope, bled of the fantastic, otherworldly presences, as well as of the love, that abide in the classical chronotope.

Although it constitutes the majority of Orual's life, the medieval chronotope occupies little of the novel itself; the classical soon returns with bitter force. Now at the end of her life, Orual makes a pilgrimage to a sanctuary in a neighboring kingdom, a modest temple "built of pure white stone, with fluted pillars in the Greek style" (240). There she sees an image of a woman carved of pale, unstained wood and wearing a black veil, a local hero named Istra, who, the temple priest explains, "has only just begun to be a goddess. For you must know that, like many other gods, she began by being a mortal" (241). Orual pays the priest to tell her a "sacred story," which begins: "Once upon a time in a certain land there lived a king and a queen who had three daughters, and the youngest was the most beautiful princess in the whole world . . ." (241–242). Readers of Apuleius will know that this is a close translation of *Metamorphoses* 4.28, the very beginning of the 'Cupid and Psyche' tale (*Erant in quadam civitate rex et regina. Hi tres numero filias forma conspicuas habuere . . . At vero puellae iunioris tam praecipua, tam praeclara pulchritudo*).

As the priest continues, it becomes clear that Orual has entered the *heroön* ('hero tomb') of Apuleius' Psyche. Orual reacts with a rage at the dissonant interpretations: the priest "was telling it all wrong—hideously and stupidly wrong" (*TWHF* 243). (One has the sense that Lewis would have been sympathetic to Orual's frustrations; in the postscript to the American edition, Lewis also takes issue with the idea that the sisters have sight of the god's palace (313).) Not only did both sisters see the god's secret palace, but "[t]hey also wanted to destroy [Istra] because they had seen her palace . . . because they were jealous" (244). Orual's resistance springs from a response to an allegorical reading of her life, as she is coerced to witness her love for Psyche rewritten as envy, assimilated to the vile and flat impulses of her trampish younger sister. In another sense, her reaction provides a metatextual commentary on the experience of fantasy or, more precisely, on the reading of the myth of Cupid and Psyche without fantasy. From her own vantage, Orual's has been the story of a person who, confronted with equivocal intimations of the supernatural, hesitates and ultimately makes a wrong decision between explanations for seemingly unnatural events; her error was to misconstrue supernatural phenomena as merely 'uncanny.' The gods, in her view, defy comprehension; they suspend the laws of nature; they riddle, hide, torment with glimpses, and leave truth uncertain. Hesitation between supernatural and scientific explanation lies at the core of her account. In the priest's (i.e., Apuleius') version, in contrast, the natural world, 'our world' is self-evidently supernatural; there is nothing fantastic about it, and there can be no fantastic hesitation—"no guessing and no guessing wrong" (244)—because there is nothing to guess about; the supernatural is not a violation of nature or a suspension of its laws; it is the law of Nature. Gods are opaque, apprehended by the senses, and expect obedience as though they have fashioned a world without ambiguity.

As the narrative proceeds, the play of chronotopes continues, its structure and *topoi* becoming ever more classicizing and allegorically compounded. Orual undergoes a series of eschatological visions in which she is forced to face herself and see who she has become. She voyages to the underworld and reads her charge against the god before a divine judge—Minos, Rhadamanthus, Persephone, or all of them at once—only to discover that the text has been transformed into a crabbed and embittered version of her book, emptied of all narrative and filled only with envy. This act of reinterpretation—in which Orual's biography is stripped of its charm and medieval heroism and reread as resentment—leads to *anagnorisis*. Her godlike love, she is led to acknowledge, is her *hamartia*; her true motive has been a love that, like Ungit's, is undifferentiated from jealousy and a meanness of soul that matches her appearance. Apuleius' version, she realizes, was right.

The meaning of the god's pronouncement is finally made clear in multiple layers of equivalencies: Orual's alienation has been a reenactment of Psyche's wanderings; but, more important, Orual has also been Ungit; the attributes for which she condemns the gods—vicious caprice, brutality, blood-thirstiness, semantic ambiguity, a jealous love that seeks to possess and consume—are hers as well.[40] Yet, when Orual, accompanied by the Fox as her psychopomp, sees Psyche's trials engraved on a temple frieze, and conducts an ecphrasis thereof, she discovers that it was she who became the ants that sorted the seeds, and she whom the golden sheep trampled as Psyche collected their wool. Despite having wounded her beloved sister, it is Orual "[w]ho bore the anguish. But [Psyche] achieved the task" (301). At the climax of the story, as Psyche completes her third task and returns to give Ungit the casket of the Queen of the Dead, allegorical matrices multiply; Orual is the final shrouded figure whom Psyche must pass in silence, but she is also Ungit who receives the casket, is beautified, and becomes Psyche. In this palimpsest of allegorical interpretation and reinterpretation, classical time and space provide a framework within which

---

[40] Throughout this sequence, in which plot structures and motifs are markedly classicizing, temporality and space break down. The visions that haunt Orual's final days occur in a lurid atemporality, anchored in no discernible space, in which the present may occur before, concurrently with, and even after the moment of experience. Cf. Donaldson (1991: 162).

to see divine presence entering and remaining in the primary world, 'our world.'

CONCLUSION

TWHF, I have argued, may be read as a commentary on the status of medievalizing as opposed to classicizing fantastic chronotopes, and as an exploration of rationalistic and allegorical explanations of fantastic experience. Orual's life begins in classical time and space, only to merge into primitive and Biblical chronotopes. Psyche's exile inaugurates a new, medieval chronotope, in which Glome morphs into a feudal city inhabited by knights gallant, courtly intrigue, and chivalrous duels, and Orual becomes its warrior queen. Medieval Glome, however, is devoid of one crucial fantastical element: contact with a secondary, super- or preternatural world. Despite its feudalistic trappings, the medieval chronotope is the least fantastic time and space in the novel. The tragic-epic conclusion triggers a restoration of the classical chronotope in which primary and secondary worlds converge. Throughout this retelling, thematization of interpretation of fantasy—that is, of events that exist impossibly—has been a recurring motif: How are Orual and the reader to interpret seemingly unnatural phenomena in the natural world, make sense of the god's oracle and relate it to the events of her autobiography, understand her psychology and the motives of those around her, and decipher the natural world within an allegorical frame? In a gesture to further interpretative possibilities and, finally, to indeterminacy, Orual's autobiography ends mid-sentence: "Long did I hate you, long did I fear you. I might—" (*TWHF* 308).

What, then, does the classical offer fantasy? Among the primary appeals of fantastic literature is the experience of what Tolkien referred to as 'enchantment,' the sidestepping of our scientifically exhausted experiences, and venturing, albeit temporarily, into a different world.[41] To (mis-) appropriate Orual's words, in Lewis's classicizing allegory, our world—the primary world—also becomes "a story belonging to a different world,

---

[41] Tolkien (1966: 73). On 'enchantment,' see discussions in Flugt and Stevens (both this volume).

a world in which the gods show themselves clearly . . ." (244). In Orual's allegorical journey through the generic possibilities of classical and medieval time and space, the classical figures as the spatiotemporal domain in which presence impinges directly upon the natural world, in which there is no wish or need to leave the world as we know it, because, in a mystery, the otherworldly inhabits our own.

Part III

Children and (Other) Ancient Monsters

8

The Classical Pantheon in Children's Fantasy Literature

Sarah Annes Brown

"Tell us about it, Pete," she said.

"Well, it's a book of old stories. About gods and things. Not Zeus and his crowd—a much better lot. Odin and Frigga. And Thor. And—Frey."

—Hilda Lewis, *The Ship That Flew*

Whereas fantasy draws heavily on legends and folklore of all kinds, classical myth is a comparatively subdued presence in the genre, overshadowed by Norse and Celtic stories as well as by Judeo-Christian traditions—those relating to demonology, for example. In Hilda Lewis's Nesbit-inspired time-travel adventure *The Ship That Flew* (1939), the children would much rather visit Asgard than Olympus, and this preference resonates in later fantasy works for both adults and children; most seem drawn to northern European folklore, rather than Greek or Roman myth.

It may seem surprising that a tradition that has been so richly influential in Western culture and that is so full of monsters, marvels, and metamorphoses should not hold a more prominent place within fantasy literature. Modern fantasies take many different forms. Some are set in imaginary 'secondary' worlds that are governed by magic rather than science. Some take place in our own 'primary' world, but with the incongruous addition of magical elements. Still other fantasies feature portals between worlds, or present us with an alternate Earth where magic is an accepted given of existence. The term 'fantasy' may also embrace works that capture subtler forms of metaphysical difference and could instead be categorized as magic realism or 'weird fiction.' Greek myth has little place in pure 'secondary world' fantasy, as it is too enmeshed in human history. Almost all the texts discussed in this chapter are very clearly set in our world—or something very like it. Sometimes, as with Riordan's *Percy Jackson* novels, the sole fantastic premise is the reality of classical myth. In others, Greek myth is just one ingredient in a more promiscuously magical universe.

Possible reasons for classical myth's comparative absence from fantasy may be suggested by an exploration of some of the texts that buck this trend; in this chapter, I track the relationship between children's fantasy literature and Greek myth from the early twentieth century to the present day and seek to explain why there is not a closer relationship between these two genres. Perhaps an association with the study of dead languages has contributed to this unpopularity. Fantasy appeals to our interest in the strange and the wonderful, and a dry schoolroom setting may have made the tales of Olympus both overfamiliar and wearisome for many children. In more recent years, because of a sharp decline in the study of classical languages, such an explanation would lose its force. However, other tensions begin to be identifiable. An examination of the fault line between children's fantasy and the classics reveals a recurring preoccupation with power—both the Greek gods themselves and the classical tradition of which they form part are invested with conspicuous authority. Writers use a range of methods to call into question both the dominance of the classics as a locus of cultural capital and the power and majesty of the gods themselves. When fantasy writers do turn to the Olympians for inspiration, the pantheon is often treated with ambivalence, irony, or even resentment.

C. S. LEWIS AND E. NESBIT: THE PANTHEON
ON THE MARGINS

Reasons and methods for marginalizing Greek gods differ between authors. For some, religion is the motive for a certain wariness. Many beings from classical myth feature in C. S. Lewis's *Chronicles of Narnia* (1950–1956), but these are not permitted to disrupt or distract from the novels' strong Christian overtones. Although everyone remembers that, in *The Lion, the Witch and the Wardrobe* (1950), the White Witch outlawed Christmas, Mr. Tumnus (as a faun, a classical creature himself) looks back with nostalgia to quite different celebrations (1979 [1950]: 20–21):

He told . . . about summer when the woods were green and old Silenus on his fat donkey would come to visit them, and sometimes Bacchus himself, and then the streams would run with wine instead of water and the whole forest would give itself up to jollification for weeks on end.

Dryads, fauns, even minor rural deities (e.g., Bacchus, Silenus, Pomona) are allowed into Narnia, but major Olympians would be as out of place there as nylons or lipstick.[1] Classical beings, particularly those with any claim to authority, are consigned firmly to the decorative margins of the text.

Although she did not share Lewis's religious agenda, E. Nesbit also undermines the pantheon's authority. In *The Enchanted Castle* (1907), the gods are most obviously diminished by the uncertainty surrounding their status; they are not full-blown Olympians but neoclassical statues that come to life at night and welcome the four children to their banquet.[2] They only figure in a single episode, towards the end of story, and are simply one more manifestation of the enchantment of the magical ring that sets the children's adventures in motion. Their dignity and power are undercut. Nesbit manipulates the gap between the authority and antiquity of the classical pantheon and the children's lack of reverence for their

---

[1] Susan Pevensie, as she grew up, stopped believing in Narnia, and was only interested in "nylons and lipstick and invitations," in Lewis (2001 [1956]: 168). For a discussion of Narnia's mythical creatures, see Nikolajeva (1988: 52–53).

[2] For an analysis of the place of magic in the novel, see Briggs (2008 [1987]: 288–292).

new friends to create an effect of humorous bathos that diminishes the gods further. Psyche was "a darling, as anyone could see" and Eros "a really nice boy, as the girls instantly agreed" (1979 [1907]: 205). The gods code-switch rather comically between archaic, courtly language and the schoolboy slang used by the children. Here, Phoebus Apollo orders the two boys to be fetched to join the feast: "Hermes, old chap, cut across and fetch them, and explain things as you come" (207). The adult reader will appreciate the humor here, and is also likely to become aware of yet another way in which the gods are questioned by Nesbit: their moral authority is compromised for the more knowing reader.

While the gods are presented in a benign enough light, even in this early children's fantasy novel, we are reminded that they have a darker side. Kathleen is charmed by Apollo (199):

"And I've been thinking," said Mabel brightly, "we might find out a lot about this magic place, if the other statues aren't too proud to talk to us."

"They aren't," Kathleen assured her; "at least, Phoebus wasn't. He was most awfully polite and nice."

Readers with some classical knowledge may remember other episodes when Apollo was rather less "nice," and Nesbit uses 'double address' to add a nudge of her own and place the god's over-attentive attitude towards Mabel in particular—"I am your slave, little lady"—in a slightly different light.[3] Here Nesbit uses a sly ellipsis to reinforce the hint: "'Late again, Phoebus!' someone called out. And another: 'Did one of your horses cast a shoe?' And yet another called out something about laurels" (204). The reference to laurels is an allusion to the metamorphosis that saved Daphne from rape (e.g., Ovid *Metamorphoses* 1.452–567), and the confused report of this comment reflects the children's failure to understand its meaning.

BATHOS AND INCONGRUITY: P. L. TRAVERS AND JOAN AIKEN

Bathos is used to similarly comic effect in the Mary Poppins novels of P. L. Travers. In the first book of the series, *Mary Poppins* (1984 [1934]),

---

[3] The term 'double address' was coined by Barbara Wall (1991) to describe the effect created when a text is designed to signal different meanings to its adult and child readers.

Maia of the Pleiades joins the Banks family for their Christmas shopping. A certain starriness aside, she seems every inch an English schoolgirl, and carefully chooses presents such as a skipping rope and a copy of *The Swiss Family Robinson* for her six sisters (125–126). The third book of the series, *Mary Poppins Opens the Door* (1943), contains a chapter entitled "The Marble Boy." The title character, young Neleus, is not Christianized; however, as in *The Enchanted Castle*, possible theological problems are softened by making him an animated statue rather than a 'real' deity. The presence of a wider pantheon seems indicated when Neleus, in myth a son of Poseidon, explains that Mary Poppins is "a very old friend of my father's" (405), but it is soon revealed that the statue was part of a larger family group, broken up by collectors. This undermines—without entirely denying—the initial suggestion that the major Olympians exist in the world of Mary Poppins. The obscurity of Neleus also perhaps encourages us to see him less as a divine figure than as a magical stone boy. Like Nesbit's statues, both Maia and Neleus seem minor characters, no more or less significant than the many other magical figures that populate the novels. There is no hint that full-blown Olympians are lurking behind the scenes; any such suggestion would weaken the power and mystique attached to Mary Poppins herself.

Travers's most significant treatment of Greek mythological figures comes in a late work, *Mary Poppins in Cherry Tree Lane* (1982), an extended short story rather than a full-length collection. It seems that their greater prominence in this tale requires more decided containment strategies that further delimit such beings' divine and cultural authority. Whereas C. S. Lewis largely sidesteps the potentially awkward discrepancies between paganism and Christianity, here the legendary characters that join the Banks children in the park are 'Englished' and Christianized. Appropriately enough, a key intertext for the story is William Shakespeare's *A Midsummer Night's Dream*, another classical/English hybrid. As in Shakespeare's play, the action in Cherry Tree Lane depicts a collision between magical and mortal beings on Midsummer's Eve. Authority is overturned for a night, and characters search for their true loves under the eye of immortal beings. In search of coltsfoot for their horses, Castor and Pollux visit the park's herb garden, where they are joined by the hunter Orion. The pompous Park Keeper at first refuses to believe the twins are really gods, although he does know their story: "Castor and Pollux! Get along! They're characters in a story. Lily-white boys turned into stars. Tamed horses, that's what they did. I read it when I was a boy" (690). Travers seems conscious that Greek myth can be presented in an unappealingly dry or austere way. Perhaps an association with prep school Latin lessons is what made Hilda Lewis's Pete so decisive in his preference for Norse gods, as we see in the epigraph to this chapter. A similar impulse may have prompted Travers to strip away any potentially alienating Latinity (691):

"Pegasus!" scoffed the Park Keeper. "He's another of them taradiddles. You learn about them when you're at school. Astronomy for Boys and Girls. But whoever saw a horse with wings? He's just a bunch of stars, that's all. And Vulpecula, and Ursa Minor and Lepus—all that lot." "What important names." The two boys giggled. "We call them Foxy and Bear and Hare."[4]

Although she does not alter the better-known classical names, Travers allows Mr. Banks to mishear "Orion" as the more familiar and homely, if not, of course, English, "O'Ryan" (705).

Perhaps the most strikingly anti-classical aspect of the story is Orion's enthusiasm for English folk songs. He complains that the stars sing the "same old plainsong day in and day out" (698), whereas he much prefers tunes such as "Green Grow the Rushes-O." This looks back to the Park Keeper's earlier reference to Castor and Pollux as "lily-white boys." The "plainsong" Orion dismisses is itself a Christian and liturgical tradition, whereas "Green Grow the Rushes-O" is an enigmatic song that weaves together Christian and pagan references:

Twelve for the twelve Apostles
Eleven for the eleven who went to heaven,
Ten for the ten commandments,
Nine for the nine bright shiners,
Eight for the April Rainers,
Seven for the seven stars in the sky,
Six for the six proud walkers,
Five for the symbols at your door,
Four for the Gospel makers,
Three, three, the rivals,

---

[4] This move to disassociate the classics from pedantry and authority, making them more playful and anarchic, echoes E. M. Forster's short story "The Celestial Omnibus" (1911), where the unnamed boy protagonist, rather than the dry scholar Mr. Bons, is welcomed and accepted by Achilles.

Two, two, the lily-white boys,
Clothèd all in green, Ho Ho
One is one and all alone
And evermore shall be so.

Some references, such as that to "Gospel makers," are unambiguous, and the "seven stars" are probably the Pleiades, but it has proved more difficult to identify the "lily-white boys" with certainty. They have been associated both with Jesus and John the Baptist and with Castor and Pollux. Travers's fondness for cross-pollination between classical myth and other European beliefs, including Christianity, is, as we will see, something of a recurring theme in fantasy literature; here it works, yet again, to detach minor personalities of Greek myth from an Olympian system (or perhaps 'system of knowledge' or *episteme*) that would be incongruous in a world seeming to rotate around Mary Poppins.

We find yet another example of classical forces being decoupled from the pantheon, their power diminished by the comedy of incongruity, in Joan Aiken's short story "The Apple of Trouble" (2008 [1968]). Like Nesbit and Travers, Aiken depicts a magical world in which classical figures must compete for the readers' attention with ghosts, witches, unicorns, and others marvels. Young Mark Armitage swaps his unwanted bicycle for a mysterious golden apple, bought from a shifty man who is anxious to make a quick getaway. The apple has a distinguished, if checkered, provenance: "Original bite marks of Adam and Eve before apple carried out of Eden ... Apple of Discord—golden apple same which began Trojan War ... Apples of Asgard too ... Not to mention Apples of Hesperides, stolen by Hercules" (172–173). When Mark's unpleasant Uncle Gavin takes charge of the apple, he receives three unexpected visitors calling for his blood. Just as Nesbit's children cut the gods down to size with their affectionate over-familiarity, Uncle Gavin's patronizing scorn similarly undermines the authority of the Furies—Tisiphone, Alecto, and Megaera—usually presented as figures to be dreaded (179):

"Didn't you see the notice on the gate, my good women? It says "No Hawkers or Circulars." I give handsome checks to charity each year at Christmas and make it a rule never to contribute to door-to-door collections. So be off, if you please!"

"We do not seek money," Tisiphone hungrily replied.

The Furies' sojourn in suburbia continues to go badly. Their dragon, Ladon, bothers the cook and frightens the cat, although they are finally appeased when Uncle Gavin wounds his heel (causing blood to flow) and the apple is returned to them. Like Nesbit's slangy gods, the Furies seem to have been forced to adapt to their modern middle-class environment, and exchange well-bred pleasantries with Mark's sister Harriet when they eventually depart (185):

Alecto even turned and gave Harriet a ghastly smile. "Thank you for having us, child," she said. "We enjoyed our visit."

"Don't mention it," Harriet mechanically replied, and only just stopped herself from adding, "Come again."

DIANA WYNNE JONES AND THE MYTHOSPHERE

Diana Wynne Jones felt a similar attraction to the incongruous, turning to a classical frame of reference late in her fantasy-writing career. *The Game* (2007) largely ignores the more powerful gods and goddesses, and that sidelining of the pantheon here has a more purposeful and political charge than was apparent in the earlier works so far discussed. This shift, as we shall see, is repeated in the works of several other recent writers of fantasy. The central character, Hayley, is the daughter of one of the Pleiades and the mortal Sisyphus. Just two of the better-known gods have significant roles to play: Jupiter, or 'Uncle Jolyon,' is a spiteful bully, determined to impose his will on the minor deities; Mercury is 'Mercer,' a character who never fully comes into focus, but whose loyalties ultimately seem to lie with Jolyon.

Not content with consigning Hayley's parents, Merope and Sisyphus, to torments in the underworld, Jolyon has forbidden the rest of the Pleiad family to enter the 'mythosphere,' banishing them to the mortal world. The mythosphere is a kind of literal worldwide web, and Hayley first glimpses it on the computer of her grandfather, Atlas, when he shows her an image of the Earth (29):

The mist seemed to be made up of thousands of tiny pale threads, all of them moving and swirling outwards. Each thread shone as it moved, gentle and pearly, so the effect was as if Earth spun in a luminous rainbow veil. While

Hayley watched, some of the threads wrapped themselves together into a shining skein.

Each of these skeins represents a different mythical tradition, and Wynne Jones cleverly uses this conceit to draw attention to the way cognate stories from quite different cultures cluster together, like Aiken's reminder of the many stories in which a magic apple has played a part.

When Hayley first finds her way into the mythosphere, guided by a mysterious musician she calls 'Flute,' she encounters a series of hunters and their prey: first Orion, then northern European swan maidens and swan princes, and finally Leda and the swan. "There was something about that big swan that Hayley did not like at all" (53). That swan is of course another manifestation of her uncle Jolyon—we may compare a similar childlike failure to recognize references to the seamier side of Greek myth in Nesbit, and this reminder of the sinister and predatory side of the major Olympians is compounded by Hayley's next encounter, this time with a young man to whom she is immediately drawn. "He was a good looking boy, not much older than Hayley, and he seemed as happy and excited as his dogs. . . . 'Oh I liked him!' Hayley said. 'Who is he?'" (55). However, she is then forced to witness him fleeing from his hounds in terror, for this is Actaeon, yet another victim of Olympian power. The reader who knows just how blameless Actaeon was, at least in the best-known versions of the story, will appreciate the dryness in Flute's response to Hayley's question (56):

"Do they catch him?"
Flute nodded. "I'm afraid so."
Hayley was horrified. "Why?"
"He managed to be really offensive to a goddess."

The Olympians' problem is not so much settled malignity as a ruthless sense of entitlement. Wynne Jones's negative response to the gods, in particular Jupiter/Jolyon, seems part of a larger pattern of sympathy for the underdog, for those who are marginalized by a lack of power or through being outside the dominant culture. Travers sought to distance her gods from the library and schoolroom, and Jolyon's attitude could also be seen as a reflection (and implicit criticism) both of the cultural hegemony of the classics and of entrenched power and privilege. In his modern incarnation, Jolyon is aligned with corporate success, and his faux-jovial manner grates on Hayley (61).

"Why are you so dishonest?" she said. . . .

Uncle Jolyon . . . leant his head back and laughed heartily.

"Because I have to be," he said. "Nobody expects a businessman to be honest, child." And he shouted with laughter again.[5]

Wynne Jones interprets the category of 'myth' capaciously; both *Alice's Adventures in Wonderland* and science fiction tropes find their place in the mythosphere. As well as updating the myth of Sisyphus to make Hayley's father's punishment a never-emptying in-tray, Wynne Jones offers us a glimpse of another strand on this underworld skein, as related myths blur into one another (130–131):

She marched on. The passage went from arched stone to dingy brick and then to modern-looking concrete with strip lights in the ceiling, but there were still prison cells on either side. She came to a squarer part, where soldiers with guns were kicking someone who was writhing about on the floor. . . . The woman soldier who seemed to be in charge snapped "Shoot her," without looking up from kicking.

It is significant that the one identifiable modern example of a torture 'myth' does not feature a communist, fascist, or Ba'athist villain; instead Wynne Jones chooses to highlight atrocities carried out by U.S. forces in Abu Ghraib.[6] An implicit link is thus drawn between American and Olympian power.

Those marginalized within the Greek hierarchy, such as Orion, join forces with mythical beings from less canonical traditions. Towards the opening of the novel, Hayley's old-fashioned grandmother dismisses her

---

[5] Uncle Jolyon is in some senses a reincarnation of Mr. Wednesday, or Wodin, from Wynne Jones's earlier story *Eight Days of Luke* (1975). There David, like Hayley, lives with coldly detached relatives, and is suddenly confronted with a powerful male guest who represents a threat. But Mr. Wednesday, although he is not fully on David's side, has a charm and warmth quite missing in Jolyon (81).

[6] For a discussion of Abu Ghraib as a version of apocalyptic phantasmagoria, see Warner (2008: 352–353).

Russian maid, Martya. Later it is revealed that Martya is the witch Baba Yaga, more than happy to help push back against the arrogant Jolyon. Many readers have been intrigued by the engaging but mysterious Flute and Fiddle, brother musicians who do not seem to map onto the better-known European traditions that dominate the strands of the mythosphere explored by Hayley. Whereas Flute can be found in daylight, Fiddle must remain in darkness. The brothers challenge the readers' attempts to interpret them, leaving clues that may simply be red herrings. "My ways are not your ways," Fiddle tells Hayley (37), echoing Isaiah 55: 8-9. Hayley herself remarks that Flute reminds her of the Pied Piper, although he is in fact dressed all in green. There are echoes of various other mythic traditions here, legends of twins who represent opposing but complementary principles, such as an Iroquois creation story in which fighting brothers end their quarrel by agreeing that one shall always dwell in night, the other in daylight. This composite quality is perhaps suggested by Hayley's response when, rather than telling her his name, Flute asks her what she wants to call him: "All sorts of names flooded through Hayley's mind, so many that she was surprised into taking a deep, gasping breath. 'Flute,' she said, in the end" (42). Perhaps, given the emphasis on Flute's green clothes (41), it is not too fanciful to identify the brothers with the "lily-white boys" of "Green Grow the Rushes-O," another mysterious pair who invoke several figures from quite different traditions. Whatever their provenance—they are excluded from the key to the characters based on Greek myth Wynne Jones provides at the end of the novel—it is significant that this subversive pair seem to be pulling most of the story's strings, ensuring that the Olympians do not have it all their own way. *The Game* thus builds on the equivocal relationship with Greek myth found in earlier fantasy novels, adding a layer of further distrust reflecting a cultural climate where multiculturalism is embraced in reaction against imperialism and neo-conservatism. This is partly manifested through the privileging of minor classical deities and the myths of other cultures over Olympian exceptionalism.

RICK RIORDAN: OLYMPIAN EXCEPTIONALISM AND THE WEST

Mythological outliers also have an important role to play in Rick Riordan's *Percy Jackson* series, where the link between Olympus and

Western civilization is emphasized to similarly equivocal effect. How and why Olympus has migrated westwards over the centuries is explained by Chiron, teacher and guide to the young demigod heroes sent to Camp Half-Blood (*The Lightning Thief* [*LT*] 72–73):

What you call "Western civilization." Do you think it's just an abstract concept? No, it's a living force.... And yes, Percy, of course they are now in your United States. Look at your symbol, the eagle of Zeus. Look at the statue of Prometheus in Rockefeller Center, the Greek facades of your government buildings in Washington.... Like it or not—and believe me, plenty of people weren't very fond of Rome, either—America is now the heart of the flame.

The gods' move to America is the basis for some good jokes, in the style of the Disney *Hercules* (1997), in which Thebes is known as the 'Big Olive' (in a riff on New York City's 'Big Apple') and Hercules has a meeting scheduled with the Daughters of the Greek Revolution. Similarly, Percy Jackson's friend Annabeth, daughter of Athena, warns him that they are beset by dangerous cannibals from the far north, Laestrygonians: "'Laistry- I can't even say that. What would you call them in English?' She thought about it for a moment. 'Canadians,' she decided" (*The Sea of Monsters* 26). We also learn that franchise stores represent a successful attempt to harness the life force of the Lernean hydra back in the 1950s, explaining their ability to multiply so fast (143).

However, there are also some darker notes in Riordan's satire, and the series' conflicted attitude towards Olympus is framed in terms that mirror American liberal anxieties. Percy's instinctive tribal loyalty towards the gods—he is the son of Poseidon—is challenged by mounting evidence that they can be negligent, callous, and unjust. The rage of the Titans against them can be seen, not as unmotivated evil, but as predictable blowback following extreme provocation from the arrogant Olympians. For example, we are reminded that 'Aunty Em,' the terrifying Medusa, was transformed into a monster by Athena as a punishment for having sex with Poseidon in her temple. Poseidon, of course, remained unpunished. The reader is not encouraged to dwell too long on the fact that Percy's father and Annabeth's mother could be seen as the root causes of Medusa's hostility to the two children, but the information is provided nonetheless.

Percy, like many of the other demigods, is torn between a wish to secure his divine father's approval and resentment at the gods' apparently self-serving agenda. Percy's main antagonist amongst his peers is Luke Castellan, a son of Hermes, who defects to the Titans (*LT* 365):

All the heroics—being pawns of the gods. They should've been overthrown thousands of years ago, but they've hung on, thanks to us half-bloods.... Their precious "Western civilization" is a disease, Percy. It's killing the world. The only way to stop it is to burn it to the ground, start over with something more honest.

Luke, who finally overcomes his dark side to destroy Kronos, is interestingly named. He is more than a little like the title character of Diana Wynne Jones's *Eight Days of Luke* (1975). Here, too, the hero, David, meets an engaging older boy who turns out to be morally ambiguous. Wynne Jones's Luke is Loki, the Norse trickster god who is torn between gods and giants as Luke Castellan is between the Olympians and the Titans. Riordan's Luke perhaps also recalls Luke Skywalker. Each Luke discovers that he has a powerful father, and each, for different reasons, turns against him. However, in his decisive turn to evil and final redemption in death, Luke Castellan is rather more like Skywalker's father, Anakin, who becomes Darth Vader.[7]

Although the reader is invited to see Luke's final return to the Olympian side as an entirely redemptive move, it is impossible to ignore the fact that he is half correct. His nihilistic support for his enemies' enemies may be wrong, but the Olympians are presented as, at best, the least-worst camp. They treat the minor gods, such as Janus, with disdain, and it is implied that their eventual decision to mend their ways on this score is strategic rather than moral. In a discussion of the novels' moral ambiguities, Mandy Pietruszewski observes a curious irony in the series' conclusion, the decision to adopt a more egalitarian approach to the lesser deities and their children: "That's the strangest and best part of the *Percy Jackson* series. In the end, the world is made the sort of place the main villain wished it would be."[8]

---

[7] The name Luke is originally derived from Greek *lykos* ('wolf') and may thus be associated with other Greek trickster figures such as Autolycos and Lycaon.

[8] Pietruszewski (2013).

Percy's loyalties are perhaps challenged most sharply by his encounter with the kind and selfless Calypso. He finds her artless beauty preferable even to that of Aphrodite, and is shocked to find out that she is being punished with eternal exile because she is a Titan, a daughter of Atlas.[9] Percy knows that there are 'good Titans,' but Calypso cannot be categorized quite so comfortably as his friend Zoë Nightshade, who chose to transfer her allegiance to Artemis (*The Battle of the Labyrinth* 217):

"But that's not fair," I said. "Just because you're related doesn't mean you support him. This other daughter I knew, Zoë Nightshade—she fought against him. She wasn't imprisoned."

"But Percy," Calypso said gently. "I did support him in the first war. He is my father."

"What? But the Titans are evil!"

"Are they? All of them? All the time?" She pursed her lips. "Tell me Percy. I have no wish to argue with you. But do you support the gods because they are good, or because they are your family?"

This mildly Hesperophobic undercurrent in Riordan's works is far from unique in modern American children's fantasy, although unusual in more realistic fiction. In her study of children's literature influenced by the 9/11 terror attacks on the United States, Jo Lampert observes that most responses, either subtly or more emphatically, reinforce patriotism. Just a few might be said to challenge the reader's moral bearings. One example is this ambiguous image from DC Comics:[10]

[T]he illustration shows a child's hand playing with superhero action dolls, rather as a puppeteer. He is flying Wonderwoman [sic] toward a tower draped in an American flag. Yet the image of play, with its disembodied hands and dark hues, seems oddly ominous. Why is Wonderwoman flying into the iconic Tower, looking suspiciously like a terrorist aircraft? Whose puppet is she? Are these hands of color, or white hands? Male or female? Is Wonderwoman a villain or a hero?

---

[9] Gellar-Goad (2014) briefly discusses the *Percy Jackson* novels as part of a wider survey of the significance of depictions of the Titanomachy in contemporary culture.

[10] Lampert (2010: 165).

Although it does not engage directly with 9/11, the *Percy Jackson* series does offer a model for a more complex and self-critical response to finding oneself caught up in a clash of civilizations. Its approach may be atypical of most children's literature, but it chimes with much contemporary science fiction in its destabilization of moral certainties and tribal allegiances. Here, for example, is Stacy Tacaks's analysis of the television series *Invasion* (2005-2006); this series both reprised and challenged the film *Invasion of the Body Snatchers* (1956; remake 1978) by destabilizing the binary between sympathetic humans and hostile aliens:

The hybrid nature of the monsters in *Invasion* belies the Manichean logics separating "us" from "them" and dictating that "we" are good and "they" are evil. Indeed, it is possible to argue that *Invasion* constitutes an exploration of imperial guilt, designed to short-circuit the anti-democratic politics of fear embraced as the route to salvation post-9/11.[11]

MCCULLOUGH AND WRIGHT: SUBVERTING THE PANTHEON

Whereas Riordan only intermittently confuses the reader's (and Percy's) moral compass, Kelly McCullough undermines the Greek pantheon more radically in his urban fantasy *WebMage* (2006). The novel does not intersect so clearly with geo-strategic issues as the *Percy Jackson* series does, but manifests a similar politically inflected distrust for established authority figures who take the allegiance of subalterns for granted and hide their ruthlessness under a specious liberal veneer. The protagonist, Ravirn, a descendant of one of the three Fates, Lachesis, lives in a modern world in which the gods have both embraced and enhanced the possibilities of modern technology. Gods are aided by artificial intelligences (AIs)—WebTrolls or smaller WebGoblins—who perform their bidding. It is eventually revealed that these beings are fully sentient and have set up a secret network to enable them to subvert the control of the autocratic immortals. Although ostensibly the only divine beings in this world are derived from Greek myth, it is significant that their AI

---

[11] Takacs (2009: 7).

antagonists are associated with the vocabulary of a rival tradition, that of northern European folklore. When Ravirn, who eventually allies with the rebel AI, finds himself in one of their secret hideaways, he describes how he wakes up "on a rounded green hill next to a faerie circle made from crushed beer cans" (28), an appropriate location for such conspicuously unclassical magical creatures as trolls and goblins. (They could quite as easily have been named WebFauns and WebSatyrs.)

Subversion is effected from within as well as from without. The action begins when Ravirn realizes that another of the three Fates, Atropos, wants to launch a digital virus called 'Puppeteer' that will destroy man's free will. At first we imagine, as does Ravirn, that even though his great aunt Atropos has bad intentions, Clotho and Lachesis are more reasonable and humane. However, he is shocked to discover that all three Fates approve of Atropos' plan, and it is Eris, goddess of discord—whom we are first led to believe is purely evil—who proves herself an ally, albeit an edgy one.

As in Wynne Jones's *The Game*, the protagonists are battling, not forces of darkness precisely, but autocratic arrogance. Lachesis, Ravirn's grandmother, has no wish to cause mankind suffering, just to bring a little more order to their chaotic and ill-regulated lives. She is the more chilling for being sincere, for wanting to limit choices for people's own good. She denies that she wishes to turn humans into puppets, describing them as " 'Children who need a bit of firm guidance. Just as you do.' She shook her head sadly. 'If only Atropos had come to me first, I might have been able to present the thing to you in its proper light' " (*WebMage* 286).

Although the main focus is on the shortcomings of the Fates, who are Titans, when the distant Olympians themselves are invoked, it is clear they have no greater moral authority: "At times like these I wished I could put my faith in prayer. Unfortunately, I'd met Zeus. When you know a god personally, it's very hard to believe in him, especially if he's a lecherous idiot" (159). Ravirn faces a situation similar to that of Riordan's Luke Castellan: he is in the uncomfortable position of having to pick a side in a complex and imperfect world, painted in shades of gray rather than black and white. But whereas Luke ultimately sacrifices himself to enable the flawed Olympians to triumph, Ravirn makes the less conventional choice to ally with Eris against the forces of order (244):

I wasn't entirely sure where the journey would lead, but it was changing the way I looked at things in a deep and fundamental way. I was coming to believe that my grandmother didn't deserve my allegiance. It was a very painful realization, and one I would rather have done without, but change is a necessary corollary of life.

The arrogance of the Olympian establishment is also targeted in John C. Wright's *Orphans of Chaos* (2005), which, like the *Percy Jackson* series, focuses on young demigods who slowly discover their inheritance. It is predicated on a complex theogony that, yet again, brings minor scions to the forefront and pits them against more established forces. The major Olympians are in turmoil, following a revolt led by Dionysus against Zeus, and the "orphans" are Uranians, a branch of the Titans who have been taken from Tartarus as hostages to ensure the Titans' good behavior, transformed into human babies and brought up in a very strange boarding school where they are the only pupils. Miss Daw, a Siren, explains to the heroine, Amelia, that while Saturn, who deposed Uranus, was bad enough, the Olympians who replaced him in turn "were far worse than Saturn had ever been" (293). One incident on which Miss Daw particularly broods is the rape of Persephone; she is disgusted that Zeus allowed her to be married off to Hades rather than rescued (294):

What kind of punishment is it to a rapist, to have the victim of his outrages be given to him in bounds [sic] of matrimony, his victim be his, forever after? . . . Honor was satisfied, but we were not satisfied. The Sirens began to work against the Olympians. Secretly at first, and then more openly, we began to undermine their power.

There is an odd disjuncture between the Siren's concern for a rape victim and Wright's dubious sexual politics, reflected in his young narrator heroine's persistent and unchallenged haziness about issues of consent: "But I wanted him to kiss me. Worse yet, I wanted not to want it, and to have him steal a kiss from me nonetheless" (10).

MARIE PHILLIPS: GODS BEHAVING BADLY

The clash between modern and Olympian sexual mores is treated more consistently in Marie Phillips's *Gods Behaving Badly* (2008). It is not a children's book, but seems marketed for a youthful audience and shares many of the patterns and preoccupations of recent children's fantasy.

Yet again, both the power and the moral authority of the Olympians are undermined. Tonally, the novel is rather uncertain. The cover of the British edition features a scantily clad Aphrodite against a London back-drop; she clutches a mobile phone as Cupid flies above her. Although the reader will find the comedy and romance promised by the 'chick-lit' cover, there are some surprisingly dark moments in this novel. Its premise is that the Greek gods are down on their luck, their powers reduced, and they are forced to share a rather grand but decaying house in London. As one would expect, incongruity and bathos drive the novel's humor.[12] Phillips makes much of the gap between mighty characters familiar from revered ancient texts and the humdrum modern setting in which she has placed them. Artemis is a professional dog walker who wears a tracksuit, and Apollo is a low-rent TV psychic.

However, Phillips, even though she eventually provides us with a perhaps overly sweet ending, makes it difficult for the reader simply to laugh at her gods. An interesting contrast could be made with the satirical treatment of Satan in the BBC Radio 4 comedy program *Old Harry's Game* (1995–2012). Here, although Satan is presented as evil, his character is softened by a lurking warmth, an attraction to the good in others. Despite having a better reputation than Satan, Apollo in *Gods Behaving Badly* quickly alienates the reader. He tries to rape the heroine Alice—only failing because he had earlier been forced to take an oath on the Styx not to harm humans—and, when she escapes him, provokes his father Zeus to strike her down with a thunderbolt. Apollo's thoroughly vindictive attitude sounds a surprisingly sour note in a novel that seems to bill itself as a romantic comedy. Here Apollo explains his feelings to Dionysus (104):

"The most beautiful, amazing, incredible girl in the world," said Apollo.

"Right," said Dionysus.

"The fucking bitch whore," said Apollo.

"Right," said Dionysus again.

---

[12] *Gods Behaving Badly* echoes, perhaps by chance, Thorne Smith's 1931 screwball fantasy, *Night Life of the Gods*, in which statues from New York's Metropolitan Museum of Art are brought to life by magic and embrace modern life—particularly its loucher elements—with enthusiasm.

Another oddly bleak moment is this description of his joyless coupling with Aphrodite (147–149):

Apollo was fucking Aphrodite in the bathroom. Again. . . . How many times, thought Apollo? How many times had he fucked Aphrodite in this precise position in this precise bathroom? How many times would he? . . .

"I'm thinking of redecorating my bedroom," said Aphrodite.

He had forgotten she was there.

"Didn't you just redecorate it?" he said.

"No," said Aphrodite. "At least I don't think so. Maybe I did."

They both fucked on, lost in their own confusion.

Although the novel has since been given the Hollywood treatment, relocated to New York, it might more appropriately have been adapted by the master of British suburban anomie, Mike Leigh. A resentment of entrenched authority, a contempt for the careless irresponsibility of the powerful, darkens the comedy.

One possible influence on the later texts discussed in this chapter is Neil Gaiman's *American Gods* (2001). This influential novel largely omits references to classical myth, but depicts the gods from other native traditions—Norse, West African, Russian, and Egyptian, for example— as diminished and dislocated by the rise of new modern 'gods' of media, finance, and the internet. Even though Gaiman's Greek gods are displaced by, rather than aligned with, the culture of the United States, his preoccupations, as well as his distinctive blend of myth, urban fantasy, and Americana, appear to find an echo in many later works of children's fantasy. A factor that unites all these texts, to a greater or lesser degree, is the way they combine myth with modernity. This combination is not unique to classicizing fantasy. Wynne Jones's *Eight Days of Luke*, mentioned above, is an inventive updating of Norse myth, and Pratchett's and Gaiman's *Good Omens* (1990) weaves Christian eschatology together with modern popular culture to amusing effect. However, classical myth seems particularly amenable to updating. As demonstrated by many of the texts discussed above, modernization is a strong driver of comedy.

However, it can also be accompanied by darker, more political undercurrents. One explanation for the persistent presence of such undercurrents in these texts may lie in the particular character of the Greek pantheon. The Greek gods, both individually and as a group, offer an unsettling combination of contradictory traits. Even Hades is not a figure of metaphysical evil, by contrast with Satan or such modern fantasy villains as J. R. R. Tolkien's Sauron or J. K. Rowling's Lord Voldemort. Gods associated with positive qualities—wisdom (Athena) and music and healing (Apollo)—commit acts of cold and ruthless violence and murderous revenge. Yet they are not chaotic beings, or without their own kind of moral authority, and they can certainly be beautiful, creative, or indeed benign. This complex combination of opposing qualities, combined with their great power, maps onto some elements of the way the modern West, in particular the United States, has been viewed over the last few decades. Its actions are perceived by many to be destructive, its methods of warfare criticized for their cold lack of concern for collateral damage, and its policies on surveillance denounced as sinisterly Orwellian. Yet even its critics will find much to value in its democratic government, commitment to free speech, and richly creative culture. Greek gods are far from easy, obvious villains, which is why they seem to have increasingly offered writers of modern children's fantasy a vehicle for engaging with the complex moral and political questions that exercise the modern world.

9

Orestes and the Half-Blood Prince: Ghosts of Aeschylus in the *Harry Potter* Series

Brett M. Rogers

HARRY POTTER AND THE CLASSICAL QUOTATION

On the eve of July 21st, 2007, some 11 million children, geeks, and other assorted sociopaths were awaiting perhaps the most eagerly anticipated literary event of the early twenty-first century: the midnight release of *Harry Potter and the Deathly Hallows* (*DH*), the seventh and final installment in J. K. Rowling's *Harry Potter* series (1997–2007).[1] (I know this, of course, because I was right there in line.) Though the release of *Deathly Hallows* produced many surprises—including legal action over

[1] In the United States, 8.3 million copies of *Deathly Hallows* were sold within the first 24 hours; in the United Kingdom, 2.65 million. For news reports on the sales figures, see Rich (2007) and Associated Press (2007) from Fox News. Although the seeds for this essay were sown on that delightful night in July 2007, they did not take proper shape until several years later, including talks for the Classical Association of the Atlantic States meetings (New York City, fall 2012), the University of Puget Sound Honors Program (Tacoma, WA, spring 2013), and *Swords, Sorcery, Sandals and Space: The Fantastika and the Classical World* (Liverpool, U.K., summer 2013); I thank those audiences for their enthusiasm, questions, and insights. I offer my deepest gratitude to Liz Gloyn, the anonymous reviewers of this volume, and, as ever, Benjamin Eldon Stevens, from whose comments I profited greatly. All mistakes, of course, are mine and mine alone.

pre-released scans of the novel, debate about the book release's violation of Shabbat in Israel, and the actual conclusion of the narrative—one of the biggest surprises confronted readers the moment they opened the book. For *Deathly Hallows*, unlike its predecessors in the series, included an epigraph (xi) consisting of two quotations: a meditation on death from William Penn's *More Fruits of Solitude* (1702) and a choral song from Aeschylus' *Libation Bearers* (Greek title *Choephoroi* [*Cho.*], 466–478):

Oh, the torment bred in the race,
    the grinding scream of death
    and the stroke that hits the vein,
  the hemorrhage none can staunch, the grief,
the curse no man can bear.

But there is a cure in the house,
    and not outside it, no,
    not from others but from *them*,
  their bloody strife. We sing to you,
dark gods beneath the earth.

Now hear, you blissful powers underground—
  answer the call, send help.
Bless the children, give them triumph now.[2]

This ode is sung by the Chorus of Libation Bearers, slaves in the palace of the slain king Agamemnon. The Chorus here accompany Agamemnon's

---

[2] Rowling uses the translation of Fagles (1984). Here is the original Greek text (following Page [1972: 220]), which Rowling does not include:

ὦ πόνος ἐγγενής,
καὶ παράμουσος ἄτας
αἱματόεσσα πλαγά,
ἰὼ δύστον' ἄφερτα κήδη,
ἰὼ δυσκατάπαυστον ἄλγος.   470

δώμασιν ἔμμοτον
τῶνδ' ἄκος οὐκ ἀπ' ἄλλων
ἔκτοθεν, ἀλλ' ἀπ' αὐτῶν,
δι' ὠμὰν ἔριν αἱματηράν·
θεῶν ⟨τῶν⟩ κατὰ γᾶς ὅδ' ὕμνος.   475

ἀλλὰ κλύοντες, μάκαρες χθόνιοι,
τῆσδε κατευχῆς πέμπετ' ἀρωγὴν
παισὶν προφρόνως ἐπὶ νίκῃ.

daughter, Electra, who has been sent to offer libations at the tomb of Agamemnon by her mother, Clytemnestra, Agamemnon's wife and murderer. Here, beside Agamemnon's tomb, Electra has just reunited with her brother Orestes, who has been in exile for seven years and is returning to Argos with his comrade Pylades to avenge his father by killing the tyrants of Argos—namely, Clytemnestra and Aegisthus, Agamemnon's cousin. In this ode, the Chorus of Libation Bearers beseech the ghost of Agamemnon and the "blissful powers underground" (μάκαρες χθόνιοι; *Cho.* 476) to aid the young trio in these bloody acts to come.

What was not surprising for readers was Rowling's use of the Greco-Roman classics in the *Harry Potter* (*HP*) series. Rowling studied Classics at the University of Exeter, with such professors as Peter Wiseman and Richard Seaford;[3] it is even rumored that she modeled the character of Hogwarts headmaster Albus Dumbledore on Wiseman, although Wiseman has denied this claim.[4] Moreover, the *HP* novels abound with classical allusions, including Greek and Latin character names and mythical creatures—all this in addition, of course, to the pervasive use of Latin in magical spells and Hogwarts's motto, *draco dormiens nunquam titillandus* ('A sleeping dragon must never be tickled').[5] However, as Alice Mills rightly notes, "[u]ntil the start of volume 7 . . . these classical allusions could be dismissed as playful flourishes of erudition," incidental to a story whose world view is more Judeo-Christian and medieval than classical.[6] The overt quotation of *Libation Bearers* at the beginning of *DH*—and the only page of quotation in the entire seven-book series—thus raises a fundamental question: What does this ghostly apparition of Aeschylus portend? Does this quotation merely add one more spirit to Rowling's crowded séance of the classical dead? Or has Rowling

---

[3] On her study of Classics, see Rowling (1998b) and her 2008 commencement speech delivered at Harvard University. Wiseman, using the pseudonym Petrus Sapiens (2002), offers an account of what Rowling studied at Exeter. Levy (2001) discusses Rowling as a student of Seaford, and it may be subsequently inferred that Seaford is 'Dr. Y' in Rowling (1998b).

[4] For this speculation and Wiseman's refutation, see [Uncredited] (2008) from *BBC News*.

[5] Mills (2009: 243–244). On the use of ancient languages (or what sounds like them) in the *HP* series, see also Casta (2014).

[6] Mills (2009: 244). Compare the interaction of classical and medieval in C. S. Lewis's *Till We Have Faces*, as discussed by Folch (this volume).

deliberately invoked the spirit of Aeschylus in order to tell readers something important about her series as a whole?

This chapter explores the relationship(s) between the *HP* series and the dramas of Aeschylus, exploring the reading practices we use to identify and describe such relationships. I want not only to advance a particular argument about the importance of Aeschylus for the *HP* novels but also to offer readers of the novels ways of thinking about the strategies used to claim that a reception has taken place. One of the greatest challenges faced by readers of modern fantasy is figuring out how to make productive sense of an increasingly diverse pool of possible source texts and ideas. Benjamin Eldon Stevens and I have argued elsewhere that we see ourselves as living in "an advanced postmodern moment marked by recomposition of past cultural products that is omnivorous and, from a scholarly perspective, generally uncritical . . . [marked by] an advanced postmodern encyclopedism that is . . . not hierarchical but associative and, so, willfully apolitical about its cultural recompositions."[7] In this world of mashed-up mythic narratives and icons, how are we to recognize the difference between when we are merely 'seeing things' and when a classical ghost truly haunts Hogwarts (and not just Nearly Headless Nick)? And are such hauntings merely "associative" and "uncritical," or do they reveal some deeper truth? I propose that these 'ghosts' of Aeschylus offer crucial insight into the spirited debates about how exactly Rowling's series works with respect to tyranny, education, and knowledge. Consequently, I argue that the *HP* novels are best understood as fictions about knowledge, sharing with Aeschylean drama a particular concern for how young adults not only come to know and 'unlearn' society in its complexity, but also respond compassionately and effectively to violence and tyranny.

HARRY POTTER AND THE LIBATION BEARERS

Let us return to the quotation of *Libation Bearers* in the epigraph of *DH* and consider the two most extensive readings of the epigraph, those offered by Alice Mills and John Granger; these readings raise important

---

[7] Rogers and Stevens (2012: 131).

questions about our methods of reading and interpretation.[8] Mills argues that the plot of the *Oresteia* trilogy (458 BCE)—consisting of the dramas *Agamemnon, Libation Bearers,* and *Eumenides*—cannot be mapped onto the narrative of the *HP* series.[9] Focusing primarily on the theme of kin-slaughter, Mills argues that *HP*'s many instances of violence against one's own kin, if not outright kin-slaughter, are hardly Aeschylean in form or tone.[10] Although Mills suggests, somewhat weakly, that Dumbledore "is the one who most closely resembles Aeschylus' Orestes"—this on the basis of Dumbledore's lifelong anguish over his sister Ariana's death—Mills instead identifies He-Who-Must-Not-Be-Named as the most prominent kin-slayer in the series.[11] Mills suggests that "Voldemort's story is an anti-*Oresteia*" in which the Dark Lord's final attempt to murder Harry backfires and he kills himself. In contrast, Harry and his friends find "enduringly happy, fertile marriages" in the epilogue of *DH*.[12] One might argue, however, that Mills, in focusing narrowly on kin-slaughter, fails to consider other themes or structural parallels—for example, to consider whether these "enduringly happy, fertile marriages" in the epilogue evoke the processional song at the end of the *Eumenides* (*Eum.*), the play concluding the *Oresteia* trilogy, wherein the Furies-turned-Eumenides offer a paean to happiness, fertile marriage, and social stability (916–1047).

John Granger offers a rather different interpretation of the *Libation Bearers* quotation, claiming the epigraph operates on three levels, two of

---

[8] I pass over Spencer (2015), whose monograph is dedicated solely to Greek and Roman allusions in the *HP* series yet offers only a brief and somewhat superficial discussion of the quotation from *Libation Bearers* or the *Oresteia* as a whole. This may result in part from the general emphasis in scholarship on (what Spencer calls) "the detection of point-by-point parallel[s] between Orestes and Harry"; see also my discussion below.

[9] Mills (2009: 246). According to the hypothesis for *Agamemnon*, the *Oresteia* also included a satyr-drama, the lost *Proteus*; see Page (1972: 137, lines 21–23).

[10] Mills (2009: 246–252). Her examples: Barty Crouch sentences his own son to Azkaban; Sirius Black repeatedly closes the curtains on his dead mother's portrait; Bellatrix 'kills' Sirius Black (although Mills does offer some caveats about whether Bellatrix actually *kills* Black; 247–248); Ariana Dumbledore kills her own mother, who then may or may not be killed by her own kin. See also Adney and Hassel (2011: 325) on the Malfoy family and Marvolo Gaunt's murder of his own children.

[11] Mills (2009: 252). Although initially drawing comparisons between Harry and "the fate-driven Oedipus," Hopkins (2009: 67) similarly argues that the Oedipus parallel is "dislocated onto" the parricide Barty Crouch Jr.; see also Grimes (2002), Spencer (2015), and the discussion of Oedipus and Voldemort later in this chapter.

[12] Mills (2009: 254).

which I recount here.[13] First, Granger offers a "surface reading" drawing a parallel between each moment in the narratives of *Libation Bearers* and *DH*: just as the trio of adolescents (Orestes, Electra, and Pylades) stands beside Agamemnon's tomb planning to avenge the death of a parent, so the trio of adolescents (Harry, Hermione Granger, and Ron Weasley) stands beside Dumbledore's tomb planning to avenge the death of the man who was often *in loco parentis* for them, as well as Harry's biological parents.[14] Second, Granger offers a "moral reading" arguing that both Orestes and Harry must recognize the serpentine elements in themselves in order to commit to "murdering murderers" and thereby avenge a kin-murder: Orestes identifies himself as the serpent of Clytemnestra's dream that will slay her (*Cho.* 523–550); Harry, as Horcrux for the Heir of Slytherin, is linked closely to serpents and even speaks their language, Parseltongue.[15] Furthermore, Harry does not ultimately commit murder like Orestes does: Harry first lets Voldemort 'kill' him so as to destroy the part of Harry that is Horcrux; then Harry redirects the *Avada Kedavra* or 'Killing Curse' so that the now-vulnerable Tom Riddle kills himself. For Granger, this difference between Orestes the killer and Harry the proto-Auror is crucial to Rowling's focus on the purity of the soul, Christian self-sacrifice, and compassion for one's enemy.[16]

These two different interpretations of the *Libation Bearers* quotation in *DH* raise important questions about how we, in the words of Joanna Paul, "address the fundamental question of what *constitutes* a [classical] reception."[17] Here Mills and Granger take the same literary quotation,

---

[13] Granger (2008). Granger's third, "spiritual" or "anagogical" reading focuses on the interaction between the *Libation Bearers* and *More Fruits of Solitude* quotations, arguing that Rowling uses Harry to symbolize *logos* and "represent the noetic faculty of soul and its purification."

[14] Granger's comments suggest that Harry and company will avenge the death of Harry's parents, but he does not seem to include Dumbledore as a figure *in loco parentis*, as I do here, even though Dumbledore increasingly becomes a father figure for Harry throughout the series.

[15] Granger's third "spiritual" reading takes into account one other noteworthy parallel—namely, how other characters comes to recognize Orestes/Harry and the meaning of such tokens of recognition (i.e., Electra's recognition of Orestes through his footprint and lock of hair, and the recognition of Harry's scar throughout the series).

[16] The god Apollo may object to Granger's reading here of 'Orestes the killer' since Orestes is acquitted of murder by Athena and the court on the Areopagus (thanks to Apollo's defense) in *Eumenides*.

[17] Paul (2010: 138, her emphasis).

but draw rather different conclusions about the relationship established between the new text (*DH*) and the quoted source text (the *Libation Bearers* and/or the *Oresteia* as a whole). Mills attempts to establish a strong 'equivalence' between the entire *Oresteia* and *DH*;[18] she uses the *Oresteia* as a master text to decode the *HP* novels, aiming to 'map' a single theme ('kin-slaughter') from the ancient trilogy onto the modern series, to find a literal, consistent, one-to-one correspondence between characters.[19] Ultimately, Mills's narrow interest in the single term 'kin-slaughter' (as opposed to 'inter-generational strife' or 'children *qua* tyrant slayers') and her narrow focus on finding equivalences in a given character's biography (Is Dumbledore the 'equivalent' to Orestes? Is Voldemort the 'anti-Orestes'?) do not illuminate much about either the *HP* books or the *Oresteia*.

In contrast, Granger's "surface" and "moral" readings treat the epigraph as an allusion.[20] Granger does not claim that the *Libation Bearers* quotation establishes an ongoing 'equivalence,' but that its scope applies primarily to one particular moment in both narratives. Yet Granger's reading, conservative in scope as it may be, also invites consideration not just of the theme of 'kin-slaughter' but also of a much wider system of symbols and themes operating between these two texts, many of which are not explicitly referred to in the quotation itself: trios and communal action, the image of the serpent, the theme of self-sacrifice. If Rowling had not included the *Libation Bearers* quotation in the epigraph of *DH*, we still might have reached many of Granger's conclusions, although Granger would then have to argue that Rowling had 'ghosted' the *Oresteia*.[21] Granger's method thus asks not how *DH* is the *Oresteia*, but in what discrete or partial ways, by which image or sets of images,

---

[18] By 'equivalence' I follow the definition of Hardwick (2003), where the theme is "fulfilling an analogous role in source and reception but not necessarily identical in form or content" (9).

[19] My use here of the phrase 'master text' is influenced by the discussion of Winkler (1985: esp. 4–8), although the language of allusion and intertextuality for reception studies has been significantly advanced over the past three decades by such scholars as Conte (1996), Hinds (1998), Hardwick (2003), Keen (2006), Martindale and Thomas (2006), Hardwick and Stray (2008), and Marshall (2015: 19–23).

[20] Here I follow Keen (2006), who describes the function of 'allusion' thusly: "classical allusion [is] used to comment on the situation in which the characters find themselves."

[21] I also borrow this term from Keen (2006) and discuss ghosting in the next section.

Rowling 'transplants' the *Libation Bearers* into the Potterverse, and to what end.[22]

HARRY POTTER AND THE GHOST OF AESCHYLUS

I suggest that the epigraph to *DH* is not the only indication of Rowling's engagement with the *Oresteia* and the dramas of Aeschylus, but that Rowling 'ghosts' Aeschylus in (at least) one more passage from *Harry Potter and the Half-Blood Prince* (2005 [*HBP*]). This earlier Aeschylean 'ghost' has implications for our understanding of the *HP* series as a whole, at least in retrospect. I remain agnostic as to whether Rowling started out the *HP* series with Aeschylus in mind, although these Aeschlyean hauntings notably do not appear until the last two novels, where she most expressly engages with the history and tyranny of Voldemort, and thus may suggest a sharpening or revision in her thinking over the course of the series.

Before we turn to this second passage, we need first to develop further Tony Keen's model of ghosting. In an influential discussion of models for studying classical receptions in science fiction, Keen writes that:[23]

[Ghosting] covers stories where no direct influence of classical originals can be established, but where nevertheless there are strong hints of themes derived from antiquity. Once [sic] could in this category talk of the possible influence of the Jason myth upon *2001*[: *A Space Odyssey*]—both are stories in which an adventurer goes beyond the limits of the known universe in order to recover wondrous artefacts. However, this category is inherently nebulous, and such connections can be difficult to establish. Moreover, one can start to see them everywhere, especially since . . . western civilization is deeply rooted in the Classics.

In other words, ghosting describes a situation in which we have a hunch that there may be a particular source text or myth lurking in the background, but no more than a hunch. Since Keen notes the category is "inherently nebulous" and that "such connections can be difficult to

---

[22] Hardwick (2003) defines 'transplant' as 'to take a text or image into another context and allow it to develop" (10).

[23] Keen (2006). Marshall (2015: 19–23) provides a useful response to Keen.

establish," he does not offer any criteria by which we might demonstrate or even recognize that one text has ghosted another. However, if ghosting is going to be a productive tool for identifying that a classical reception has taken place, then we must develop some criteria or reproducible technique to make ghosting more than mere gut feeling.

One way we might develop some testable criteria would be to think in terms of the concept of 'syntagms.'[24] A 'syntagm' is "an ordered combination of signifiers forming a meaningful whole."[25] Scholars of linguistics tend to stress the importance of (temporal) sequence in a syntagmatic relationship (since spoken language unfolds over time); in contrast, scholars of semiotics, who are more interested in visual signs, tend to stress the assemblage of signifiers—that is, the whole picture seen at once. If we treat the different elements of a narrative—such as icons, plot points, and narrative themes—as 'signifiers,' then perhaps we might examine different ordered combinations or assemblages of signifiers as representing distinct syntagms. We need not follow linguists in laying stress on temporal sequence (plot point A, then B, then C), although attention to sequence within a given assemblage may help us distinguish one 'syntagm' or 'ghost' from another.

To use the example in the excerpt above, Keen identifies an assemblage made up of (at least) three distinct elements—an adventurer, travel beyond the limits of the known universe, and the goal of recovering wondrous artifacts—in order to suggest that *2001: A Space Odyssey* may be a ghosting of the myth of Jason and the Argonauts. Perhaps Keen is right that these three distinct elements produce an assemblage or syntagm that is shared between the Argonaut myth and *2001*, although we may consider whether these are elements really fit both texts, or whether this assemblage describes other possible sources for *2001*, such as Homer's *Odyssey* or (older still) the *Epic of Gilgamesh*.[26] Nevertheless, for the purpose of studying classical reception, I think we can use Keen's notion of ghosting productively if we revise the term to mean 'a situation in which

---

[24] Much of my discussion here is inspired by Martin (1997), who argues for the study of Homeric formulae in terms of paradigmatic and syntagmatic relationships.

[25] *Oxford English Dictionary*, s.v. syntagm 2b. I use the definition drawn from the field of semiotics.

[26] Compare the somewhat different discussion of the *Odyssey*, the Jason myth, and *2001: A Space Odyssey* in Rogers (2015: 217–222, including n. 21).

a receiving text uses a particular narrative syntagm—a particular assemblage, possibly in an ordered sequence—identifiably derived from classical antiquity."[27]

With a working definition of ghosting provisionally in hand, we may return to Aeschylus and Rowling. During their final lesson together, Dumbledore explains to Harry how a prophecy uttered by Divination professor Sybill Trelawney led Voldemort to attempt to kill Harry, and, in the process, implanted in Harry both the desire and ability to seek vengeance (*HBP* 510):

"Harry, Harry, only Voldemort made a grave error, and acted on Professor Trelawney's words! If Voldemort had never murdered your father, would he have imparted in you a furious desire for revenge? Of course not! If he had not forced your mother to die for you, would he have given you a magical protection he could not penetrate? Of course not, Harry! Don't you see? Voldemort himself created his worst enemy, just as tyrants everywhere do! Have you any idea how much tyrants fear the people they oppress? All of them realize that, one day, amongst their many victims, there is sure to be one who rises against them and strikes back! Voldemort is no different! Always he was on the lookout for the one who would challenge him. He heard the prophecy and he leapt into action, with the result that he not only handpicked the man most likely to finish him, he handed him uniquely deadly weapons!"

The speech here is unusually abstract and detailed, even for Dumbledore, telling more than showing.[28] Dumbledore connects three distinct elements—prophecy, tyranny, and action motivated by fear—and places them in a particular sequence. A prophetic utterance inspires fear in the tyrant, who in turn commits a rash action (here, murder) in order to protect his power. As a consequence of his own action, the tyrant continues, out of fear, to oppress the people he rules; subsequently, the tyrant creates the circumstances for a future opponent, an offspring of this intergenerational strife, to defeat him.

---

[27] It is important to stress, as does Marshall (2015: 20–22), a reader need not recognize that the ghosting of the ancient source is present in order to derive meaning or pleasure from the modern text.

[28] Birch (2009: 113–114) observes that, throughout the *HP* series, Dumbledore largely prefers to let Harry and his friends figure things out for themselves; as Harry observes in *Sorcerer's Stone* (1997, a.k.a. *Philosopher's Stone*), "I reckon [Dumbledore] had a pretty good idea we were going to try, and instead of stopping us, he just taught us enough to help. I don't think it was an accident he let me find out how the mirror worked" (302).

The narrative Dumbledore has sketched out here probably draws from a particular syntagm found in the *Oresteia*, from the backstory for the scene in *Libation Bearers* quoted in the epigraph of *DH*. Before she murders Agamemnon, Clytemnestra sends the young Orestes away; once she murders her husband, Clytemnestra does not recall Orestes to Argos, fearing that he will seek his inheritance and vengeance for his father's death; thus making an enemy of Orestes. Moreover, by forcing Electra to remain unmarried and thus without an heir, Clytemnestra makes a second enemy of Electra and creates a force for vengeance within the household. When a prophetic dream suggests that a snake will bite her breast, Clytemnestra 'leaps into action' by sending Electra to the tomb of Agamemnon to pour libations, thus making possible the reunion of Orestes and Electra and, ultimately, the death of the tyrants.

One might reasonably object that the syntagm I have identified may not be exclusive to the *Oresteia*. There may be a case that Rowling is ghosting portrayals of tyrants found throughout Greek drama. Interestingly, one of Rowling's professors from Exeter, Richard Seaford, is renowned in part for his research on the Greek 'stage tyrant'—that is, the figure of the tyrant as he appears in Greek drama. Seaford has identified three key characteristics of the stage tyrant: he commits impiety, he distrusts his *philoi* (Greek for 'relatives' and 'friends'), and he shows a concern with greed and money.[29] Although these characteristics are not identical to those in the syntagm we have identified in Dumbledore's speech, they complement Dumbledore's syntagm, and characteristics from Seaford's typology appear elsewhere in the *HP* novels. For example, Seaford observes that Clytemnestra abuses ritual language as she kills Agamemnon and Cassandra;[30] ritual impiety is also fundamental to Voldemort's action, in particular to his resurrection at the end of *Goblet of Fire* (2000), when he (with the aid of Wormtail) uses his father's exhumed bones and the blood of Harry Potter to regenerate his own physical body (641–643). Perhaps then Voldemort is modeled in part on the Greek stage tyrant and not merely the particular presentation of the tyrant in the *Oresteia*.[31]

[29] Seaford (2003: 96).
[30] Ibid. (99–101).
[31] Note that Dumbledore does not explicitly link ritual impiety to tyranny in his speech to Harry in *HBP*.

Yet Seaford also sets tyrants in the dramas of Aeschylus apart from those found in the later dramas of Sophocles and Euripides, usefully observing that the depiction of tyranny in the *Oresteia* is most similar to that found in another drama attributed to Aeschylus, *Prometheus Bound* (also known by the Latin title *Prometheus Vinctus* [*PV*]).[32] It is compelling that we find in *PV* the three elements articulated in Dumbledore's speech: prophecy, tyranny, and action motivated by fear. Moreover, these three elements occur in the same ordered combination of cause-and-effect as they do in the *Oresteia*: tyrant learns prophecy; tyrant exercises violence out of fear, robbing friends and committing violence against kin; tyrant indirectly undermines his own actions, although here the youthful tyrant Zeus will eventually reconcile with Prometheus and thus not be overthrown.[33] If we are not persuaded that Rowling draws upon the *Oresteia* in particular for her depiction of tyrannical fear and intergenerational strife, there is nevertheless a strong case that Rowling is ghosting a particularly Aeschylean syntagm.

HARRY POTTER AND THE EDUCATION IN TYRANNY

Thus far we have seen that Rowling's direct quotation in *DH* draws complexly on *The Libation Bearers* (for its trio of adolescents and communal action, its serpent imagery, its themes of intergenerational violence and self-sacrifice), while in *HBP*, Dumbledore propagates an Aeschylean view that prophecy motivates tyrannical action grounded in fear of the future. I want to press further the relationship between these narratives, but reframe the discussion in terms of education, school, and knowledge. I argue that Rowling draws on the ancient *Oresteia* as one of the primary 'ghosts in the machine' for the modern *HP* series because Rowling sees in Aeschylus' emphasis on certain themes—knowledge, education, and kinship—solutions to the problems of failing social institutions and tyranny.

---

[32] Seaford (2003: 99–101, 104–111). On the question of the authorship of *PV*, see (e.g.) Herington (1970), Griffith (1977), Bees (1993), and Podlecki (2005: 195–201).

[33] The resolution to *PV* is not entirely known, as we have scant few fragments of the sequel or sequels (*Prometheus Unbound* and possibly *Prometheus the Fire-Bearer*), though we do know that Prometheus will be freed by Zeus' son Herakles. For an outline of the problem of the Prometheus plays and the remaining fragments, see (e.g.) Griffith (1983: 281–305).

Broadly speaking, both the *Oresteia* and the *HP* series are educational narratives about adolescents who undergo rites of passage amid intergenerational familial violence and political discord. However, in reframing our discussion in such terms as 'education' and 'school,' we must exercise caution, since these terms mean something quite different in the *Oresteia* than in the *HP* series. In classical Athens, where the *Oresteia* was first performed in spring 458 BCE, what we recognize as 'schools' did not have the long history of an institution like Hogwarts, having only recently come into existence, and only offering education in *grammatikê* (reading and writing), *mousikê* (music, poetry, and dance), and *gymnastikê* (physical exercise).[34] The mythic world of the *Oresteia* does not acknowledge such practices, as its events take place hundreds of years earlier; however, as Anne Lebeck has observed, the notions of 'teaching' and 'learning' are nevertheless prominent throughout the trilogy.[35] Teaching and learning are tied not to such practices as the discovery of technical knowledge and knowledge acquisition but to moral action, ritual appropriateness, and political interaction.[36] Education takes place not in the school but in two other institutions: the seat of prophecy and the nascent law court. This is clear from the two gods who secure Orestes' safe passage from ephebic political exile to restored king of Argos: Apollo, who is quite literally Orestes' "teacher" (διδασκάλου; *Eum.* 279),[37] instructing Orestes on both moral/political action (matricide/tyrannicide, *Cho.* 900–902) and ritual purification (*Eum.* 64–93); and Athena, whose pronouncements establish the law court as a form of civic instruction (*Eum.* 707–708). As Yun Lee Too has observed, in the newly established Athenian law court of Eumenides, citizens literally "teach" (*didaskei*) one another.[38]

Aeschylus also offers in the *Oresteia* two ideas about the process of learning that merit additional attention: 'learning through suffering'

[34] See (e.g.) Marrou (1956), Wise (1998), and Griffith (2001).

[35] Lebeck (1971: 26). See also Zeitlin (1978, rev. 1995) on male rites of passage in the *Oresteia*.

[36] My phrasing here is influenced by Hopkins (2003), who notes the great emphasis in the *HP* series on the discovery of technical knowledge (e.g., learning how to conjure a particular spell), historical knowledge (e.g., learning one's past), and natural aptitude (e.g., learning one has a knack for Quidditch).

[37] Orestes doubly emphasizes this point for Athena when he claims that "educated in evils.... I was ordered to speak by a wise teacher" (ἐγὼ <u>διδαχθεὶς</u> ἐν κακοῖς ... φωνεῖν ἐτάχθην πρὸς σοφοῦ <u>διδασκάλου</u>; *Eum.* 276, 279).

[38] Too (2001).

(πάθει μάθος) and 'unlearning' (*metamanthanein*). Both of these principles are established in *Agamemnon* by the Chorus of Argive Elders and remain important throughout the trilogy. In the 'Hymn to Zeus' (160–183), the Chorus claim that Zeus is "he who set mortals on the road to good sense, he who has established that it is learning through suffering that holds authority" (τὸν φρονεῖν βροτοὺς ὁδώ-/σαντα, τὸν πάθει μάθος / θέντα κυρίως ἔχειν; 174–176); the Chorus later express a variation of the sentiment, asserting that "Justice weighs out learning for those who have suffered" (Δίκα δὲ τοῖς μὲν παθοῦ-/σιν μαθεῖν ἐπιρρέπει; 250–251).[39] Later, when the Chorus offer an account of the fall of Troy, they sing that "the aged citadel of Priam, unlearning the marriage hymn, groans a mass dirge loudly" (μεταμανθάνουσα δ' ὕμνον / Πριάμου πόλις γεραιὰ / πολύθρηνον μέγα που στένει; 709–711), suggesting that the process of 'unlearning'—in this case, the Trojans' changing understanding that the marriage of Helen and Paris led not to joy but to grief—is one part of the process of learning through experience or, in this case, suffering. Thus we may say that the *Oresteia* posits that learning is accompanied by experience, suffering, and, in some events, unlearning or revising one's previous understanding.

As the *HP* novels progress, Rowling's view of education draws increasingly closer to these Aeschylean perspectives on teaching and learning: emphasis falls not on the importance of passing one's O.W.L.s (Ordinary Wizarding Level examinations) but on becoming educated in moral virtue and civic action against tyranny. Harry's most significant actions often take place outside of the formal boundaries of the classroom and, after *Chamber of Secrets* (1998), further and further away from the grounds of Hogwarts, often resulting in suffering and death for Harry's friends and loved ones, including Cedric Diggory, Sirius Black, Dumbledore, Hedwig the owl, even Harry himself.[40] It is perhaps no

[39] For further discussions of the history of interpretation on *pathei mathos* and the 'Hymn to Zeus,' see Fraenkel (1950: ii.99–114), Smith (1980: ix, 21–23), Bollack (1981: ii.197–248, esp. 223–228, 245–247), and Raeburn and Thomas (2011: 86–87, 95–96). Also useful are the interpretations of Lebeck (1971: 25–26), Gagarin (1976: 139–150), and Clinton (1979).

[40] Cf. Elster (2003), who notes that, on their face, "the *Harry Potter* books depict a traditionally dichotomous view of learning: school learning, which is stodgy and bookish, and 'real [or life] learning,' which involves solving the big problems of life" (204); however, Elster sees Harry as "an active seeker after knowledge" and participant in "inquiry based learning," ultimately arguing that the series offers "a complex representation of knowledge and learning" (220). See also Birch (2009: 114–119).

coincidence that Dumbledore's theory of tyranny in *HBP* is the last formal lesson we see Harry receive, taking place just two chapters before
the chain of events resulting in the death of Dumbledore and Harry's
decision beside Dumbledore's tomb to leave Hogwarts. Harry's choice of
real-world action instead of a final year at Hogwarts suggests a broader
skepticism about the ability of any teacher, curriculum, or institutional
structure to offer the "real learning" needed to resolve the deep problems
of intergenerational familial strife and tyranny.[41] The resolution to the
HP series, consequently, does not take place within the mechanisms of a
formal institution like the Ministry of Magic with its dysfunctional court
system (as we see in both *Order of the Phoenix* [2003] and *DH*),[42] but
rather on the battle-torn grounds of Hogwarts, no longer a traditional,
structured school but now a site for the performance of civic heroism.[43]

If Rowling's faith does not lie in institutional structures or the Rule of
Law, it is instead found in networks of kinship and chosen friendship.[44]
Kinship and friendship, of course, are not without their own problems in
the world of Harry Potter. On one hand, Harry is born into a family and
circumstances beyond his control: he possesses enormous wealth and
celebrity; he is an immediate object of prophecy and a target for murder. As Farah Mendlesohn has rightly observed, the children in the *HP*
novels operate within a caste system, constrained by birth, social hierarchies, and sorting within the school.[45] On the other hand, Harry actively
chooses to construct new networks of filiation that do not always align

[41] I pass over here the generally conventional representations of teachers at Hogwarts
(with some exceptions), for which see Birch (2009: 104–114). Such skepticism towards civic
institutions is also prominent in Rowling's first novel after completing the *HP* series, *The
Casual Vacancy* (2012).

[42] Hall (2003) argues that legal concepts and the Rule of Law are weak in Rowling's wizard world, and anticipates the Ministry of Magic's inability and ultimate failure to admin-
ister justice to Voldemort. Writing between *Goblet of Fire* (2000) and *Order of the Phoenix,*
Hall rightly predicts that the Ministry will require fundamental restructuring and rebuild-
ing, although she could not have known that this would be literally true (since the Ministry
also suffers much physical damage at the end of *Order of the Phoenix*).

[43] Cf. Skulnick and Goodman (2003), who analyze the role of ritual at Hogwarts in order
to cultivate civic heroism.

[44] Cf. Ibid. (276): "the *Harry Potter* series suggests that where evil may usurp goodness,
a hero relies on his friends."

[45] Mendlesohn (2002). Concerns about the constraints of social and economic class in
the *HP* novels factor into several essays in Whited (2002), Anatol (2003) and (2009), and
Heilman (2003) and (2009).

with his pedigree. He befriends Hermione, a 'Mudblood' who defies the expectations of her low birth and embodies timocratic virtue, excelling as a student at Hogwarts. (In this respect, Hermione is similar to Aeschylus' Electra, who is treated like a slave by Clytemnestra, but actively seeks to learn from the Chorus of Libation Bearers how to act otherwise, as seen at *Cho.* 112–119.) Wealthy Harry also befriends Ron and is informally adopted into the impoverished Weasley family; eventually Harry marries Ginny Weasley, giving permanence to his filiation with the Weasleys. Harry's network of care extends not just to his fellow students in Gryffindor, but also to those in other houses, teachers, staff, students at other schools, and even non-human creatures who occupy the edges of Hogwarts. Even if kinship and friendship require reorganization, they offer in the *HP* novels the possibility for a durable plasticity where more rigid institutions have failed.[46]

Rowling's solution to the problem of intergenerational strife, failing institutions, and constraint by birth is compelling because it is strikingly conservative and Aeschylean in its focus on the household. Ximena Gallardo C. and C. Jason Smith have argued that the *HP* series involves a "quest for the domestic," ending in the epilogue with the restoration of the traditional nuclear family, although they further add that this "focus on the family [is] part of an extended community."[47] This view seems right, as long as we understand "domestic" in terms of both 'house' and 'household.' The crucial importance of the household (broadly defined) and its restitution can be observed in the *Libation Bearers* quotation in *DH*: "There is a cure *in the house* / and not outside it" (emphasis added). In the *Oresteia*, the "house"—or, rather, the poetic plural "houses" (δώμασιν; *Cho.* 471)—refers most obviously to the royal palace where Clytemnestra and Aegisthus will be murdered. However, "house" also may refer to: the trio of adolescents (Orestes, Electra, and Pylades) as members (and future members) of the House of Atreus; the aid of servants within the palace, such as the Chorus of Libation Bearers and the

---

[46] As Liz Gloyn points out to me, not all characters in the *HP* novels view the notion of 'family' as possessing such plasticity, such as the Malfoys and Tom Riddle.

[47] Gallardo C. and Smith (2009: 104–105). They conclude that, despite the normative status accorded to the household, Rowling does challenge the masculine–feminine gender dichotomy within the household itself. On home and family, see also Kornfeld and Prothro (2009).

Nurse; and the house's broader social connections in the form of *prox-enia*, the (often) hereditary practice by which a foreign host (*proxenos*) advocates for a guest with whom he shares *xenia* (the 'guest–host friend-ship'), an extension of the household across *poleis*.[48] Thus the final cure for the Argive political crisis lies not only in the communal action of the Argive youth but also in the aid of Orestes' new *proxenos*, Athena/Athens.

This Aeschylean emphasis on the "house" is also crucial to Rowling's solution to the threat of Voldemort. In *DH*, "house" refers not only to the literal "house" structure of Hogwarts in the final battle scenes but also to: our trio of adolescents (Harry, Hermione, and Ron) from Gryffindor house (who will all become legal family in the epilogue); the many other low-status individuals and servants who inhabit Hogwarts and help fight Voldemort (most notably Hagrid and Dobby the House-Elf); the presence of many of their family members at the Battle of Hogwarts; and finally, the four different "houses" of Hogwarts fighting together as one, such that Hogwarts becomes a symbol of the cumulative bonds of kinship produced through the schooling experience for the entire wizarding society.[49] Rowling suggests that our ability to discover the Aeschylean "cure in the house" is predicated on an understanding of and willingness to accept the "house" in its various possible forms: birth family, adopted family, chosen friends, classmates-as-kin, and even (for-mer) servants-as-kin.

To put this all in slightly different terms, Rowling poses a riddle in the *HP* series through the figure of Tom Riddle, asking an ethical and politi-cal question: 'What makes a man become an evil tyrant?'[50] Rowling's rid-dle bears some resemblance to Sophocles' Oedipus in *Oedipus Tyrannus* (c. 429–425 BCE), in which drama the hero Oedipus—who has solved the riddle of the Sphinx with the self-aware answer *anthrôpos* ('man' or 'humankind')—attempts to solve another mystery and learns that he does not even know himself, in the process isolating himself from the advice of others, becoming a 'stage tyrant,' destroying his family, and blinding

---

[48] This is an oversimplified distillation of the sophisticated argument of Griffith (1995).

[49] As Kornfeld and Prothro (2009: 127) point out, such cooperation among houses is first anticipated towards the end of *Goblet of Fire*, when Harry and Cedric Diggory decide to grasp the Triwizard Cup together, although this leads unwittingly to Cedric's murder by Voldemort.

[50] Cf. Grossman (2005) on the developing character of Voldemort: "*Half-Blood Prince* goes a long way, finally, to working through Rowling's take on the psychology of evil."

himself. So, too, does Tom Riddle become a tyrant, which we learn along with Harry during his Pensieve-aided lessons throughout *HBP*; Riddle's relentless pursuit of knowledge and immortality leads him to murder his family, become Voldemort, and lay the foundation for his many forms of self-destruction.[51]

However, while Voldemort may trace the arc of the Sophoclean tragic hero, Harry follows an Aeschylean course. Through Harry, we see Rowling's attempt at an answer to her riddle, suggesting that tyranny is the product of a failure in what the ancient Greeks called *philia* ('love,' 'affectionate regard,' and 'friendship'), the relationship that exists among *philoi*. Tyranny arises from the failure of parents (who could be called *philoi*) to love their child, of kin (likewise *philoi*) to protect their own, and of friends (also *philoi*) to trust one another and join together to protect the shared house.[52] (Recall that one of Seaford's characteristics for the stage tyrant is distrust of one's *philoi*.) As we follow Harry's development from 'Boy Who Lived in the Cupboard Under the Stairs' to savior of the wizarding world, we see the crucial role *philia* and Harry's *philoi* play in steering him away from becoming the next Tom Riddle or tyrant.[53] While Rowling's riddle is no doubt partly a product of her own life experience— for example, as a single mother caring for a child in the face of poverty, or as a researcher working for Amnesty International with former political prisoners who had escaped totalitarian regimes in Africa[54]—much of the framework for and solution to Rowling's riddle is strikingly Aeschylean, if not distinctively Oresteian.[55] The quotation of *Libation Bearers* in *DH*,

---

[51] Kornfeld and Prothro (2009) note that Riddle's actions result from being abandoned by his father: "Voldemort's descent into evil ... provides an object lesson in the destructive consequences of a father's (and grandfather's) broken covenant with his family" (128). This suggests that Riddle's father and Oedipus' father Laius are also analogues. Voldemort's forms of self-destruction include: dividing himself into seven Horcruxes; his near death when attempting to kill the infant Harry; and his final self-destruction in *DH* when he is killed by his own *Avada Kedavra* spell.

[52] In Grossman (2005), Rowling remarks "'That's where evil seems to flourish, in places where people didn't get good fathering.'"

[53] Cf. the observation of Grossman (2005) that "Granted, we know Harry will not succumb to anger and evil. But we never stop feeling that he could." Other readers have similarly read the *HP* novels in terms of something akin to *philia*, such as the non-profit, human rights organization the Harry Potter Alliance (http://thephalliance.org), whose rallying cry goes: "'The weapon we have is love.'"

[54] Rowling (2008) discusses both experiences.

[55] There are also crucial differences between the solutions offered by Aeschylus and Rowling. Most importantly, Rowling eschews Aeschylus' misogyny: whereas Lily Potter's

then, is not merely a playful flourish of erudition, but reveals the importance of Aeschylus as a form of knowledge that structures the *HP* series,
as both a crucial 'ghost in the machine' for the series' theory of tyranny
and part of its warm, beating heart.

HARRY POTTER AND THE FANTASTICAL KNOWLEDGE

This reading of the *HP* novels argues that Rowling draws on a number
of Aeschylean elements and syntagms that link tyranny, education, and
the household/networks of *philia*; it also enables us to better understand
the *HP* series' relationship to the larger field of modern fantasy. Here I
conclude by suggesting the *HP* novels are best understood not merely as
works of modern fantasy but more specifically as fictions about knowledge
that share with the *Oresteia* a concern for how young adults come to know
and respond to the political problem of tyranny. In other words, I suggest
that Rowling is interested in fantasy, not as the genre of the 'impossible'
or 'unreal,' but as a form of suppositional fiction, as a narrative that deliberately displaces action into an alternate wizarding world only to reflect
back upon the social and political complexities of the real world.

As Richard Mathews quips, the task of writing about fantasy is "like
grasping water."[56] And so it may be productive to start by noting that
Rowling has claimed outright in interviews that she did not initially consider the *HP* novels to be works of 'fantasy.' As Lev Grossman reported in
a 2005 *Time* magazine article coinciding with the release of *HBP*:

The most popular living fantasy writer in the world doesn't even especially
like fantasy novels. It wasn't until after *Sorcerer's Stone* [a.k.a. *Philosopher's
Stone*] was published that it even occurred to her that she had written one.
"That's the honest truth," she says. "You know, the unicorns were in there.
There was the castle, God knows. But I really had not thought that that's what

---

love for her son protects Harry in multiple direct and indirect ways, Orestes' survival is
based on the rejection (and murder) of his mother in *Libation Bearers,* and in *Eumenides*
on both Apollo's rejection of the mother as a child's blood-relation (657–666) and Athena's
deferral to the father in all things (735–740).

[56] Mathews (1997: xi). Readers interested in criticism on fantasy are perhaps best served
starting with Clute and Grant (1997), Sandner (2004), James and Mendlesohn (2012), and
the Introduction to this volume.

I was doing. And I think maybe the reason that it didn't occur to me is that I'm not a huge fan of fantasy." Rowling has never finished *The Lord of the Rings*. She hasn't even read all of C. S. Lewis' *Narnia* novels, which her books get compared to a lot. . . . And unlike Lewis, whose books are drenched in theology, Rowling refuses to view herself as a moral educator to the millions of children who read her books. "I don't think that it's at all healthy for the work for me to think in those terms. So I don't," she says. "I never think in terms of 'What am I going to teach them?' "[57]

For our purposes, Rowling's remarks merit attention in two respects. First, she resists the common notion that a novel is a fantasy simply because it includes unreal creatures or medieval settings; in her mind, unicorns and castles do not automatically denote fantasy.[58] Immediately after the publication of the *Time* article, famed fantasy writer Terry Pratchett publicly criticized Rowling by focusing on such features: "I would have thought that the wizards, witches, trolls, unicorns, hidden worlds, jumping chocolate frogs, owl mail, magic food, ghosts, broomsticks and spells would have given her a clue?"[59] Interestingly, Pratchett revised his remarks a few days later in an online newsgroup (alt.fan. harry-potter), stating "Id [sic] like to know how an author can write in a genre she doesn't like—really. I'd like to know what she thinks she *is* writing."[60] Pratchett's revised statement usefully concedes that we may need to revise our criteria in order to make sense of the *HP* series: either the novels are a different species within the genus 'fantasy,' or we are looking at the wrong traits altogether.

The *Time* interview also deserves attention for Rowling's criticism of C. S. Lewis and rejection of fantasy as a moral education for readers. Given that the series focuses so closely on Hogwarts and the schooling experience, it is somewhat surprising that Rowling does not intend the novels to be morally didactic—at least, not explicitly.[61] To what ends, then, does Rowling focus so much attention on school and education? In the previous two sections, I have argued that Rowling ghosts Aeschylean drama in order to produce a theory of tyranny. I have also suggested that while Rowling,

---

[57] Grossman (2005). See also Hopkins (2003: 33).

[58] On fantasy and 'false medievalism,' see the chapters in Part II of this volume.

[59] In a letter to *The Sunday Times*, reported in [Uncredited] (2005) for *BBC News*.

[60] Pratchett (2005).

[61] "Although," Rowling concedes, "undeniably, morals are drawn," in Grossman (2005). Rowling's approach to the moral didacticism of the *HP* series stands in some contrast to a British literature of children's school stories, such as Enid Blyton's *St. Clare's* and *Malory*

unlike Aeschylus, expresses a general skepticism towards civic institutions, she nevertheless locates in education the possibility for a strengthening of the "house" and the reorganization of one's kith and kin, in a manner similar (but by no means identical) to that in the *Oresteia*. In other words, Rowling seems interested not in being didactic but rather in making both education and knowledge themselves objects of scrutiny, in examining how the schooling experience contributes to particular ways of knowing.

This puts the series into productive dialogue with other ways of thinking about fantasy. One particularly intriguing theory of fantasy is that of Eric Rabkin, who has similarly sought to explain fantasy in terms of knowledge: "the very nature of ground rules, how we know things, on what bases we make assumptions, in short, the problem of human knowing infects Fantasies at all levels, in their settings, in their methods, in their characters, in their plots."[62] For Rabkin, the fantastic complicates human knowledge by challenging the base assumptions or 'ground rules' upon which all other knowledge has been erected, thus contradicting our ordinary perspectives.[63] In the *HP* novels, Harry and the reader are first invited to un-learn the ground rules of the Muggle world and come to know instead the wizarding world—not only its impossible creatures and settings, but also its unfamiliar Latin-based language of magic, its spells in place of techno-science, its curious snack foods, its alternate modes of transit, its differing customs, laws, and institutions. The fact that Harry and the reader at first learn these things primarily at Hogwarts—a space that gives physical form and structure to the struggles of learning new rules and acquiring knowledge—only makes the interest in knowing more obvious, if heavy-handed.

From this perspective, the *HP* series becomes more remarkable when we take into account the notion of unlearning discussed above. As the novels progress, Rowling requires her readers not only to unlearn their

---

Towers series (both of which similarly follow children through their course in school) and the *Chalet School* novels, in which the authors tend to offer heavy-handed moral lessons. I thank Liz Gloyn for this observation. We find a still starker contrast in the responses of some Christian literalists in the United States, who interpreted the novels as a form of indoctrination for young readers into magic and witchcraft, and subsequently staging book burnings and other forms of protest against the series. On the various schools of interpretation for the *HP* novels with respect to Christian theology, see Taub and Servaty-Seib (2009: 14–17), Ciaccio (2009), and Attebery (2014: 160–168).

[62] Rabkin (1976: 37).

[63] Ibid. (38). Cf. 4: "The fantastic does more than extend experience; the fantastic contradicts perspectives."

Muggle perspective, but also to unlearn and revise their initial understanding of Hogwarts and wizardry, to see their limits and shortcomings.
In discovering that, contrary to expectation, the wizarding world shares
the fundamental problems and dangers of the Muggle world, the initial
wonder we feel at the discovery and strangeness of magic is supplanted by
the even stranger and more disturbing similarity in the horrors that exist
among witches and wizards. For example, Ron's seemingly innocuous pet
rat, Scabbers, turns out to be Voldemort's adherent Peter Pettigrew, who
lives in Harry's dorm room for three years and could easily have murdered Harry in his sleep. Several of Voldemort's Horcruxes—including
the diary of Tom Riddle, the serpent Nagini, and even Harry himself—sit
in plain sight before we learn in *HBP* what a Horcrux is and its role in
Voldemort's ascendant tyranny. Put differently, we may, along with Farah
Mendlesohn, see the *HP* novels as relying first on the rhetoric of the
'intrusion fantasy' (Harry is brought to the Dursleys), then "very rapidly
transmut[ing] into almost archetypal portal fantasies, reliant on elaborate
description and continual new imaginings" (Harry goes to Hogwarts).[64]
However, as Harry progresses through school from year to year, and,
concomitantly, as Voldemort grows increasingly stronger and more violent, intruding back into the Muggle world, Harry and readers are forced
to unlearn the Otherness of the wizarding world and see it anew in political terms with which readers are all too familiar.[65] In this, Rowling's fantasy looks less and less like fantasy as the genre of the 'impossible' or the
'unreal' and more like the genre of the (barely) 'displaced.'[66]

Given this emphasis on knowledge and its revision, the *HP* novels may
also deserve consideration alongside other genres within the broader category of speculative fiction, including science fiction (SF). For example, we

---

[64] Mendlesohn (2008: 2; cf. 246–247).

[65] Elsewhere in *Rhetorics of Fantasy*, Mendlesohn (2008) describes Voldemort as "the
evil intrusion," arguing "one rhetorical function of the intruder in an otherworld fantasy,
is to render that otherworld more 'real' by virtue of its juxtaposition" (114). In the terms
used by Rabkin (1976: 4), we may say that Rowling's depiction of tyranny brings the textual
and extratextual perspectives into closer alignment so as to produce the feeling that the *HP*
novels are 'realistic.'

[66] Here I am inspired by the language of Sandner (2004: 9), although for the *HP* novels,
I resist the full force of Sandner's intent (hence my addition of the word "barely"): "The
fundamental characteristic of the fantastic is displacement; the fantastic signifier does not
point, even superficially, to any clear signified and so causes the reader to experience a lack,
a disruption, inviting (if not provoking) an interpretation."

might profitably examine the *HP* series with respect to the concept of the *'novum'*—a work's most significant conceptual difference or innovation from its present cognitive environment—as developed by the SF critic Darko Suvin. Suvin has observed that "much valid SF uses the plot structure of the 'education novel', with its initially naive protagonist who by degrees arrives at some understanding of the novum for her/himself and for the readers."[67] Suvin's framework encourages looking at the *HP* series as a seven-part 'education novel' or *Bildungsroman* with an initially naïve protagonist (Harry) who by degrees arrives at some understanding. Less obvious, however, is what exactly Harry comes to understand: at first we may be distracted by Harry's interactions with a secondary or misleading novum—a magic spell or centaur that does not belong to our own material and metaphysical reality—but it turns out that the most crucial novum for Harry is the nature of Voldemort's tyranny and the importance of utilizing networks of *philia* to overcome such tyranny. Thanks to Dumbledore's final lesson, it is this innovation in Harry's cognitive environment—this knowledge—that makes possible Harry's ability to recognize himself as the "handpicked ... man most likely to finish [Voldemort]" (*HBP* 510) and maneuver into the situation in which Voldemort destroys himself in *DH*. As I hope to have shown, it is in this conceptual framework that Rowling displays her greatest debt to Aeschylus.

In suggesting that we may profitably read the *HP* novels in terms of knowledge and knowing, I am of course bucking one of the most fundamental tenets in discussions of modern fantasy, one that has been part of how critics have discussed fantasy since 1712, when Joseph Addison first discussed "the fairy way of writing"—namely, that fantasy is a genre based on the fundamental cognitive principle of not knowledge but imagination.[68] Rowling herself has stressed the importance of imagination for the *HP* series:

Imagination is not only the uniquely human capacity to envision that which is not, and therefore the fount of all invention and innovation. . . . Unlike any other creature on this planet, humans can learn and understand, without having experienced. They can think themselves into other people's places.

---

[67] Suvin (1979: 79).

[68] Addison in Sandner (2004: 21–23). On 'imagination' as a key term in early fantasy criticism, see Wolfe (2012).

Of course, this is a power, like my brand of fictional magic, that is morally neutral. One might use such an ability to manipulate, or control, just as much as to understand or sympathise. And many prefer not to exercise their imaginations at all. They choose to remain comfortably within the bounds of their own experience, never troubling to wonder how it would feel to have been born other than they are. They can refuse to hear screams or to peer inside cages; they can close their minds and hearts to any suffering that does not touch them personally; they can refuse to know. We do not need magic to change the world, we carry all the power we need inside ourselves already: we have the power to imagine better.[69]

While Rowling's notion of 'imagination' here is by no means identical to 'knowledge,' the two are closely linked through the other conceptual terms we have explored in *HP*'s reception of Aeschylus' *Oresteia*: tyranny, education (*pathei mathos*), *philia*. Imagination, Rowling suggests, is the human ability to "learn and understand," to learn through the "suffering" of others, a kind of sympathetic knowing. In the wrong hands, imagination can become a tool "to manipulate or control," even exercise tyranny, while others may not exercise their imagination, "close their minds and hearts," and simply "refuse to know." Imagination is, in other words, not only our "brand of fictional magic" but also a kind of knowing, a cognitive process by which we educate ourselves emotionally and learn better responses, perhaps even more loving responses, to ourselves and others. Thus Rowling not only reveals in the *HP* series a deep understanding of the conceptual terms Aeschylus uses in the *Oresteia*, but she innovates upon Aeschylean thought by making explicit the crucial role imagination plays in education, in producing knowledge, and in resisting tyrannies of the mind and body. One cannot help but wonder if Rowling, when she reads the epigraph to *DH*, hears the prayer "Now hear, you blissful powers underground—answer the call, send help," as a hymn calling not for *pathei mathos*, learning through suffering, but for *phantasiai mathos* (φαντασίᾳ μάθος): learning through imagination/fantasy.

---

[69] Rowling (2008).

10

Filthy Harpies and Fictive Knowledge in Philip Pullman's *His Dark Materials* Trilogy

Antonia Syson

"Liar! Liar! Liar!"

And it sounded as if her voice were coming from everywhere, and the word echoed back from the great wall in the fog, muffled and changed, so that she seemed to be screaming Lyra's name, so that *Lyra* and *Liar* were one and the same thing.

—The Amber Spyglass

Lyra, the heroine of Philip Pullman's *His Dark Materials* (*HDM*)—published in three parts in 1995, 1997, and 2000, though structured as a single triple-decker novel—is honored for her inventive eloquence with the name "Silvertongue."[1] But eventually Lyra faces a violent attack on her

---

[1] The armored bear Iorek Byrnison substitutes 'Silvertongue' for Lyra's family name, Belacqua (*Northern Lights* 348). For valuable advice on drafts of this chapter, I am grateful to Melissa Mueller and my writing group at Purdue (Kathy Abrahamson, Katie Brownell, Cara Kinnally, and Stephanie Zywicki), as well as the editors of this volume.

identity as a storyteller. She has been passing off the clichés of adventurous romance as her own real experience, but now she is jolted out of her habit of beguiling trickery. At this point, Lyra, her friend and traveling companion Will (the bearer of the 'subtle knife,' who entered the trilogy in its second volume), and we as readers are asked to sift "lies and fantasies" (*The Amber Spyglass* 317) from real memories and from the visionary reach of imagination as "a form of seeing" (494).

The attack on Lyra's identity therefore takes on programmatic force. In this crisis, *HDM* invites readers to distinguish the imaginative knowledge it offers from "fantasies" and to question their own expectations of 'fantasy' as a genre. Many elements of the three novels are familiar from fantasy earlier in the twentieth century: travel between multiple worlds, tools endowed with supernatural force, witches, talking animals, and so on. But in *HDM*, these overtly unreal elements do not mark out a fictional world (or series of worlds) detached from readers' own reality. Instead, the trilogy insistently uses fantasy's capacity for imaginative travel as a means to restate the value of material, bodily existence in the here and now.[2]

The assault on Lyra's identity occurs during a Virgilian journey to visit the dead, which heightens anxieties surrounding the work of lies and fantasies in the trilogy.[3] Accounts of the world of death are overtly fictive. These accounts have a special place in the classical epic tradition precisely because they invite readers to contemplate what kind of truths may be offered by tales of an unknowable sphere of existence—or non-existence. Moreover, Lyra's attacker is the leader of the harpies; these monsters are demonic underworld deities from Greek and Roman myth who drip filth and embody cosmological pollution. The authority Pullman grants the filth-ridden harpies seems at odds with the main thrust of the trilogy,

---

[2] Pullman's version of what Oziewicz and Hade call 'fantastic realism' has received an unusual amount of attention, partly because it operates at a cosmological level; his personal interviews present his vision as vehemently opposed to what he sees as the specifically Christian form of escapism in C. S. Lewis's *Narnia* books, above all. But in other ways, Pullman's insistence on truthfulness in fantasy is far from unique. For example, many of Diana Wynne Jones's novels explore this theme: in *Fire and Hemlock*, the central character reflects that "there were ways of thought that were quite unreal, and the same ways went on being unreal even in hero business" (281).

[3] For Virgilian underworlds in another modern fantasy work, Tolkien's *The Hobbit*, see Stevens (this volume).

which is to challenge the force of discourses that associate embodied knowledge with corruption, dirt, and decay.

The first section of this chapter explores the role of the harpies in framing the kind of knowledge offered by the three novels that make up *HDM: Northern Lights* (a.k.a. *The Golden Compass* [*NL*]), *The Subtle Knife* (*SK*), and *The Amber Spyglass* (*AS*). Part two of this chapter addresses the problems posed by the harpies for the novels' commitment to upending traditional discourses that visualize embodied, material knowledge as a form of defilement. On one level, it is relatively straightforward to understand the harpies' pivotal role as a means for *HDM* to challenge traditional views of what counts as 'dirty'. But a difficulty emerges from Pullman's almost collage-like assembly of earlier literary materials in the service of a progressive program that seeks to question the fundamental polarities and hierarchies assumed by—and sometimes upheld through—those literary traditions. The narrative does not so much eliminate as invert existing discourses of dirt. So the trilogy reinvigorates these discourses even in the process of challenging them.

"LIAR! LIAR! LIAR!"

Journeys into death are transgressive and potentially contaminating. They cross the boundaries of readers' and authors' knowledge, venturing into a space that *must* be imaginary and yet at the same time is all too real—we know we will meet death one day. In many cultures—including the Greco-Roman tradition evoked by figures such as the harpies—the dirt of death emblematizes the kind of ritual or cosmological pollution famously summarized by Mary Douglas as "matter out of place."[4] So, when living heroes visit the dead in the story worlds of classical epic, they not only expose themselves to unimaginable forms of dirt. These heroes also risk still more cosmological defilement due to the anomalous position they take up, 'out of place' in the most absolute sense. These problems of defilement prompt a need for crucial assistance, for example, of the sort Virgil's Cumaean Sibyl provides for Aeneas in his descent

---

[4] Douglas (1966/2002: 44). The most richly nuanced study of ancient Greek *miasma* ('defilement', 'pollution') remains Parker (1983), while Lennon (2013) draws attention to Roman ritual pollution.

into the underworld in *Aeneid* (*Aen.*) book 6. The Sibyl, as priestess and prophet, paves the ritual way for Aeneas' boundary-crossing and informs Aeneas about the Tartarean regions of death. He may see much of the underworld for himself, but the defilement of Tartarus is so extreme that it is impermissible for the pure to enter (*nulli fas casto . . . insistere*; 6.563).

In Pullman's vision, the world of the dead has been established by the "Authority" as a "prison camp" (*AS* 33), which needs guards. Though this image reflects peculiarly modern systems of oppression, the guards here are thoroughly classical. Their leader is "a great bird the size of a vulture, with the face and breasts of a woman" (289). She is a harpy, as Will recognizes, since "he had seen pictures of creatures like her" (289). She harasses Lyra and Will with mocking scorn for their living presence in her realm, and after a brief attempt to fight back fails, Lyra instead comes to an agreement with her. "We could tell you where we've been, and maybe you'd be interested, I don't know" (292). If she tells her story, Lyra suggests, perhaps she and Will can pass through the door to the dead, to find the ghost they are looking for. The harpy invites her to try. At this decisive moment, Lyra makes a mistake. She pulls out a retelling of the kind of romance that has duped listeners many times on her travels: "*Parents dead; family treasure; shipwreck; escape. . .*" (292). The harpy, "No-Name," attacks and re-attacks with screams and claws: "*Liar! Liar! Liar!*"

The harpies' identity as embodiments of dirt is deeply bound up in their commitment to truthful stories and real memories. The harpies themselves deal in the memories that the dead bring with them; these defiled and defiling creatures twist memories into filth. Long ago, No-Name eventually explains, they were granted the power to see the worst in every one. "We have fed on the worst ever since, till our blood is rank with it" (*AS* 316). In the *Aeneid*, the Harpies' dirt is the only filth to give off a stench that makes it explicitly into the narrative (3.228).[5] Pullman's narrative also emphasizes the force of that stench, but the harpies' dirt-filled utterances are woven into the power they wield through smell, sight, and touch. Sometimes they go in for painfully expressive sounds rather

---

[5] Modern editions of classical texts usually capitalize names like 'Harpies' and 'Furies' to distinguish such animate beings from (lowercase) abstractions (e.g., *Harpyiae* in Latin). I follow this convention to make it easier for readers to see when I am referring to Pullman's (lowercase) harpies and when to classical (capitalized) Harpies.

than words. The first harpy answers Lyra's question "Who are you?" with a scream, a "jet of noise," which turns into "wild, mocking peals of laughter" that evoke "the merciless cruelty of children in a playground" (*AS* 290).

Despite these guards, Lyra and Will do reach the dead. Her friend Roger, now a ghost, explains how the harpies work on the imprisoned dead (*AS* 308):

"and them bird-things.... You know what they do? They wait till you're resting—you can't never sleep properly, you just sort of doze—and they come up quiet beside you and they whisper all the bad things you ever did when you was alive, so you can't forget 'em. They know all the worst things about you ... they shame you up and they make you feel sick with yourself."

The Amber Spyglass transfers to the specific physical form of the harpies the capacity for memory, knowledge, and anonymous communication that Virgil grants to the rumor-goddess Fama. The *Aeneid* personifies talk as a "filthy goddess" (*dea foeda*; 4.195) who defiles human mouths, thus sharing many of the sickening characteristics of Pullman's "bird-things." Yet the goddess Fama also monstrously embodies the discursive mode of *fama* ('fame' or 'tradition' as well as 'rumor' and 'gossip') constituted by the epic narrative. In Virgil, Fama is equipped with feathers, tongues, mouths, and ears in precisely equal yet unimaginable proportions (4.181–183), both to transmit and to twist the truth.[6] Fama flies screeching through the night, sets up as guard in daytime, and sows terror (184–188). Thus Pullman's harpies evoke Virgil's Fama but wield still more power over mortal knowledge, as they probe individual consciences.

The fact that the harpies base their cruelty on some kind of truth provides a pivot for the transformation of their role that occurs when they become guides instead of guards. The ghost children clamor "for Lyra to tell them about the things they remembered, the sun and the wind and the sky, and the things they'd forgotten, such as how to play" (*AS* 313). Lyra begins by telling them stories that readers recognize from the first

[6] Will would have been hard put to recognize Fama from an artistic tradition. As Hardie (2009: 95) points out, the very precision with which Fama's balanced proportions of feathers, tongues, eyes, and ears are described contributes to the difficulty of fully visualizing her.

volume of the trilogy. Next the narrative dwells more on visible, sniffable, tangible, audible sights, scents, textures, and unformed sounds that the living experience through their "flesh and skin and nerves and senses" (315), as well as through their minds. She expresses "how it felt to squish your fingers into the cracks and slowly lever up a dried plate of mud." She describes the "smoke from the kilns, the rotten-leaf-mold smell of the river when the wind was in the southwest, the warm smell of the baking potatoes the clayburners used to eat" (314–315). The senses merge; we smell the warmth of the baking potatoes. When the emphasis shifts to sounds, the prose becomes onomatopoeic. Lyra tells of "the sound of the water slipping slickly over the sluices and into the washing pits; and the slow, thick suck as you tried to pull your foot out of the ground; and the heavy, wet slap of the gate paddles in the clay-thick water" (315). The harpies join the children in listening to all this, attentive and still.

The harpies' acknowledgement of what truthful storytelling can do leads into a grand bargain that completely changes their identity. In return for hearing true stories from the lives of those who have recently died, the harpies are to guide the ghosts toward the new opening that Will's subtle knife will make to release them where they can merge with the world. The ghosts will follow their daemons, which "en't just *nothing* now" as Lyra tells the dead. After consulting the alethiometer (the 'truth-meter,' which allows access to depths of information that would normally be out of reach), Lyra explains: "All the atoms that were them, they've gone into the air and the wind and the trees and the earth and all the living things. They'll never vanish. They're just part of everything. And that's exactly what'll happen to you. . . . You'll drift apart, it's true, but you'll be out in the open, part of everything alive again." The ghosts' silent response to Lyra's account indicates the high value set by the trilogy on the truthful reach of imagination: "Those who had seen how daemons dissolved were remembering it, and those who hadn't were imagining it" (*AS* 319).

Lyra's account of how the atoms of the dead will "drift apart" and become "part of everything alive again" (*AS* 319) evokes Lucretius' *De Rerum Natura* (*On the Nature of Things*), the great Roman hexameter poem that communicates the materialist philosophy of Epicurean atomism. This is an important predecessor to *HDM*, not only because its materialist perspective and vocabulary is so influential in the scientific traditions evoked by Pullman, but also in the fundamental rhetorical structure of its didacticism. *De Rerum Natura* sets out to free mortals of fear, much as in Pullman's modern prose epic Lyra sets out to crush the notion that a move from ignorance to experience is something sinful, fearful, and defiling. Lucretius' poem does this in part by convincing readers that no human identity survives after bodily disintegration in death.

Pullman's modern fantasy shows striking overlap with the implied rhetorical claims underpinning the imaginative expansiveness of classical epic–and raises as well the same questions arising from such claims. What kinds of experience may be categorized as 'knowledge'? Do imaginative experiences count? Always? Sometimes? Partly to avoid pre-emptive answers that would shut down these questions, I would categorize the communications of both classical epic and modern novels under the term 'fictive knowledge.' This term acknowledges that fictive communications may permeate consciousness so deeply that they join the category of things that readers know.[7] But they are nonetheless irreducibly fictive. They enter our reality and may merge with readers' previous perceptions of reality through allegory and through recognizable elements of history, science, or the more tangible familiarity of "the slow, thick suck" of mud pulling on your foot (*AS* 315). Yet the ingredients of fictions remain meaningful in their own terms; they do not rely on being recognizable as fact for their entire communicative efficacy.

Fictive knowledge is not specific to fantasy but can be conveyed by any kind of fiction. However, the key distinguishing characteristics of nineteenth- and twentieth-century English-language fantasy closely link that genre with overtly myth-making genres in the classical tradition. Fantasy, as the name implies, is one of the genres that most explicitly acknowledges the potential force of the imagination. This may be heightened by specific programmatic discussions, as we see in *The Amber Spyglass*, but it is most uniformly achieved simply by bending everyday beliefs (that are conventional in modern Western societies) about what is

---

[7] By contrast, some critics have adopted 'fictive knowledge' to denote the content of fiction as opposed to the content of works of history: for instance using the term prescriptively to keep 'fictive' knowledge safely contained in fictional worlds that are separate from our reality. For further discussion, see Syson (2013). Attebery (2014: 29) analyzes George MacDonald's emphasis on "the irreducibility of fantastic symbols"; as Attebery puts it, "[f]antasy, like myth, is meaningful, but the significance cannot be translated into other terms than its own."

possible. Unlike science fiction, fantasy's strategies for bending such beliefs about possibility usually evoke traditional magic, myth, or ritual.[8] *HDM* rarely alludes to Greek and Roman traditions, however (except via *Paradise Lost*).[9] So it is striking that texts from the classical canon make their presence felt most strongly when *The Amber Spyglass* confronts most directly what it means to exist and not exist: to be dead or alive, to be true or a lie.

After the chief harpy's initial attack, Lyra and Will reappraise Lyra's romancing and seem to share the harpy's condemnation of her earlier stories as mere lies. When Lyra tells Will that she can no longer lie, despairing that "it's all I can do, and it doesn't work!" Will points out: "It's *not* all you can do. You can read the alethiometer, can't you?" (*AS* 294). He contrasts Lyra's facile inventions with her intuitive, quasi-prophetic ability to grasp the meanings projected by the allusively telegraphic combinations of symbols on the device that measures truth. The contrast Will draws is surprising, given that, in the first novel of the trilogy, we learn that Lyra's artistry as a liar closely resembles the feeling of mastery she obtains from reading the alethiometer, a "sense of complexity and control" (*NL* 282). But by the end of the trilogy, the angel Xaphania has defined imagination as "a form of seeing" rather than "pretending" or "making things up" (*AS* 494). This "seeing," the angel suggests, may allow travel between worlds even when the children give up using the subtle knife and the openings made by it because of the resultant pollution.

William Gray notes that the opposition here is "between fantasy (in a negative sense) and the imaginative intuition of reality."[10] Yet the role of imagination envisaged by Xaphania is not a window through which to perceive a restrictive 'reality' limited to everyday life. Its potential to bridge worlds suggests that this kind of vision can range widely, as long as it does so with specificity, precision, and care for the worlds observed.

Gray and others have suggested that Pullman's personal interviews have at times expressed (in a less violent form) a hostility to 'fantasy'

---

[8] For Attebery (2014), it is important that myths (when part of a still living tradition) are sacred narrative (12), while fantasy "speaks with no cultural authority" (21). However, as he acknowledges, the ritual status of myth-making narratives is often unstable (22), even when the traditions they participate in and shape are still dominant in a culture.

[9] In the chapter epigraphs of *The Amber Spyglass*, John Milton and William Blake far outnumber any other named author; the only text that dominates still more is the King James Bible.

[10] Gray (2009: 157).

almost as vehement as the harpies' hatred of 'fantasies,' though Pullman's hostility in no way diminishes his commitment to imaginative storytelling.[11] Pullman invites us, in a sense, to see the novels of *HDM* as having more in common with the historical adventures of Sally Lockhart (the main character of the progressive political novels that first made his name as a children's writer) than with *The Lord of the Rings* or the *Narnia* books.[12] Pullman has described some critics as chiding him for writing fantasy: "everyone knows that there are no such things as elves or hobbits, so nothing interesting or truthful can be said about them."[13] He admits in this *New York Times* "Opinion" piece that his previous standard response ("to deny that I'm writing fantasy at all, and to maintain that all my work is stark realism") is inadequate, because it merely reinforces the notion that "realism is the highest form of literary art." Instead, let imagination reign, if it will, but "[r]eason, memory, emotional experience, whatever we know of social and political truth . . . all these things must come into play."

The Amber Spyglass emphasizes play as one the tangible experiences that the ghost-children are forgetting—the experiences that entice the harpies into listening to Lyra's spellbinding stories. This emphasis confirms that Pullman's novel is not opposing fiction and truth, or even fiction and lies. The opposition is between fictions that expand knowledge via the imagination and fictions that distort or neutralize experience.

"GRACIOUS WINGS"

Distortions of experience may occur through pervasive discourses, as well as in particular fictional creations. *HDM* explores a fear that the transition to adulthood may corrupt childhood innocence. The novels combat with equal vehemence the unobservant fantasy that children are innocent and the oppressive belief that adulthood (in its increased

---

[11] Ibid. (152–157). See also, e.g., Cox (2011: 3–4).

[12] Pullman's resistance to the forms of Christian ideology underpinning the *Narnia* books has perhaps been exaggerated (partly by Pullman himself, and partly by critics) into the claim of a complete separation from the strand of fantasy so dominated by Tolkien and Lewis; as Oziewicz and Hade (2010) show, such a claim would be unconvincing.

[13] Pullman (2003).

knowledge and mature sexuality) could in any sense defile human beings. Pullman challenges a particular loathing of female sexuality, a loathing seen in many cultures, which in some strands of Judeo-Christian traditions exemplifies a dread of all embodied knowledge as somehow contaminating. As part of this head-on confrontation, the novels celebrate materiality. So the biblical dust of Genesis 3:19 ("For dust thou art, and unto dust shalt thou return") becomes Dust, a mysterious entity needed for the ecological stability of all the possible worlds in the universe.

Although it is barely perceptible, Dust marks in material form the growth of understanding. "Dust," we are told near the start of *The Amber Spyglass*, "is only a name for what happens when matter begins to understand itself" (31). Much later, we hear that Dust "came into being when living things became conscious of themselves" (*AS* 451). Human maturity, which extremists in Lyra's world regard as a kind of disease, is visible because of another kind of material embodiment. The wisest and most reflective part of a person's consciousness is embodied in the form of a 'daemon' (a word with a Latinate spelling whose pronunciation as 'demon' Pullman himself has clarified in interviews and journalism).[14] Children's daemons are flexibly metamorphic; they take many different animal shapes to suit the state of awareness a person is in at any given moment. Adult daemons, however, remain fixed with one identity, and at this point more Dust gathers around them.

Northern Lights links this with the doctrine of Original Sin, famously rewriting the opening chapters of Genesis to explain the church's view of what it means to be human in Lyra's world (372):

And when the woman saw that the tree was good for food, and that it was pleasant to the eyes, and a tree to be desired to reveal the true form of one's daemon, she took of the fruit thereof, and did eat, and gave also unto her husband with her; and he did eat.

[. . .]

But when the man and the woman knew their own daemons, they knew that a great change had come upon them, for until that moment it had seemed that they were at one with all the creatures of the earth and the air, and there was no difference between them:

---

[14] The harpies' transformation from demonic monsters into kindly guides parallels Pullman's reassertion of the classical heritage of the 'daemon' (or Greek *daimon*); instead of

And they saw the difference, and they knew good and evil; and they were ashamed, and they sewed fig leaves together to cover their nakedness.

After reading this 'Genesis' to her, Lyra's father explains that the discovery of Dust by the experimental theologian Rusakov provided at last "a physical proof that something happened when innocence changed into experience" (373).

But the extremist wing of the church in Lyra's world is obsessed with purging and cleaning, even if that means destroying what is purified. For these extremists, Dust is something that "infects" adults because they have lost their innocence (*NL* 284). Seeing maturity as a state of infection, they have developed horrific technology that severs children from their daemons before this fixed identity can develop. Readers comprehend the fictive reality of this particular strange evil—an evil that could only occur in Lyra's world—through practices familiar from past and current oppression in our own world. The extremists use methods that are recognizable from Nazi death-camps, female circumcision, the use of the guillotine for mass-murder, and the slaughter of 'heretics' during the Counter-Reformation. A euphemistically softened account explains this 'intercision' as a way of protecting children from "something evil and wicked," that is, Dust: "Grown-ups and their daemons are infected with Dust so deeply that it's too late for them" (*NL* 284). The plot's turning point at the end of *Northern Lights* comes when Lyra realizes that she should not yield to the pervasive belief that Dust is bad; she and her daemon, Pantalaimon, will search for it in the hope of— what? Well, "when we've found it we'll know what to do" (398). After Lyra escapes the danger of intercision in *Northern Lights*, her hope of challenging the pervasively negative view of Dust drives much of the storyline of the second and third novels. And when, eventually, Lyra and Will intentionally touch one another's daemons (*AS* 498–499), the moment of contact does far more than merely standing in for a kind of erotic consummation more familiar to readers from our own world. It is crucial that this meeting of minds is also, in some sense, a meeting of bodies.[15] The novels' concern is with emphatically embodied consciousness: matter, in many forms.

---

being a medieval Christian agent of the devil, Pullman's daemon/demon becomes a quasi-Socratic guide and embodiment of spirit.

   [15] The daemons' animal-forms also achieve crucial rhetorical effects for readers. We are asked to imagine beings that are part of ourselves but separate; they are certainly *not* pets. But the narrative helps us along the imaginative path by sketching the relationship between

So it is logical enough to understand the complexity of the harpies'
role as another way for Pullman's trilogy to question what role Dust and
dirt may play in perceptions of human knowledge. When the harpies
are still operating as guards instead of Sibyl-like guardians, the chief
harpy's identity resides entirely and only in various forms of filth; she is
called No-Name. Pullman's harpies are more birds than goddesses, but
they are akin to at least three kinds of defiling divinities in Greek and
Roman literature: not only Virgil's Harpies and Fama but also the Furies
(Greek *Erinyes*). As we saw previously, *The Amber Spyglass* invites readers to recognize the harpies' place in a mythical tradition. Will consciously names the first of the vulture-sized bird-women a 'harpy.' (Of
the many possible worlds in the story universe of *HDM,* which differ
according to the contingencies realized in each, Will's is closest to our
own reality and shares the iconography of Greco-Roman myth.) This
moment of recognition echoes a scene in Aeschylus' *Oresteia* trilogy.
As the last of the three tragedies opens, Apollo's priestess, flounder-
ing through a series of attempts to convey the unimaginable horror
of the sleeping Furies in the Delphic shrine, compares them to the
Harpies, whom she once saw in a picture carrying off Phineus' dinner
(*Eumenides* 50–51).

Aeschylus' Furies give shape to the most nauseating forms of ritual,
ethical, and cosmological pollution. In *Agamemnon* (the first play of
the *Oresteia*), the Argives visualize the curse on the house of Atreus in
terms of the Furies, figures that instantiate the defilement caused in the
previous generation, when Agamemnon's father paid out his brother
Thyestes by feeding him his own children. At the end of the second play,
Libation Bearers, Orestes sees the Furies as they begin to hound him with
madness—they are now signs of his blood-guilt, and seen only by him.
Eventually their fully materialized horror becomes visible on stage in the
Eumenides as they resist Apollo, who argues that he has purified Orestes
of guilt. Like the *Eumenides*, Pullman's narrative asks us to imagine smelling the "putrescent stink" (*AS* 290) of death that emanates from the chief
harpy and the "hideous smells of corruption and decay" (292) that bring
the travelers close to fainting.

---

human and daemon partly in terms that many child and adult readers will recognize from
the cats, dogs, rodents, and birds they have lived with, and from wild animals they have
watched.

Throughout the *Aeneid*, with its allusions to complex Greek and Roman literary traditions and through its internal web of verbal associations, Virgil provides chthonic deities with shifting identities that render Harpies close kin to Furies.[16] John Milton follows Virgil's lead in this blending: "harpy-footed furies" (*Paradise Lost* 2.596) take the damned back and forth between burning and frozen torments. The oozing filth and stench that mark out Aeschylus' Furies as embodiments of pollution belong firmly to the Harpies in the *Aeneid*. Apollonius of Rhodes' *Argonautica* provides a midpoint between Aeschylus' Harpy-like Erinyes and Virgil's Harpies and other "dread goddesses" (Dirae); this epic tells how Jason and the Argonauts end the story of Phineus (punished for indiscreet prophecies by having his food stolen and befouled by the stinking Harpies) by driving off the defilers, though even on their departure "an unendurable stench is left behind" (2.272). In the *Aeneid*, though the Harpies are briefly mentioned in the underworld journey of book 6, they play their most prominent role in book 3. Aeneas is the narrator here, and he picks up where Apollonius had left off, explaining that the Harpies had moved to the Strophades after being driven in fear from Phineus' home and their earlier tables. Aeneas describes them in gruesome detail as the foulest imaginable embodiments of the gods' wrath (3.215). Angry that the Trojans are feasting on their unguarded cattle, the Harpies fly down on the attack, and release the foul stench that Apollonius had emphasized, as well as a terrible sound: "then there was a terrible utterance amidst the foul stench" (*tum vox taetrum dira inter odorem*; 3.228). Aeneas says that the crowd of Harpies polluted the Trojans' feast with their mouths (*polluit ore dapes*; 3.234), but does not specify whether this pollution consists of sound or some more tangible filth. One Harpy, Celaeno, is briefly singled out. Her oral dirt takes the form of a prophecy predicting a strange meal (table-munching!) due to precede the Trojans' fated Italian settlement, a prediction that Aeneas later refers to as "disgusting hunger" (*obscenam . . . famem*; 3.367).

The Amber Spyglass makes the most of a traditional misogynistic horror of female bodies and their sexual capacities in visualizing No-Name. She wears decaying body fluids as a kind of makeup. Instead of being

---

[16] See Syson (2013: 94–96) for further discussion and bibliography on the partly overlapping identities of Dirae, Erinyes, Eumenides, Furiae, and Harpyiae.

made up with eyeliner and mascara, her eye sockets are "clotted with filthy slime." Her mouth is bedaubed with a grotesque equivalent of lipstick: "the redness of her lips was caked and crusted as if she had vomited ancient blood again and again" (*AS* 290). On being threatened with opposition, "[t]he harpy's sickening red mouth moved again, but this time it was to purse her lips into a mock kiss" (290).

It eventually becomes clear that this grotesquely parodic eroticism reflects the role of the harpies as incarnations of the Authority's perverse insistence on seeing human life as something essentially filthy (*AS* 316). The misogyny evoked by Pullman is implicit to varying degrees in ancient representations of Harpies and Furies and is ubiquitous and unmistakable in Greek and Roman literature more generally.[17] Virgil describes the Harpy-birds' faces as virginal (*virginei*; *Aen.* 3.216), while the face of Pullman's No-Name is "smooth and unwrinkled," though aged by the cruelty and misery experienced over thousands of years (*AS* 289–290). William Blake, in "Europe: A Prophecy" provides in the imperatives of the "distant heavens" a crucial model for Pullman's satire of Judeo-Christian and Greco-Roman misogyny (vv. 94–98):

Go! Tell the human race that Woman's love is sin,
That an eternal life awaits the worms of sixty winters   95
In an allegorical abode where existence hath never come.
Forbid all joy, and from her childhood shall the little female
Spread nets in every secret path.[18]

The harpy's regurgitation of ancient blood also recalls Aeschylus' Furies. This regurgitation is a physical manifestation of the dredging up of wrongs, to prevent any recovery from past evils, just as the *Oresteia*'s

---

[17] One of the most ambiguous kinds of dirt emitted by the Virgilian Harpies is the "utterly foul discharge from their bellies" (*foedissima ventris / proluvies*; *Aen.* 3.216–217). Felton (2013) shows that for Roman readers this discharge could denote diarrhea or menstrual blood.

[18] Burton Hatlen (2005: 82) emphasizes how Pullman has chastised C. S. Lewis for his denial of salvation to Susan in *The Last Battle*; as Lewis writes, "She's interested in nothing nowadays except nylons and lipstick and invitations. She always was a jolly sight too keen on being grown-up" (quoted in ibid.). Hatlen quotes Pullman's *Guardian* essay, "The Dark Side of Narnia" (October 1, 1998), in which Pullman observes "Susan, like Cinderella, is undergoing a transition from one phase of her life to another. Lewis didn't approve of that."

Furies try to prevent Orestes from expiating his blood-guilt after he has killed his mother.

Yet even before the grand bargain turning guards into guides comes fully into effect, the narrative begins to glide over the filth-oozing horror that had previously defined these "bird-things." No-Name rescues Lyra from a nearly disastrous fall, and Lyra thanks her by "kissing and kissing" the harpy's face. That face is now merely "ravaged" (*AS* 361), instead of "repulsive" in its smooth and unwrinkled bitterness and caked gore, as it was five chapters earlier. It is left up to readers to choose whether or not to remember that the "same claws" that enclose Lyra's wrist to bring her to safety (360) were poisonously dirty when they gashed her scalp as punishment for her "lies and fantasies" (293).

To make disgusting figures of material disorder into keepers of ethical and cosmological order is not a new thing. It is still less new to change their role and shift attention away from their bodily filth—that is exactly what Aeschylus' *Oresteia* does with the Furies. The dealings with the "bird-things" in *The Amber Spyglass* echo the negotiations between Athena and the Furies when their honor is restored at the end of the *Oresteia*. Aeschylus' Furies are allotted new tasks that include keeping order in Athens; they are needed because of the horror and fear they have inspired as embodiments of criminal pollution. Pullman's harpies, too, are offered the chance to give up "seeing only the wickedness and cruelty and greed of the ghosts" in favor of hearing "the truth about what they've seen and touched and heard and loved and known in the world" (*AS* 317). They agree to this only when they receive "a duty and a task to do, one that will bring us the respect we deserve!" (318).

CONCLUSION

Pullman's trilogy rearticulates traditional discourses of dirt even while challenging them. On one hand, the powerful brutality of the harpies' dirt remains in play as a source of prescriptive authority governing what kinds of storytelling are in some sense 'clean' or 'dirty.' As so often in mythical accounts of embodied defilement, the harpies make heightened disorder manifest so as to impose order. Their new job includes the right to refuse help to ghosts who have not brought some truth-filled memories with them from life. The criteria remain much the same as in the original attack on Lyra. On the other hand, readers are invited to imagine that the previously "rank" blood of the harpies will now be sweetened by the variety of memories that the dead will share with their strange guides. In that sense, any more fundamental dissolution of a binary opposition that hierarchically sets purity against and over dirt is limited. Yes, Dust is praised as a positive force, and the joys of embodied experience are fêted. But the narrative avoids going further; it does not unequivocally present the newly named 'Gracious Wings' as still stinking with filth even after she has shown her gracious beneficence. Even the tremendous changes that occur in this section of the trilogy do not destroy a basic polarity opposing punitive dirt to kindly purity.[19]

Yet while the harpies' filth disappears from the narrative, they are not physically cleaned up. When the "bird-things" alter their ways and begin to derive their power from human knowledge, contained in human stories, instead of from the Authority, their shift from prison guards to guardian-guides appears to be entirely verbal, even within the story world of *The Amber Spyglass*. We are no longer actively invited to continue smelling the harpies' old stench. But we are not directed to imagine a full-scale metamorphosis into some purified form. The resulting tension between the reassertion and redefinition of 'clean' and 'dirty' categories gives readers freedom in our choices about how far to align material experience with evaluative principles.

This freedom emerges also in the way Pullman's novels simultaneously disavow and revel in the fantastic elements of the fictive knowledge they offer. The trilogy is fascinated by the potential for speaking truth as the alethiometer speaks truth, transformed through metaphor and symbol.

---

[19] Butler (2012: 232) comes to a similar conclusion regarding Pullman's depiction of puberty as "*the* life-defining event": "Having overturned the Christian-Romantic model of human development, however, Pullman surprisingly preserves its structure intact." However, Butler risks exaggerating the continued pull of that model's ideology when she argues that "the conclusion of his story is still in thrall to a moral and aesthetic vision that defines satisfying artistic closure in terms of self-sacrifice and self-denial—exemplified in . . . Will's and Lyra's decision to part forever." The novel does not celebrate sacrifice for its own sake. The purposeful, materialist logic of that final parting denies special privileges that absolve singular individuals from ecological constraints—why should Lyra and Will allow themselves a route that would damage the universe by its continued existence? At the same time, the reasons for Lyra and Will's separation re-emphasize the centrality of a specific worldly existence, in contrast not only with a monarchical kingdom of heaven but even with the republic of heaven that Lord Asriel has envisaged.

But Lyra's intuitive understanding of the alethiometer (though that intuition deserts her) and the emphatic materiality of the harpies (though the narrative ceases to dwell on this materiality) resist any attempt to impose narrow allegories that would limit the imaginative scope of the narrative. Despite the ways No-Name and, later, the angel Xaphania privilege visions of reality over 'fantasies' and 'pretending,' readers are not encouraged to decode and remold the fantastic into something acceptably 'real.' We are each asked to return, ultimately, to our own material here and now. Nevertheless, the here and now that closes the trilogy is Lyra's, not ours. The novels defy interpretations that would limit the scope of the trilogy's imaginative journeys into possible worlds.

11

Girls in Bears' Clothing in Greek Myth
and Disney/Pixar's *Brave*

Elizabeth A. Manwell

The animated film *Brave* (2012) tells the story of a young girl, Merida, on the brink of womanhood. Her mother, the queen, wishes to marry her to the son of one of the three clans who owe fealty to the royal family, but Merida rebels. Such a film—not the typical Disney princess fare to begin with—relates a story not of romance and marriage but of the stage before that, focusing on a young woman's identity formation, the choices attendant upon her at the brink of womanhood, and the problem of negotiating this territory with her mother in tow. Yet, in addition to being a coming-of-age tale, *Brave* is set squarely in the genre of fantasy. Set in a fantastic version of tenth-century Scotland, the world of *Brave* is inhabited by impossible and unworldly elements: a witch, will-o'-the-wisps, and—most significantly—the transformation of humans into bears.[1]

---

[1] Fantasy is notoriously difficult to define. David Sandner (2004: 9) offers a model of the fantastic as a genre that is "radically unstable," where the fantastic elements displace, unsettle, and overwhelm, causing "the reader to experience a lack, a disruption, inviting (if not provoking) an interpretation." Rosemary Jackson (1981: 4, 14) notes that modern fantasy relies on earlier genres such as "myth, mysticism, folklore, fairy tale and romance" and is subversive, in that it disrupts the "'rules' of artistic representation." Farah Mendlesohn's

The bear has been a figure of fascination for Indo-European and Near Eastern cultures since time immemorial, including among northern European societies.[2] Yet the most significant mythic resonances here appear to be Greek, where myths such as that of Callisto and the worship of Artemis Brauronia detail the journey of girls to women in story, metaphor, and ritual practice that liken them to bears. This chapter examines some of the similarities in bear imagery between Greek culture and the animated film. I focus first on how *Brave's* use of transformation into a bear appears more naturalized than other Disney 'marvels' and how this is accomplished; and second on how the use of bears in Merida's coming-of-age tale might offer us insight into the interpretation of bears in Greek myth and ritual.

TO BEAR AND BACK AGAIN

While Disney's princesses have been subject to cultural change no less than the rest of us, some constants tend to be present.[3] From Snow White to the Rapunzel of *Tangled* (2010), the princess is pursued by a malevolent force that must be overcome, often with the aid of a male hero who is himself usually of royal lineage; the tale typically ends with the reunion of the princess and her male assistant.[4] Much scholarship on Disney princess films has focused on how these figures promote or are complicit

---

(2008) categories of fantasy may be useful in thinking about the breadth of fantasy (and in attempts to create a typology), where portal-quest, immersion, intrusion, and liminality describe the fantastic in relation to the plot. See also Attebery (2014) on the interrelation of fantasy and myth.

[2] 'Indo-European' refers to a family of related languages, which scholars posit derive from a single prehistorical language and culture that altered as populations separated and migrated; see Mallory and Adams (1997). Pastoureau (2011) details the history of the bear in Europe, beginning in the Paleolithic Age.

[3] In discussing Disney princesses, I examine those most commonly referred to in scholarship and also included in Disney's gallery of princesses: Ariel, Rapunzel, Tiana, Belle, Merida, Cinderella, Pocahontas, Aurora, Mulan, Snow White, and Jasmine (found at http://princess.disney.com/; accessed November 24, 2013); see Pugh and Aronstein (2012). More recent are the films *Maleficent* (2014) and *Frozen* (2013), which, like *Brave*, focus on female-female relationships. Yet, while these tales spend significant time discussing the growth and development of their female protagonists in girlhood, nonetheless all—Maleficent, Aurora, Elsa, and Anna—are represented as adult and marriageable figures.

[4] Henke, Umble, and Smith (1996) and Bradford (2012: 173).

with a patriarchal system that supports heteronormative sexuality. Non-white princesses carry an additional cultural burden, which many critics have seen as conflicted at best, as films such as *Aladdin, Mulan,* and *Pocahontas* both offer representations of the non-European cultures from which they hail and yet denigrate them as backward.[5] Yet all of these female figures—whether singing "Someday My Prince Will Come" or working explicitly for the right to choose her own mate—view the goal as marriage, in which princess and prince live happily ever after.

Conversely, Merida is figured much more like a hero, although not one that is intentionally gender-bending. Merida is female in both her sex (i.e., biologically female) and her gender (i.e., she performs acts that are socially and culturally coded as feminine).[6] While she also engages in stereotypically masculine, heroic behavior—she rides a warhorse, is expert with bow and arrow, climbs sheer cliffs, drinks from a sacred waterfall, and correctly interprets a riddle—this heroic activity does not threaten the social order because she is not yet nubile. Her physical representation (e.g., shorter in stature than both her parents, with small breasts and more plastic features) marks her as occupying an intermediate stage between girlhood and adulthood.[7] While she prefers male-coded activities such as horseback riding to the female-coded tasks her mother attempts to impose upon her (such as elocution lessons), the divide thus appears not only as one of gender but also as one of age. At the film's beginning, for example, upon returning from her climb to the Fire Falls, Merida rushes into dinner, slyly slips muffins to her younger brothers, and breathlessly recounts her adventures to her family, as her tangled hair falls in her face. While her activity might be marked as masculine, her demeanor is like that of her young brothers. The dynamics at table pit Merida's mother, Elinor, against her children and her husband, King Fergus, who piles his plate as high as his daughter's, deems it fit that his daughter should learn to fight, and welcomes the castle dogs onto his lap in mid-meal. Elinor's exasperation with husband and children alike highlights the contrast

---

[5] Bradford (2012) and Mitchell-Smith (2012).

[6] On the distinction between biological sex and gender representation (or 'performance'), see Butler (1990).

[7] Merida's physique is notably younger than her peers' among Disney princesses. Controversy erupted in the spring of 2013 when Disney, about to induct her into the gallery of princesses, performed a makeover, rendering her older and sexier. Backlash against the 'new' Merida caused Disney to restore the 'old' Merida; see (e.g.) Morrison (2013).

between her attempts to act as a civilizing force and her family's untamed nature.[8] In the process, one can see an initial moment where behavior is coded to set the context in which Merida operates: boring/civilized/feminine is set against a nexus of fun/uncivilized/masculine.

All Disney princesses undergo a transformation in their tales, though, as noted above, in most this is a transition from unmarried girl to bride.[9] Merida's evolution is thus distinct, since the story culminates in her successful negotiation of a new relationship, but with her mother rather than with a potential spouse. In addition, while, like that of most other Disney heroines, Merida's transformation is assisted by magical processes, those are benign or ambivalent (e.g., wisps and the witch). This fantastic milieu draws upon those elements that Rosemary Jackson has noted underpin fantasy in general: the possibility of magical transformation, the fairy-tale-like setting, the mythic elements of quest and adventure.[10] Moreover, magic alone is not what makes the setting fantastic; rather, the Disney princess movies operate according to a logic of their own, where the stories they tell and the depth of knowledge they offer is possible only under metaphysical conditions that are different from the real world and realistically impossible.[11] The unboundedness and openness of fantasy, to be filled with a 'reality' that is coherent within the world of the story, reflects what J. R. R. Tolkien calls the tension between 'dyscatastrophe' and 'eucatastrophe' in fairy tales—that is, between the evil unexpected turn and the fortunate, which produces not only energy but, more important, wonder.[12] Wonderment on the part of both the audience and the characters themselves activates their investment in the transformation at the heart of Merida's story.

---

[8] The natural similarity of Merida, her brothers, and her father is likewise coded physically, in that they all have unruly red hair, unlike Elinor, who has a straight, kempt brown bun.

[9] There are two notable exceptions. Pocahontas, while involved in a love triangle, does not ultimately marry, but chooses to stay in Virginia while her beloved returns to England. In *The Princess and the Frog* (2009), Tiana desires to possess her own restaurant, a goal that is achieved by the movie's end. See Bradford (2012) and especially Mitchell-Smith (2012).

[10] Jackson (1981).

[11] Sandner (2004: 1–13) offers a helpful way of thinking about fantasy in this way. For Sandner "the fundamental characteristic of the fantastic is displacement," requiring the reader to juxtapose the metaphysical requirements of the fantastic alongside her own reality.

[12] Tolkien sets the fairy tale up as 'otherworld,' where the reader does not deny the world beyond the fairy tale but acknowledges it as separate and qualitatively different (1984: 153); cf. Sandner (2004: 5).

This kind of fantasy setting, reliant on a vaguely medieval context and on folkloric or mythic themes, is consonant with other Disney films in which unreal transformations occur and in which the fantastic elements are crucial not for plot alone but also for that sense of wonderment inherent to the greater message of the tale. Other princesses' transformations are frequently spurred by fantastical creatures or phenomena: e.g., Snow White lives among dwarves, eats an enchanted apple, and is revived by a kiss; Cinderella has not only a fairy godmother, but also a crew of talking mice who assist her; and *The Little Mermaid*'s Ariel is granted a chance to become human by her merman father. Merida's development, however, is facilitated by entities that are only quasi-magical or whose magic is downplayed—the wisps (a supernatural rendering of a biological phenomenon) and the witch (a hag, who represents herself as an artisan). Moreover, the transformation and its solution are entirely in Merida's control. She has requested a way to make her mother stop controlling her, and it is only by solving the riddle that Merida saves her mother and restores order, requiring the exertion of her wit and skill alone. She is agent of Elinor's metamorphosis as well as her counter-metamorphosis. Thus the fantastic elements here are subordinated, so that Merida's journey reads more like that of an Odysseus or an Oedipus, a voyage of self-discovery located, like those heroes' journeys, in a fantastic context.

Merida's mother, Queen Elinor, once transformed into a bear, struggles to retain her humanity. The moments when she forgets her role as a human mother or embraces her bear-ness literalize the wildness that Merida feels within herself. Merida's desires—to remain unwed, to spend time outdoors, to ride, to practice archery—are not wholly uncivilized pursuits. More constraining are the expectations of a girl on the brink of womanhood. Marriage plays a large role, but these constraints are symbolized in other ways: the snood that ill-keeps her wild red curls from view; and her mother's admonitions that she sit still, sit up straight, speak clearly, and not leave her bow on the dining room table. Yet, once transformed, Queen Elinor shows how quickly one might revert to one's wild nature and the danger of giving free rein to it. Elinor serves as a mirror for Merida, reflecting both what Merida should ultimately become—namely, an educated, self-disciplined, and authoritative queen—and (in bear form) Merida's inner nature.

Initially, Elinor is embarrassed by her nakedness, tries to wear her crown, and attempts to set a table. She has to be taught by Merida to act like a bear; for example, to fish in a stream with her mouth. Yet, once used to it, she quickly assimilates, delighting in her ursine behavior and temporarily forgetting that she is human and a human mother—much to Merida's surprise and horror. As Merida and her mother search for a way to reverse the spell, Elinor experiences more moments when she becomes, in her daughter's words, "a bear on the inside." Although she saves her daughter from an encounter with the fierce bear Mor'du, she turns on Merida thereafter: when they attempt to re-enter the castle; later in the tapestry room while attempting to mend the tear; and finally, in the stone circle just before her counter-metamorphosis. Indeed, the challenges of returning to the castle nearly thwart Elinor-as-bear, causing her to consider giving herself over wholly to her bear nature; it is Merida who asserts that she is as stubborn as her mother and refuses to give up on the hope of Elinor's restoration to her mortal form. The film culminates in a hunt—the castle denizens, including Fergus, pursue Elinor to a stone circle (à la Stonehenge), thinking she is Mor'du. Merida arrives in the nick of time, having mended the tapestry, but must first intervene to keep her father from killing Elinor. At this moment the real Mor'du appears and threatens Merida, and only Elinor in bear form can defeat him. Yet, even as Merida covers her mother with the tapestry and professes her grief and her guilt, Elinor still appears on the brink of becoming fully bear, until Merida, telling her mother she loves her, enables Elinor's transformation back into a queen. The struggles in this film over the acculturation of humans to societal values—over the breakdown in the system and its eventual restoration—ultimately reinscribe the limits of societal value: after all, Elinor and the triplets are human once more, and Merida has learned the value of her mother and the life Elinor strives to secure for her family and nation. Yet there remains a sense that the borders are slightly more permeable or flexible than first thought, where femininity is refashioned as brave and strong, where some moments are deemed appropriate for females to fight, and where female autonomy is validated.

In the end, Merida restores her mother to humanity by solving the witch's riddle, which requires her to stitch together a tapestry (on which Elinor has woven a family portrait) that Merida rent in anger. Though this seemingly signifies a return to civilization, Merida completes the sewing while on horseback, riding into the woods with her bear-cub brothers. Far from an acceptance of her need, now, to embrace the world of the adult female, Merida's unconventional needlework points to a blending of conventional female behavior and innate wildness. Likewise, when Merida covers Elinor with the tapestry, there is a moment when she believes that she has made an error and the transfiguration will be permanent. Though Elinor is returned to her earlier form, she remains naked beneath the tapestry, signaling both her rebirth and an acknowledgement of her natural state (though it makes both mother and daughter blush). Moreover, the newly gained sympathy between mother and daughter suggests that each now perceives the value in the other's nature—and indeed shares it.

While the story resides within the genre of fantasy, its fantastic elements are downplayed: there are, for example, no talking animals, and very limited kinds of fantastic creatures that offer only a modicum of help.[13] The wisps are given no anthropomorphic shape or voice, and while we are meant to see them as spirits that guide Merida, on the occasions when they fail to appear, Merida must—and does—find a path for herself.[14] The witch's status is likewise ambiguous. Unlike the evil entities in *Snow White and the Seven Dwarves* (1937) or *Sleeping Beauty* (1959), *Brave*'s witch is benign. While she does concoct the cake that brings about transformation, she balks at the designation 'witch' and instead portrays herself as a woodcarver and shopkeeper. The supernatural elements in *Brave* are therefore limited both in number and in their fantastic representation. Most of the interpretation and the quasi-magical resolution must be achieved by human agency.

Brave thus offers the Disney princess story with a twist. Drawing upon traditional themes that have been staples of Disney fare—the princess thwarted in her ambitions by a mother-figure must face a life-threatening situation in order to achieve her heart's desire—*Brave* alters the calculus by making the mother–daughter relationship the crisis, and the happy ending a reunion between the two. Though set in a fantastic world inhabited by supernatural elements, *Brave* is remarkable in its reliance upon the women of the tale—especially Merida—to bring about a positive outcome, through use of intellect, skills (that are coded both masculine and feminine), and courage.

---

[13] On the use of a nebulous and indistinct medieval ecology in Disney princess films, see Coyne-Kelly (2012).

[14] One possible exception occurs at the end of the film, where the spirit of Mor'du, freed from his bearish countenance, becomes a wisp himself.

'BRAVE' GREEK GIRLS?

Many cultures tell fantastic bear tales. Michel Pastoureau identifies three common kinds of mythic stories about bears: tales of magical transformation of humans into bears; episodes where human infants are taken in, protected, and nourished by benevolent mother bears; and stories of women abducted by male bears, with whom they have intercourse and by whom they are often impregnated.[15] These kinds of tales figure in ancient Greek myth and legend as well, and in addition give rise to rituals in which girls and bears figure prominently. There is no explicit connection between the Greek tales of girls and bears and the story that features in *Brave*; whereas both screenwriters for *Brave* have mentioned in interviews the influence of Scotland, including tales they heard there and their own Scottish heritage, neither has suggested that they drew upon Greek (or other) bear myths.[16] Yet the resonances between these two sets of tales are provocative. In this section I set the tale of Merida alongside ancient Greek tales and rituals that link girlhood and bearhood, not because one is influenced by the other but rather because I think that Merida's tale may offer us a new lens through which to examine a perplexing set of ancient stories and experiences.

Even if *Brave*'s screenwriters aver that they had no model for their story, the prominence of bear tales worldwide—especially in European prehistory and history—might suggest that there would be many stories we could use to think with Merida's story. Although nearly every culture incorporates bears into their mythology or folklore, most such stories are distinct from Greek tales in a few important ways. If we revisit Pastoureau's categories, while some tales are of bears that steal and impregnate women, the emphasis tends to be on the woman's subsequent offspring, 'were-bears.'[17] Likewise, a handful of stories feature a mother bear who nurses a human or otherwise acts as a mother.[18] Most tales and

---

[15] Pastoureau (2011: 28).

[16] The storyline for *Brave* was created by Brenda Chapman and modified by Mark Andrews.

[17] For example, the French folktale of Jean de l'Ours, who is the offspring of a young woman and a bear; the Haida tribe of North America has a similar tale. See Pastoureau (2011: 24) and Kroeber (1998: 95–109).

[18] Various cultures focus on the bear mother. We can see this in European prehistory, where we find a carving of a mother bear holding a cub in her arms as one would hold an infant; see Gimbutas (1982: 194). Likewise, the Korean Ungyo is a bear that becomes the

rituals, however, center on the transformation of humans into bears (and perhaps back again), but these tales almost exclusively feature men.[19] This is not to say that worldwide there are no other tales about bears that involve young girls and their transformative experience. Yet it is striking that Greek myths and rituals about bears tend to focus on women and girls, especially the journey from girl to woman, in a way that appears to be unique. Thus the affiliation between *Brave* and Greek myth and ritual, though not intentional, may offer fruitful comparisons.

First, we should separate out myth from ritual. The mythic stories told about bears are not voluminous—as compared with, say, those about bulls—but they occur with regularity, and the bears in the tales frequently evidence human-like qualities, consonant with representations of bears in ancient scientific texts.[20] Many bear myths involve Artemis, whose role as goddess of the hunt, protector of the young, and patroness of nubile women makes her a logical participant in such tales.[21] The most notable transfiguration involves Callisto, a devotée of Artemis, who, like the goddess, had vowed to lead a chaste life. Callisto finds herself the object of Zeus' desire, is raped by him, and impregnated. Though Callisto attempts to hide her pregnancy, Artemis comes upon her while bathing, discovers her treachery, and transforms her into a bear. Callisto dies when shot

---

wife of the divine king and gives birth to a son, Tangun, who founds Korea; see Lee and de Bary (1997: 4–6).

[19] Examples here are numerous. Most obvious might be: Scandinavian *berserkers* ('bear-shirts'), who adopt bear-like behavior in battle; the Russian fairy tale "Ivanko the Bear's Son," in which a were-bear tries to become part of the human community; the Cherokee tale of the young hunter adopted by a bear, who becomes a bearman; and the Scottish fairy tale "Brown Bear of Norway," in which a girl marries a prince who is turned into a bear, and only her love (and some fantastic adventures) can restore him to his human form. See Kroeber (1998: 115–117), Eliade (1995: 81–84), Afanas'ev (1945: 221–223), and Kennedy (1891: 52–60). Pastoureau details how the bear is viewed by many cultures as a king of the animals, and thus is revered by men as a totem or incorporated into rituals for proving mettle. He observes that, for example, while numerous bear artifacts and representations appear in northern European graves of men, none appear in those of women (2011: 34–59).

[20] For example, Aristotle *Historia Animalium* 7.17, Plutarch *Moralia* 494, and Pliny *Natural History* 8.126.

[21] Albert Schachter (1990: 49–50) observes that Artemis' duty was to nurture animal and human young and "bring them to terms with their own destinies by seeing them through the crises in their lives"; as such, she is a "goddess of margins." On the vulnerability of women undergoing rituals, see Cole (1998: 28–29), Herodotus (Hdt.) *Histories* 6.138, and Pausanias (Paus.) 4.4.2 with Goff (2004: 109–110).

either by Artemis or, years later, by her son Arcas, who, while hunting, happens upon his mother. Zeus then places her in the sky as Ursa Major.[22]

Likewise, Iphigenia is offered as a sacrifice at Aulis by her father Agamemnon, in order to appease Artemis, who was holding back the winds and preventing the Greek army from sailing to Troy. Agamemnon lures his daughter to her death by sending word that he has prepared a wedding for her to the hero Achilles, and begging her to come before they depart. In some versions, at the moment of sacrifice, Iphigenia is transformed into an animal, or an animal takes her place—a deer, heifer, or she-bear. In those versions where an animal is substituted, Iphigenia is spirited away to a remote temple to serve as a priestess of Artemis.[23]

Tales such as those of Callisto and Iphigenia share commonalities with Merida's. These are all girls on the cusp of marriage, yet no union occurs. Both Merida and Callisto are skilled with the bow and show no desire to marry. In the cases of Callisto and Iphigenia, Artemis acts as a merciless force, showing no compassion for the young women, who, through no fault of their own, find themselves the objects of her wrath. Artemis' world operates under immutable prescriptions. The metamorphoses of Callisto and Iphigenia into bears (or a like creature) metaphorically capture a duality in their natures. As unmarried creatures, they are wild, fierce things, as yet ungoverned by society's strictures for young women. Yet each metamorphosis presages the more symbolic transformation girls of this age typically endure, as they transition to a new (i.e., married) state and will soon witness the alteration of their forms through pregnancy and lactation.

Elsewhere the motif of the ursine form signaling the potentiality of the female body manifests itself in stories of foundlings adopted and nursed by bears. The two most notable of these tales, about Paris and Atalanta, are marriage plots. Paris—known for his judgement of a divine beauty pageant, his abduction of Helen, and the subsequent Trojan War—was, as an infant, exposed by his family to die, nurtured by a bear, and then raised by shepherds.[24] Pastoureau suggests something of his "ursine

---

[22] Hesiod *Astronomia* 3, Ovid *Metamorphoses* (*Met.*) 2.405–531, Paus. 8.3.6, and Apollodorus (Apollod.) *Bibliotheca* (*Bibl.*) 3.8.2. In some versions, Arcas is also transformed into a bear and is set in the sky as Ursa Minor.

[23] Hdt. 4.103, Euripides *Iphigenia at Aulis* and *Iphigenia Among the Taurians*, Apollod. *Epitome* 3.22, Dictys Cretensis 1.19, and Tzetzes *On Lycophron* 183.

[24] Apollod. *Bibl.* 3.12.5.

nature" remains, and that at the root of the story of Paris and Helen may lie the first example of Beauty and the Beast.[25]

Atalanta's story more clearly ties to that of Callisto and Iphigenia. Not only is she nursed by a bear after being abandoned as an infant, but Atalanta also hails from Arcadia ('Bearland,' named for Callisto's son, Arcas). A follower of Artemis, she refuses to marry anyone who cannot beat her in a footrace. Those who fail are executed. One youth, Hippomenes, however, distracts her attention by throwing three golden apples in the course of the race; Atalanta chases after them, fails to overtake Hippomenes, and so must marry him.[26] Both Atalanta and Paris find themselves in contests that lead ultimately to marriage. An echo of the marriage contest is found in Merida's tale as well. Irritated that she will have to marry one of the scions of the three clans, she chooses an archery contest as the method by which her hand will be won, and then bests all three of the suitors—to her mother's dismay and the three clans' outrage. Like Merida, Atalanta strategically selects a marriage contest that favors her own skill set, offering her a measure of control over the selection of a potential mate. Yet, unlike in the Greek myths, both Merida and her suitors elect to remain unmarried a while longer, to linger in adolescence. Whereas Atalanta makes a clear transition from wild girl to wife (unlike Callisto and Iphigenia), Merida instead chooses to remain liminal, untamed but, unlike devotées of Artemis, not eschewing marriage completely. Her attitude is instead "not now."

In addition to the mythic stories, bears also appear in a significant way in at least one festival, the Arkteia, a celebration in honor of Artemis. It was centered at Brauron, in Attica, at a sanctuary to Artemis.[27] According to ancient sources, as compiled in the Byzantine encyclopedia the *Suda*, the ritual found its basis in myth (s.v. Ἄρκτος ἢ Βραυρωνίοις):

Women playing the bear used to celebrate a festival for Artemis dressed in saffron robes, not older than ten years nor less than five, appeasing the goddess. The reason was that a wild bear used to come to the deme of Phlauidoi and spend time there; and it became tamed and was brought up with the

---

[25] Pastoureau (2011: 31–32).

[26] Ovid *Met.* 10.560–637, Apollod. *Bibl.* 3.9.2.

[27] The Arkteia may have also been celebrated at other sanctuaries to Artemis. There is evidence for a similar festival at Mounichia; see Goff (2004: 105) and Golden (1990: 78).

humans. Some virgin was playing with it and, when the girl began acting recklessly, the bear was provoked and scratched the virgin; her brothers were angered by this and speared the bear, and because of this a pestilential sickness fell upon the Athenians. When the Athenians consulted the oracle, [the god] said that there would be a release from the evils if, as blood price for the bear that died, they compelled their virgins to play the bear. And the Athenians decreed that no virgin might be given in marriage to a man if she had not previously played the bear for the goddess.[28]

Thus young girls must serve the goddess by 'playing the bear' in order to propitiate her.[29] Beyond this, we know little about the ritual, though this has not stopped—perhaps has even encouraged—debate about the components of the festival.[30]

There were two festivals associated with the temple of Artemis at Brauron, the Brauronia and the Arkteia. Many believe the two to have occurred simultaneously, though there is no definitive proof for this, and in some ways the evidence seems to argue against it. It appears that prepubescent girls were called upon to become *arktoi*, 'bears,' and to engage in parades, dances, and a variety of contests (including footraces and spinning). Much of this is conjecture, based in part upon vase paintings, which in no way specify their subject. Scholars argue for participants anywhere from the ages of five to fourteen. Some believe that all

[28] ἀρκτευόμεναι γυναῖκες τῇ Ἀρτέμιδι ἑορτὴν ἐτέλουν, κροκωτὸν ἠμφιεσμέναι, οὔτε πρεσβύτιδες ι ἐτῶν, οὔτε ἐλάττους ε, ἀπομειλισσόμεναι τὴν θεόν· ἐπειδὴ ἄρκτος ἀγρία ἐπιφοιτῶσα διέτριβεν ἐν τῷ δήμῳ Φλαυιδῶν· καὶ ἡμερωθεῖσαν αὐτὴν τοῖς ἀνθρώποις σύντροφον γενέσθαι. παρθένον δέ τινα προσπαίζειν αὐτῇ καὶ ἀσελγαινούσης τῆς παιδίσκης παροξυνθῆναι τὴν ἄρκτον καὶ καταξέσαι τῆς παρθένου· ἐφ' ᾧ ὀργισθέντας τοὺς ἀδελφοὺς αὐτῆς κατακοντίσαι τὴν ἄρκτον, καὶ διὰ τοῦτο λοιμώδη νόσον τοῖς Ἀθηναίοις ἐμπεσεῖν. χρηστηριαζομένοις δὲ τοῖς Ἀθηναίοις εἶπε λύσιν τῶν κακῶν ἔσεσθαι, εἰ τῆς τελευτησάσης ἄρκτου ποινὰς ἀρκτεύειν τὰς ἑαυτῶν παρθένους ἀναγκάσουσι. καὶ ἐψηφίσαντο οἱ Ἀθηναῖοι μὴ πρότερον συνοικίζεσθαι ἀνδρὶ παρθένον, εἰ μὴ ἀρκτεύσειε τῇ θεῷ. Translation: Jennifer Benedict. Eustathius records a similar myth for Mounichia (*Commentarii ad Homeri Iliadem* 2.732).

[29] See also *Suda* s.v. Ἀρκτεῦσαι: "Lysias used [the verb] 'to be a bear' of consecrating virgins, before marriage, to Artemis. For the virgins are called 'being bears,' as Euripides and Aristophanes show" (Λυσίας τὸ καθιερωθῆναι πρὸ γάμων τὰς παρθένους τῇ Ἀρτέμιδι ἀρκτεύειν ἔλεγε. καὶ γὰρ αἱ ἀρκτευόμεναι παρθένοι καλοῦνται, ὡς Εὐριπίδης καὶ Ἀριστοφάνης δηλοῖ; trans. David Whitehead).

[30] The bibliography on the Arkteia is especially abundant since the excavations of Brauron by J. Papadimitriou from 1948 to 1963. The most current bibliography can be found in Beaumont (2013: 264–265 n. 236).

Athenian girls were required to participate; others suggest that only girls
of some means or status would 'dance the bear.'[31] They are represented on
vase paintings either naked or in gowns being chased by a bear (imagined
or actual).[32] There was a priestess in charge of the cult and this ritual,
who probably had the title of 'Iphigenia.'[33] Thus, while there is some textual and material evidence for girls worshipping Artemis through a bear
ritual, what happened, who participated, and what was being re-enacted
or symbolized remain obscure and open to interpretation.

A recent examination of the evidence by Lesley Beaumont attempts
to strip away what we think we know about the Arkteia, focusing on
interpreting the literary and iconographic imagery separately before considering them in conjunction.[34] Beaumont suggests, following a scholi-
ast on Aristophanes, that the girls were between five and ten years old,
which, as Christine Sourvinou-Inwood suggests, would ensure that all
girls participating in the Arkteia had not yet begun to menstruate.[35] She
further argues for separating the Brauronia from the Arkteia, since it is
hard to reconcile the Arkteia, a *mysterion* ('mystery cult'), with a large,
publicly sponsored festival like the Brauronia. It appears that only the
girl participants and perhaps adult female chaperones could enter the
Brauron sanctuary.[36] The same scholion on Aristophanes attests that part
of the ritual required the girls to put on and them remove the *krokotos*,
a saffron-colored garment. Apart from these tidbits, we can say nothing
for certain.[37]

---

[31] Perlman (1983) argues for participants from ten to fourteen; Sourvinou-Inwood
(1988: 21) for ages five to ten. Other scholars tend to follow one or the other. Simon
(1983: 86), Golden (1990: 78), and Mikalson (2005: 150) all argue for widespread participation; limited participation is advocated by Cole (1984: 242), Dillon (2002: 221), and
Beaumont (2013: 184); Demand (1994: 107–112) presents both sides.

[32] Bevan (1987: 19) and Dillon (2002: 221).

[33] Dillon (2002: 93).

[34] Beaumont (2013: 175).

[35] Σ Aristophanes (Ar.) *Lysistrata* (*Lys.*) 645: οὔτε πρεσβύτεραι δέκα ἐτῶν οὔτ' ἐλάττους
πέντε. Sourvinou-Inwood (1988: 25) observes that the earliest date we have for the onset of
menses in ancient Greek sources is at age eleven, and that the common age was fourteen.
Thus an age-range of five to ten ensures all participants are prepubescent.

[36] Beaumont (2013: 175), Sourvinou-Inwood (1988: 21–31), and Σ Ar. *Lys.* 644–645.

[37] Σ Ar. *Lys.* 644–645. It is also worth mentioning that the written sources we do have are
quite late, adding yet another measure of uncertainty to the little we think we do know; see
Golden (1990: 78) and Dillon (2002: 220).

Looking at material culture provides more information but requires further speculation. One of Beaumont's most interesting observations is that the *krateriskoi* (little *kraters* or mixing bowls) commonly found at Brauron and at other sanctuaries to Artemis are frequently decorated with both prepubescent girls and *parthenoi* (virginal girls of marriageable age). Girls who are represented as running or dancing naked are almost always *parthenoi*, easily identifiable by their long hair (either loose or collected in a bun) and their noticeable breasts.[38] In addition, fragments of two *kraters* show scenes that appear to concern Artemis. One depicts females of varying ages, both young girls (short, with short hair, wearing short, sleeveless *chitons*) and older females (taller, with long hair pulled into a bun, wearing *chiton* and *himation*). The second *krater* shows four naked *parthenoi* running (or dancing?) and holding wreaths, another girl with breasts but long, loose hair, and a sixth female who is shorter, flat-chested, and with short hair.[39] Thus these images depict a precinct of Artemis in which girls, *parthenoi*, and occasionally adult women are all involved. In addition, whatever race or chase is represented seemingly involves not only prepubescent but also adolescent girls.

Beaumont believes that given the distribution of these *kraters* and *krateriskoi* with the iconography of running and dancing girls being found exclusively at Brauron and Mounichia—both being locales where an Arkteia was celebrated—these vessels should be associated with the Arkteia. The trouble then becomes reconciling this with what we know from the literary sources: that the girls, who 'play the bear,' put on, and then take off the *krokotos*, were prepubescent, since many of the females represented are far beyond this stage of life.[40] Through this ritual, they dedicated themselves to Artemis in expiation for killing her bear. Yet, as Beaumont and others have argued, it is also likely to have been a coming-of-age ritual, in which girls anticipated the moment when they would become a 'bear'—that is, a mother.[41] Indeed, Elinor Bevan observes that

---

[38] Beaumont (2013: 176).

[39] For detailed discussions of these figures and reproductions of the images, see ibid. (177–180).

[40] Kahil (1979:73–87) connects the *krokotos* to a saffron-colored garment that Iphigenia removes before her sacrifice (Aeschylus *Agamemnon* 239), and suggests that the *arktoi* re-enact the sacrifice of Iphigenia.

[41] Dillon (2002: 175), Goff (2004: 108), and Beaumont (2013: 182–83).

bears were regarded as the "emblem and supreme pattern of mother-hood."[42] Thus, Beaumont considers that the representations should not be considered 'photographic' images but rather symbolic representations, where the females who appear to be *parthenoi* are those who have undergone the ritual and are ready for the onset of puberty, whereas the younger girls have not yet made the transition.[43] For Beaumont, 'playing the bear' is a way of acknowledging and perhaps actuating the potential inherent in the girls' bodies.

While etiological myth for the Arkteia and the ritual itself bear few resemblances to Merida's story, there is consonance in Merida's prepa-ration for life as an adult, her mother's coaching, and her ability when confronting the clan elders to draw upon that knowledge, thereby dem-onstrating that she has, in some sense, made the transition from girl to young woman. As she does so, her mother, the bear, stands in the back-ground offering her support. Yet the Arkteia appears to manifest none of the warmth of this tale. While the festival may highlight Artemis' kou-rotrophic (i.e., child-nurturing) nature, the bear tales about her likewise emphasize her anger and implacability. The etiological myth, for exam-ple, offers both a bear as a tame playmate and Artemis' rage in the form of a plague. Girls would be smart to be wary of such a deity, who is owed their fealty and honor and who was felt to have sway over the health of their future children—as the numerous dedications of thanks at Brauron, honoring the birth of both healthy male and female children, attest.[44]

In the end, however, there is still disagreement about how we are to interpret what we know of the Arkteia, and what we might know, if we are reading the evidence correctly. When added to the mythic tales of both beneficent she-bears and transformations of girls into bears, the evidence for the Arkteia leaves us still with a mixed picture, where girls are 'bears' twice over: unmarried girls are wild things; they are bears by nature and objects of sacrifice as such.[45] Yet girls who have made the transition are bears as well, in that they become mothers, are aligned with the aims of kourotrophic Artemis, and potentially impart some of that bearish

---

[42] Bevan (1987:19).

[43] Beaumont (2013: 184).

[44] On votives of children at Brauron, see Beaumont (2003) and Neils (2003). On their contextualization within Greek sanctuaries, see Straten (1990).

[45] On the wildness of the girls, see Cole (1984: 242) and Goff (2004: 107–108).

nature to their offspring. Is the point of these stories and rituals to get girls to leave their bearish natures behind? Or to embrace a new bearish nature? Or both?

WRITING THEIR OWN STORY

Most work on the classical tradition states or suggests that understanding the classical model will offer a richer appreciation of the modern adaptation. Yet this is one instance where the modern tale may shed some light or offer suggestions on how to think about the ancient myths. *Brave* presents an original tale that is steeped in Indo-European notions of bear mythology, yet the film reworks these stereotypical mythemes: the mother bear is not innately caring and must be returned to human form; and metamorphosis, while a punishment, is reversed in order to effect a happy ending.[46]

When first trying to explain to Merida her duty as a princess—the duty to marry and to learn how to rule—Elinor tells a tale about a kingdom that was bequeathed to four sons. The kingdom was divided, but the oldest prince wanted to be the sole ruler and selfishly thought only of himself. When Merida retorts that this is only a story, Elinor chides her, "Legends are lessons. They ring with Truths." Though Merida remains skeptical of her mother's words, she comes to see her mother's point of view. Later, as Merida attempts to soothe the clansmen who are still furious that she refuses to marry any of their offspring, she tells them the same tale in an attempt to maintain peace in the kingdom and show their strength when they work cooperatively. When the leaders of the clans jeer her, she repeats—much to her astonishment—her mother's words, that "legends are lessons." At that moment, admitting her own selfishness, she is poised to commit to marriage until she spies her mother-as-bear

---

[46] *Brave* does not explicitly invoke the third bear mytheme, though it is there implicitly in the form of Mor'du. This bear appears in the opening scene where Merida, as a toddler, is surprised by the fierce male animal and protected from him by her father. Later in the film, Merida discovers that Mor'du was once a human prince, who through selfishness and hunger for power destroyed his kingdom. There is, then, the implicit sense that Elinor could become Mor'du's consort; that, mimicking Beauty and the Beast, Mor'du might be restored and become an appropriate mate for Merida; or more menacingly, that Merida's fate is to become Mor'du's bride in death.

in the background, encouraging her to break with tradition: she declares instead, with her mother's approval, "We should be free to write our own story."

Admittedly, Greek women—both the young and the already-married—were never free to 'write their own stories' in the manner *Brave* advocates. The lives of ancient women were circumscribed by a host of factors, not least of which were the patriarchal underpinnings of their culture that left many women with little room to maneuver. Yet I want to think for a moment with Elinor and Merida, as they contemplate the truths that legends can hold, and how that knowledge can be—literally and figuratively—transformative.

Brave values the skills that Merida brings to her quest: bravery, intelligence, daring, stubbornness, curiosity, eloquence, temperance, and even needlework. This assemblage of skills is variously coded as masculine or feminine, but all are required for the successful resolution of the tale. The human efforts required for Merida's transformation throw the mystical elements into the background, allowing her to be the agent of her own transformation. Moreover, Merida does not accomplish this alone but relies heavily on her mother, who acts as a reflection of both who Merida is and who she will become. As the end of the film demonstrates, the transformation and counter-transformation serve to cement not only the relationship between mother and daughter but also the stability of the family itself. All are reintegrated and better understand their places, both in the family and society. In becoming a bear, Elinor is now able to facilitate Merida's transition, allowing her to employ the skills and knowledge that she will require as an adult.

This story—like those of Iphigenia, Callisto, and Atalanta—ultimately concerns the transition of a girl to marriageable young woman. Where the details in the Greek ritual are vague and the myths fantastic, bloody, and horrific, the progress of Merida in *Brave* may offer insight into the matrix of Greek bear lore. Merida's journey requires separation from her childish nature as a wild thing, a transition that she is loath to make, and the process engenders resentment of her mother and the societal position as wife and queen for which Elinor explicitly prepares her. Conversely, Elinor's sojourn as a bear reminds Elinor of her own youthful desires and the part of her that remains untamable. While we understand that Greek girls would not have had the option, as Merida does, of postponing matrimony or choosing their own spouses, the use of this ritual as one of reinforcing the upcoming transition—not only for the girl, but also for her family—seems congruent here. More suggestively, Merida's tale results in a rewoven bond between mother and daughter, where each must recognize the other's position. In the end, although the status and relationship between the two will be altered, the bond itself remains stable.

Certainly, while myths about bears are often monstrous, and scholars like Beaumont are right to emphasize the fear that might well attend a girl at the brink of transition in the face of a temperamental Artemis, we should not forget the duality of the she-bear: ferocious yet nurturing, playful and fierce, a punishment and a blessing. Even as the myths emphasize the fantastical nature of the bear (and its patron goddess), it may well be that the rituals of the Arkteia serve to naturalize the supernatural qualities of these tales, in much the same way that such naturalization is accomplished in *Brave* through the agency of its participants. The *arktoi* perhaps dressed and undressed, processed, raced, were chased by a 'bear,' and spun wool. There is, likewise, much we do not know about the rites, but in other rituals, including *mysteria*, there are often words to be spoken, food to be prepared and eaten, songs to be sung. In any case, in becoming Artemis' 'bears,' the girls are no longer helpless victims of fate, but agents in a complex ritual, where it appears that they both act symbolically and perhaps also engage in activities that will be necessary for them to perfect as they transition to wives and mothers.[47]

In one of the red-figure *kraters* that Beaumont reproduces, three older women are attending to four girls of varying ages.[48] The women are clearly adults: their hair is bound up and they wear both a *chiton* and *himation*. One has placed one hand on a girl's shoulder, while her other hand appears to be making sure the child's *chiton* is girt securely about her middle; another woman looks to be distributing branches or fronds to two girls; a third woman holds bowls in either hand. These women could be any adult females especially tasked with assisting in this ritual, but you will indulge me, I hope, when I note that it looks not unlike the sidelines of my four-year-old's soccer matches before play begins.

---

[47] Goff (2004: 108–113) specifically sees this as an opportunity for girls to experience themselves as both subjects and objects of an emerging sexuality that will be requisite for marriage.

[48] Beaumont (2013: 178).

True, these women cannot securely be identified as mothers, yet I certainly hope they are (and, I offer, that it is not an unreasonable suggestion).[49] *Brave* shows how Merida's ordeal has made her bond with her mother more secure, how both not only better understand each other, but also have confidence in Merida's ability to negotiate her coming life as an adult. In the same way that Elinor-as-bear facilitates Merida's transition and is integral to it, likewise, the presence of female relations at the Arkteia would offer a measure of security, not only to the girls as they perform the ritual, but also—and perhaps more importantly—to the mothers who know from experience the road their daughters will have to walk. The duality of the bear makes the most sense in this context, for the mothers, then, *are* bears as well. As women who once underwent the same ritual (if it was indeed as universal as some posit), they are now the beneficent bears, ushering their wild cubs through this transition. In such a matrix, one does not need to choose between the different iterations of the bear, provided that the transition is not arrested (as it is in the cases of Iphigenia and Callisto).

While we know comparatively little about ancient Greek girls, let alone their family members, Greek literature suggests that girls felt anxiety about the impending separation from their mothers. So it may be worth a moment or two to think through the way other tales in other times handle similar themes and motifs. *Brave*'s appropriation of ancient Greek coming-of-age motifs, which are naturalized and incorporated into a tale of literal and physical metamorphosis, may offer us a new path to considering the value of such rituals. This is not to say that the two are identical, but that by exploring the power and strength of the mother–daughter dyad in *Brave*'s modern reading of bear-related mythemes, we may find a way back not only to ancient girls but also to their mothers.

---

[49] Likewise, Goff (2004: 106) surmises that girls were accompanied by mothers and other female relatives.

Part IV

(Post)Modern Fantasies of Antiquity

12

Fantasies of Mimnermos in Anne Carson's "The Brainsex Paintings" (*Plainwater*)

Sasha-Mae Eccleston

In "The Brainsex Paintings," the first section of her 1995 collection *Plainwater*, Anne Carson translates, critiques, and 'interviews' the archaic Greek poet Mimnermos (seventh century BCE). A few extant poems offer scholars a tantalizing glimpse into Mimnermos' body of writing, the poet himself, and the archaic Greek past of which he was part. We have enough traces of the man, the breadth of his work, and his cultural context to be intrigued, but not much we can be certain about. Carson plays upon this elusive allure of Mimnermos: 'interviews' seem to promise historical facts from the man himself; an essay suggests an elucidation of Mimnerman poetics; translations of an ancient, foreign language (Greek) into a modern language (English) could make what Mimnermos wrote accessible to contemporary readers. But Carson does not use these three genres to flesh out the historical facts of a figure from the remote past. Nor does she make her scholarly voice the sole authority with regard to the poet and his contemporary world. Rather, Carson's play with language and literary convention in "The Brainsex Paintings" exposes how all intersubjective experiences—whether from the remote past or in the present—rely on elements of 'fantasy' to construct 'reality.'

'Fantasy' and the 'fantastic' are often defined in opposition to 'reality' and 'realism.'[1] 'Realism' developed as a full-blown literary term in the nineteenth century, but its conceptual foundation lies in notions of imitation (*mimesis*) from Greek antiquity.[2] These ideals measured a cultural product's artistic merit according to how well it imitated reality. But what constitutes reality? Tzvetan Todorov defined 'the fantastic' as a genre that sustains the reader's hesitation to reject what she knows defies the "laws of nature" or to accept the "apparently supernatural."[3] This framework defined 'reality' using scientism, a mode of facticity understood as predictable, verifiable, and consensus-based ('in the common opinion').[4] 'Nature,' in this case, functions as shorthand for everything that seems objectively inviolable and universal, leaving what does not conform a matter of subjective surrender or defiance.[5] Subsequent critics have redefined 'fantasy' as different trends have emerged within the genre.[6] They challenge scientism and the underlying metaphysics of Todorov's definition by exposing 'reality' and 'realism' as being open to dispute: since imitation cannot be severed from the limits and limit-defying powers of human perception, even realistic fiction reimagines, alters, and restructures 'reality.' It simply does not foreground—or even admit to—that process.[7] Fantasy does, probing both what does not exist and what could not exist under the rubrics (e.g., history, physics) used to define reality.[8] Accordingly, readers of modern fantasy become displaced from this world's certainties, however much they are just a construct, as

[1] The term 'fantastic' often refers to a way of describing phenomena, while 'fantasy' indicates the genre that sustains that mode throughout; see, e.g., Attebery (1992: chapter 1). In the case of "The Brainsex Paintings," separating genre from mode may inhibit understanding the nuances of Carson's artistry. Therefore, I have used the term 'fantasy' throughout to signal Carson's challenge to realistic genres, techniques used in those genres, and realism as a literary value system.

[2] See the survey of literary 'realisms' in Wellek (1963: chapter 8) and Horstkotte (2000) 29.

[3] Todorov and Scholes (1975: 25).

[4] Ibid. (41); on different modes of facticity, including scientism, and their relationship to 'fantasy,' see Collins (1982) 114–115 and Hume (1984) 39–44.

[5] Whereas Todorov focuses on 'hesitation,' Attebery (1992: 16) settles on 'wonder' as the emotional response garnered by fantastic phenomena that makes us more aware of 'reality.' Both hesitation and wonder seem germane to Carson's process here.

[6] One can find many overviews, including Sandner (2004) and Horstkotte (2000: chapter 2).

[7] Cf. Hume (1984: esp. 20–25) and Attebery (1992: 3).

[8] See the Introduction to this volume. Cf. Clute and Grant (1999: 338).

they become immersed in another construct with its own parameters of certainty, possibility, and reality.[9]

Carson's "The Brainsex Paintings" highlights how a 'reality' defined by and valued in terms of objective criteria insufficiently reconstructs human experiences. Carson, who is a scholar of Greek antiquity as well as an artist, knows the dynamics of this value system well. But, after claiming "Mimnermos is plainly not interested in explaining historical references," she avoids making the historical record the focal point of her engagement with the poet and his work.[10] The interview's very format challenges the information gathered: any biographical holes filled in by the interviewer's questions will come from a source that has been conjured supernaturally and thus 'unrealistically.' Moreover, Carson's Mimnermos is fond of the lacunose, and she allows his disruptive presence to recall the problems of transmitting information across historical periods that lead to these gaps in knowledge.[11] Scholarly writing conventionally seeks to make arguments, including those about such gaps, based on objective research and analysis. But Carson's impressionistic insertions thrust subjective experience into the logic of her essay so that the scholarly and personal both lead to an understanding of Mimnerman poetics. Finally, her renderings of Mimnerman elegy challenge the universalizing worldview present in the Greek poems in favor of private, irretrievable moments fading from history. These Mimnermos-inspired poems fixate upon the private experiences of contemporary figures in such a way that they seem both as fantastic and as real as archaic Greece is for us.

THE INTERVIEWS AND THE ESSAY

Although they end "The Brainsex Paintings," I will begin with the three interviews because they include Carson's most obvious engagements with

---

[9] On displacement and the impossible, see Sandner (2004: 9).

[10] Carson (1995: 14).

[11] Carson expands upon the lacunose in her intriguing and more recognizably fantastic *Autobiography of Red* (1998) and its quasi-sequel, *Red Doc>* (2003). Both texts follow a mythological creature named Geryon who appears in recently discovered fragments of a work by Stesichorus, another archaic Greek poet. Like *Plainwater*, *Autobiography of Red* juxtaposes scholarship with creative work: an essay and several appendices accompany the 'novel in verse.'

fantasy. The physically impossible face-to-face conversation between Mimnermos and the interviewing 'I' defies the laws of nature and is the stuff of scholarly dreams. Interviews offer what many literary critics and historians long for—a chance to question their object of inquiry directly. If only we were to speak with the poet about his work and world, we would have unassailable knowledge about the archaic Greek past—or so the dream goes. The desire to fill in the gaps of scholarly knowledge is even more pressing in the case of Mimnermos because his fragmentary corpus makes our distance from his world and our ignorance about it more apparent.[12]

In the interviews, Carson upends conventions that would under-score the supernatural circumstances of the Mimnerman encounter. Her Mimnermos immediately inverts the model of the supernatural visitor as interloper. Rather than transgressing the divide between this world and the next (or the past and the present), he expresses his surprise at the interviewer's willingness to come "all this way" in order to see him.[13] The location of the interviews is never specified, though Mimnermos does know New York City exists. Taking cues from the normalization of the supernatural as found in magical realism, Mimnermos seems comfort-able with some aspects of the present, as he refers to the contemporary publishing industry, expresses little to no surprise at the term 'psycho-analysis,' and uses a metaphor involving a telephone.[14]

Rather than belabor the supernatural aspect of the encounter, Carson belabors the quest for information. The interviewer's efforts to retrieve information lost to the historical record from the poet himself are often in vain. For example, the second interview begins with the unnamed speaker asking Mimnermos to share his opinion on a sustained inward turn in the study of contemporary human values. He responds poeti-cally: "Secrets save me from dissolving."[15] Nowhere is Mimnermos' pref-erence to preserve secrets more evident than in the treatment of Nanno, a flute girl whom an ancient source names as Mimnermos' lover and whose

---

[12] On the conflation of the bibliographic and the biographic in the reception of Mimnerman fragments, see West (1974: 74–76) and Caspers (2006: 21, 25–29). For exam-ples of how questions about Mimnermos and his works influence interpretations of his poems, see Podlecki (2011: 57–61).

[13] Carson (1995: 18).

[14] Ibid. (19, 22, 25).

[15] Ibid. (21).

name is attached to a collection of his poems.[16] When the interviewer mentions Nanno by name in the third exchange, the space next to "M" is filled by a dash indicating Mimnermos' silence. Eventually Mimnermos admits that he had written a poem about her but that it was never published. Because this admission comes after he angrily claims that the constant investigations into his life and writing force him to lie, his relationship to Nanno remains uncertain.[17] Was that the truth or just another lie? Is there another (now lost) poem we should call "Nanno"? Carson, the interviewer, and Mimnermos never resolve this uncertainty.

Instead, Carson couples Mimnermos' biographical reticence with his refusal to act as a privileged source about a singular, universal human existence. Supernatural visits can presage the future or reveal the past to those who normally know only as much as their lifespan allows. Thus such visits challenge reality in terms of time, materiality, and mortality, as well as in the limitations those conditions impose upon human understanding. That Mimnermos, a figure from the past and from a culture fetishized for its wisdom (i.e., ancient Greece), could be the source of some preternatural knowledge would fit within this paradigm. That Carson, a trained Classicist, and her narrators could be gatekeepers for this culture from the past fits, too.

Yet, when the interviewing 'I' labels Mimnermos' statement, "[i]n my day we valued blindness rather more," as "mystical," he hesitates to agree.[18] After repeating the term, he counters, "I don't think we had a word mystical," and replaces "mystical" with a misquoted proverb, "hidden in the scrutum [*sic*] of Zeus."[19] The proverb should read "scrotum," referring to an origin story of the god Dionysus.[20] But one mistyped letter and an easily consumed proverb becomes arresting and more difficult to construe: "scrutum" resembles a Latin word for bits of trash.[21]

---

[16] West (1974: 75): "Nowhere [in the fragments] do we catch a whiff of Nanno herself."

[17] Carson (1995: 26).

[18] Ibid. (19–20).

[19] Ibid. (20): The square-bracketed "[*sic*]" is Carson's, letting the poet signal the typographical error of "scrutum" for "scrotum." A Latin adverb (*sic*) creeps into a Greek proverb via a Latin word inserted in the place of a translated Greek word: a clear example of learned philological play where something readers can passively receive becomes problematic instead of neutral.

[20] Variants of the story place Dionysus in the thigh (a proxy for the scrotum) of Zeus; cf. Euripides *Bacchae* 88–91 and Nonnus *Dionysiaca* 5–8.

[21] *Oxford Latin Dictionary*, s.v. 'scruta.'

The tongue-in-cheek typo underscores how tenuous the process of transmitting information across media—as well as across time, space, and cultures—can be. Classicists may be comfortable with this precariousness: they often deal with fragmentary bits of text discovered amongst trash heaps and corrupted by repeated copying from Greco-Roman antiquity to the present. However, if the point of Mimnermos' presence is clarity, preserving the error resists it. Furthermore, the physicality of the metaphor (i.e., scrotum) and the flippant mistake (i.e., trash) undercut the delicate term 'mystical' as well as the the awe it represents: it becomes more difficult for the interviewer (and the reader) to latch onto Mimnermos' first statement as a profound apothegm from the past, and the uncertainty about the proverb inhibits passive acceptance.[22] Mimnermos' refusal to "distill [his] history into this or that home truth" works similarly.[23] His history remains his, too big to be encapsulated for easy consumption and unable to be scrutinized, verified, and made 'real' according to objective criteria.

Likewise, Carson defies the expectations of scholarly writing to challenge objectivism's reach in the essay that precedes the interviews, "Mimnermos and the Motions of Hedonism." The essay has a scholarly appearance: it is in prose and includes historical dating—e.g., "thirty-seventh Olympiad (632–629 BCE)"—and scholarly references.[24] Moreover, for readers less familiar with Greco-Roman poetry, Carson's analysis of Mimnerman meter strikes a particularly learned note. Nevertheless, the essay straddles the ground between objective investigation and individual response. What begins with explanatory statements about Mimnerman lyric goes on to include bodily responses to his verse, sentence fragments, and other poeticisms. For example, Carson writes, "When you pass from sun to shadow in his poems you can feel the difference run down the back of your skull like cold water."[25] The corporeality of "skull" paired with the chill of water recalls descriptions of supernatural visitations in fantasy and horror that cause mortals to feel cold or shudder because they have come into contact with death. It is as if the supernatural aura so carefully avoided in the interviews

---

[22] Rae (2008: 239) sees gender and cultural ideology brought into relief in this moment.
[23] Carson (1995: 25).
[24] Ibid. (12).
[25] Ibid. (13).

has seeped into the essay and the analytical reading process that is supposed to produce it. Furthermore, Carson uses the second person ('you') rather than an impersonal third person ('one'), giving this observation a more intimate register.[26]

Here and elsewhere, Carson is not trying and failing to achieve scholarly distance from her subject matter. Rather, she deliberately gets into the thick of what it means to understand Mimnermos' work. Her body, her personal experiences—as well as her scholarly acumen—are bound to this endeavor. If, as her essay argues, "everything in his verse bristles with [hedonism]," the decision to include her own experiences of pleasure in her exposition of Mimnermos' writing is a fitting tribute to the effectiveness of his poetry.[27]

THE POEMS

Carson's English translations of Mimnerman verse significantly alter the poems' viewpoint on humankind and the mortal condition to account for a lacunose conception of reality as well. Her poems are not neutral renderings (i.e., so-called 'faithful translations'). The Everyman figure who bridges universal experiences and personal preference in the Mimnerman fragments becomes an isolated individual whose memories and identity remain hauntingly abstract. As we struggle to understand him, the unidentified subject of her poems tiptoes on the boundary between distance and proximity. As a result, this figure differs little from the historical Mimnermos or the Mimnerman corpus. Understanding the recent past of her subject and the remote past of Mimnermos becomes bound to analytical and imaginative work while appealing to both experience and intellect. I offer readings of the first three poems in the Mimnerman corpus as examples, giving my own translation of the Greek, then the Greek, with Carson's adaptation in each following discussion.[28]

---

[26] Another instance of the same technique: "We had been seduced into thinking that we were immortal and suddenly the affair is over" (15).

[27] Carson (1995: 12).

[28] For Mimnermos' fragments in Greek, see West (1989).

Fragment 1

In fragment 1, Mimnermos' poetic persona reveals his view of human reality:

What life is there, what pleasure is there without golden Aphrodite?
Let me die, when I no longer care about these things,
secret love affairs and sweet gifts and bed,
the sort of tender blossoms of youth that happen
to men and women; but when comes along baneful
old age, which makes a man shameful and ugly alike,
base cares always assail his mind,
and beholding the sun's rays he does not find pleasure,
instead hateful is he to children on the one hand, dishonored by women on
   the other.
God made old age difficult in this way.

τίς δὲ βίος, τί δὲ τερπνὸν ἄτερ χρυσῆς Ἀφροδίτης;
   τεθναίην, ὅτε μοι μηκέτι ταῦτα μέλοι,
κρυπταδίη φιλότης καὶ μείλιχα δῶρα καὶ εὐνή,
   οἷ᾽ ἥβης ἄνθεα γίνεται ἁρπαλέα
ἀνδράσιν ἠδὲ γυναιξίν· ἐπεὶ δ᾽ ὀδυνηρὸν ἐπέλθηι
   γῆρας, ὅ τ᾽ αἰσχρὸν ὁμῶς καὶ κακὸν ἄνδρα τιθεῖ,
αἰεί μιν φρένας ἀμφὶ κακαὶ τείρουσι μέριμναι,
   οὐδ᾽ αὐγὰς προσορῶν τέρπεται ἠελίου,
ἀλλ᾽ ἐχθρὸς μὲν παισίν, ἀτίμαστος δὲ γυναιξίν·
   οὕτως ἀργαλέον γῆρας ἔθηκε θεός.

The broad, generalizing force of the question that begins line 1 ('What is life?') yields to a more idiosyncratic interpretation of life expressed in the second ('What pleasure is there without golden Aphrodite?'). For the speaker, life (βίος; 1.1) is allied with pleasure (τερπνόν). The speaker's choice to die (1.2) when those things are absent is based on a rationale about life that is dependent on the gifts of the goddess of love, Aphrodite (1.3). But the speaker constantly channels the general human experience to inform this rationale: the sort of things he cares about happen to all "men and women" (1.5). Likewise, having delayed specifying what "baneful thing" (ὀδυνηρὸν; 1.5) is bound to arrive until the beginning of line 6 ('old age,' γῆρας), he homes in on what makes it so grievous: old age disconnects an individual (ἄνδρα) from the community. Because he has aged, that individual cannot even enjoy the sunlight that he shares with every other member of humankind. Old age can have such a stable connotation ('baneful') because its effects are universal. The choice to die no longer seems subjective and unique.

The poem's final line supports this universalizing impulse: old age is so harsh for everyone because it has been made so by a force outside of, beyond the reach of, and unaffected by mortals—namely, the god (θεός; 1.10). Difficult (ἀργαλέον) changes from mere descriptor to an enunciation of the undeniable in the final line. There is a thing difficult in the way that he has mentioned, that thing is old age, and that is the way it is. The same verb that appeared in the present tense ('make,' τιθεῖ) in line 6 occurs in line 10 but in the past tense ('made,' ἔθηκε). The verb 'to make or render' thus unites the first half of the poem, which reads as subjective and personal, with the second half, which reads as objective and universal. By the time we arrive at the poem's last word, 'god,' this unity becomes even more arresting. A god made old age terrible (and incontrovertibly so), just like a god(dess), Aphrodite, gave it meaning in the first place. The truth of our experiences as a class of mortal beings was determined outside of the space of this poem, beyond any single human's control.

This general condition of humanity is not the thrust of Carson's translation of fragment 1, "What Is Life Without Aphrodite?" Carson creates distance between the poet, the poem's protagonist, and the world in which he lives. She abandons the first-person voice and represents the Mimnerman "he" of her epigraph addressing a "you" about a "her" only known to them. Her choice excludes the reader as a member of a general class of human beings, allowing us only a glimpse into a world of private experience. Furthermore, Carson individualizes the experience of death and pleasure. She thus changes the dynamic between the individual decision to die (τεθναίην; 1.2) and the inevitable end of mortal life (1.5–10) found in Mimnermos' verses.

A quick glance at my attempt at a neutral translation above should show the originality of Carson's beautiful poem. From the first line, Carson's reader is in the middle of a subjective worldview:

fr. 1
What Is Life Without Aphrodite?

> *He seems an irrepressible hedonist as he asks his leading question.*

Up to your honeybasket hilts in her ore—or else
    Death? for yes
how gentle it is to go swimming inside her the secret swimming
    Of men and women but (no) then

The night hide toughens over it (no) then bandages
    Crusted with old man smell (no) then
bowl gone black nor bud nor boys nor women nor sun no
    Spores (no) at (no) all when
God nor hardstrut nothingness close
    its fist on you.

Carson's reader starts from the center of Mimnermos' implied condi-
tional statement, "If life is pleasure, what sort of life is there when pleasure is absent?" In the beginning, Carson does pay heed to the Greek—if
not in translating the actual meaning of a word, then by bringing to the
surface some of its associations.[29] As the poem continues, however, her
departures from the Greek point to a full acceptance and exploration of
the subjective viewpoint from which she starts. The phrase "up to one's
hilts" suggests excess, and 'honey' seems indulgent. Carson thus hints at
the excess of the pleasure that constituted life in the Greek text. But there
is no broadly generalizing term like 'life' in line 1. Instead, in line 2, death
stares us in the face as the more easily understood option of a disorient-
ing dilemma because of the oddness of the phrase "up to your honeybasket hilts in her ore." What does it mean to have "honeybasket hilts"?
The phrase could suggest a surfeit of honey and gold. But the entire line
can also be read as a threat ("—or else"). One need not think the phrase
definitely means 'drowning' to acknowledge its disquietude, though that
reading is attractive. Since it is death that eventually ends the phrase and
frames the dilemma, the question could also be a choice between the
lesser of two evils—death and the unknown. Moreover, note that instead
of naming the female character like Aphrodite, Carson's threat comes
after a reference to an unidentified "her." The equally unidentified "your"
and this "her" form a closed circuit, offering a choice whose parameters
the reader cannot fully comprehend.

In several ways, Carson's poem moves ever closer to interiority and
away from Mimnerman universality. "How gentle it is to go swimming
inside her the secret swimming" brings the "her" from the first line back

---

[29] "Up to your honeybasket hilts in her ore—or else" distills Mimnermos 1.1–4 with
"ore" recalling the χρυσῆς ('golden') that described Aphrodite and "honeybasket" capturing
the imagery Mimnermos attached to the goddess, that of fecundity, harvesting, and sweet-
ness connoted by μείλιχα ('sweet') and ἄνθεα ('flowers') and, possibly χρυσῆς as well (i.e.,
his baskets would be filled with a gold-colored substance, honey).

into the picture as the location of a private action. There is no attempt to characterize "the swimming" with Mimnermos' imagery of blossoming (cf. 'flowers,' ἄνθεα; 1.4), no use of the language of exposure to balance the private experience in the Greek ('secret,' κρυπταδίη; 1.3).[30] Though the phrase "of men and women" imitates the Greek by virtue of position, this "swimming" is wholly "secret." As we read on, Carson embraces the hardness of Mimnermos' ἀργαλέον as things toughen or become "crusted."[31] But the toughening happens "over" something else and "bandages" appear, covering something unidentified. In line 7, "boys" nods towards the intergenerational, familial, community-based connotations of "children" (παισίν), "shame" (αἰσχρὸν), and "honor" (ἀτίμαστος). But the image of sterility in the phrase "Nor bud . . . no spores" counteracts those connotations. Moreover, the homophonic punning of "nor sun" (i.e., nor son) invokes sterility. The wider world isn't rejecting someone unable to connect with it, as happened in the Mimnerman context: in this poem, "you" had no tangible connection to it in the first place; he was "inside" of and overwhelmed by "her," and eventually becomes altogether severed from it. A fist, like a coffin-lid, is being closed upon him. Carson does not, as happens in the Greek, negate the perception of human-fortifying light (cf. "nor beholding the rays of the run does he find pleasure," οὐδ'. . . προσορῶν τέρπεται; 1.7), but the very existence of its source with "nor sun." Her subject is absolutely displaced.

Likewise, she localizes the ill effects of old age. Instead of ending with a god, this poem ends with "you." Mimnermos' final word recapitulated the inextricability of Aphrodite and the divine realm from the poet's concept of life and, when coupled with "made" (ἔθηκε; 1.2), underscored the powerlessness of humanity in the face of the divine. Carson retains the divine presence at the beginning of line 9, but it is figured harming the individual, instead of creating a life-stage. As a result, the oblivion is the subject's alone to bear, just as when he was overwhelmed in the 'ore' of line 1 and secluded in the 'swimming' of line 3. All gentleness from being inside has been lost, as the external object is no longer "her,"

---

[30] Carson imagines "*harpaleon* . . . sounds like a secret trout on the slip down the fathoms" (17); her translation reproduces the association between secrecy and water.

[31] Notice the synesthetic quality of "*crusted* with old man *smell*." This confused sensual perception becomes a hallmark of Geryon in *Autobiography of Red* (1998) and of Carson's ruminations on her brother's death in *Nox* (2010).

but a "fist." Seclusion has become a matter of deprivation and isolation rather than intimacy and privacy.

Fragment 2

In the second fragment, Mimnermos focuses on the mortal condition more explicitly:

We are like leaves the many flowered season bears,
Spring, when they shoot up quickly aided by the light of the sun,
like them for a cubit of time in youth's flowers
we find pleasure, knowing of the gods neither bad
nor good. Two gloomy fates stand at hand,
one having the end that is baneful old age
and the other death. The fruit of one's youth is
short-lived, as long lasting as the sun scatters its light upon the earth.
But truly when the season has reached its end and gone by,
indeed immediately it is better to be dead than to keep living.
For many bad things affect the heart.
Sometimes one's household wastes away, and then come poverty's wretched
    tasks.
Another person, in turn, lacks children and desiring these very much
he goes below the earth to Hades.
Yet another has a fatal disease. There is no one
of mortal men to whom Zeus does not give many bad things.

ἡμεῖς δ᾽, οἷά τε φύλλα φύει πολυάνθεμος ὥρη
    ἔαρος, ὅτ᾽ αἶψ᾽ αὐγῆις αὔξεται ἠελίου,
τοῖς ἴκελοι πήχυιον ἐπὶ χρόνον ἄνθεσιν ἥβης
    τερπόμεθα, πρὸς θεῶν εἰδότες οὔτε κακὸν
οὔτ᾽ ἀγαθόν· Κῆρες δὲ παρεστήκασι μέλαιναι,
    ἡ μὲν ἔχουσα τέλος γήραος ἀργαλέου,
ἡ δ᾽ ἑτέρη θανάτοιο· μίνυνθα δὲ γίνεται ἥβης
    καρπός, ὅσον τ᾽ ἐπὶ γῆν κίδναται ἥλιος.
αὐτὰρ ἐπὴν δὴ τοῦτο τέλος παραμείψεται ὥρης,
    αὐτίκα δὴ τεθνάναι βέλτιον ἢ βίοτος·
πολλὰ γὰρ ἐν θυμῶι κακὰ γίνεται· ἄλλοτε οἶκος
    τρυχοῦται, πενίης δ᾽ ἔργ᾽ ὀδυνηρὰ πέλει·
ἄλλος δ᾽ αὖ παίδων ἐπιδεύεται, ὧν τε μάλιστα
    ἱμείρων κατὰ γῆς ἔρχεται εἰς Ἀΐδην·

ἄλλος νοῦσον ἔχει θυμοφθόρον· οὐδέ τίς ἐστιν
ἀνθρώπων ὧι Ζεὺς μὴ κακὰ πολλὰ διδοῖ.

Comparing a human's life to that of springtime leaves, Mimnermos describes how the sorrows of old age pale in comparison to the pleasures of youth. Acknowledging that humans may not experience old age identically ('at one time,' ἄλλοτε, 2.11; 'another,' ἄλλος, 2.13; 'another,' ἄλλος, 2.15), he ends the poem by stating that all human experiences ultimately have a common origin in Zeus (15–16). The option to die once announced as a personal choice (τεθναίην; 1.2) appears as one of two eventualities presented to all humankind by the Fates here (2.5): the individual is a community member at the outset. The first person voice is no longer singular (1.2) but plural ('we,' ἡμεῖς; 2.1). Like old age, our existence was designed in a particular way and outside of the realm of human agency. Human life includes inexorable evils (κακά; 10) and for that reason, we are all very much alike.

Mimnermos reappraises the human experience as the poem develops. The simile "we are like leaves," becomes less apt as the poem continues. All of the indications of time are cyclical in the poem's earlier lines. Springtime does not die; it moves on and changes into another season. The sun and its light do not, as they seem to do in Carson's translation of fragment 1, expire; they merely shift location.[32] The truth is we all are not like the products of spring, because they reappear with the season. No human can return once he has died and been buried (14).[33] Quite to the contrary, Mimnermos highlights the possibility of sterility ('another lacks children,' ἄλλος . . . παίδων ἐπιδεύεται; 2.13). Though spring is described as the season that has "many blooms" (πολυάνθεμος) in line 1, we learn in line 16 that the only multiplicity germane to the human lifespan is of "troubles" (κακὰ πολλά). Humans are not guaranteed children, and the one creative act that might dispel oblivion, reproduction, slips from our

---

[32] Cf. the sun's permanence in Mimnermos 12.1–3: "[t]he sun has been allotted toils for all his days / nor is there ever any rest for his horses or for him" (Ἠέλιος μὲν γὰρ ἔλαχεν πόνον ἤματα πάντα / οὐδέ ποτ' ἄμπαυσις γίνεται οὐδεμία / ἵπποισίν τε καὶ αὐτῶι).

[33] Mimnermos recalls Homer's *Iliad* (6.149). Unlike that scene, there is no glimmer of the next generation here.

grasp—however desperately we long for it (14–15). For Mimnermos, the uncertainty of happiness is our reality.

Carson's poem embraces that view of mortality as her adaptation points to the human lifespan, however indirectly:

fr. 2
All We as Leaves

> *He (following Homer) compares man's life with the leaves.*

All we as leaves in the shock of it:
    spring—
one dull gold bounce and you're there.
    You see the sun?—I built that.
As a lad. The Fates lashing their tails in a corner.
    But (let me think) wasn't it a hotel in Chicago
Where I had the first of those—*my body walking out of the room*
    bent on some deadly errand
and me up on the ceiling just sort of fading out—
    brainsex paintings I used to call them?
In the days when I (so to speak) painted.
    Remember
that oddly wonderful chocolate we got in East
    (as it was then) Berlin?

In line 1, Carson translates many-flowered season (πολυάνθεμος ὥρη) as "shock" as if the season were a single, startling instant. "Spring" stands alone on line 2 and yet, for all this visual, positional power, a power enhanced by "gold" as a translation for 'by the light of the sun' (2.2), the poet uses "dull" to describe its arrival. By rendering 'shoot up' (αὔξεται) as "bounce," Carson introduces an inspired pun on "spring." The English word "spring" may denote a season, a motion, or an object that stores potential energy. It is impossible, at the moment that we read line 2, to know which meaning is active, but "bounce" suggests interplay between all three since bouncing is characterized by repetition; it is the movement both upwards and downwards. "Spring" may signify the repetition of the season and its innate potential. But the pat "you're there" does not communicate hope or excitement. However brilliant the season is for the individual (gold), the fact that it is bound to reappear and blossom once more makes it less spectacular (dull). Since humans cannot reappear, however, that instant is all we ever know. It is quickly upon us, and just as quickly it has passed.

As her poem continues, Carson injects an element of fantasy into the view of mortal reality she inherited from Mimnermos by focusing on what cannot be known and verified by consensus. The subject of "All We as Leaves" is very much like the childless man of Mimnermos 2.13 as he yearns to identify his creative offspring. First he tries to claim the sun, with its cyclical immortality, for his own. "I built that" reveals a mistake. He did not build the sun. He simply enjoyed its presence, and the fact that it still exists is irrelevant to his actions. When the subject tries to pinpoint other construction projects, they become increasingly less tangible. He struggles to recall his "brainsex painting," whose initial description (7–9) half-heartedly points to a tangible, visual object.[34] Note that he merely "called" them paintings and he admits to only having painted "(so to speak)." The speaker's final memory is that of acquisition, "got" (11), a substitute for production. By commenting that the chocolate was "oddly wonderful" and was bought in "East Berlin" the subject reveals two important points. Because he knows its quality, he must have consumed it. More importantly, it was purchased in a place that no longer exists on a map. The parenthetical statement "as it was then" highlights this loss. Despite this erasure, East Berlin remains real to the people who were there.

Just like the lack of children alluded to in poem 2, Carson's speaker longs for memories that elude him. Recall that, in the Greek, the possibility of sterility exacerbates old age because no one remains to remember the individual. In Carson's poem, the subject himself fails to remember his past and appeals to a second person for help in line 13. The subject's first act of creation was a misconstrued act of perception, but as we move on to what could have been actual creations, the speaker expresses himself in interrogatives rather than statements. "Wasn't it?" obviously communicates uncertainty. "Remember," like "spring" before it, could be interpreted as a desperate imperative said by the subject to himself. By the

---

[34] Carson likens poetry to painting in D'Agata (1997). It is likely these 'paintings' were poems, since this section of *Plainwater* is entitled "The Brainsex Paintings," with Carson rejecting firm generic boundaries. Nevertheless, her subject's memories have a hallucinatory air that shrouds his art in potential rather than execution.

time he says "we" in line 13, it becomes clear that he is asking someone to corroborate his memories, but because the external audience never hears the response of the other person, we cannot be sure if he created anything, and the subject's past grows further riddled with uncertainty. It cannot be ignored that the other person, like the children of 2.13, might not exist at all. In that case, the memories are irretrievable and the reality of these creations remains uncertain.[35] If an answer had been given, it was only heard by the "we" of line 13. The audience can merely mourn its inability to help recover that memory and to ever observe the speaker's creations. Here we might recall the loss of Mimnermos' Nanno and the possibility of it ever existing.

Fragment 3

When Mimnermos documents the experience of the singular subject in fragment 3, that subject is again placed in relation to the community: "Though he was, in former times, the most noble, when the season has changed / a father is neither honored nor cherished by his children" (τὸ πρὶν ἐὼν κάλλιστος, ἐπὴν παραμείψεται ὥρη, / οὐδὲ πατὴρ παισὶν τίμιος οὔτε φίλος). The couplet explores the movement from exceptionality to sub-normalcy on account of time; the season changes and, with it, the state of the subject. Because Mimnermos uses a superlative adjective (κάλλιστος; 3.1) to describe the father in the past, he is associated with surpassing what is normal.[36] But, in one line, this exceptional man does not possess what any father normally should: honor and affection from his offspring. Through a normal occurrence, the passage of time, the same man goes from one extreme to the other, from the heights of admiration to the depths of rejection.

[35] Since "All We as Leaves" follows "What Is Life Without Aphrodite," where Carson highlights a relationship between one "you" and one "her," I have imagined that those two constitute the "we" of line 13. Consequently, that "we" ends up being very different from its Greek equivalent (ἡμεῖς; 2.1). If not a specific *pair*, the group has to have been on a trip to a particular place at a particular time in human history. Where the Greek "we" includes the entirety of humankind, exemplified by a variety of people and situations (ἄλλοτε οἶκος 2.11; ἄλλος, 2.13; ἄλλος, 2.15), Carson's "we" remains exclusive.

[36] The adjective κάλλιστος is the superlative form of καλός, which means both 'noble' and 'beautiful.' Carson's translation acknowledges this duality, as discussed above.

The father (πατήρ) of poem 3 is a less specific figure than this exceptionality would suggest. In fragment 2, Mimnermos described spring as the season of blooms (2.1–4) and those blooms constituted the life worth living (1.1–4). No longer in the flower of his youth, the father (πατήρ) has become the man both dishonored (ἀτίμαστος) and disliked (ἐχθρός; 1.9). Convinced that all men must endure misfortune (2.14), Mimnermos depicts the future of this particular subject with a precision guaranteed by the shared human condition. Old age's shared fate makes even the exceptional person feel frighteningly isolated.

Though Carson's poem is nearly bereft of any traces of direct translation, it captures this sense of isolation by lingering on the questions that singular perception can generate:

fr. 3
However Fair He May Once Have Been

In the offing he sees old age.

Yes lovely one it's today forever now what's that shadow unzipping your every childfingered wherefrom?

In her previous responses to Mimnerman verse, Carson displaced some words (cf. god/θεός in 1); however, it was possible, though challenging, to read the texts, if not just side-by-side, but very nearly line-by-line. Here, only two words, "lovely" (cf. 'most noble,' κάλλιστος) and "childfingered" (cf. 'father,' πατήρ), approach the Greek this way. Through these deviations, Carson focuses on the uncertainty of the speaker's viewpoint rather than his social status. Downgrading the initial adjective from the superlative, 'most noble/beautiful' (κάλλιστος) to the positive form of the adjective, 'beautiful' (καλός), she translates it as a description of appearance (lovely) rather than morality or social standing. 'Father' (πατήρ) is echoed by the difficult non-word "childfingered." Whereas the Greek word and its adjectives depend on the relationship between community and household members, "childfingered" may not have that same meaning. "Childfingered" suggests offspring, but it functions as one part of a modifying sequence that includes "your" and "every." What exactly those modifiers are attached to remains ambiguous. Even "it's today" stands on progressively shakier ground. Line 1 ends with a question swathed in murkiness ("shadow") and possible revelation ("unzipping"). Moving on to the second line, we know neither what exact temporal frame to grab hold of—"today," "forever," or "now"—nor whether a question is being asked ("what") or if a clause has been lost. That clause would have begun with "wherefrom."

This confusion makes it difficult to verify what is being perceived and, as a result, to disambiguate what is 'real' from what is not. "Forever" stands in the center of the 11-word line, creating two symmetrical halves. Consequently, "yes lovely one it's today" and "what's that shadow unzipping" mirror each other. It would follow, then, that "lovely one" would find its parallel in "that shadow." Because the addressee is only known as "lovely one," that description seems objectively true: the addressee's loveliness is unflinchingly posited, a facet to be appreciated instead of interrogated. But, on the other side of the line, "that shadow" appears, "unzipping" something. Something had been obscured and is still being revealed. Because there is still so much that the subject cannot "see in the offing," the speaker's sight is exposed as an untrustworthy means of perception. It is as difficult for the reader as it is for the speaker to ascertain what exactly exists at any point in time, including "forever." One wonders how lovely "the lovely one" truly is—never mind what it is and how to represent that for others.

The poem also suggests that interpretive certainty may not be so important as the experience of wading through the uncertainties of the subject's perception. Because the fragment is a couplet, like the bounce of fragment 2 and the Mimnerman lifespan (2.2), the entire scene has passed us by in a "brief cubit of time" (2.3). Mimnermos also used adjectives like 'darkness' and 'gloom' to portray old age. In turn, Carson removes the narrator's omniscience and dramatizes the poetic subject trying to make sense of that opacity. Furthermore, "forever" exposes a mistake the very length of the utterance dramatizes. Reading the fragment ropes the reader into the banes of old age and mortality because making sense of the poem cannot be separated from their effects. We, too, are in the thick of it.

CONCLUSIONS

Carson's poems recreate the state of Mimnermos and his work as it exists for modern audiences without resolving the uncertainties his corpus generates. Her interventions emphasize that the tasks necessary for understanding Mimnerman verse are motley and not merely a matter of verification or inviolable authority. Gone are Mimnermos' universalizing gestures that situate the life cycle of humankind in opposition to that of the gods and coincided with scientism. The contemporary figure in her poems remains estranged from broad consensus, material evidence, and categorical experience. Although her protagonist has memories from the recent past—East Berlin being a particularly useful if ghostly reference—we are as certain about those experiences of his 'reality' as we are about those of the historical Mimnermos, his output (e.g., "Nanno"), and his relationships (e.g., Nanno). The subject of these poems seems to be falling out of the audience's grasp. And yet the reader cannot sit idly by and not wrestle with his situation. Objectivism simply will not suffice.

The poems thus complement Carson's play with the language and literary conventions used to demarcate 'fantasy' from 'reality' in other sections of "The Brainsex Paintings." The poems immerse the reader in a world brimming with the improbable, the displaced, and the unverified. The interviews downplay the supernatural in order to highlight the mystery of the everyday and frustrate the quest for consensus. Carson's essay valorizes subjective response and hints at the supernatural where objective analysis usually prevails. In each genre, Carson could have relied on the values of realism, scientism, and classical philology, especially because of her scholarly training and the special relationship between Greek literary history and realism. Instead, she draws attention to the variety of methods available for understanding Mimnermos as both poet and person. Carson's approach suggests that this situation is not unique. If we want to grapple with human reality, the elements of fantasy—uncertainty, potentiality, and the sensitivity to the dynamics of perception—that constitute our existence and representations of it should not be excluded. For the stuff of real life is complicated, like working with the fragments of a long-lost poet.

13

Aeneas' American New World
in Jo Graham's *Black Ships*

Jennifer A. Rea

Jo Graham's 2008 novel, *Black Ships*, re-envisions the Roman poet Virgil's epic, the *Aeneid* (published after Virgil's death in 19 BCE [*Aen.*]), as a fantasy novel.[1] Central to Aeneas' story is his struggle to come to terms with his destiny as the leader whose actions will lead to the rise of the Roman Empire, and how he must sacrifice his home and his identity to accomplish this goal. The poem culminates in a battle between Aeneas and his rival Turnus, and ends abruptly, with the slain Turnus' ghost flee-ing to Hades.[2] Graham asks the critical question—'What happens next?' for Aeneas following Turnus' death.

[1] I presented an earlier version of this paper at the International Conference of the Fantastic in the Arts in Orlando, Florida, in 2014. My thanks go to Avery D. Cahill and Velvet L. Yates for their thoughtful critiques of this work. I also want to thank Oxford University Press's anonymous readers and the editors of this volume, Brett M. Rogers and Benjamin Eldon Stevens.

[2] Turnus' death, according to Edwards (2007: 24), is not "beautiful . . . but one which raises problems, provokes deep discomfort, even if it was necessary to the foundation of Rome." Edwards observes that, at *Aen.* 2.317, Aeneas looks at the smoking ruins of Troy, and his youthful wish is that he had died in battle. Cox (2011: 262) argues the poem's final moments offer a lack of redemption that guarantees the ending's grief and loss will resonate more with modern audiences than if Aeneas had appeared triumphant in war.

Black Ships engages with the theme of boundaries, both psychological and geographical, that encroach on Aeneas and his men as part of their post-war existence, and in particular, the freedom Aeneas has lost.[3] Throughout Virgil's poem, Aeneas is affected by the sacrifice of giving up his Trojan identity and by the fact that he cannot break away from his past. At the start of *Black Ships*, Aeneas and his men appear to have moved beyond the agony of losing their homeland and are ready to begin a new life. At the novel's end, however, Aeneas' final reflections on his post-war existence prove he has lost much more than just his Trojan identity and that his past can never be denied or abandoned.

Graham reinvents Aeneas as what Carl Rubino terms an 'American' version of the hero, who initially appears to be able to leave his past behind him.[4] Graham has chosen to diminish the role the gods play in Virgil's text and to dismiss any notions that a murderous rage overcame Aeneas in the poem's final scene; her Aeneas no longer fights Turnus in a one-on-one battle. Yet the battle he fights in destroys the promise of a fresh start for him and his men. Although it seems as though Aeneas will be granted an 'American hero' ending, in truth the reader will find Aeneas' post-war reality shaped by the anxiety of not knowing when the enemy will strike again. In this chapter, I argue Graham offers in *Black Ships* a critique of this 'American' ending as an impossible goal in a society that is preoccupied with post-war homeland security.

Graham's engagement with Virgil's text—specifically the *Aeneid*'s ending—offers but one of many illustrations of how fantasy authors confirm the *Aeneid*'s relevance for contemporary American society.[5]

---

[3] Other recent fantasy novels that reimagine Aeneas' epic story include Ursula K. Le Guin's *Lavinia* (2008) and David Gemmell's *Troy* series (2005–2007).

[4] Rubino (2011: 3) defines the American dream as containing "the hope that we can escape the past, make a completely fresh start, and create a new world free from the troubles that haunted our ancestors. This hope . . . is largely absent from the European tradition, with its clearly defined sense of the importance and weight of the past."

[5] As Cox (2011: 248) notes, "America is indebted to ancient Rome." Cox observes that *Aen.*'s themes, which include immigration and colonization, are not far removed from modern apprehension about societal change due to migration. James (2009) notes not only that modern adaptations of classical texts can inform our study of the original sources but also that an enhanced knowledge of classical sources can deepen our enjoyment of and critical responses to works like Graham's novel: contemporary works can offer "a fresh and reinvigorated perspective" on the ancient epic (237). Cf. Hardwick (2003: 32), who notes works from Greco-Roman antiquity can function "as a base from which subsequent generations might analyze and critique not just the ancient world, but their own."

She employs the fantasy genre's discursive nature to consider narratives about national security.[6] While Graham focuses on Aeneas fighting primarily defensive wars, Aeneas' engagement with the enemy does not put an end to the cycle of violence. Rather, fear, isolation, and an uncertain future come from the final battle's aftermath. Aeneas lives long enough to see his son Ascanius grow up and to realize the cost of his violent actions for the Trojans.[7] To analyze how Graham highlights Aeneas as a hero who cannot escape his past, I first look at themes of sacrifice and loss in the *Aeneid*, and then loss and sacrifice of personal freedoms in *Black Ships*. Finally, I explore Rubino's comparison of 'American' and 'ancient' heroes. The former, who are freed from tradition and fate, possess a future in which to accomplish great new things. But the latter cannot escape the past.

THE SACRIFICES OF AENEAS IN VIRGIL'S *AENEID*

Understanding the motif of personal sacrifice in the *Aeneid* can enrich our reading of Graham's novel. After I discuss the poem's ending, I offer an overview of how Aeneas gives up pieces of his former life—his homeland and his Trojan identity—but can never leave the past behind. This is critical to understanding Graham's interpretation of Aeneas' character,

---

[6] For this chapter, I am using John Clute's definition of 'fantasy' in Clute and Grant (1997: 338): "A fantasy text is a self-coherent narrative. When set in this world, it tells a story which is impossible in the world as we perceive it . . . when set in an otherworld, that otherworld will be impossible, though stories set there may be possible in its terms." I am also following Branham (1983: 75), who argues that fantasy does not offer inadequate or incomprehensible worlds, but rather stories that test our sense of security: "If the alien nature of world and events strips us of our comfortable systems of thoughts and expressions, we are forced to be open to new ways of seeing, knowing and living." For consideration of the various divisions, or 'frontiers,' within the fantasy genre, see Bozzetto and Huftier (2004); in particular, Bozzetto (2004: 303–313) focuses on the distinction between the fantastic and the magical. For a brief overview of Western and non-Western proto-fantasy stories (including epic), see Mendlesohn and James (2009: 7–23).

[7] Graham's story takes liberties with the versions of Aeneas' life as found in Livy and Virgil. In *Ab Urbe Condita* (*AUC*), Livy describes how Aeneas won the war, founded Lavinium, and then died later on in another battle while his son, Ascanius, was still too young to rule (1.2). Aeneas' untimely death is also foreshadowed in *Aen.* when Dido prays for it (4.619–620). See Kepple (1976: 356): "The curse against Aeneas becomes, consequently, a malevolent portent of an uncertain future."

since she engages with the theme of Aeneas as a hero who escapes Troy's burning ashes to found a new city.

Scholars have long identified the *Aeneid*'s ending as problematic.[8] Richard Thomas argues for a reading of the ending that clarifies Aeneas' understanding of his actions' significance:

When we turn back to the ending of *Aeneid* 12, no matter how comprehensible the vengeance is, we are left with a sense that it might not have happened and therefore might not needed to have happened (Aeneas' hesitation shows the reality of that possibility).[9]

For Thomas, to see Aeneas as the hero who has considered a different ending means Virgil's audience should consider the moral ambiguity in the conclusion of the *Aeneid* and the likelihood of Aeneas' internal conflict over what he is about to do (12.919–927):

Aeneas, hesitating, brandishes the deadly weapon against him,
choosing fortune with his eyes, and with his whole body
he hurls it from a distance. Rocks moved violently from a war engine
never resound thus, nor have such great clashes burst forth from thunder.
The spear, bearing fearful destruction, flies like a black whirlwind
and pierces the edges of his cuirass, and the extreme layers of his sevenfold
    shield.
Hissing it passes through the middle of his thigh.
Proud Turnus struck falls to the ground with bended knee.

Cunctanti telum Aeneas fatale coruscat,
sortitus fortunam oculis, et corpore toto   920
eminus intorquet. murali concita numquam
tormento sic saxa fremunt nec fulmine tanti
dissultant crepitus. volat atri turbinis instar
exitium dirum hasta ferens orasque recludit
loricae et clipei extremos septemplicis orbis;   925

---

[8] For discussions of how various scholars have interpreted *Aen.*'s ending, see in particular Horsfall (1995: 192–216) and Thomas (2001: 289–296). The unfinished nature of Virgil's work complicates the issue. Hardie (1997: 142–151) suggests the shield's description in *Aen.* book 8 provides more resolution than the epic's last lines because it offers a look at Rome's future. More recently, Putnam (2011: 116) has offered an analysis of the poem's last 30 lines. He argues Virgil's wish to destroy the epic was due to his uncertainty as to how the community of Augustan Rome would receive Aeneas' final actions.

[9] Thomas (2001: 291); see also Farron (1992: 260–276).

per medium stridens transit femur. incidit ictus
ingens ad terram duplicato poplite Turnus.[10]

Aeneas stops for just a moment to reflect on using a *telum fatale*, a
"deadly weapon," against Turnus. His choice to throw his weapon, which
rings out like a "war engine," brings the reader back to Aeneas' inner turmoil at 1.208–209, where he pretends to be optimistic for his crew's sake.
Prior to killing Turnus, Aeneas offers his companions the hope of further
adventures and a chance to found a new city (1.200–207):

You have approached the madness of Scylla and the rocks deeply
  resounding:
And you have tested the Cyclopean rocks: recall your courage and set aside
  sorrowful
fear; perhaps one day it will delight us to have recalled also these things.
Through various perils we enter Latium, through so many dangers,
where the fates reveal peaceful seats to us: there it is right that the kingdom of
Troy should rise up again. Hold fast and save yourselves for prosperous
  events.

vos et Scyllaeam rabiem penitusque sonantis	200
accestis scopulos, vos et Cyclopia saxa	
experti: revocate animos maestumque timorem	
mittite; forsan et haec olim meminisse iuvabit.	
per varios casus, per tot discrimina rerum	
tendimus in Latium, sedes ubi fata quietas	205
ostendunt; illic fas regna resurgere Troiae.	
durate, et vosmet rebus servate secundis.	

Aeneas' speech is tinged with anticipation, as he speaks of the potential "delight" that the Trojans may someday experience in recalling past
trials and predicts that "prosperous events" are to come. Yet Aeneas the
Trojan exile has lost much of his crew. His search for a place where he
can repair his remaining seven damaged ships has taken its toll, and the
Trojans' arrival in North Africa is tainted with sadness: "He says such
things with his voice; and sick with great cares, he feigned hope with his
face and pressed back mighty grief in his heart" (*talia voce refert curisque
ingentibus aeger / spem vultu simulat, premit altum corde dolorem*; *Aen.*

---

[10] The Latin text is from Mynors (1969). All translations are my own.

1.208–209). While Aeneas puts on a brave front to encourage his companions, he does not believe the words he is telling them. He speaks of a time when Troy will rise again—even though he will eventually learn Troy's resurrection will not come to pass. He remains mired in sorrow over his losses.

When Virgil's audience hears Aeneas speak for the first time, he is comforting his people even as he hides his anguish: "O comrades (for we are not ignorant of troubles before), / you who have suffered more grievous things, / the god will give an end also to these" (*O socii, (neque enim ignari sumus ante malorum), / o passi graviora, dabit deus his quoque finem; Aen.* 1.198–199). As Aeneas promises his men that an end will come to their trials, he acknowledges that his companions have endured the same tragedies along with him before he goes on to detail their specific ordeals. Virgil allows his audience to feel the hero's anguish at his lost crewmates and his torment at the devastation of his former city, Troy.[11] Aeneas did not think he could break away from the cycle of misfortune when the epic's audience first sees him, and once he decides to go through with killing Turnus, he perpetuates the cyclical nature of war's violence and vengeance.

The ending does not present closure or resolution. What it does offer the audience is a chance to reflect on what Aeneas' actions might mean for his future. Such reflection involves the perspective of multiple characters.[12] Turnus begs for his life, and if Aeneas will not spare him, he asks for his body at least to be returned to his father for burial (*Aen.* 12.928–939):

He, humble and submissive, stretching forth his eyes and his right hand
    begging, says,
"Indeed I have deserved it, nor do I pray to avert it, use your fortune.
If any care of an unfortunate parent is able to touch you, I beg you pity

---

[11] Smith (2005: 21) describes Aeneas' first appearance before his crew as one that "commands attention and respect" due to his ability to remain in "psychological proximity to the world in which he lives."

[12] Thomas (2001: 296). Galinsky (1988: 326–343), however, argues for more closure, which allows for a reading of the poem's ending that marks Aeneas' killing of Turnus as within the scope of civilized behavior. Lowrie (2005: 950) discusses the civilized aspect of Aeneas' behavior within the context of legal action. She questions whether or not the formation of a state regulated by laws is required before Aeneas can be judged for killing Turnus. Williams (2003: 208–243) defines Aeneas as a 'Law-Giver.' For more on the legal context of Turnus' death, see Shelfer (2011: 295–319).

the old age of Daunus (there has also been for you such a father Anchises)
and return me, or if you prefer, my body, deprived of life, to my family.
You have conquered and the Ausonians have seen me, defeated, extend my
   hands;
Lavinia is your wife, do not reach out further in hate."
Aeneas stood fierce in arms rolling his eyes and drew back his right hand.

ille humilis supplex oculos dextramque precantem
protendens 'equidem merui nec deprecor' inquit;
'utere sorte tua. miseri te si qua parentis   930
tangere cura potest, oro (fuit et tibi talis
Anchises genitor) Dauni miserere senectae
et me, seu corpus spoliatum lumine mavis,
redde meis. vicisti et victum tendere palmas
Ausonii videre; tua est Lavinia coniunx,   935
ulterius ne tende odiis.' stetit acer in armis
Aeneas volvens oculos dextramque repressit.

Turnus' speech to Aeneas recalls Anchises' words at the end of *Aeneid*
book 6. Anchises addresses Aeneas as *Romane* ('o Roman') and reminds
him, as Putman argues, "it was the duty of the empowered Roman warrior
to abase the prideful but also to practice forbearance on those brought
low" (6.851–853).[13] Aeneas' decision to ignore Turnus' plea highlights his
determination. Aeneas ends the battle, but it is not on Anchises' terms; he
defies his father's wish and does not spare Turnus.[14] Thus, his act will not
bring the "prosperous events" he spoke of at 1.207. Instead, the audience is
left with an image of Aeneas' destructive achievement (*Aen.* 12.940–952):

And just now his speech had begun to move him delaying more,
when the unlucky belt of the youth Pallas came into view
on his high shoulder and the belt shone with the familiar studs;
the one whom defeated Turnus had slain with a wound
and he was wearing the hostile badge on his shoulder.
After he received with his eyes the reminders of cruel grief

---

[13] Putnam (2011: 102). Shelfer (2011: 314), however, interprets Aeneas' decision to kill
Turnus within the political and legal context of Virgil's time. Thus, Aeneas' actions in the
epic are restorative in that they will repair broken laws.

[14] James (2009: 18) argues Aeneas demonstrates his independence at the end: "in not
sparing the suddenly meek Turnus, Aeneas has graduated into autonomy and refused to
accept what Anchises identified as the Roman way, that the submissive would be spared."

and the spoils, inflamed with rage and terrible in anger, he said,
"Will you, clothed with the plunder of one of my friends,
be snatched from me hence? Pallas, Pallas sacrifices you
with his wound and exacts this penalty from your profaned blood."
Saying this, burning, he concealed the sword within his hostile chest;
but his limbs grow slack with cold and his life fled indignant
with a lamentation to the shades.

Et iam iamque magis cunctantem flectere sermo   940
coeperat, infelix umero cum apparuit alto
balteus et notis fulserunt cingula bullis
Pallantis pueri, victum quem vulnere Turnus
straverat atque umeris inimicum insigne gerebat.
ille, oculis postquam saevi monimenta doloris   945
exuviasque hausit, furiis accensus et ira
terribilis: 'tune hinc spoliis indute meorum
eripiare mihi? Pallas te hoc vulnere, Pallas
immolat et poenam scelerato ex sanguine sumit.'
hoc dicens ferrum adverso sub pectore condit   950
fervidus; ast illi solvuntur frigore membra
vitaque cum gemitu fugit indignata sub umbras.

This final scene is a stark reminder that those who do not fit into the new
Trojan-Roman assimilated culture will always be regarded as the enemy—
and in a case like Turnus', be eliminated. Aeneas' decision to remove Turnus
as a potential threat to Rome leaves the audience with a lasting sense of
devastation, even as they can see the potential for Rome's future.

Putnam has questioned why Aeneas, who should be the poem's
civilization-builder, appears destructive in the end: "Aeneas' actions tend
toward imitating the more brutal deeds that he or his people have endured
in the past. Witness to a city's ruin, city destroyer, and city founder are
with some irony one and the same."[15] This leaves the audience wondering,
"Who killed Turnus? Trojan Aeneas—whose recall of Troy's destruction
would lead to brutal deeds—or Roman Aeneas—who should be looking
to Rome's future?"[16] The only words we get from Aeneas on this topic are

---

[15] Putnam (2011: 73).

[16] Burnell (1987: 198) concludes Aeneas demonstrates Roman values in the work.
Although Aeneas is lacking in the Roman value of clemency when he kills Turnus, his
actions would be "understandable but regrettable" to a Roman. For a discussion of Trojan
versus Roman Aeneas, see Fratantuono (2007: 386–390).

that it is Pallas, a young man in Aeneas' charge, not Aeneas, who killed Turnus.

Aeneas ends Turnus' life when he realizes Turnus is wearing Pallas' belt. He is inflamed with rage when he kills Turnus: "Aeneas has won Lavinia, he has won the Lavinian shores (1.2–3)—but at a great cost."[17] The epic's end offers no resolution. Turnus' body lies unburied, and the audience, lacking closure, is left to puzzle over Aeneas' actions in the final scene:

> There is a relentless negativity to this conclusion that the poet leaves unresolved. . . . The poet offers us no relief from Aeneas' all-consuming fury, no transcendence into a different emotional or intellectual sphere. Neither through the words of his hero nor within the narration does Virgil come to the defense of his violent action. He gives us no sense that Aeneas kills either to secure his own heroic stature as his poem concludes or to rid the world of negative opposition to his immediate fate or to more distant Roman accomplishments.[18]

The audience comes to realize Aeneas has lost not only his wife and city but also his identity as a Trojan.[19] Yet Aeneas is destined to be the founder of the Roman race, not just the city.[20] In order to be a founder of Rome and the Roman people, he, along with the rest of the Trojans, will lose everything about their society except the Penates, 'household gods' that will become part of Roman religion.[21] Rome's foundation requires Turnus' death and, as Juno commands, the death of Troy: "[Troy] has fallen, and with the name Troy allow [the city] to have fallen (*occidit, occideritque sinas cum nomine Troia*; *Aen.* 12.828). It is the *Aeneid's*

---

[17] Fratantuono (2007: 396). Fratantuono's reading of the poem, which understands Aeneas' character as *choosing* to make Pallas the killer by naming him twice at the end, emphasizes the importance of understanding that "Madness is certainly alive and well at the end of Book 12," thus Madness creates uncertainty about the future for Aeneas and the Trojans (397).

[18] Putnam (2011: 103).

[19] Livy relates that the post-war Trojans had lost everything but their swords and ships (*AUC* 1.1–2). He then states that Aeneas calls his people 'the Latins' in order to strengthen the bond between the Trojans and the native Latins and to hasten the integration of the two groups into one cohesive society.

[20] Papaïoannou (2003: 691).

[21] Lowrie (2005: 954) frames this loss of identity as an act of violence committed by Juno against the Trojans.

anticipation of new beginnings, along with the realization of loss, that will be critical to Graham's treatment of Aeneas as a hero who cannot escape his past, regardless of the circumstances.

JO GRAHAM'S *BLACK SHIPS*

Black Ships (*BS*) tells the story of Gull, a young girl whose Trojan mother was enslaved and raped by the Greeks. Aeneas plays a major role in the story since Gull joins his crew and sails to Italy with them. The addition of Gull's character to Aeneas' story adds a fantasy element since she is a seer whose visions guide the Trojans. As a young girl, Gull's mother had given her to the Pythia at Pylos after she was hurt in an accident and was no longer useful to the Greeks as a slave laborer. It is her ability as a seer that weaves Aeneas' and her stories together, and the audience sees Aeneas' character through Gull's eyes as he struggles to found a new city, lead his people, and secure a future for the Trojans.

Aeneas initially appears to Gull in dreams, when she sees a vision of black ships that hold the Trojans who are fleeing burning Troy. But when Aeneas arrives at Pylos in person, it is in contrast to the audience's first glimpse of him in the *Aeneid*. Aeneas and his men are attempting a daring rescue mission to take any Trojan survivors away from Pylos and King Neoptolemus.[22] Gull stops the violence between the Greeks and the band of men that constitutes the remaining Trojans by physically placing herself between the two groups. Instead of a bloody war, a bittersweet reunion takes place, when the Trojans learn at last who survived the war only to be taken captive by the Greeks.

Aeneas appears at first as a confident leader who seeks advice from Gull and a few other trusted advisors. He meets Gull formally after she stops the battle. When Gull makes his acquaintance, she learns he is a favorite of the Roman goddess Venus. In Virgil's version of the story, Aeneas has divine parentage through his mother, Venus. In *Black Ships*, Aeneas is the son of a mortal woman, Lysisippa, but has Venus' protection. He is called "the Beloved of the Lady of the Sea," and Gull is told he

---

[22] Instead of participating in a raid on a Greek city, Aeneas will hear about this from Helenus in *Aeneid* book 3.

is "the son of Aphrodite Cytherea" (105). It is then explained he is really the son of the mortal Lysisippa, a priestess of Aphrodite Cytherea who raised him in the shrine until he was six. His mother's special devotion to the goddess means he is favored in battle (109):

> No man on any ship he has captained has ever been lost and no ship under his command has foundered, unless you count Menace, which was far from him at the time. He is lucky. Blessed. If it can go well for him, it does. If She can stretch forth Her hand and help him, She does.

Divine support carries Aeneas and his men through their travels without major losses in battle until the final fight with the Greeks near the novel's end. This protection means he does not struggle as he did in the *Aeneid* to find safe passage to Italy. He easily emerges from combat as the victor, and once he has taken the remaining Trojan captives from Greece, he is no longer the aggressor when he faces enemies such as the Greeks or the Rutoli.

Graham repeatedly presents her audience with characters, including Aeneas, who appear to be able to make a fresh start in a new place. Aeneas is absent from Troy during the Greek attacks, for example, so when he returns, the city's devastation is complete and he has not witnessed any destruction firsthand. Aeneas' beloved wife Creusa is raped and killed at Troy while he was away, so, although he does experience her loss, it is not the same as in the *Aeneid* in which he has to leave her behind. Rather, Aeneas, his son Ascanius, and his father Anchises flee Troy knowing there is nothing left for them in the city. By the time Aeneas remarries and starts a new family with Lavinia, Creusa is long forgotten.

Aeneas arrives on Italy's shores expecting to trade with Latinus' men but finds them hostile. They remain armed and refuse to give him any supplies. King Latinus describes how he is engaged in an ongoing war with an enemy known as the Rutoli. The king explains to Aeneas that the Rutoli are waiting until it is convenient (after the harvest) for them to finish the war: "They know we cannot leave, and that they may return in force at any time and finish what they have begun" (*BS* 361). Aeneas offers his crew's labor in exchange for food from the harvest and indicates the crew will assist Latinus' men in defending the city when the Rutoli return to attack. Aeneas fights alongside his men, and Turnus is never singled out when the Rutoli are defeated; in fact, he is never even mentioned by name in the novel. In Graham's version, Aeneas gains the kingdom and Lavinia while fighting alongside his men, all of whom are equally responsible for the victory and the deaths that led to it.

Graham has the warriors quickly recover from the battle with the Rutoli and has one Trojan warrior commenting on how lucky Aeneas and his men are to have found Latium and the residents of Latium to have found the Trojans (*BS* 374):

But here everyone gains. We get a city ready built with people who want us, women who are ready for marrying, good walls and good land. They get men who can defend what they have, and who won't loot them out or take them as slaves.

There is no sense from the residents of Latium that they have been colonized, or that a feeling of being disposed or displaced by the Trojans' arrival is an issue for them.[23] In fact, the two cultures blend seamlessly. Even Aeneas' fear that his two sons, Ascanius and Silvius, will not be able to share one kingdom is alleviated by building another city for Silvius to rule over. Graham's Aeneas lives to see his sons Ascanius and Silvius take over separate kingdoms. He is middle-aged at the novel's end, although one of the characters has a vision that suggests he will live to old age. This means he gets to see the long-term consequences of his actions, including the cost of war. Despite the scenes such as the one above where the audience is told "everyone gains," Aeneas does not get to enjoy his newfound kingdom via his hard-won victory for long. Instead, he must worry about border security, safety, and lack of personal freedom, and he mourns the lives lost in war. When Gull looks at the future site of Rome, all she can see is "too much potential, too many paths, and too many roads . . . too many shadows of the future" (*BS* 384). The promise of future Roman glory is never revealed as it is on the shield in *Aeneid* book 8.

AENEAS' 'AMERICAN DREAM' ADVENTURE

Carl Rubino has suggested "perennial themes" exist that have occupied humankind for "millennia, perhaps even from the very beginnings of human history," which we can acknowledge still today for their relevance.

---

[23] Le Guin takes up this theme of the Trojans' colonization and oppression of the Latins in her fantasy novel *Lavinia*. See Rea (2010: 126–131) for Le Guin's reading of *Aen.* as a tragedy and a discussion of the ways in which violence's cyclical nature fails to offer heroes closure or resolution. Both Graham and Le Guin engage in post-9/11 discourses regarding the loss of personal freedoms in exchange for order and security.

One of those themes is the hero being "called to sacrifice everything," which recalls Aeneas' situation. He must give up almost everything to achieve Rome's eventual founding. Both in the *Aeneid* and in *Black Ships*, Aeneas is required to fulfill his destiny as Rome's founding father. Virgil's audience knows, however, that the sacrifices will lead to the founding of the Roman Empire. The freedom Aeneas gives up in *Black Ships* goes beyond the epic tradition of what Rubino calls the hero's inability to escape from "the importance and weight of the past."[24] Graham's novel questions whether the sacrifices Aeneas must make in order to achieve a secure society for himself and his fellow Trojans are too great, given that the Trojans exist in fear, with an uncertain future ahead of them.[25] Her vision of Aeneas' aftermath reminds us Aeneas does not know what lies ahead, only that he has nothing left of his former life. His new life consists of waiting for the next enemy to seek him out.

The idea that the hero does not have to be concerned with history repeating itself is vital to Graham's novel at key points. At first, her Aeneas appears to have escaped the wars of the past and put his fear of the enemy behind him; he is on an 'American' adventure where he has a chance to give the Trojans a fresh start. But the book's final scenes suggest Graham has added an innovative twist to the 'American' adventure: her ending casts doubt on what the new, post-war world has to offer war heroes besides fear and isolation. Rubino argues that stories such as *Star Wars*, which contain modern adaptations of the hero's journey based on ancient Greco-Roman myth, add a "uniquely American touch" when they allow the hero to escape the past and make a fresh start:

Unlike the great heroes of Greek and Roman epic, American heroes—and thus all Americans—are called to make their own destiny, not merely to follow in the steps of their forebears. There is more to this than the notion that individual human beings, be they "real people" or characters in myth or works of fiction, can escape the call of destiny. The "American dream" includes the hope that we can escape the past, make a completely fresh start, and create a new world free from the troubles that haunted our ancestors.[26]

---

[24] Rubino (2011: 3).
[25] Tarrant (2012: 27) reminds readers the epic does not offer an "idealized" ending and perhaps the best that can be hoped for is that "lust for violence" is prevented from taking over the Empire.
[26] Rubino (2011: 3).

Yet, in Graham's book, there is a loss of freedom the Trojans experience when they put the past behind them. In the *Aeneid*, the final battle takes place between the Trojan Aeneas and the Rutulian prince Turnus. Graham includes a fight between the Rutoli and the Trojans, but the final combat scene in her book is between the Trojans and the Greeks, who have sought out the Trojans for one final fight following the war. When the Trojans defeat the Greeks for the last time, it would seem there is a chance Aeneas and his comrades can have a better life.

It becomes clear, however, that peace consists of an uneasy state, and there is no more resolution to be found here than in the *Aeneid*. Aeneas recounts to Gull that now, instead of sailing around to look at other civilizations, he has been reduced to hearing from foreign traders the state of world affairs (*BS* 396): "Men do not measure grain in tallies anymore, or write down the number of their measures. They do not build on the coast, but in strong places inland, and do not send their ships to trade far from home. The world has ended and the great days are past." Aeneas' final comment is in contrast with the *Aeneid*'s ending, where the audience knows that, despite Aeneas' killing of Turnus, Rome's future greatness lies ahead. But more than that, there is a caution in Aeneas' statement that contrasts with his past bravery. Here the future is uncertain, with Aeneas hesitant and doubting whether even the Shades of Hades would recall his deeds. Although the novel ends with the phrase "and the world was mended," Aeneas' 'mended world' can break apart again at any time. For Aeneas and his men, "the promise of a new world" or a 'mended' one has been replaced by anxiety about the future. There is no great adventure for the Trojans to begin once they put their past behind them, and no real future to anticipate. Aeneas has chosen a remote existence for his community as he regrets how the world has changed: his people have settled inland, they are cut off from other cultures, and there are no new heroes among the next generation.

Rubino contrasts the ancient heroes who can never fully "seek the promise of a new world" because of their emphasis on tradition, or the "importance and weight of the past," with what he labels the 'American heroes' who are not bound by the concept that the past will define their future. Graham's Aeneas seems at first like he could be Rubino's 'American hero,' but in the end his ability to escape the past is limited by his fear of the future.[27] He

---

[27] Ibid. (3).

should have a promising future, but by shunning encounters with foreign cultures, travel, and resisting new adventures, he has nothing left. Graham's novel suggests the world cannot ever be the same after the devastation of war.

BLACK SHIPS AND AMERICAN HOMELAND SECURITY

Black Ships' treatment of Aeneas and the remaining Trojans' post-war existence reflects an American consciousness of the world after the attacks of September 11, 2001.[28] In particular, the emphasis on being in a state of perpetual war due to the possibility of attacks on American soil has shaped the political dialogue and transformed thoughts about the future:

The horrific events of September 11, 2001, are seared into the collective unconscious of the American public. Indeed it has become almost cliché to say that the 9/11 attacks were a watershed moment in U.S. history—one that forever changed the social lives of Americans and the foreign policy of the U.S. government.... Over time, public fear has subsided though not vanished, paranoia has diminished though not disappeared, and a sense of normalcy has returned, although the nation has not forgotten.[29]

September 11, 2001, demonstrated for Americans that one event can mark a shift in both how a population understands history and foreign policy and how a society redefines normal existence: "History itself seemed to pivot on a singular moment in which past and present were replaced by before and after." Along with the idea that "civilians were no longer safe or secure even at home," came distrust of others, fear, and increased travel restrictions.[30] This is reflected in Graham's novel as the

---

[28] See Adler (2008: 596–600), for an overview of why, post-9/11, academic scholars have renewed their interest in the Roman Empire as relevant for discussing American foreign policy. Adler identifies Rome's "defensive imperialism" as significant for our understanding of direct versus indirect rule within American contemporary contexts (600).

[29] Ott (2008: 12–13).

[30] Ibid. (13). Ott argues that this kind of discourse allows us to confront our fears and, in a post-9/11 world, establish not only a common enemy but also what he terms as a "collective challenger" to those fears (21). Thus, the theme of establishing a common, cohesive identity for the Trojans and the Latins in Virgil's epic relates well to post-9/11 American political policy.

characters take on a similar attitude towards their post-war means of survival. Her story creates a space for a discourse on the effects of violence on a society.

Aeneas' laments about no longer traveling and a fear of building too close to the coast reflect contemporary concerns regarding travel restrictions and homeland security. The ending of Graham's book tackles tough social issues relevant to our times, such as how acts of war can cause the loss of personal freedoms and security.[31] The awareness of 'before and after' is striking as the reader contrasts the Trojans' travel and adventures prior to the final battle with the Greeks. I would argue the novel invites its modern audience to consider the consequences of an existence limited by boundaries both psychological and geographical. *Black Ships'* fantasy world may engage the audience in an imaginary story but it also creates a critical thinking space for us by distorting our reality in a way that forces us to think about "the culture that produced it."[32] The Trojans' desire to give up their personal freedoms to travel and seek new conquests does not appear remote from post-9/11 fears about homeland security and foreign occupation.

Black Ships also invites us to consider whether or not the characters can be happy living in the post-war world. Can the Trojans find happiness with an existence that requires them to be content with what they have and not to seek new conquests? Their world was once full of brave deeds and the knowledge they had suffered tragic circumstances and yet had gone on to search for better lives for themselves.[33] The final line of the novel, "And the world was mended," seems to suggest the realization of happiness has been achieved, and that the Trojans, having done what was required of them, should now be content to accept living out the rest of their lives in mundane circumstances. But the final line contrasts with Aeneas' concern that there are no new adventures or heroes to come, suggesting one should read more into it. The 'mended' version of

---

[31] Ibid. (16): "As social anxieties change over time, so do the discourses that address them."

[32] Ibid. (16).

[33] Cf. Baldwin (2008: 3–14), who argues Aristotelian and Stoic ideals can be applied to works in which the world as the characters know it ends. According to Baldwin, when the characters choose to be happy in their post-apocalyptic existence, it is because they accept what happened and want only what has been given to them.

the Trojans' world requires its inhabitants to renounce their former lives and to give up daring to explore the kind of adventure that would allow them to escape their past.

CONCLUSION

Part of Rubino's claim for why the non-American heroes cannot let go of their past has to do with the hero's prior actions determining their future. However, by eliminating Virgil's focus on Aeneas' losses through Troy's destruction and any potential turmoil over Turnus' death, Graham leads her audience to believe that Aeneas might have a chance to let go of his past and attain the 'American dream' ending. Her Aeneas does not have a final, dramatic, fight-to-the-death scene with Turnus. Instead, at every opportunity to make a truce or reduce the bloodshed, he is a willing ally. Turnus is merely one of many who must die in order for Aeneas to succeed in his destiny as king. These pacifist efforts do not pay off, since Aeneas is left waiting until the next enemy rises up to defeat him.

In order to highlight the similarities between the post-war anxieties of antiquity and present apprehensions regarding the loss of personal freedoms in a post-9/11 world, Graham subverts the tradition of the hero who has no place in the new world and offers us a glimpse of a middle-aged Aeneas being forced to live out his days knowing the best times are behind him.[34] Only a vague future exists for him, instead of his knowing Rome's glory awaits his descendants. He is no better off than he was at the *Aeneid*'s end. It could be argued he is even worse off, since Aeneas becomes his own worst enemy—indeed he embodies the perennial theme, identified by Rubino, of the hero who is unable to escape his past. Viewed thus, Aeneas lets Graham offer her readers a critical look at how fantasy narratives can strip us of our complacency and encourage us to evaluate our existence in new ways. Graham has given us a world "mended" to reveal the American dream has been compromised in the post-9/11 realm of anxiety.

---

[34] The scope of this paper does not allow for an extensive discussion of how Graham also subverts the promise of a Golden Age. For more on the Golden Age in *Aen.*, see Evans (2008: 66–68) and Rea (2008: 80–84); for a more extensive treatment of the Golden Age in Rome, see Gatz (1967).

Graham's central narrative draws upon Greco-Roman antiquity's tradition of the war hero who does not have a place in the post-war world he helped create (e.g., Achilles, Agamemnon, and Aeneas). Her work also draws attention to how Virgil's epic demonstrates that the cycle of violence is not broken at the end: even Rome's foundation will not stop the bloodshed. *Black Ships* may engage the audience in a fantasy world, but it also initiates a discourse on what would constitute homeland security for the Trojans that does not appear distant from post-9/11 anxieties about national defense. In particular, I suggest Graham draws on a post-9/11 interest in the Roman Empire, an interest that turns to Rome as the key to comprehending the deepest fears regarding the price paid for living in a post-war world where individual liberties are ceded to communal security.

14

Genre, Mimesis, and Virgilian Intertext in George R. R. Martin's *A Song of Ice and Fire*

Ayelet Haimson Lushkov

Wolfgang Petersen's *Troy* came out in 2004 to little critical acclaim.[1] Classicists in particular had reason to be cagey, if not downright hostile, towards the many liberties the film took with Homer's epic.[2] For Romanists, however, there was one small reason to rejoice, since *Troy* features one of the relatively infrequent cinematic appearances of the Roman hero Aeneas.[3] As the city burns all about him, the young hero, equipped with aged father but minus the burden of wife and child, eagerly

[1] I am grateful to Brett M. Rogers, Benjamin Eldon Stevens, Pramit Chaudhuri, and audiences at both the 2012 meeting of the Pacific Ancient and Modern Language Association and the 2013 meeting of the American Philological Association (now Society for Classical Studies) for comments on this and earlier versions of this paper. I should also like to thank my former students Adriana Casarez, Dusty Rhodes, and Andrew Zigler, to whom this paper is dedicated, for their initial enthusiasm for this project and their continued tolerance since.

[2] Academic responses to the film: see Winkler (2007), Mendelsohn (2008), and Paul (2013).

[3] For a survey of the *Aeneid* in film and television, see Solomon (2013).

accepts from Paris the golden 'sword of Troy,' a talismanic reassurance—albeit invented for the film—of the survival of the Trojan race. As a miniaturized version of the second book of Virgil's epic *Aeneid* (*Aen.*), the moment leaves more out than a young Iulus, Aeneas' son, but it captures rather neatly the transference of cultural capital with which the *Aeneid* is so concerned—from the epic realm of Troy to the muddled history of Rome and Italy.[4]

As cinematic good fortune would have it, the author of Aeneas' brief appearance, *Troy*'s scriptwriter David Benioff, has since gone on to write and produce HBO's televised adaptation of a very different sort of text, George R. R. Martin's *A Song of Ice and Fire* (*SIF*), a sprawling fantasy saga, which narrates a protracted civil war in the medieval- and chivalric-inspired land of Westeros.[5] The coincidence of Benioff having a hand in both properties is precisely that, but it is also serendipitous, because it provides a sharp reminder of the shared idiom of the two genres. Feasting, warring, dying, an incessant quest for fame, and a pronounced streak of self-reflexivity unify both epic and fantasy in the familiar language of the heroic, translated from ancient hexameter to modern prose and celluloid.[6]

Three degrees of separation notwithstanding, in this chapter I want to take rather more seriously the presence of the classics, and specifically of Virgil's *Aeneid*, in Martin's Westeros and to argue that the *Aeneid*, as well as the Homeric resonances it carries along with it, helps us untangle some of the modern work's bewildering mass of detail. I argue that Virgil's episode of Nisus and Euryalus, the two young Trojans who go raiding

---

[4] Paul (2013: 75) notes that scenes such as these, however poorly executed, "gesture towards the existence of an epic tradition." They thus replicate the oral tradition in which Homer's *Iliad* developed.

[5] The HBO series is called *Game of Thrones*. The book series *SIF* is currently made up of five volumes, of which I refer by name only to the first three. They are *A Game of Thrones* (1996), *A Clash of Kings* (1998), and *A Storm of Swords* (2000). I use the following editions: Martin (2011a) for *A Game of Thrones* (*GT*); Martin (2003) for *A Clash of Kings* (*CK*); and Martin (2011b) for *A Storm of Swords* (*SS*).

[6] By 'epic' I refer to classical—ancient Greek and Roman—epic, which has much in common structurally and thematically with the heroic literature of other cultures; cf. Weiner (this volume). The definition of 'fantasy' is more complex, as the editors lay out in their Introduction, but my interest here is in Martin specifically rather than the genre more broadly. I take 'modern fantasy' as fiction in which the normal rules of physics, biology, evolution, or technological development are suspended, and which was authored in what is commonly understood as the modern era.

through the Rutulian camp (*Aen.* 9.176–449), offers a structuring device for one of Martin's minor plot lines, the relationship of Renly Baratheon with Loras Tyrell and their movement together from the ludic context of chivalric tournaments in *SIF*'s first book to the martial plot of the second.[7] Concomitantly, I want to use this reading not as a strictly philological or historical exercise but rather as a test case for classical reception as a reading practice. What emerges from this experiment, I suggest, is a symbiosis of ancient and modern that yields benefits both for literary criticism and for classical outreach.

In the present context, my approach sets to one side the historically contingent questions of authorial intent or the audience's knowledge of Virgil and focuses instead on the possibility of a broader intertextual relationship. Indeed, *SIF*, at five volumes and 6,000 pages, makes no direct gestures to any classical text, nor have the responses to the series to date focused on the classical content of Martin's library; furthermore, for many of *Game of Thrones*' viewers or *SIF*'s readers, the *Aeneid* is probably relatively unknown.[8] This state of affairs effectively inverts the usual models of reception that classical reception is accustomed to, where the classical text is a privileged model, to which both authors and readers respond critically and from a shared background. Instead, *SIF* offers a reception context in which the Virgilian 'source' exists primarily in the mind of a relatively small group of readers, and in which the considerable authority of the *Aeneid* is brought to bear more obviously by the interested reader rather than by the author.

That the intentions of the author or of the majority of readers should not determine a work's interpretation is a longstanding canon of literary criticism, both outside and within Classics.[9] An exclusive focus on either author or reader, however, necessarily ignores the text itself as a locus

---

[7] The bibliography on Nisus and Euryalus is considerable; see Hardie (1994: 23–34) and Horsfall (1995: 170–178), with bibliographical highlights collected in Whittington (2010: 594 n. 19). For the episode's use of Homer's *Doloneia* and its scholiastic tradition, see Casali (2004).

[8] The work of cataloguing potential allusions is largely done by fans, which may account for the predominance of other works of fantasy, especially the *Lord of the Rings* trilogy. A representative example can be found at Ran (2005). I have not contacted Martin myself; indeed, my argument questions the tendency to afford ancient texts greater freedom from authorial control than modern—especially popular—works.

[9] For the theory, see Wimsatt and Beardsley (1946), Barthes (1977), Foucault (1977), Fish (1982), Martindale (1993), and Hinds (1998).

of transmission, where formal mechanisms such as allusion and intertext preserve a distinctive reading practice.[10] The genre of fantasy, partly
defined by its concerns with chivalric heroism and the supernatural, exists
in a clear genealogical relationship with the genre of chivalric romance
and epic, and hence classical epic. This family tree, which preserves
salient characteristics from Homer down to Martin, should encourage
critics to attend to the evolutions and variations that unify and differentiate the tradition and its local exemplars. Moreover, as Stephen Hinds has
shown, the apparent inertness of a typical feature of a tradition—a 'mere'
commonplace—can always be animated through pointed juxtaposition
with other commonplaces: whether as a self-reflexive commentary on the
topos itself or as a startling invocation of a competing subtext or mood,
intertextuality offers the potential to enlarge our understanding of a work
by bringing texts together for productive comparison at the micro and
macro levels.[11]

With all of that in mind, this essay does not seek to pin down a causal
relationship of influence between Virgil and Martin. Instead, it engages
the question of intertextuality between the two authors on many such
levels: local similarities of characterization, action, and narrative features
such as the *mise en scène*; commonplaces running through the epic and
romance traditions; and the plot structures associated with particular
genres. The *Aeneid* is to be found in Westeros, whether or not Martin
took Virgil as an explicit literary guide.

For a reader versed in the *Aeneid*, the Nisus and Euryalus episode provides a template for Renly and Loras, but it is a template they follow partially and with interesting variations. The setting aside of intentionality
frees us to ask what work the Virgilian intertext, and the logic of Virgilian
epic more generally, enables Martin's characters and plots to do, and how
it helps bring out some important points in higher relief. It does not seek
to establish the *Aeneid* as a primary explanatory paradigm, but rather as
one option among many. The *Aeneid* provides, nevertheless, a salutary
comparison, and I conclude by suggesting that similarities and differences in Martin's handling of the type-scene have further implications for
the dynamics of plot and genre in the work.

---

[10] Kallendorf (2006).
[11] Hinds (1998: 17–51).

What do I mean by 'the logic of Virgilian epic'? Within the *Aeneid*, the Nisus and Euryalus episode performs various functions beyond narrating the tragic deaths of those young warriors. For example, the episode reflects on youth and its characteristics in a time of war and obliquely offers an alternative view of epic emplotment. As Nisus doubles back to find Euryalus, he recalls Aeneas' pointed failure to find Creusa during the last fatal night at Troy, a gender-bending allusion that is characteristic of the episode's reception tradition.[12] Within this allusion is embedded also a generic commitment to teleological narrative: Aeneas as an epic hero cannot look backwards, whereas Nisus, a more romantic figure, must retrace his steps towards an inevitable death. Even as a minor narrative, and in fact because of being such, the subplot of Renly and Loras responds precisely to the digressive quality of Nisus and Euryalus' night raid. Each episode is likewise a *mise en abyme*, a miniature narrative of failed conquest within works dedicated to narratives of failed leadership.[13] And the topos more generally functions as a cautionary tale against youthful excess, as well as offering a tragic view of lost hopes and might-have-beens.[14] In that light, Martin's characters participate in an elaborate type scene, which exists within a European tradition that stretches from the Homeric *Doloneia* (*Iliad* book 10) through the Latin epic of Statius,

[12] Nisus: "he tracked back footsteps already seen" (*vestigia retro / observata legit*; *Aen.* 9.393); Aeneas: "I follow back footsteps already seen" (*vestigia retro / observata sequor*; 2.753–754). All translations are my own. Whittington (2010: 604) points out that in Milton's *Paradise Lost* (*PL*), of three variations on Nisus' speech, *me me adsum qui feci* ("I'm here, here, I who did it"; *Aen.* 9.427), Eve's "me me only just object of his ire" (*PL* 10.936) is "the closest to Vergil in both syntax and situation." Virgil's episode alludes to the *Georgics'* accounts of Orpheus and Eurydice; see Hardie (1994: 26). In *SIF*, gender bending is more explicit, through Loras's good looks and the presence of the mannish Brienne, who mirrors him in some important aspects (see n. 32, this chapter).

[13] On *mise en abyme* with specific reference to the Nisus and Euryalus episode, see Fowler (2000). On *Aen.* book 9 and narratives of failed (or immature) leadership, see Hardie (1994: 14–18). On the Nisus and Euryalus episode as an epyllion, see Mendell (1951: 216–219) and Hardie (1994: 24–25). The *SIF* saga is a kaleidoscope of juxtaposed *mise en abyme* narratives. Renly's camp is, however, perhaps the most explicitly self-referential (*CK* 256): "'Because it will not last,' Catelyn answered sadly. 'Because they are the knights of summer, and winter is coming.' 'Lady Catelyn, you are wrong.' Brienne regarded her with eyes as blue as her armor. 'Winter will never come for the likes of us. Should we die in battle, they will surely sing of us, and it's always summer in the songs. In the songs all knights are gallant, all maids are beautiful, and the sun is always shining.'" The issues of identity here are worth noting: Catelyn's inability to see the world in other than stark terms is paralleled by her husband (see *GT* 470, quoted below). The difference between song and real life, and the resultant disappointments, are a preoccupation of *SIF*, and almost all of the main characters suffer disillusionment at some stage.

[14] For adulthood and childhood in *Aen.*, see, e.g., Petrini (1997: 21–47); for the fetishization of the heroic death, see Reed (2007: 16–43).

to the Italian epic of Ariosto and beyond, and which is formative for and emblematic of our broader understanding of epic, especially in its concern with heroism, pathos, and eros.[15]

CLASSICAL CONTINUITIES: STRUCTURE AND THEMES

The intertextuality between *SIF*'s Renly–Loras episode and the *Aeneid*'s Nisus–Euryalus episode is cued by two structural elements: first, the ambiguous sexual status of each pair's relationship; and second, the sequence of killing and frenzy operative in both episodes. The nature of the relationship between Renly and Loras has been somewhat controversial, especially after the HBO adaptation presented it decisively, and with Martin's approval, as sexual.[16] Nisus and Euryalus, too, whether Virgil meant them as lovers or the best of friends, certainly echo other such doomed pairs, chiefly Homer's Achilles and Patroclus.[17] More specific verbal echoes support the intertextuality as well, especially with the younger half of the pair. Both Loras and Euryalus are young, beautiful, and characterized by floral imagery. Loras is known as the Knight of Flowers, whose armor and other chivalric equipment display all manner of flowers, and whose sigil is the rose (*GT* 297): "Sansa had never seen anyone <u>so beautiful</u>. His plate was intricately fashioned and enameled as a bouquet of a <u>thousand different flowers</u>, and his snow-white stallion was draped in a blanket of <u>red and white roses</u>." Euryalus, meanwhile, is introduced as the loveliest of the young Trojans, in possession of verdant youth—"Euryalus, noted for his beauty and flourishing youth" (*Euryalus forma insignis viridique iuventa*; *Aen.* 5.295)—and is famously likened to a drooping flower at the point of his death (9.433–437):

Euryalus collapses in death, his blood flows over his beautiful
limbs, and his neck, bent, droops on his shoulders:
just as a crimson flower, cut by the plow,   435
languishes dying, and the poppy flower with weary neck
lowers its head when, by chance, rains weigh it down.

---

[15] See Pavlock (1990: esp. 87–112) on Nisus and Euryalus.

[16] Martin confirmed that he "did intend those characters to be gay" at a convention in May 2005; see 'Odiedragon' (2005).

[17] Servius (*ad Aen.* 9.180) kicks off the debate by explaining Virgil's "one love" (*unus amor*) as a shared pursuit of common interest: "that is, they burned with the same passion" (*id est eodem studio flagrabant*). The modern opinions are summarized in Hardie (1994: 31–34).

volvitur Euryalus leto, pulchrosque per artus
it cruor inque umeros cervix conlapsa recumbit:
purpureus veluti cum flos succisus aratro   435
languescit moriens, lassove papavera collo
demisere caput pluvia cum forte gravantur.

The similarities extend to the level of plot structure. We encounter both pairs—Renly and Loras; Nisus and Euryalus—in two separate
phases: first a ludic context, games or tourneys, followed by actual, and
deadly, war. When the narrative refocuses on each pair during the war,
both pairs further follow the same pattern: expedition, separation, death,
and frenzy. So, Nisus and Eurylaus compete in a footrace in *Aeneid* book 5,
while Loras and Renly participate in a chivalric tournament early in *GT*,
the first novel of the series. Both Loras and Euryalus win their events with
the aid of a trick: Loras rides a mare in heat in order to agitate his opponent's stallion, while Nisus trips up a competitor to help Euryalus win
the race. After the victory, in each case there is some argument about the
awarding of prizes. Loras faces the wrath of the knight he had defeated
and ends up forfeiting his reward, while Nisus, who had slipped on a
patch of blood in the race, demands some prize as compensation for his
bad luck.[18] Some time later, after both texts shift to a context of civil war,
both pairs embark on a daring military enterprise. On the eve of battle,
Renly and Loras are separated when they tend to their own commands,
while Nisus and Euryalus are involuntarily separated as they get lost
during their raid of an enemy camp. One of each pair dies (Renly and
Eurylaus) and the other (Nisus and Loras) goes mad and seeks revenge.

IMITATION AND THE REAL

Even this very schematic outline already points to some interesting differences; in particular, the neat equivalence between the pairs is often
complicated. For instance, Renly, unlike Nisus, leads an army—rather
than just a single companion—and not for a mere night raid, but with

---

[18] Loras: *GT* 314–316. Nisus and Euryalus: *Aen.* 5.353–358. Nisus will eventually be
promised "worthy gifts" (*digna dona*) by Iulus in reward for the night raid (9.257–280); on
the problems of the gift exchange, see Casali (2004: 327–335).

the rather grander aim of asserting his claim to the throne. If he is the Nisus to Loras's Euryalus, however, he is nevertheless an unwarlike itera- tion of the trope. Crucially, where Nisus has a glorious *aristeia* ('moment of excellence in battle') to his name, Renly's participation in combat is patchy: where his brothers are warriors of renown, Renly was a young child during the war that brought his family to power, and his subse- quent appearances track him as he comes ever nearer to fighting, mov- ing steadily from court schemer, to royal spectator, to an almost-warrior. Thus, he jousts in the Tournament of the Hand but is eliminated in the early rounds; he presides over, but does not participate in, the war games held during preparations for his campaign; and his premature death stops short what would have been his first full-scale military engagement.[19]

What this pattern exposes, however, is a deeper consistency between the two texts, one that engages one of Virgil's fundamental concerns in *Aeneid* book 9. Nisus, who is introduced as a companion of Aeneas (*comitem Aeneae*; 9.177), is also one of a set of younger and less expe- rienced men left behind when Aeneas departs to seek reinforcements. Indeed, Nisus and Euryalus embark on their doomed mission in order to find Aeneas and bring him back to the Trojan camp, which is mean- while run by Iulus and a council of elders, all of whom are barely able to sustain the Trojan line against Rutulian attacks. Book 9 is thus in important ways both suggestively counterfactual and proleptic, expos- ing the worrying consequences of removing Aeneas from the epic plot, and establishing his centrality to the epic present as well as the Roman future. This situation parallels the situation in *SIF*: a king who is absent first due to drink and then, more permanently, due to his death, and a kingdom run by councilors and later on by children. Much like Renly's campaign, populated by young and optimistic soldiers—the 'knights of summer' in one character's phrase—the build-up to Nisus' and Euryalus' raid offers a view of youthful excess when left unsupervised, their good intentions notwithstanding.[20] In a very obvious sense, therefore, both

[19] Tournament of the Hand: *GT* 294–296; mêlée at Bitterbridge: *CK* 247–254; death before battle: *CK* 365–367.

[20] *CK* 256 "'Because it will not last,' Catelyn answered sadly. 'Because they are the knights of summer, and winter is coming.'" Renly's 'extreme youth' is emphasized in his first appearance (*GT* 147), in pointed contrast to Barristan the Bold, whom Renly nick- names 'Barristan the Old.'

texts demand that their heroes mature quickly in order to achieve success, and derive their poignancy from the heroes' failure to do so. This miniature *Bildungsroman* or 'story of maturation' is figured also in the broader plot, which progresses relentlessly from heroic play to a full-fledged, and deadly, war.

Like Iulus, and like Nisus himself, Renly also substitutes for, but fails to improve upon, a stronger character.[21] Renly, in fact, is described as the living image of his elder brother, the late King Robert (*CK* 250; italics original):

> In their midst, watching and laughing with his young queen by his side, sat a ghost in a golden crown. *Small wonder the lords gather around him, with such fervor,* she thought, *he is Robert come again.* Renly was handsome as Robert had been handsome; long of limb and broad of shoulder, with the same coal black hair, fine and straight, the same deep blue eyes, the same easy smile.

The ghost metaphor, compounded by the anaphoric "same," has various ramifications, but it immediately establishes Renly as an imitation, a shade of the real thing—the brother whom he seeks to replace. The ghost image finds full realization in Renly's own death, when he becomes more literally a ghost in the morning mist (*CK* 369). Moreover, in a later battle, fought after Renly's murder, rumor has it that Renly's ghost appeared to fight beside Loras, but this turns out to be a substitution of a different kind—not a ghost in reality but merely someone dressed in Renly's armor. Like the Homeric Patroclus dressed in Achilles' armor, Renly is confirmed as another iteration of a mimetic figure, with all the literary

---

[21] Iulus tries to imitate his father Aeneas; Nisus feels a less specific impulse to imitate, but, as Hardie points out (1994: 108), Nisus' opening speech, wherein he lays out his motivation for the expedition, combines elements from both Nestor's speech at *Iliad* (*Il.*) 10.204–17 and Diomedes' reply (10.220–26) preceding the *Doloneia*. The evocation of these two characters is here poignant, not only because Nisus and Euryalus will fail to replicate the successes of the *Doloneia*, but also because they (Nestor in *Il.* and Diomedes in his Virgilian reception in *Aen.* 11) typify heroic vigor past its prime, in counterpoint to Virgil's young heroes, who are doomed never to reach theirs. It is also worth noting that both texts feature a council scene with surrogate father figures: Nisus and Euryalus with Iulus, who stands in relation to them as *pater* Aeneas does to the older Trojans; and Renly with his elder brother Stannis and Catelyn Stark, who provides a maternal view onto events. It is perhaps significant in this context that when Renly first appears, he is described jokingly as a "prancing jackanapes" (*GT* 147), an early modern phrase for a monkey, the quintessential imitative animal.

allusivity such repetition entails.[22] The closer we seem to move to an imitation of the Virgilian intertext, and the closer Renly comes to battle, the more superficial or illusory is the character himself.

The abortive movement from imitation to the real is replicated in Loras's story arc as well, though here it manifests itself in aesthetic rather than political terms. In Loras's formal entrance into the plot quoted above, he is introduced as the 'Knight of Flowers.' Sansa's gaze, which focalizes the episode, fetishizes the armor of the young man, just as the poet's gaze lingers on Euryalus' beauty in death. The moment lies at the intersection of a number of thematic concerns. At the tournament, Loras rides a mare in heat to distract his opponent's horse, and he himself has much the same effect on Sansa, who gazes at him with somewhat mindless adoration. The eroticism of the tournament also intersects with a systematic Virgilian concern, as Euryalus is only one of a sequence of young virgins whose death evokes the blood of virginal defloration.[23] Flowers thereby become a loaded symbol, and indeed both youths are attended by floral imagery. The opening description of Loras informs the reader that his armor is worked into a "bouquet of a thousand different flowers, and his snow-white stallion was draped in a blanket of red and white roses" (*GT* 297). The detail of the roses is meant to catch the eye, both of the internal audience, to whom Loras offers the flowers, and of the reading audience, for whom roses might hold a range of symbolic meanings, from the Wars of the Roses to the emblem of romantic love. When Loras appears next, however, his floral armament changes tellingly (*GT* 314):

When the Knight of Flowers made his entrance, a murmur ran through the crowd, and he heard Sansa's fervent whisper, 'Oh, he's so beautiful.' Ser Loras Tyrell was slender as a reed, dressed in a suit of fabulous silver armor polished to a shining sheen and filigreed with twining black vines and tiny blue forget-me-nots.... Across the boy's shoulders his cloak hung heavy. It

---

[22] Pramit Chaudhuri points out to me that Loras's frustration here is at not being able to be identical with Renly, although, ironically, in falling (quite literally) short of his brother, he does in fact replicate Renly in another way. Note, too, the reversal of the Patroclus motif: Garlan Tyrell—the counterfeit—not only appears after, rather than before, his model, but he also in some sense supersedes both Renly and his own brother Loras.

[23] The clearest case is Camilla (*Aen.* 11.801–804), but as Fowler (1987: esp. 188–189, on Euryalus and the poppy simile) has shown, the collocation of floral and bloody imagery is consistent in Latin literary history.

was woven of forget-me-nots, real ones, hundreds of fresh blooms sewn to a heavy woolen cape.

The description this time is focalized through Sansa's father, Lord Eddard Stark, and despite the differences in gender and age, Lord Eddard responds to Loras in much the same terms as his daughter: a fascination with the details of the armor.[24] Unlike the previous joust, where cape and arms bore different flowers, now the flowers on Loras's cape and suit of armor are identical, a similarity to which the text draws explicit attention ("forget-me-nots, real ones"). The difference between the two appearances is explicable as the vanity of a young knight, and both occasions are clearly meant as a spectacle of wealth and excess, a token of Loras's nom de guerre. However, the flowers betoken identity and its stabilization, and their duplication calls attention to the gap between what is real and what is imitative. Loras himself, a storybook knight whose prowess, at least so far, is ludic rather than martial, hovers between the two realms.

Here the shapes begin to rearrange themselves. I have so far treated Loras's and Renly's allusive traits as two parallel lines, but, in the following section, I discuss the plot not as the linear and teleological progression of epic but as the cyclical and repetitive wanderings of romance. The change is triggered by Renly's death, which in turn orders the allusions chiastically. Renly becomes Euryalus, and therefore also Loras; Loras becomes Nisus, and therefore also Renly. At a greater remove, the catastrophe of Renly's death forces Loras from the idyllic world of song into the frenzied *realia* of warfare, while in Virgil, the young lovers' death forces them out of the world of war and into immortality in verse (*fortunati ambo!*).[25]

DEATH, ROLE REVERSAL, AND THE CYCLICAL PLOT

Before focusing on the cyclical plot, it is worth dwelling for a moment on Renly's death itself, which also participates in the sequence from

---

[24] The description of Eddard's gaze includes the bucolic metaphor "slender as a reed," which might be taken as alluding to Virgil's Tityrus, playing on a slender reed (*tenui avena*; *Eclogues* 1.2). If so, we might also say that Eddard has a richer allusive world than his daughter, and one that reaches for the less heroic world of Roman pastoral.

[25] "Fortunate pair! If my songs have any worth, no day shall snatch you from the memory of the ages, not while the people of Aeneas dwells on the immovable rock of the Capitol,

imitation to the real discussed above. Renly's death, and his aborted first battle, both take place below the castle of Storm's End, the family's ancestral seat and the place of his birth. Our last view of Renly in life is of dressing for battle, the classic build-up for the epic *aristeia*, and he is slain, by a mysterious shadow cutting through his gorget, just at the point when he is about to pick up his helmet to complete the arming scene (*CK* 367):[26]

'Cold,' said Renly in a small puzzled voice, a heartbeat before the steel of his gorget parted like cheesecloth beneath the shadow of a blade that was not there. He had time to make a small thick gasp before the blood came gushing out of his throat. . . . The king stumbled from her arms, a sheet of blood creeping down the front of his armor, a dark red tide that drowned his green and gold. More candles guttered out. Renly tried to speak, but he was choking on his own blood. His legs collapsed, and only Brienne's strength was holding him up.

There is much of interest in the scene: blood and shadow have been thematic concerns throughout *CK*, programmatic not only of the family drama of the Baratheons, but also of the developing unrest throughout the kingdom. Blood, and especially its dark red color, is also characteristic of epic heroic death and defloration, and as such the scene recalls also the death of Euryalus, quoted above, a role Renly takes up through his death.

Two more elements are worth drawing out. First, Renly's death itself participates in the broader pattern of progression from imitation to reality, corresponding to, and making real, his only appearance in combat. In a brief passage during the Tournament of the Hand, in which we first meet Loras, Renly is driven from his horse in the early rounds, where the detail of the antlered helm once again appears (*GT* 296):[27]

---

and the Roman father holds dominion" (*Fortunati ambo! si quid mea carmina possunt, / nulla dies umquam memori vos eximet aevo, / dum domus Aeneae Capitoli immobile saxum / accolet imperiumque pater Romanus habebit; Aen.* 9.446–449). On the passage, see Hardie (1994: 153–154); on the irony of Virgil's judgement, see Quinn (1968: 206–207), Fitzgerald (1972: 117), and Fowler (2000: 104).

[26] Helmet: "Brienne brought the king's gauntlets and great helm, crowned with golden antlers that would add a foot and a half to his height. 'The time for talk is done. Now we see who is stronger'" (366).

[27] It appears for the first time at Renly's first introduction (*GT* 144–147), where he is armored and holding his helm, thus forming a ring composition with his last appearance.

Renly was unhorsed so violently that he seemed to fly backward off his charger, legs in the air. His head hit the ground with an audible crack that made the crowd gasp, but it was just the golden antler on his helm. One of the tines had snapped off beneath him.

The moment dissolves quickly into humor, as the crowd fights over the golden antler until Renly walks among them to restore order, foreshadowing his attempt to claim the throne through popularity and alliance. The breaking of the tine, however, is ominous, especially in the symbolic economy of *SIF*, in which heraldic symbolism is strongly referential of its owner's characteristics, and here it stands explicitly for the snapped neck the tournament audience fear and proleptically for the severed neck that will mark Renly's eventual death. As so often in epic, what is farcical in games becomes all too real in war. The fact that the movement of Renly's life and death follows the sequence from imitation to reality has important consequences, not least in suggesting that Renly and Loras each moves towards becoming the other. This idea of such a character inversion has some textual support. The switching of roles is marked in particular by the violent frenzy with which Loras responds to Renly's death.[28] The motto of Renly's family, House Baratheon, their 'words' in Martin's terminology, reads "Ours is the Fury." And yet that fury is one that Loras, in his maddened response to his lover's death, takes upon himself. Thus, Renly becomes Euryalus, and Loras Nisus.

This technique, whereby identities blur, usually at the climax of a duel or in the heat of battle, is a familiar Virgilian technique, as Alessandro Barchiesi and David Quint have observed, as well as a particularly salient feature of the episode's reception history.[29] In Statius and later in Ariosto (who relies equally on his Virgilian and Statian models), the Nisus and

---

Each of these details is first described in the author's voice, and then enumerated by Sansa, a doubling of both appearance and focalization thus intratextually connected to Loras's first appearance. In fact, Sansa thinks Renly "the handsomest man [she] had ever set eyes upon" (144), until she sees Loras at the joust.

[28] The frenzy, too, participates in a variation on the sequence from imitation to reality. We first hear of it indirectly, in a report based on a rumor heard by non-witnesses ("It's said the Knight of Flowers went mad when he saw his king's body, and slew three of Renly's guards in his wrath," *CK* 387). Loras himself later confirms the rumor, admitting obliquely to killing the guards (*SS* 925).

[29] Barchiesi (1984: 30–43) and Quint (2001).

Euryalus roles are regularly switched between the heroic pairs—Hopleus and Dymas in Statius' *Thebaid* and Medoro and Cloridano in Ariosto's *Orlando Furioso*.[30] Statius and Ariosto go further than simple switching, however. Both poets, for instance, sever the pair's games-to-warfare sequence: Ariosto completely, Statius by relegating Dymas to a minor appearance in the funeral games and transferring the Nisus/Euryalus model instead to Parthenopaeus (as his name suggests, yet another virgin) in the footrace.[31] The reception tradition is therefore inherently flexible, and against its background the Virgilian intertext stands out as uniquely fitting for Renly and Loras's plot. This flexibility accounts also for the presence of Brienne of Tarth at the crucial moment of death, since it is she, rather than Loras, who first assumes the role of Nisus through her view of Renly's death and consequent grief. Her anger anticipates Loras's, and in both cases the anger and the violence that follow stand metonymically for the battle Loras and Brienne now have no purpose in fighting.[32]

Loras's fury also corresponds to Nisus' reaction to Euryalus' death and closely traces the movement from frenzy to revenge (*Aen.* 9.423–439):

At once [Volcens] drew his sword and went for Euryalus. Then Nisus, frightened witless, shouts, unable to hide in the shadows any longer, or bear such anguish . . . the sword was thrust with force and pierces the ribs and bursts the white breast. Euryalus collapses in death . . . but Nisus rushes amidst them and through them all seeks only Volcens, dwells only on Volcens.

>   simul ense recluso
> ibat in Euryalum. tum vero exterritus, amens,

---

[30] On the reception of the episode in Statius, see Markus (1997), Pollman (2001), and Ganiban (2007: 131–6); in Ariosto, see Burrow (1993: 62–67) and Wiley Feinstein (1990); in Milton, see Whittington (2010).

[31] Lovatt (2005: 59–71).

[32] Brienne of Tarth is an interesting parallel for Loras throughout, and they form mirror images of each other. Brienne is a tall woman and broad-shouldered, Loras is a slender boy; he is marked throughout as beautiful, she as ugly. When they both fight Renly's guards after seeing Renly dead, her duel is defensive, his is aggressive. This parallelism is sustained by other characters as well: Renly assigns Brienne to the van with Loras (*CK* 383); Jamie Lannister points out to Loras that both he and Brienne cheat in their first (on-record) competition (*SS* 924). Twinning and tripling are preoccupations of Martin through all five books, as they are of epic more generally; see Hardie (1993: 10–11). The best example is Statius' *Thebaid*, on which see Henderson (1991).

conclamat Nisus nec se celare tenebris   425
amplius aut tantum potuit perferre dolorem. . .
                    sed viribus ensis adactus   431
transadigit costas et candida pectora rumpit.
volvitur Euryalus leto. . .
at Nisus ruit in medios solumque per omnis   438
Volcentem petit, in solo Volcente moratur.

Most striking here is Nisus' terrified madness—he is both *amens*
and *territus*—and his vengeful focus on Volcens, whose name Virgil
repeats to emphasize Nisus' intensity: *solumque . . . / Volcentem . . . in
solo Volcente* (438-439).[33] Madness and revenge, together and individually, are typically epic sentiments, which are often used to drive the plot.
The formative example is Homer's Achilles when he hears of the death
of Patroclus, and the hero's reaction is crucial for the narrative of the
Iliad, since it reinstates Achilles into the main plot, gives him the motivation to fight again, and sets him on the path that will lead to his own
death.[34] In miniature, that is what Nisus does, too: a maddened quest
for vengeance, followed shortly by death, and with it a resolution of the
subplot. Anger and revenge, however, likewise drive the *Aeneid*, from
Juno's vengeful ire at the opening of the poem (*memorem Iunonis ob
iram*; 1.4) to Aeneas' revenge-fueled *furor* at its close (*furiis acensus et
ira*; 12.946). Here, too, Nisus follows in Aeneas' footsteps, losing himself
in his final moments in the poem to a madness that threatens to typify
him as an epic paradigm.

Madness likewise plagues Loras. Just as Nisus loses his mind when he
witnesses Euryalus' death, so, too, Loras loses his upon seeing Renly's
corpse. But Euryalus, too, was 'raging' (*perfurit*; *Aen*. 9.343), so drenched
in battle fever that Nisus has to turn him away from the slaughter. Hence,
madness characterizes Loras through both his intertextual predecessors.
But if he successfully matches the madness of Virgil's characters, what
he singularly fails to do is to die, and thus fulfill, finally, the paradigm

---

[33] See Hardie (1994: 151 ad loc.) for other instances of the anaphora with polyptoton
(repetition of the same root in different forms) in the *Aeneid*.

[34] On *furor* as an epic emotion, see Hershkowitz (1998). On post-traumatic stress dis-
order (PTSD) and the emotive response to the death of a 'special friend' in the epic and in
Vietnam, see Shay (1994: 39-68); on PTSD in *SIF*, though without reference to Loras, see
Cole (2012).

established by Nisus and Euryalus. Vengeance here has more immediate consequences than in Virgil, since it sets up a sequence of repetitive attempts to re-enact old battles. Loras is something of a specialist in holding such grudges, even before Renly's death. Late in *GT*, he volunteers to lead an expedition against the same knight whom he had tricked to win the joust (470).

> When the echoes of his words had died away, the Knight of Flowers seemed perplexed. 'Lord Eddard, what of me?'
>
> Ned looked down on him. From on high, Loras Tyrell seemed almost as young as Robb. '<u>No one doubts your valor, Ser Loras, but we are about justice here, and what you seek is vengeance.</u>' He looked back to Lord Beric. 'Ride at first light. These things are best done quickly.'

Lord Eddard's recognition is certainly proleptic, but whereas, before Renly's death, Loras's desire for revenge seemed part and parcel of the chivalric quest for glory, Renly's death concretizes this desire and transforms it into a narrative engine, driving Loras to enact repetitively the battle Renly's murder effectively pre-empted. The first such repetition was the battle supposedly involving Renly's ghost. Despite Loras's being on the winning side in that battle, however, there is no resolution for him, nor indeed for the reader, faced with five volumes yet to come. The second iteration—a suicidal attack on an island fortress—almost realizes the Nisus-like sacrifice that Loras ought to have made some time ago. And yet we hear no confirmation of his death, and his fate is left hanging for another book. This repetition compulsion and deferral, as Quint has shown, is characteristic of a particularly epic view of the plot of romance, coded as endlessly circular, even as epic tells a more linear story of progress and victory.[35] Moreover, the fact that the bereaved Loras seems to embody the tension between epic and romance only re-enlivens the Freudian terminology underlying Quint's narrative theory: desire, repression, grief, death-wish, and transference here function at the levels of character psychology and plot structure, and in doing so they firmly place Martin's work in the most canonical of literary—and literary critical—traditions.

[35] Quint (1993).

CONCLUSIONS

The reading I have offered proceeds from a flexible model of reception, one that employs the Virgilian paradigm in multiple ways and to various effects. The Nisus and Euryalus intertext functions as a structuring device or template, certainly, but it operates in different ways for Renly than it does for Loras, and most importantly it is an imperfect paradigm. Especially when it is imperfect, it highlights important aspects of the character and the plot. Thus, for Renly, who seems to play both the Nisus and Euryalus roles somewhat passively, the campaign is an attempt to inhabit more fully his elder brother's persona en route to inhabiting his own. For Loras, on the other hand, the intertext holds up an image of failure, and reveals his drift into the repetitive plot structures of romance. Later in the series, when the dust has settled, Loras says of Renly, "He was the king that should have been. He was the best of them" (*SS* 923). He is being overly sentimental, perhaps, but between the Homeric overtones— Achilles was the best of the Achaeans—and the Virgilian pathos, he captures also the double valence of the intertext, as it reveals the vulnerability of epic to the disappointments of romance.

I want to conclude, however, with one final thought on the utility of this exercise. Given the current interest in classical outreach, there is no need to belabor the value of encountering Virgil in unexpected places; likewise, one should not exaggerate the importance Martin has for Virgilian studies. Nevertheless, the presence of a well-known Virgilian theme in this hugely popular text affords us an opportunity to assess the presence of the classics in contemporary popular culture beyond overt reinterpretations, such as Petersen's *Troy*. More practically, however, this sort of exercise models a way of reading that is classically inflected, and that connects what we do in our scholarship and in the classroom with the critical skills students are expected to take away from their university education. Such links are not, in the end, trifling, especially as the value of the humanities is increasingly questioned; and they can, perhaps, help exemplify the continued currency of ancient literature and modern criticism within contemporary culture.

Works Cited

[Anon.]. (2012) "Shelf Candy—Interview with Kinuko Y. Craft, Cover Artist for Midsummer Night." *She-Wolf Reads.* 3 September 2012. At http://shewolfreads.com/2012/09/03/shelf-candy-interview-with-kinuko-y-craft-cover-artist-for-midsummer-night. Accessed 19 December 2015.

[Uncredited]. 2005. "Pratchett Takes Swipe at Rowling." *BBC News.* 31 July 2005. At http://news.bbc.co.uk/2/hi/entertainment/4732385.stm. Accessed 5 September 2015.

[Uncredited]. 2008. "'I'm Not Dumbledore,' Says Prof." *BBC News.* 3 October 2008. At http://news.bbc.co.uk/2/hi/uk_news/england/devon/7651629.stm. Accessed 24 August 2015.

Adey, Lionel. 1998. *C. S. Lewis: Writer, Dreamer, Mentor.* Grand Rapids, MI: William B. Eerdmans.

Adler, Eric. 2008. "Post-9/11 Views of Rome and the Nature of 'Defensive Imperialism.'" *International Journal of the Classical Tradition* 15.4.587–610.

Adney, Karley, and Holly Hassel. 2011. *Critical Companion to J. K. Rowling: A Literary Reference to Her Life and Work.* New York, NY: Facts on File.

Adorno, Theodor W. 1974. *Minima Moralia: Reflections from a Damaged Life.* Trans. E. F. H. Jephcott. London: Verso.

Adorno, Theodor W. 1984. *Aesthetic Theory.* Eds. G. Adorno and R. Tiedmann. Trans. C. Lenhardt. London: Routledge.

Adorno, Theodor W., and Max Horkheimer. 1997. *Dialectic of Enlightenment.* Trans. J. Cumming. New York, NY: Continuum.

Afanas'ev, Aleksander. 1945. *Russian Fairy Tales.* Trans. N. Guterman. New York, NY: Pantheon.

Aiken, Joan. 2008. *The Serial Garden: The Complete Armitage Family Stories.* Easthampton, MA: Big Mouth House.

Aldiss, Brian. 1976. *Space Odysseys: A New Look at Yesterday's Futures.* New York, NY: Doubleday.

Anatol, G. L. ed. 2009. *Reading Harry Potter Again: New Critical Essays.* Santa Barbara, CA: Praeger.

Anatol, G. L., ed. 2003. *Reading Harry Potter: Critical Essays.* Westport, CT: Praeger.

Andrews, Mark, dir. 2012. *Brave.* Screenplay by Brenda Chapman and Mark Andrews. Walt Disney/Pixar.

Anzinger, Silke. 2010. "Von Troja nach Gondor. Tolkiens 'The Lord of the Rings' als Epos in vergilischer Tradition." In *Vestigia Vergiliana. Vergil-Rezeption in der Neuzeit.* Eds. T. Burkard, M. Schauer, and C. Wiener. Berlin and New York, NY: De Gruyter. 363–401.

Armstrong, Isobel. 2012. "The Pre-Raphaelites and Literature." In *The Cambridge Companion to the Pre-Raphaelites.* Ed. E. Prettejohn. Cambridge, UK: Cambridge University Press. 13–31.

Arthur, Elizabeth. 1991. "Above All Shadows Rides the Sun: Gollum as Hero." *Mythlore* 18.1.19–27.

Ashley, Mike. 2010. *Dreams and Wonders, Stories from the Dawn of Modern Times.* New York, NY: Dover Publications.

Asimov, Isaac. 1961. *Words from the Myths.* New York, NY: Signet.

Associated Press. 2007. "'Harry Potter and the Deathly Hallows' Breaks Records." *Fox News.* 24 July 2007. At http://www.foxnews.com/story/0,2933,290346,00. html. Accessed 24 August 2015.

Atherton, Catherine, ed. 1998. *Monsters and Monstrosity in Greek and Roman Culture.* Bari, Italy: Levante Editori.

Attebery, Brian. 1988. "Fantasy's Reconstruction of Narrative Conventions." *Journal of the Fantastic in the Arts* 1.1.85–98.

Attebery, Brian. 1992. *Strategies of Fantasy.* Bloomington, IN: Indiana University Press.

Attebery, Brian. 2014. *Stories About Stories: Fantasy and the Remaking of Myth.* Oxford, UK: Oxford University Press.

Auerbach, Erich. 1953. *Mimesis: Dargestellte Wirklichkeit in der abendländischen Literatur.* Bern: Franke Verlag.

Auerbach, Erich. 1993. *Literary Language and Its Public in Late Latin Antiquity and in the Middle Ages.* Trans. Ralph Manheim. Princeton, NJ: Princeton University Press.

Austin, R. D. 1986. *Aeneidos Liber Sextus.* Oxford, UK: Oxford University Press.

Baker, Daniel. 2012. "Why We Need Dragons: The Progressive Potential of Fantasy." *Journal of the Fantastic in the Arts* 23.3.437–459.

Bakhtin, Mikhail M. 1981. "Epic and Novel." In *The Dialogic Imagination.* Ed. M. Holquist. Austin, TX: University of Texas Press. 3–40.

Baldwin, Erik. 2008. "How to Be Happy After the End of the World." In *Battlestar Galactica and Philosophy: Knowledge Here Begins Out There.* Ed. J. T. Eberl. Malden, MA: Wiley-Blackwell. 3–14.

Barceló, Pedro. 2001. "Pompaelo." In *Der Neue Pauly. Enzyklopädie der Antike* 10. Stuttgart and Weimar: Metzler. 88.

Barchas, Janine. 2003. *Graphic Design, Print Culture, and the Eighteenth-Century Novel.* Cambridge, UK: Cambridge University Press.

Barchiesi, Alessandro. 1984. *La Traccia del Modello: Effetti omerici nella narrazione Virgiliana.* Pisa: Giardini.

Barthes, Roland. 1972 [1957]. *Mythologies.* Trans. Annette Lavers. New York, NY: Farrar, Straus and Giroux.

Barthes, Roland. 1977. "The Death of the Author." In *Image, Music, Text.* Trans. S. Heath. New York, NY: Hill and Wang. 142–148.

Batteux, Charles. 1970 [1747]. *Les Beaux arts réduits à un même principe.* New York, NY: Johnson Reprint Corporation.

Baudrillard, Jean. 1981. *Simulacra et Simulation.* Paris: Éditions Galilée.

Baumbach, Manuel. 2013. "Proteus and Protean Epic: From Homer to Nonnos." In *Transformative Change in Western Thought: A History of Metamorphosis from Homer to Hollywood.* Eds. I. Gildenhard and A. Zissos. London: Legenda. 153–162.

Beall, Hazel S. 1960. "Historical Fiction on Classical Themes." *Classical World* 54.8–12.

Beaumont, Lesley. 2003. "The Changing Face of Childhood." In *Coming of Age in Ancient Greece.* Eds. J. Neils and J. Oakley. New Haven, CT: Yale University Press. 59–83.

Beaumont, Lesley. 2013. *Childhood in Ancient Athens: Iconography and Social History.* London: Routledge.

Bees, Robert. 1993. *Zur Datierung des Prometheus Desmotes.* Stuttgart: Teubner.

Bentley, D. M. R. 2009. "'Polysemos Hoc Est Plurium Sensum': Dante Rossetti's Paintings of Jane Morris." *The Journal of Pre-Raphaelite Studies* 18.59–80.

Bentz, Martin, and Christian Mann. 2001. "Zur Heroisierung von Athleten." In *Konstruktionen von Wirklichkeit. Bilder im Griechenland des 5. und 4. Jahrhunderts v. Chr.* Eds. R. von den Hoff and S. Schmidt. Stuttgart: Steiner. 225–240.

Berman, Ruth. 2007. "Tolkien as a Child of *The Green Fairy Book.*" *Mythlore* 26.1/2.127–135.

Berman, Ruth. 2012. "Watchful Dragons and Sinewy Gnomes: C. S. Lewis' Use of Modern Fairy Tales." *Mythlore* 30.3/4.117–127.

Bettelheim, Bruno. 2010. *The Uses of Enchantment: The Meaning and Importance of Fairy Tales.* New York, NY: Vintage.

Bevan, Elinor. 1987. "The Goddess Artemis, and the Dedication of Bears in Sanctuaries." *Annual of the British School at Athens* 82.17–21.

Biow, Douglas. 1996. Mirabile Dictu: *Representations of the Marvelous in Medieval and Renaissance Epic.* Ann Arbor, MI: The University of Michigan Press.

Birch, Megan L. 2009. "Schooling Harry Potter: Teachers and Learning, Power and Knowledge." *Critical Perspectives on Harry Potter,* Second Edition. Ed. E. E. Heilman. New York, NY: Routledge. 103–120.

Blackall, Eric. 1983. *The Novels of the German Romantics.* Ithaca, NY and London: Cornell University Press.

Bloom, Harold. 1982. "*Clinamen:* Towards a Theory of Fantasy." In *Bridges to Fantasy.* Eds. G. E. Slusser, E. S. Rabkin, and R. Scholes. Carbondale, IL: Southern Illinois University Press. 1–20. Reprinted as 2004. *Fantastic Literature: A Critical Reader.* Ed. David Sandner. Westport, CT: Praeger. 236–254.

Bloom, Harold. 2000. "Can 35 Million Book Buyers Be Wrong? Yes." *The Wall Street Journal.* 11 July 2000.

Bollack, Jean. 1981. *L'Agamemnon d'Eschyle:* Agamemnon *I.* 2 vols. Lille: Presses universitaires de Lille.

Booker, M. Keith. 2009. "The Other Side of History: Fantasy, Romance, Horror, and Science Fiction." In *The Cambridge Companion to the Twentieth-Century English Novel.* Ed. R. L. Caserio. Cambridge, UK: Cambridge University Press. 251–266.

Bost-Fiévet, Mélanie, and Sandra Provini, eds. 2014. *L'Antiquité dans l'imaginaire contemporain: Fantasy, science-fiction, fantastique.* Paris: Classiques Garnier.

Bould, Mark, and Sherryl Vint. 2012. "Political Readings." In *The Cambridge Companion to Fantasy Literature.* Eds. E. James and F. Mendlesohn. Cambridge, UK: Cambridge University Press. 102–112.

Bozzetto, Roger, and Arnaud Huftier. 2004. *Les Frontières du fantastique: Approches de l'impensable en littérature.* Valenciennes: Presses Universitaires de Valenciennes.

Bradford, Clare. 2012. "'Where Happily Ever After Happens Every Day': The Medievalisms of Disney's Princesses." In *The Disney Middle Ages: A Fairy-Tale and Fantasy Past.* Eds. T. Pugh and S. Aronstein. New York, NY: Palgrave. 171–188.

Branham, R. 1983. "Fantasy and Ineffability: Fiction at the Limits of Language." *Extrapolation* 24.1.66–79.

Branham, Robert Bracht, ed. 2002. *Bakhtin and the Classics.* Evanston, IL: Northwestern University Press.

Bratton, J. S. 1981. *The Impact of Victorian Children's Fiction.* London: Croom Helm.

Brawley, Chris. 2007. "The Fading of the World: Tolkien's Ecology and Loss in *The Lord of the Rings.*" *Journal of the Fantastic of the Arts* 18.3.292–307 and 435.

Bredsdorff, Elias. 2005. "Introduction to Hans Christian Andersen." In *Hans Christian Andersen.* Ed. H. Bloom. Philadelphia, PA: Chelsea House Publishers. 1–6.

Bremmer, Jan N. 2004. "Attis: A Greek God in Anatolian Pessinous and Catullan Rome." *Mnemosyne* 57.534–573.

Briggs, Julia. 2008 [1987]. *A Woman of Passion: The Life of E. Nesbit.* Harmondsworth, UK: Penguin.

Brink, C. O. 2011. *Horace on Poetry.* Cambridge, UK: Cambridge University Press.

Bronkhurst, Judith, and William Holman Hunt. 2006. *William Holman Hunt: A Catalogue Raisonné.* New Haven, CT: Published for the Paul Mellon Centre for Studies in British Art by Yale University Press.

Brown, Sarah Annes. 2002. *The Metamorphosis of Ovid: From Chaucer to Ted Hughes.* Bristol: Bristol Classical Press.

Brown, Sarah Annes. 2008. "'Plato's Stepchildren': SF and the Classics." In *A Companion to Classical Receptions.* Eds. L. Hardwick and C. Stray. Malden, MA, and Oxford, UK: Blackwell. 415–427.

Bruce, Alexander M. 2012. "The Fall of Gondolin and the Fall of Troy: Tolkien and Book II of *The Aeneid*." *Mythlore* 30.3/4.103–115.

Burleson, Donald R. 2013. "On 'The Dunwich Horror.'" In *New Critical Essays on H. P. Lovecraft*. Ed. D. Simmons. New York, NY: Palgrave Macmillan. 105–116.

Burnell, Peter. 1987. "The Death of Turnus and Roman Morality." *Greece and Rome*, Second Series 34.186–200.

Burrow, C. 1993. *Epic Romance. Homer to Milton*. Oxford, UK: Oxford University Press.

Butler, Catherine. 2012. "Modern Children's Fantasy." In *The Cambridge Companion to Fantasy Literature*. Eds. E. James and F. Mendlesohn. Cambridge, UK: Cambridge University Press. 224–235.

Butler, Judith. 1990. *Gender Trouble: Feminism and the Subversion of Identity*. London: Routledge.

Byock, J. L. 2013 [1990]. *The Saga of the Volsungs*. New York, NY: Penguin Classics.

Caldecott, Stratford, and Thomas Honegger, eds. 2008. *Tolkien's The Lord of the Rings: Sources of Inspiration*. Zurich and Jena: Walking Tree Publishers.

Canevaro, Lilah Grace. 2014. "The Homeric Ladies of Shalott." *Classical Receptions Journal* 6.2.198–220.

Cantor, Paul A. 2007. "The Politics of the Epic: Wordsworth, Byron, and the Romantic Redefinition of Heroism." *The Review of Politics* 69.3.375–401.

Carpenter, Humphrey. 1978. *The Inklings: C. S. Lewis, J. R. R. Tolkien, Charles Williams, and Their Friends*. London: Allen and Unwin.

Carpenter, Humphrey. 1981. *The Letters of J. R. R. Tolkien*. Boston, MA: Houghton Mifflin.

Carpenter, Humphrey. 2000. *J. R. R. Tolkien: A Biography*. New York, NY: Houghton Mifflin.

Carson, Anne. 1995. *Plainwater: Essays and Poetry*. New York, NY: A. A. Knopf.

Carswell, John. 1948. "Introduction." In R. E. Raspe et al., *Singular Travels: Campaigns and Adventures of Baron Munchausen*. Ed. J. Carswell. London: Cresset Press. ix–xlvi.

Carter, Lin. 2001. "H. P. Lovecraft. The Books (Annotated by Robert M. Price and S. T. Joshi)." In *Discovering H. P. Lovecraft*. Ed. D. Schweitzer. Holicong, PA: Wildside Press. 107–147.

Casali, S. 2004. "Nisus and Euryalus: Exploiting the Contradictions of Vergil's 'Doloneia.'" *Harvard Studies in Classical Philology* 102.319–354.

Caspers, C. L. 2006. "The Loves of the Poets: Allusions in Hermesianax Fr. 7 Powell." In *Beyond the Canon*. Eds. A. Harder, R. F. Regtuit, and G. C. Wakker. Leuven: Peeters Publishers. 21–42.

Casta, I.-R. 2014. "*Petrificus Totalus!* Langue du sacré, langue du secret: L'usage des langues anciennes—ou de leur fac-similé—dans *Harry Potter* et la 'bit lit' en général." *L'Antiquité dans l'imaginaire contemporain: Fantasy, science-fiction, fantastique.* Eds. M. Bost-Fiévet and S. Provini. Paris: Classiques Garnier. 359–374.

Ciaccio, Peter. 2009. "Harry Potter and Christian Theology." In *Critical Perspectives on Harry Potter.* Second Edition. Ed. E. E. Heilman. New York, NY: Routledge. 33–46.

Clark, George. 2000. "J. R. R. Tolkien and the True Hero." In *J. R. R. Tolkien and His Literary Resonances.* Eds. G. Clark and D. Timmons. Westport, CT, and London: Greenwood Press. 39–52.

Clark, Raymond J. 1979. Catabasis: *Vergil and the Wisdom-Tradition.* Amsterdam: B. R. Grüner.

Clement, Clara E., and Laurence Hutton. 1897. *Artists of the Nineteenth Century and Their Works.* Ninth Edition, revised. Boston, MA: Houghton Mifflin.

Clinton, Kevin. 1979. "'The 'Hymn to Zeus,' πάθει μάθος, and the End of the Parodos of 'Agamemnon.'" *Traditio* 35.1–19.

Clute, John, and John Grant, eds. 1997. *The Encyclopedia of Fantasy.* New York, NY: St. Martin's Press.

Cole, M. 2012. "Art Imitates War. Post-Traumatic Stress Disorder in *A Song of Ice and Fire.*" In *Beyond the Wall: Exploring George R. R. Martin's* A Song of Ice and Fire. Ed. J. Lowder. Dallas, TX: SmartPop. 73–88.

Cole, Susan. 1984. "The Social Function of Rituals of Maturation: The Koureion and the Arkteia." *Zeitschrift für Papyrologie und Epigraphik* 55.233–244.

Cole, Susan. 1998. "Domesticating Artemis." In *The Sacred and the Feminine in Ancient Greece.* Eds. S. Blundell and M. Williamson. London: Routledge. 27–43.

Collins, Robert A. 1982. "Fantasy and 'Forestructures': The Effect of Philosophical Climate upon Perceptions of the Fantastic." In *Bridges to Fantasy.* Eds. G. E. Slusser, E. S. Rabkin, and R. E. Scholes. Carbondale, IL: Southern Illinois University Press. 108–120.

Conte, G.-B. 1996. *The Rhetoric of Imitation: Genre and Poetic Memory in Other Latin Poets.* Ed. C. Segal. Ithaca, NY: Cornell University Press.

Cox, Fiona. 2011. *Sibylline Sisters: Virgil's Presence in Contemporary Women's Writing.* Oxford, UK: Oxford University Press.

Cox, John. 1984. "Tolkien's Platonic Fantasy." *Seven* 5.53–69.

Cox, Katherine. 2011. "Introduction." In *Critical Perspectives on Philip Pullman's His Dark Materials: Essays on the Novels, the Film and the Stage Productions.* Jefferson, NC: McFarland & Company, Inc. 1–10.

Curry, Patrick. 1998. *Defending Middle-Earth.* London: HarperCollins.

Curry, Patrick. 1999. "Magic vs. Enchantment." *Journal of Contemporary Religion* 14.3.401–412.

D'Agata, John. 1997. "A Talk with Anne Carson." *Brick* 57.14–22.

De Armas, Frederick A. 1994. "Gyges' Ring: Invisibility in Plato, Tolkien, and Lope de Vega." *Journal of the Fantastic in the Arts* 3.4.120–138.

de Mott, Benjamin. 1957. "Agonists and Agonizers, and a Utopian." *Hudson Review* 10.140–48.

Dean, John. 1980. "Strangely Familiar Forms: Exploitations of Romance in American Science Fiction and Fantasy." *Revue française d'études américaines* 9.149–158.

Decker, Wolfgang. 2002. "Theogenes [1]." In *Der Neue Pauly. Enzyklopädie der Antike* 12.1. Stuttgart and Weimar: Metzler. 350.

Dégh, Linda. 1991. "What Did the Grimm Brothers Give to and Take from the Folk?" In *The Brothers Grimm and Folktale*. Ed. James M. McGlathery. Urbana, IL, and Chicago, IL: University of Illinois Press. 66–90.

Demand, Nancy. 1994. *Birth, Death, and Motherhood in Classical Greece*. Baltimore, MD: Johns Hopkins University Press.

Dentith, Simon. 2000. *Parody*. London and New York, NY: The New Critical Idiom, Routledge.

Dillon, J. 1977. *The Middle Platonists*. London: Duckworth.

Dillon, Matthew. 2002. *Girls and Women in Classical Greek Religion*. London: Routledge.

DiTerlizzi, Tony. 2011. "Books: The Many Colors of Andrew Lang and H. J. Ford." 22 August 2011. At http://diterlizzi.com/home/books-the-many-colors-of-andrew-lang-h-j-ford. Accessed 19 December 2015.

Donaldson, Mara E. 1988. *Holy Places Are Dark Places: C. S. Lewis and Paul Ricoeur on Narrative Transformation*. Boston, MA: University Press of America.

Donaldson, Mara E. 1991. "Orual's Story and the Art of Retelling: A Study of *Till We Have Faces*." In *Word and Story in C. S. Lewis*. Eds. P. J. Schakel and C. A. Hunter. Columbia, MO: University of Missouri Press. 157–170.

Dougherty, Carol. 2005. *Prometheus*. London: Routledge.

Drout, Michael D. C., ed. 2007. *J. R. R. Tolkien Encyclopedia: Scholarship and Critical Assessment*. New York, NY: Routledge, Taylor & Francis Group.

duBois, Page. 1982. *Centaurs and Amazons*. Ann Arbor, MI: University of Michigan Press.

Duriez, Colin. 1993. "Sub-creation and Tolkien's Theology of Story." In *Scholarship and Fantasy*. Ed. K. J. Battarbee. Turku, Finland: University of Turku. 133–150.

Durst, Uwe. 2007. *Theorie der phantastischen Literatur*. Berlin: Lit Verlag Dr. W. Hopf.

Eckhardt, Jason C. 2011. "Cthulhu's Scald: Lovecraft and the Nordic Tradition." In *Dissecting Cthulhu: Essays on the Cthulhu Mythos*. Ed. S. T. Joshi. Lakeland, FL: Miskatonic River Press. 210–215.

Edwards, Catharine. 2007. *Death in Ancient Rome*. New Haven, CT: Yale University Press.

Edwards, Mark J. 1992. "The Tale of Cupid and Psyche." *Zeitschrift für Papyrologie und Epigraphik* 94. 77–94.

Eliade, Mircea. 1995. *Rites and Symbols of Initiation: The Mysteries of Birth and Rebirth*. Trans. W. Trask. Woodstock, CT: Spring Publications.

Elster, Charles. 2003. "The Seeker of Secrets: Images of Learning, Knowing, and Schooling." In *Harry Potter's World: Multidisciplinary Perspectives*. Ed. E. E. Heilman. New York, NY, and London: RoutledgeFalmer. 203–220.

Evans, Jonathan. 1987. "The Dragon." In *Mythical and Fabulous Creatures: A Source Book and Research Guide*. Ed. M. L. South. New York, NY: Greenwood. 27–58.

Evans, Jonathan. 2000. "The Dragon-Lore of Middle-earth: Tolkien and Old English and Old Norse Tradition." In *J. R. R. Tolkien and His Literary Resonances*. Eds. George Clark and Daniel Timmons. Westport, CT, and London: Greenwood Press. 21–38.

Evans, Rhiannon. 2008. *Utopia Antiqua: Readings of the Golden Age and Decline at Rome*. London: Routledge.

Fagles, R., trans. 1984. *Aeschylus: Oresteia*. New York, NY: Penguin Classics.

Fantham, Elaine. 1990. "*Nymphas . . . e navibus esse*: Decorum and Poetic Fiction in *Aeneid* 9.77–122 and 10.215–59." *Classical Philology* 85.102–119.

Farron, S. 1992. "Pius Aeneas in the *Aeneid* 4, 393–6." In *Collection Latomus: Studies in Latin Literature and History* VI. Ed. C. Deroux. Bruxelles: Éditions Latomus. 260–276.

Feeney, D. C. 1991. *The Gods in Epic: Poets and Critics of the Classical Tradition*. Oxford, UK: Oxford University Press.

Feinstein, W. 1990. "Ariosto's Parodic Rewriting of Virgil in the Episode of Cloridano and Medoro." *South Atlantic Review* 55.1.17–34.

Felton, D. 2012. "Rejecting and Embracing the Monstrous in Ancient Greece and Rome." In *The Ashgate Research Companion to Monsters and the Monstrous*. Eds. A. S. Mittman and P. J. Dendle. Farnham, UK: Ashgate Publishing. 103–131.

Felton, D. 2013. "Were Vergil's Harpies Menstruating?" *Classical Journal* 108.4.405–418.

Ferrari, G. 1985. "The Struggle in the Soul: Plato, *Phaedrus* 253c7–255a1." *Ancient Philosophy* 5.1.1–10.

Finkelpearl, E. 2004. "The Ends of the *Metamorphoses*." In *Metamorphic Reflections: Essays Presented to Ben Hijmans at His 75th Birthday*. Eds. M. Zimmerman and R. van der Paardt. Leuven and Paris: Peeters. 319–342.

Fish, S. 1982. *Is There a Text in This Class? The Authority of Interpretative Communities*. Cambridge, MA: Harvard University Press.

Fisher, Jason. 2010. "Dwarves, Spiders, and Murky Woods: J. R. R. Tolkien's Wonderful Web of Words." *Mythlore* 29.1/2.5–15.

Fisher, Jason. 2011. *Tolkien and the Study of His Sources: Critical Essays*. Jefferson, NC, and London: McFarland & Company.

Fiske, John. 1991. "Popular Discrimination." In *Modernity and Mass Culture*. Eds. J. Naremore and P. Brantlinger. Bloomington, IN: Indiana University Press. 103–116.

Fitzgerald, J. 1972. "Nisus and Euryalus: A Paradigm of Futile Behavior and the Tragedy of Youth." In *Cicero and Virgil: Studies in Honour of Harold Hunt.* Ed. J. R. C. Martyn. Amsterdam: J. Hakkert. 114–137.

Flieger, Verlyn. 1986. "Naming the Unnamable: The Neoplatonic 'One' in Tolkien's *Silmarillion.*" In Diakonia: *Studies in Honor of Robert T. Meyer.* Eds. T. Halton and J. P. Willimer. Washington, DC: Catholic University of America Press. 127–132.

Flieger, Verlyn. 2000. "Taking the Part of Trees: Eco-Conflict in Middle-earth." In *J. R. R. Tolkien and His Literary Resonances.* Eds. G. Clark and D. Timmons. Westport, CT, and London: Greenwood Press. 147–158.

Flieger, Verlyn. 2002. *Splintered Light: Logos and Language in Tolkien's World.* Kent, OH: The Kent State University Press.

Flieger, Verlyn. 2005. "A Postmodern Medievalist?" In *Tolkien's Modern Middle Ages.* Eds. J. Chance and A. K. Siewers. New York, NY: Palgrave Macmillan. 17–28.

Folch, Christine. 2013. "Why the West Loves Sci-Fi and Fantasy: A Cultural Explanation." *The Atlantic.* 13 June 2013. At http://www.theatlantic.com/entertainment/archive/2013/06/why-the-west-loves-sci-fi-and-fantasy-a-cultural-explanation/276816. Accessed 14 January 2016.

Foucault, Michel. 1977. "What Is an Author?" In *Language, Counter-Memory, Practice.* Trans. and ed. D. F. Bouchard. Ithaca, NY: Cornell University Press. 113–138.

Fowler, D. 1987. "Vergil on Killing Virgins." In Homo Viator: *Classical Essays for John Bramble.* Eds. M. Whitby, P. Hardie, and M. Whitby. Bristol: Bristol University Press. 185–198.

Fowler, D. 2000. "Epic in the Middle of the Wood: *Mise en Abyme* in the Nisus and Euryalus Episode." In *Intratextuality: Greek and Roman Textual Relations.* Eds. A. Sharrock and H. Morales. Oxford, UK: Oxford University Press. 89–114.

Fowler, Howard North, trans. 1966. *Plato:* Euthyphro. Apology. Crito. Phaedo. Phaedrus. Cambridge, MA: Harvard University Press.

Fraenkel, Eduard. 1950. *Aeschylus: Agamemnon.* 3 vols. Oxford, UK: Clarendon Press.

Fratantuono, Lee. 2007. *Madness Unchained: A Reading of Vergil's* Aeneid. Rowman and Lanham, MD: Littlefield.

Fredericks, S. C. 1976. "Lucian's *True History* as SF." *Science Fiction Studies* 3.1.49–60.

Fredericks, S. C. 1978. "Problems of Fantasy." *Science Fiction Studies* 5.1.33–44.

Frye, Northrop. 1961. "Myth, Fiction, and Displacement." *Daedalus* 90.3.587–605.

Gagarin, Michael. 1976. *Aeschylean Drama.* Berkeley, CA: University of California Press.

Gaiman, Neil. 2001. *American Gods.* London: Headline.

Galinsky, Karl. 1988. "The Anger of Aeneas." *American Journal of Philology* 109.321–348.

Gallardo C., X, and C. J. Smith. 2009. "Happily Ever After: Harry Potter and the Quest for the Domestic." In *Reading Harry Potter Again: New Critical Essays.* Ed. G. L. Anatol. Santa Barbara, CA: Praeger. 91–108.

Ganiban, R. 2007. *Statius and Virgil. The* Thebaid *and the Reinterpretation of the* Aeneid. Cambridge, UK: Cambridge University Press.

Gantz, Timothy. 1993. *Early Greek Myth.* 2 vols. Baltimore, MD: Johns Hopkins University Press.

Gatz, Bodo. 1967. *Weltalter, goldene Zeit, und sinnverwandte Vorstellungen.* Hildesheim: Tübingen.

Geiger, Marion. 2013. "Kreative Mimesis—E. T. A. Hoffmanns *Die Jesuiterkirche in G.*" *Orbis Litterarum* 68.1.17–42.

Gellar-Goad, T. M. H. 2014. "Rehash of the Titans: Sequels to the Titanomachy on the American Screen (Part 2)." American Philological Association. 10 January 2014. At https://classicalstudies.org/blogs/ted-gellar-goad/rehash-titans-sequels-titanomachy-american-screen-part-2. Accessed 13 November 2015.

Georgiadou, Aristoula, and David H. J. Larmour. 1998. *Lucian's Science Fiction Novel* True Histories. *Interpretation and Commentary.* Mnemosyne. Bibliotheca Classica Batava Suppl. 179. Leiden: Brill.

Gildenhard, Ingo, and Andrew Zissos, eds. 2013. *Transformative Change in Western Thought: A History of Metamorphosis from Homer to Hollywood.* London: Legenda.

Gilliver, Peter, Jeremy Marshall, and Edmund Weiner. 2006. *The Ring of Words: Tolkien and the* Oxford English Dictionary. Oxford, UK: Oxford University Press.

Gilman, Greer. 2012. "The Languages of the Fantastic." In *The Cambridge Companion to Fantasy Literature.* Eds. E. James and F. Mendlesohn. Cambridge, UK: Cambridge University Press. 134–146.

Gilmore, David D. 2003. *Monsters: Evil Beings, Mythical Beasts, and All Manner of Imaginary Terrors.* Philadelphia, PA: University of Pennsylvania Press.

Gimbutas, Marija. 1982. *The Goddesses and the Gods of Old Europe.* Berkeley, CA: University of California Press.

Gloyn, Liz. 2015. "In a Galaxy Far, Far Away: On Classical Reception and Science Fiction." *Strange Horizons.* 27 April 2015. At http://www.strangehorizons.com/2015/20150427/1gloynb-a.shtml. Accessed 3 January 2016.

Goff, Barbara. 2004. *Citizen Bacchae: Women's Ritual Practice in Ancient Greece.* Berkeley, CA: University of California Press.

Golden, Mark. 1990. *Childhood in Classical Athens.* Baltimore, MD: Johns Hopkins University Press.

Goldhill, Simon. 2011. *Victorian Culture and Classical Antiquity: Art, Opera, Fiction, and the Proclamation of Modernity.* Princeton, NJ: Princeton University Press.

Gould, F. J. 1910. *The Children's Plutarch: Tales of the Romans.* New York, NY: Harper and Bros.

Gove, Philip B. 1961. *The Imaginary Voyage in Prose Fiction.* London: The Holland Press.

Grafton, Anthony, Glenn W. Most, and Salvatore Settis, eds. 2010. *The Classical Tradition.* Cambridge, MA: Harvard University Press.

Graham, Jo. 2008. *Black Ships.* London and New York, NY: Orbit.

Granger, J. 2008. "The Aeschylus Epigraph in 'Deathly Hallows.'" *Hogwarts Professor: Thoughts for Serious Readers.* 20 October 2008. At http://www.hogwartsprofessor.com/the-aeschylus-epigraph-in-deathly-hallows. Accessed 24 August 2015.

Gransden, K. W. 1984. *Virgil's Iliad: An Essay on Epic Narrative.* Cambridge, UK: Cambridge University Press.

Graver, Bruce. 2010. "Romanticism." In *A Companion to the Classical Tradition.* Ed. C. Kallendorf. Malden, MA: Wiley-Blackwell. 72–86.

Gray, William. 2009. *Fantasy, Myth and the Measure of Truth—Tales of Pullman, Lewis, Tolkien, MacDonald and Hoffmann.* New York, NY: Palgrave Macmillan.

Green, Roger Lancelyn. 1962. *Andrew Lang.* [First American edition]. New York, NY: H. Z. Walck.

Green, Roger Lancelyn. 1980. "Andrew Lang in Fairyland." In *Only Connect: Readings on Children's Literature.* Second edition. Eds. S. Egoff et al. Toronto and New York, NY: Oxford University Press. 244–252.

Greenberg, Clement. 1939. "Avant-Garde and Kitsch." *Partisan Review* 6.5.34–49.

Greenman, David. 1992. "Aeneidic and Odyssean Patterns of Escape and Return in Tolkien's *The Fall of Gondolin* and *The Lord of the Rings.*" *Mythlore* 18.2.4–9.

Griffith, Mark. 1977. *The Authenticity of* Prometheus Bound. Cambridge, UK: Cambridge University Press.

Griffith, Mark. 1983. *Aeschylus:* Prometheus Bound. Cambridge, UK: Cambridge University Press.

Griffith, Mark. 1995. "Brilliant Dynasts: Power and Politics in the *Oresteia.*" *Classical Antiquity* 14.62–129.

Griffith, Mark. 2001. "'Public' and 'Private' in Early Greek Institutions of Education." In *Education in Greek and Roman Antiquity.* Ed. Y. L. Too. Leiden: Brill. 23–84.

Grimes, M. Katherine. 2002. "Harry Potter: Fairy Tale Prince, Real Boy, and Archetypal Hero." In *The Ivory Tower and Harry Potter: Perspectives on a Literary Phenomenon.* Ed. L. A. Whited. Columbia, MO, and London: University of Missouri Press. 89–122.

Grossman, Lev. 2005. "J. K. Rowling Hogwarts and All." *Time Magazine.* 17 July 2005. 166.4.60–5.

Grybauskas, Peter. 2012. "Untold Tales: Solving a Literary Dilemma." *Tolkien Studies* 9.1–19.

Haigh, John D. 1991. "C. S. Lewis and the Tradition of Visionary Romance." In *Word and Story in C. S. Lewis*. Eds. P. J. Schakel and C. A. Huttar. Columbia, MO: University of Missouri Press. 182–198.

Hainsworth, J. B. 1991. *The Idea of Epic*. Berkeley, CA: UC Press.

Hall, S. 2003. "Harry Potter and the Rule of Law: The Central Weakness of Legal Concepts in the Wizard World." In *Reading Harry Potter: Critical Essays*. Ed. G. L. Anatol. Westport, CT: Praeger. 147–162.

Halliwell, Stephen. 1999. *Aristotle: Poetics*. Second edition. Cambridge, MA: Harvard University Press.

Hamilton, Andy, dir. 1995–2012. *Old Harry's Game*. BBC Radio 4.

Hammond, Wayne G., and Christina Scull. 1995. *J. R. R. Tolkien: Artist and Illustrator*. New York, NY: Houghton Mifflin.

Hammond, Wayne G., and Christina Scull. 2012. *The Art of* The Hobbit *by J. R. R. Tolkien*. New York, NY: Houghton Mifflin.

Hansen, William. 2002. *Ariadne's Thread: A Guide to International Tales Found in Classical Literature*. Ithaca, NY: Cornell University Press.

Hanson, J., trans. 1989. *Apuleius:* Metamorphoses. 2 vols. Cambridge, MA: Harvard University Press.

Hardie, Philip. 1987. "Ships and Ship-Names in the *Aeneid*." In Homo Viator: *Essays for John Bramble*. Eds. M. Whitby, M. Whitby, and P. Hardie. Bristol: Bristol Classical Press. 163–172.

Hardie, Philip. 1993. *Vergil's Epic Successors*. Cambridge, UK: Cambridge University Press.

Hardie, Philip. 1994. *Virgil: Aeneid Book IX*. Cambridge Greek and Latin Classics. Cambridge, UK: Cambridge University Press.

Hardie, Philip. 1997. "Closure in Latin Epic." In *Classical Closure: Reading the End in Greek and Latin Literature*. Eds. D. Roberts, F. M. Dunn, and D. Fowler. Princeton, NJ: Princeton University Press. 139–162.

Hardie, Philip. 2009. *Lucretian Receptions: History, the Sublime, Knowledge*. Cambridge, UK and New York, NY: Cambridge University Press.

Hardwick, Lorna. 2003. *Reception Studies*. Oxford, UK: Oxford University Press.

Hardwick, Lorna and Christopher Stray, eds. 2008. *A Companion to Classical Receptions*. Malden, MA: Wiley-Blackwell.

Hares-Stryker, Carolyn. 2009. "Doing Justice to Henry: A Biographical Study of Henry Justice Ford." *Studies in Illustration* 43.27–64.

Harmon, Austin M., trans. 2006. *Lucian: Volume I*. Ed. J. Henderson. Cambridge, MA, and London: Harvard University Press.

Harms, Daniel, and John Wisdom Gonce. 2003. *The Necronomicon Files. The Truth Behind the Legend*. Boston, MA: Red Wheel/Weiser.

Harrison, S. 2000. *Apuleius: A Latin Sophist*. Oxford, UK: Oxford University Press.

Harrisson, J. 2010. "The Domestication of Classical Mythology in *The Chronicles of Narnia*." *New Voices in Classical Reception Studies* 5.1–13.

Hathaway, Baxter. 1968. *Marvels and Commonplaces: Renaissance Literary Criticism*. New York, NY: Random House.

Hatlen, Burton. 2005. "Pullman's *His Dark Materials*, a Challenge to the Fantasies of J. R. R. Tolkien and C. S. Lewis, with an Epilogue on Pullman's Neo-Romantic Reading of *Paradise Lost*." In His Dark Materials *Illuminated: Critical Essays on Philip Pullman's Trilogy*. Eds. M. Lenz and C. Scott. Detroit, MI: Wayne State University Press. 75–94.

Heidegger, M. 1977 [1954]. *The Question Concerning Technology*. Trans. W. Lovitt. New York, NY: Garland.

Heilman, E. E., ed. 2003. *Harry Potter's World: Multidisciplinary Perspectives*. New York, NY and London: RoutledgeFalmer.

Heilman, E. E., ed. 2009. *Critical Perspectives on Harry Potter*. Second edition. New York, NY: Routledge.

Henderson, J. 1991. "Statius' *Thebaid*: Form Premade." *Proceedings of the Cambridge Philological Society* 37.30–80.

Henke, Jill, Diane Umble, and Nancy Smith. 1996. "Construction of the Female Self: Feminist Readings of the Disney Heroine." *Women's Studies in Communication* 19.229–49.

Herington, C. J. 1970. *The Author of the* Prometheus Bound. Austin, TX: University of Texas Press.

Hershkowitz, D. 1998. *The Madness of Epic. Reading Insanity from Homer to Statius*. Oxford, UK: Oxford University Press.

Heubeck, Alfred, and Arie Hoekstra. 1989. *A Commentary on Homer's* Odyssey. *Volume II: Books IX–XVI*. Oxford, UK: Clarendon Press.

Hieatt, Constance B. 1981. "The Text of *The Hobbit*: Putting Tolkien's Notes in Order." *English Studies in Canada* 7.2.212–24.

Highet, Gilbert. 1949. *The Classical Tradition: Greek and Roman Influences on Western Literature*. Oxford, UK: Oxford University Press.

Hinds, S. 1998. *Allusion and Intertext. Dynamics of Appropriation in Roman Poetry*. Cambridge, UK: Cambridge University Press.

Hinz, Evelyn J. 1976. "Hierogamy versus Wedlock: Types of Marriage Plots and Their Relationship to Genres of Prose Fiction." *Proceedings of the Modern Language Association* 91.900–913.

Hoffmann, Ernst T. A. 2008. *The Golden Pot and Other Tales*. Trans. R. Robertson. Oxford, UK: Oxford University Press.

Holberg, Ludwig. 2004. *The Journey of Niels Klim to the World Underground*. Ed. J. McNelis, Jr. Lincoln, NE, and London: University of Nebraska Press.

Holzberg, Niklas. 1995. *The Ancient Novel: An Introduction*. Trans. C. Jackson-Holzberg. London: Routledge.

Hooper, Walter. 1996. *C. S. Lewis: A Companion and Guide*. San Francisco, CA: HarperSanFrancisco.

Hooper, Walter. 2004. *The Collected Letters of C. S. Lewis: Volumes 1–3*. San Francisco, CA: Harper.

Hopkins, David. 2010. *Conversing with Antiquity: English Poets and the Classics, from Shakespeare to Pope.* Oxford, UK: Oxford University Press.

Hopkins, L. 2003. "Harry Potter and the Acquisition of Knowledge." In *Reading Harry Potter: Critical Essays.* Ed. G. L. Anatol. Westport, CT: Praeger. 25–34.

Hopkins, L. 2009. "Harry Potter and Narratives of Destiny." In *Reading Harry Potter Again: New Critical Essays.* Ed. G. L. Anatol. Santa Barbara, CA: Praeger. 63–75.

Horsfall, Nicholas, ed. 1995. *A Companion to the Study of Virgil. Mnemosyne Supplement* 151. Leiden: Brill.

Horsfall, Nicholas. 2013. *Virgil* Aeneid 6: *A Commenary.* Berlin: de Gruyter.

Horstkotte, Martin. 2000. *The Postmodern Fantastic in Contemporary British Fiction.* Trier: Wissenshaftlicher Verlag Trier.

Houellebecq, Michel. 2002. *Gegen die Welt, gegen das Leben. H. P. Lovecraft.* Köln: DuMont.

Houghton, John. 1990. "Commedia as Fairy-Story: Eucatastrophe in the Loss of Virgil." *Mythlore* 17.2.29–32.

Hoyler, Robert. 1991. "The Epistemology of C. S. Lewis's *Till We Have Faces*." In *Essays on C. S. Lewis and George MacDonald: Truth, Fiction and the Power of Imagination.* Ed. C. Marshall. Lewiston, NY: Edwin Mellen Press. 53–81.

Hume, Kathryn. 1984. *Fantasy and Mimesis: Responses to Reality in Western Literature.* New York, NY: Methuen.

Hutton, James, trans. 1982. *Aristotle's Poetics.* New York, NY: Norton.

Huyssen, Andreas. 1986. *After the Great Divide: Modernism, Mass Culture, Postmodernism.* Bloomington, IN: Indiana University Press.

Irwin, W. R. 1976. *The Game of the Impossible: A Rhetoric of Fantasy.* Urbana, IL: University of Illinois Press.

Jackson, Rosemary. 1981. *Fantasy: The Literature of Subversion.* London: Routledge.

James, Edward, and Farah Mendlesohn, eds. 2012. *The Cambridge Companion to Fantasy Literature.* Cambridge, UK: Cambridge University Press.

James, Edward. 2012. "Tolkien, Lewis and the Explosion of Genre Fantasy." In *The Cambridge Companion to Fantasy Literature.* Eds. E. James and F. Mendlesohn. Cambridge, UK: Cambridge University Press. 62–78.

James, Paula. 2009. "Crossing Classical Thresholds: Gods, Monsters and Hell Dimensions in the Whedon Universe," In *Classics for All: Reworking Antiquity in Mass Culture.* Eds. D. Lowe and K. Shahabudin. Cambridge, UK: Cambridge Scholars Publishing. 237–260.

Jameson, Fredric. 1979. "Reification and Utopia in Mass Culture." *Social Text* 1.130–148.

Jameson, Fredric. 1984. "Postmodernism, or the Cultural Logic of Late Capitalism." *New Left Review* 1.146.53–92.

Jantschewski, Patricia. 2012. "Die griechische Mythologie in ihrer Bedeutung für die Literatur des Schreckens." In *Spannungsfelder. Literatur und Mythos. Beiträge zum 2. Studierendenkongress der Komparatistik, 6. bis 8. Mai 2011,*

Universität Bonn. Eds. A. J. Haller, B. Huppertz, and S. Lenz. Frankfurt am Main: Peter Lang. 157–164.

Jenkins, Ian. 1992. *Archaeologists and Aesthetes in the Sculpture Galleries of the British Museum 1800–1939.* London: British Museum Press.

Jenkyns, Richard. 1980. *The Victorians and Ancient Greece.* Cambridge, MA: Harvard University Press.

Johnson, W. Ralph. 1976. *Darkness Visible: A Study of Virgil's Aeneid.* Berkeley, CA: University of California Press.

Jones, Diana Wynne. 2012 [1985]. *Fire and Hemlock.* New York, NY: Firebird.

Joshi, Sunand T. 2001. *A Dreamer and a Visionary. H. P. Lovecraft in His Time.* Liverpool: Liverpool University Press.

Joshi, Sunand T. 2004. *H. P. Lovecraft. A Life.* Third edition. West Warwick, UK: Necronomicon Press.

Joshi, Sunand T. 2011. "The Cthulhu Mythos. Lovecraft vs. Derleth." In *Dissecting Cthulhu: Essays on the Cthulhu Mythos.* Ed. S. T. Joshi. Lakeland, FL: Miskatonic River Press. 43–53.

Joshi, Sunand T., and David E. Schultz. 2001. *An H. P. Lovecraft Encyclopedia.* New York, NY: Hippocampus Press.

Kahil, Lilly. 1979. "La déesse Artémis: Mythologie et iconographie." In *Greece and Italy in the Classical World. Acta of the XI International Congress of Classical Archaeology, London, 3–9 September 1978.* Eds. J. N. Coldstream and M. A. R. Colledge. London: National Organizing Committee, XI International Congress of Classical Archaeology. 253–263.

Kallendorf, Craig. 2006. "Allusion as Reception. Virgil, Milton, and the Modern Reader." In *Classics and the Uses of Reception.* Eds. C. Martindale and R. Thomas. Hoboken, NJ: Wiley. 67–79.

Kallendorf, Craig. 2007. *A Companion to the Classical Tradition.* Malden, MA: Blackwell.

Kallendorf, Craig. 2015. *The Protean Virgil: Material Form and the Reception of the Classics.* Oxford, UK: Oxford University Press.

Kaster, Robert A. 1988. *Guardians of Language: The Grammarian and Society in Late Antiquity.* Berkeley and Los Angeles, CA: University of California Press.

Keen, Antony. 2006. "The 'T' Stands for Tiberius: Models and Methodologies of Classical Reception in Science Fiction." *Memorabilia Antonina.* 10 April 2006. At http://tonykeen.blogspot.com/2006/04/t-stands-for-tiberius-models-and.html. Accessed 24 August 2015.

Keen, Antony. 2015. "Mr. Lucian in Suburbia: Links Between the *True History* and *The First Men in the Moon.*" In *Classical Traditions in Science Fiction.* Eds. B. M. Rogers and B. E. Stevens. Oxford, UK: Oxford University Press. 105–120.

Kelly, Kathleen Coyne. 2012. "Disney's Medievalized Ecologies in *Snow White and the Seven Dwarfs* and *Sleeping Beauty.*" In *The Disney Middle*

Ages: A Fairy-Tale and Fantasy Past. Eds. T. Pugh and S. Aronstein. New York, NY: Palgrave. 189–207.

Kennedy, Patrick. 1891. *Legendary Fictions of the Irish Celts.* London: Macmillan and Co.

Kenney, E. J. 1990. *Apuleius: Cupid and Psyche.* Cambridge, UK: Cambridge University Press.

Kepple, Lawrence. 1976. "Arruns and the Death of Aeneas." *American Journal of Philology* 97.4.344–360.

Kermode, Frank. 1985. *Forms of Attention.* Chicago, IL: University of Chicago Press.

Kornfeld, John, and Laurie Prothro. 2009. "Comedy, Quest, and Community: Home and Family in Harry Potter." In *Critical Perspectives on Harry Potter.* Second edition. Ed. E. E. Heilman. New York, NY: Routledge. 121–137.

Kragelund, Aage. 1970. *Niels Klims underjordiske rejse 1741–1745.* Copenhagen: Gad.

Kranz, Gisbert. 1969. "Amor und Psyche: Metamorphose eines Mythos bei C. S. Lewis." *Arcadia* 4.285–299.

Kristeller, Paul Oskar. 1990. *Renaissance Thought and the Arts: Collected Essays.* Princeton, NJ: Princeton University Press.

Kroeber, Karl. 1998. *Artistry in Native American Myths.* Lincoln, NE: University of Nebraska Press.

Krueger, Frederic. 2014. *Pyramiden und Sternentore. Gedächtnisgeschichtliche Untersuchungen zur Ägyptenrezeption in* Stargate *und der zeitgenössischen Populärkultur.* Göttinger Orientforschungen 4. Ägypten 57. Göttingen: Harrassowitz.

Lampert, Jo. 2010. *Children's Fiction About 9/11: Ethnic, Heroic and National Identities.* London and New York, NY: Routledge.

Larsen, Kristine. 2011. "Sea Birds and Morning Stars." In *Tolkien and the Study of His Sources: Critical Essays.* Ed. J. Fisher. Jefferson, NC, and London: McFarland & Company. 69–83.

Le Guin, Ursula K. 1979. *The Language of the Night: Essays on Fantasy and Science Fiction.* New York, NY: G. P. Putnam's Sons.

Lebeck, A. 1971. *The* Oresteia: *A Study in Language and Structure.* Washington, DC: The Center for Hellenic Studies.

Lee, Peter, and Wm. Theodore de Bary, eds. 1997. *Sources of Korean Tradition. Volume 1.* New York, NY: Columbia University Press.

Lennon, Jack J. 2013. *Pollution and Religion in Ancient Rome.* New York, NY: Cambridge University Press.

Levy, G. 2001. "Heartache Before Harry." *Daily Mail.* 5 November 2001. 31.

Lewis, C. S. 1952. *The Voyage of the "Dawn Treader".* London: Geoffrey Bles.

Lewis, C. S. 1956. *Till We Have Faces: A Myth Retold.* New York, NY: Harcourt.

Lewis, C. S. 1964. *The Discarded Image: An Introduction to Medieval and Renaissance Literature.* Cambridge, UK: Cambridge University Press.

Lewis, C. S. 1966. *Of Other Worlds: Essays and Stories*. Ed.W. Hooper. New York, NY: Harcourt, Brace & World.

Lewis, C. S. 1969. "William Morris." In *Selected Literary Essays*. Cambridge, UK: Cambridge University Press. 219–231.

Lewis, C. S. 1979 [1950]. *The Lion, the Witch and the Wardrobe*. Harmondsworth, UK: Puffin.

Lewis, C. S. 1984. *Surprised by Joy: The Shape of My Early Life*. New York, NY: Harcourt Brace Jovanovich.

Lewis, C. S. 2001 [1956]. *The Last Battle*. London: HarperCollins.

Lewis, Hilda. 1939. *The Ship That Flew*. Oxford, UK: Oxford University Press.

Librán Moreno, Miryam. 2005. "Parallel Lives: The Sons of Denethor and the Sons of Telamon." *Tolkien Studies* 2.15–52.

Liddell, H. G., R. Scott, et al. 1925. *A Greek-English Lexicon*. Ninth edition. Oxford, UK: Clarendon Press.

Lindenberger, Herbert. 1990. *The History in Literature: On Value, Genre, Institutions*. New York, NY: Columbia University Press.

Lionarons, Joyce Tally. 1996. "*Beowulf*: Myth and Monsters." *English Studies* 77.1.1–14.

Lovatt, H. 2005. *Statius and Epic Games*. Oxford, UK: Oxford University Press.

Lovecraft, Howard P. 1965-1976. *Selected Letters, Vols. I-IV*. Eds A. Derleth and D. Wandrei. Sauk City, WI: Arkham House.

Lovecraft, Howard P. 1973. *Supernatural Horror in Literature*. New York, NY: Dover.

Lovecraft, Howard P. 1976. *Selected Letters V. 1934–1937*. Eds. A. Derleth and J. Turner. Sauk City, WI: Arkham House.

Lovecraft, Howard P. 2011. *The Complete Fiction*. New York, NY: Barnes & Noble.

Lowrie, Michèle. 2005. "Vergil and Founding Violence." *Cardozo Law Review* 27.2.945–976.

Lukács, Georg. 1971. *The Theory of the Novel*. Trans. A. Bostock. Cambridge, MA: MIT Press.

Lupack, Barbara T., and Alan Lupack. 2008. *Illustrating Camelot*. Woodbridge, Suffolk: D. S. Brewer.

Mackley, J. S. 2013. "The Shadow over Derleth. Disseminating the Mythos in *The Trail of Cthulhu*." In *New Critical Essays on H. P. Lovecraft*. Ed. D. Simmons. New York, NY: Palgrave Macmillan. 119–134.

Mallory, James, and D. Q. Adams. 1997. *Encyclopedia of Indo-European Culture*. London: Routledge.

Manlove, Colin N. 1975. *Modern Fantasy: Five Studies*. Cambridge, UK: Cambridge University Press.

Manlove, Colin. 1991. "'Caught Up into the Larger Pattern': Images and Narrative Structure in C. S. Lewis's Fiction." In *Word and Story in C. S. Lewis*. Eds. P. J. Schakel and C. A. Huttar. Columbia, MO: University of Missouri Press. 256–276.

Markus, D. 1997. "Transfiguring Heroism: Nisus and Euryalus in Statius' *Thebaid.*" *Vergilius* 43.56–62.

Marrou, H. I. 1956. *A History of Education in Antiquity.* Trans. G. Lamb. New York, NY: Sheed and Ward.

Marshall, C. W. 2015. "Odysseus and *The Infinite Horizon.*" In *Son of Classics and Comics.* Eds. G. A. Kovacs and C. W. Marshall. Oxford, UK: Oxford University Press. 3–31.

Martin, George R. R. 2003. *A Clash of Kings.* Paperback. London: Voyager (HarperCollins).

Martin, George R. R. 2011a. *A Game of Thrones.* Mass market paperback. New York, NY: Bantam Books.

Martin, George R. R. 2011b. *A Storm of Swords.* Mass market paperback. New York, NY: Bantam Books.

Martin, R. P. 1997. "Formulas and Speeches: The Usefulness of Parry's Method." In *Le style formulaire de l'épopée homérique et la théorie de l'oralité poétique: Hommage à Milman Parry.* Ed. F. Létoublon. Amsterdam: J. C. Gieben. 263–273.

Martin, Richard P. 2005. "Epic as Genre." In *A Companion to Ancient Epic.* Ed. J. M. Foley. Oxford, UK: Blackwell. 9–19.

Martindale, C. 1993. *Redeeming the Text: Latin Poetry and the Hermeneutics of Reception.* Cambridge, UK: Cambridge University Press.

Martindale, C., and R. F. Thomas, eds. 2006. *Classics and the Uses of Reception.* Malden, MA: Wiley-Blackwell.

Mathews, Richard. 1997. *Fantasy: The Liberation of Pure Imagination.* New York, NY: Twayne Publishers.

Matson, Lisa Dallape. 2010. *Re-Presentations of Dante Gabriel Rossetti: Portrayals in Fiction, Drama, Music, and Film.* Amherst, NY: Cambria Press.

McCloud, Scott. 1993. *Understanding Comics: The Invisible Art.* New York, NY: Harper Collins.

McCullough, Kelly. 2006. *WebMage.* New York, NY: Ace Books.

Medcalf, Stephen 1991. "Language and Self-Consciousness: The Making and Breaking of C. S. Lewis's Personae." In *Word and Story in C. S. Lewis.* Eds. P. J. Schakel and C. A. Huttar. Columbia, MO: University of Missouri Press. 109–144.

Mendell, C. 1951. "The Influence of the Epylion on the *Aeneid.*" *Yale Classical Studies* 12.216–19.

Mendelsohn, D. 2008. "A Little *Iliad.*" In *How Beautiful It Is and How Easily It Can Be Broken: Essays.* New York, NY: HarperCollins. 111–123.

Mendlesohn, Farah. 2002. "Crowning the King: Harry Potter and the Construction of Authority." In *The Ivory Tower and Harry Potter: Perspectives on a Literary Phenomenon.* Ed. L. A. Whited. Columbia, MO, and London: University of Missouri Press. 159–181.

Mendlesohn, Farah. 2008. *Rhetorics of Fantasy.* Middletown, CT: Wesleyan University Press.

Mendlesohn, Farah, and Edward James. 2009. *A Short History of Fantasy*. London: Middlesex University Press.

Menges, Jeff A. 2010. *Maidens, Monsters and Heroes: The Fantasy Illustrations of H. J. Ford*. New York, NY: Dover Publications.

Miéville, China. 2002. "Editorial Introduction." *Symposium: Marxism and Fantasy. Historical Materialism* 10.4.39–49.

Mikalson, Jon. D. 2005. *Ancient Greek Religion*. Malden, MA: Wiley-Blackwell.

Mills, A. 2009. "Harry Potter and the Horrors of the *Oresteia*." In *Critical Perspectives on Harry Potter*. Second edition. Ed. E. E. Heilman. New York, NY: Routledge. 243–255.

Mitchell-Smith, Ilan. 2012. "The United Princesses of America: Ethnic Diversity and Cultural Purity in Disney's Medieval Past." In *The Disney Middle Ages: A Fairy-Tale and Fantasy Past*. Eds. T. Pugh and S. Aronstein. New York, NY: Palgrave. 209–224.

Mollier, Jean-Yves, and Marie-Francoise Cachin. 2009. "A Continent of Texts: Europe 1800–1890." In *A Companion to the History of the Book*. Eds. S. Elliot and J. Rose. Chichester, UK: Wiley-Blackwell. 303–314.

Mommsen, Wolfgang, ed. 1992. *Max Weber: Gesamtausgabe. Bd. 17 Wissenshaft als Beruf*. Tübingen: Mohr Siebeck.

Montgomery, P. Andrew. 2000. "Classical Literature." In *Reading the Classics with C. S. Lewis*. Ed. T. L. Martin. Grand Rapids, MI: Baker Academic. 52–71.

Montiglio, S. 2013. *Love and Providence: Recognition in the Ancient Novel*. Oxford, UK and New York, NY: Oxford University Press.

Moritz, L. 1958. *Grain-Mills and Flour in Classical Antiquity*. Oxford, UK: Clarendon Press.

Morris, Ian. 1986. "The Use and Abuse of Homer." *Classical Antiquity* 5.1.81–136.

Morrison, Tracie Egan. 2013. "Disney Pulls Sexy Merida Makeover after Public Backlash." *Jezebel.com*. 15 May 2013. At http://jezebel.com/disney-pulls-sexy-merida-makeover-after-public-backlash-494274022. Accessed 29 November 2013.

Morse, Robert E. 1980. "Rings of Power in Plato and Tolkien." *Mythlore* 7.3.38.

Morse, Robert E. 1986. *Evocation of Virgil in Tolkien's Art*. Oak Park, IL: Bolchazy-Carducci.

Mosig, Dirk W. 1980. "H. P. Lovecraft. Myth-Maker." In *H. P. Lovecraft. Four Decades of Criticism*. Ed. S. T. Joshi. Athens, OH: Ohio University Press. 104–112.

Mosig, Dirk W. 2011. "H. P. Lovecraft. Myth-Maker." In *Dissecting Cthulhu: Essays on the Cthulhu Mythos*. Ed. S. T. Joshi. Lakeland, FL: Miskatonic River Press. 13–21.

Moul, Victoria. 2007. "Translation as Commentary? The Case of Ben Jonson's *Ars Poetica*." *Palimpsests* 20.59–77.

Murray, Will. 2011. "Behind the Mask of Nyarlathotep." In *Dissecting Cthulhu: Essays on the Cthulhu Mythos*. Ed. S. T. Joshi. Lakeland, FL: Miskatonic River Press. 131–138.

Myers, Doris T. 2004. *Bareface: A Guide to C. S. Lewis's Last Novel*. Columbia, MO: University of Missouri Press.

Mynors, R. A. B., ed. 1990 [1969]. *P. Vergili Maronis Opera*. Oxford, UK: Oxford University Press.

Nagy, Gergely. 2004. "Saving the Myths: The Recreation of Mythology in Plato and Tolkien." In *J. R. R. Tolkien and the Invention of Myth: A Reader*. Ed. J. Chance. Lexington, KY: University Press of Kentucky. 81–100.

Nagy, Gergely. 2005. "The Medievalist's Fiction." In *Tolkien's Modern Middle Ages*. Eds. J. Chance and A. K. Siewers. New York, NY: Palgrave Macmillan. 29–41.

Nagy, Gergely. 2006. "The 'Lost' Subject of Middle-Earth: Elements and Motifs of the Constitution of the Subject in the Figure of Gollum in *The Lord of the Rings*." *Tolkien Studies* 3.57–79.

Neils, Jenifer. 2003. "Children and Greek Religion." In *Coming of Age in Ancient Greece*. Eds. J. Neils and J. Oakley. New Haven, CT: Yale University Press. 139–161.

Nelson, Marie. 2008. "Time and J. R. R. Tolkien's 'Riddles in the Dark'." *Mythlore* 27.1/2.67–82.

Nesbit, E. 1979 [1907]. *The Enchanted Castle*. Harmondsworth, UK: Puffin.

Neuburg, Victor E. 1976. *Popular Literature: A History and Guide from the Beginning of Printing to the Year 1897*. London: Woburn.

Nicolson, Marjorie Hope. 1948. *Voyages to the Moon*. New York, NY: Macmillan.

Niedbala, Amanda M. 2006. "From Hades to Heaven: Greek Mythological Influence in C. S. Lewis's *The Silver Chair*." *Mythlore* 93/94.71–93.

Nikolajeva, Maria. 1988. *The Magic Code: The Use of Magical Patterns in Fantasy for Children*. Stockholm: Almqvist & Wiksell.

Obertino, James. 1993. "Moria and Hades: Underworld Journeys in Tolkien and Virgil." *Comparative Literature Studies* 30.2.153–169.

'Odiedragon.' 2005. *The Citadel: So Spake Martin*. 6 May 2005. At http://www.westeros.org/Citadel/SSM/Entry/To_Be_Continued_Chicago_IL_May_6_8/. Accessed 5 December 2013.

Ogden, D. 2013. *Dragons, Serpents, and Slayers in the Classical and Early Christian Worlds: A Sourcebook*. Oxford, UK: Oxford University Press.

Otis, Brooks. 1959. "Three Problems of *Aeneid* 6." *Transactions and Proceedings of the American Philological Association* 90.165–79.

Ott, Brian. 2008. "(Re)Framing Fear: Equipment for Living in a Post 9/11 World." In *Cylons in America: Critical Studies in* Battlestar Galactica. Eds. T. Potter and C. W. Marshall. New York, NY: Continuum. 13–26.

Oziewicz, Marek, and Daniel Hade. 2010. "The Marriage of Heaven and Hell? Philip Pullman, C. S. Lewis, and the Fantasy Tradition." *Mythlore* 28.39–54.

Page, D., ed. 1972. *Aeschyli Septem quae Supersunt Tragoedias*. Oxford, UK: Clarendon Press.

Paige, Nicholas. 2009. "Permanent Re-Enchantments." In *The Re-Enchantment of the World*. Eds. J. Landy and M. Saler. Stanford, CA: Stanford University Press. 159–180.

Papaïoannou, S. 2003. "Founder, Civilizer and Leader: Vergil's Evander and His Role in the Origins of Rome." *Mnemosyne* 56.6.680–702.

Parker, Robert. 1983. *Miasma: Pollution and Purification in Early Greek Religion.* Oxford, UK: Oxford University Press.

Pastoureau, Michel. 2011. *The Bear: History of a Fallen King.* Trans. G. Holoch. Cambridge, MA: Harvard University Press.

Paul, J. 2010. "Cinematic Receptions of Antiquity: The Current State of Play." *Classical Receptions Journal* 2.1.136–155.

Paul, J. 2013. *Film and the Classical Epic Tradition.* Oxford, UK: Oxford University Press.

Pavlock, B. 1990. *Eros, Imitation, and the Epic Tradition.* Ithaca, NY: Cornell University Press.

Peppin, Brigid. 1975. *Fantasy: The Golden Age of Fantastic Illustration.* New York, NY: Watson-Guptill.

Peretti, Daniel. 2007. "The Ogre Blinded and *The Lord of the Rings.*" *Mythlore* 25.3/4.133–143.

Pérez Diez, María del Carmen 2001. "*Till We Have Faces*: Viejas Historias, Nuevos Significados." In *Behind the Veil of Familiarity: C. S. Lewis (1898–1998).* Eds. M. Carretero González and E. Hidalgo Tenorio. Bern: Peter Lang. 327–341.

Perlman, Paula. 1983. "Plato *Laws* 833C–834D and the Bears of Brauron." *Greek, Roman, and Byzantine Studies* 24.115–130.

Petrini, M. 1997. *The Child and the Hero.* Ann Arbor: University of Michigan Press.

Petty, Anne. 2002. *One Ring to Bind them All: Tolkien's Mythology.* Tuscaloosa, AL: University of Alabama Press.

Phillips, Marie. 2008. *Gods Behaving Badly.* London: Vintage Books.

Pieri, Giuliana. 2012. "The Myth of Psyche in the Work of D'Annunzio and Burne-Jones." In *Text and Image in Modern European Culture.* Eds. N. Grigorian, T. Baldwin, and M. Rigaud-Drayton. West Lafayette, IN: Purdue University Press. 15–31.

Pietruszewski, Mandy. 2013. "Moral Ambiguity in *Percy Jackson and the Olympians.*" *Tor.com.* 16 September 2013. At http://www.tor.com/blogs/2013/09/moral-ambiguity-in-percy-jackson-and-the-olympians. Accessed 17 May 2014.

Podlecki, Anthony J. 2011. *The Early Greek Poets and Their Times.* Vancouver: UBC Press.

Podlecki, Anthony J., ed., with Introduction. 2005. *Aeschylus: Prometheus Bound.* Chippenham, UK: Aris and Phillips.

Pollman, K. 2001. "Statius' *Thebaid* and the Legacy of Vergil's *Aeneid.*" *Mnemosyne* 54.10–30.

Porter, James I. 2009. "Is Art Modern? Kristeller's 'Modern System of the Arts' Reconsidered." *British Journal of Aesthetics* 49.1.1–24.

Poulson, Christine. 1996. "Death and the Maiden: The Lady of Shalott and the Pre-Raphaelites." In *Re-Framing the Pre-Raphaelites: Historical and Theoretical Essays*. Ed. E. Harding. Brookfield, VT: Scolar Press. 173–194.

Praet, Stijn. 2011. "Reader Beware: Apuleius, Metafiction and the Literary Fairy Tale." In *Anti-Tales: The Uses of Disenchantment*. Eds. C. McAra and D. Calvin. Newcastle upon Tyne: Cambridge Scholars Publishing. 37–50.

Pratchett, Terry, and Neil Gaiman. 1990. *Good Omens*. London: Gollancz.

Pratchett, Terry. 2005. "Terry Pratchett Clarifies J. K. Rowling Remarks." From the *alt.fan.harry-potter newsgroup*. 2 August 2005. Archived on *Beyond Hogwarts*. http://www.beyondhogwarts.com/story.20050802.html. Accessed 5 September 2015.

Prettejohn, Elizabeth, ed. 2012a. *The Cambridge Companion to the Pre-Raphaelites*. Cambridge, UK: Cambridge University Press.

Prettejohn, Elizabeth. 2012b "The Painting of Dante Gabriel Rossetti." In *The Cambridge Companion to the Pre-Raphaelites*. Ed. E. Prettejohn. Cambridge, UK: Cambridge University Press. 103–115.

Price, Robert M. 2011. "Demythologizing Cthulhu." In *Dissecting Cthulhu: Essays on the Cthulhu Mythos*. Ed. S. T. Joshi. Lakeland, FL: Miskatonic River Press. 118–126.

Pringle, David. 2002. *Fantasy, The Definitive Illustrated Guide*. London: Carlton Books.

Propp, Vladimir. 1968 [1958]. *Morphology of the Folktale*. Trans. L. Scott. Second edition. Rev. and ed. L. A. Wagner. Austin, TX: University of Texas Press.

Pugh, Tison, and Susan Aronstein, eds. 2012. *The Disney Middle Ages: A Fairy-Tale and Fantasy Past*. New York, NY: Palgrave.

Pullman, Philip. 2003. "Why I Don't Believe in Ghosts." *The New York Times*. 31 October 2003. At http://www.nytimes.com/2003/10/31/opinion/31PULL.html. Accessed 2 August 2016.

Putnam, Michael C. J. 1995. *Virgil's Aeneid: Interpretation and Influence*. Chapel Hill, NC: The University of North Carolina Press.

Putnam, Michael C. J. 2011. *The Humanness of Heroes: Studies in the Conclusion of Vergil's Aeneid*. Amsterdam: Amsterdam University Press.

Quinn, K. 1968. *Virgil's Aeneid: A Critical Description*. Ann Arbor, MI: University of Michigan Press.

Quint, D. 1993. *Epic and Empire. Politics and Generic Form from Virgil to Milton*. Princeton, NJ: Princeton University Press.

Quint, D. 2001. "The Brothers of Sarpedon: Patterns of Homeric Imitation in *Aeneid* 10." *Materiali e discussioni per l'analisi dei testi classici* 47.35–66.

Raaflaub, Kurt A. 2005. "Epic and History." In *A Companion to Ancient Epic*. Ed. J. M. Foley. Oxford, UK: Blackwell. 55–70.

Rabkin, Eric. 1976. *The Fantastic in Literature*. Princeton, NJ: Princeton University Press.

Rae, Ian. 2008. *From Cohen to Carson: The Poet's Novel in Canada*. Montreal: McGill–Queen's University Press.

Raeburn, D., and O. Thomas, eds. 2011. *The Agamemnon of Aeschylus*. Oxford, UK: Oxford University Press.

'Ran.' 2005. "References and Homages." *Westeros: The A Song of Ice and Fire Domain*. At http://asoiaf.westeros.org/index.php/topic/784-references-and-homages. Accessed 4 December 2013.

Rateliff, John D. 2007. *The History of The Hobbit*. Boston and New York, NY: Houghton Mifflin.

Rea, Jennifer. 2008. *Legendary Rome: Myths, Monuments and Memory on the Palatine and Capitoline*. London: Duckworth Academic.

Rea, Jennifer. 2010. "*Pietas* and Post-Colonialism in Ursula K. Le Guin's *Lavinia*." *Classical Outlook* 87.4.126–131.

Reckford, Kenneth J. 1972. "Some Trees in Virgil and Tolkien." In *Perspectives of Roman Poetry*. Ed. G. K. Galinsky. Austin, TX: University of Texas Press. 57–92.

Reed, J. 2007. *Vergil's Gaze. Nation and Poetry in the Aeneid*. Princeton, NJ: Princeton University Press.

Reinhardt, Katja. 2008. ". . . von den allerbizarrsten Hieroglyphen. Ägyptische Motive bei H. P. Lovecraft." In *Miscellanea in honorem Wolfhart Westendorf*. Ed. C. Peust. Göttinger Miszellen Beihefte 3. Göttingen: Seminar für Ägyptologie und Koptologie der Universität Göttingen. 83–108.

Rich, Motoko. 2007. "Record First-Day Sales for Last 'Harry Potter' Book." *The New York Times*. 22 July 2007. At http://www.nytimes.com/2007/07/22/books/22cnd-potter.html. Accessed 24 August 2015.

Richter, Daniel. 2005. "Lives and Afterlives of Lucian of Samosata." *Arion* 13.1.75–100.

Riegl, Alois. 1982. "The Modern Cult of Monuments: Its Character and Its Origin." *Oppositions* 25.20–51.

Ringel, Faye. 2000. "Women Fantasists: In the Shadow of the Ring." In *J. R. R. Tolkien and His Literary Resonances: Views of Middle Earth*. Eds. G. Clark and D. Timmons. Westport, CT: Greenwood Press. 159–172.

Roberts, Adam. 2012. "Gothic and Horror Fiction." In *The Cambridge Companion to Fantasy Literature*. Eds. E. James and F. Mendlesohn. Cambridge, UK: Cambridge University Press. 21–36.

Rogers, Brett M. 2011. "Heroes Unlimited: The Theory of the Hero's Journey and the Limitation of the Superhero Myth." In *Classics and Comics*. Eds. G. Kovacs and C. W. Marshall. Oxford, UK: Oxford University Press. 73–86.

Rogers, Brett M. 2015. "Hybrids and Homecomings in the *Odyssey* and *Alien Resurrection*." In *Classical Traditions in Science Fiction*. Eds. B. M. Rogers and B. E. Stevens. Oxford, UK: Oxford University Press. 217–242.

Rogers, Brett M., and Benjamin Eldon Stevens, eds. 2015. *Classical Traditions in Science Fiction*. Oxford, UK: Oxford University Press.

Rogers, Brett M., and Benjamin Eldon Stevens. 2012. "Classical Receptions in Science Fiction." *Classical Receptions Journal* 4.1.127–147.

Rohde, Erwin. 1950. *Psyche: The Cult of Souls and Belief in Immortality Among the Greeks*. Eighth edition. Trans.W. B. Hillis. London: Routledge & Kegan Paul.

Rowling, J. K. 1997. *Harry Potter and the Sorcerer's Stone*. New York, NY: Arthur A. Levine Books.

Rowling, J. K. 1998a. *Harry Potter and the Chamber of Secrets*. New York, NY: Arthur A. Levine Books.

Rowling, J. K. 1998b. "What Was the Name of That Nymph Again? *or* Greek and Roman Studies Recalled." *Pegasus: Journal of the University of Exeter Department of Classics and Ancient History* 41.25–27.

Rowling, J. K. 2000. *Harry Potter and the Goblet of Fire*. New York, NY: Arthur A. Levine Books.

Rowling, J. K. 2003. *Harry Potter and the Order of the Phoenix*. New York, NY: Arthur A. Levine Books.

Rowling, J. K. 2005. *Harry Potter and the Half-Blood Prince*. New York, NY: Arthur A. Levine Books.

Rowling, J. K. 2007. *Harry Potter and the Deathly Hallows*. New York, NY: Arthur A. Levine Books.

Rowling, J. K. 2008. "The Fringe Benefits of Failure, and the Importance of Imagination." (Commencement Speech at Harvard University). *Harvard Gazette*. 5 June 2008. At http://news.harvard.edu/gazette/story/2008/06/text-of-j-k-rowling-speech. Accessed 24 August 2015.

Rowling, J. K. 2012. *The Casual Vacancy*. New York, NY: Little, Brown and Company.

Rubino, Carl. 2011. "Long Ago, But Not So Far Away: Another Look at *Star Wars* and the Ancient World." *Classical Outlook* 89.1.1–4.

Rudd, Niall. 1990. *Horace*: Epistles *Book II and* Ars Poetica. Cambridge, UK: Cambridge University Press.

Sabo, Deborah. 2007. "Archaeology and the Sense of History in J. R. R. Tolkien's Middle-earth." *Mythlore* 26.1/2.91–112.

Saler, Michael. 2012. *As If: Modern Enchantment and the Literary Prehistory of Virtual Reality*. Oxford, UK and New York, NY: Oxford University Press.

Sandner, David M. 2000. "'Joy Beyond the Walls of the World': The Secondary World-Making of J. R. R. Tolkien and C. S. Lewis." In *J. R. R. Tolkien and His Literary Resonances*. Eds. G. Clark and D. Timmons. Westport, CT and London: Greenwood Press. 133–146.

Sandner, David M., ed. 2004. *Fantastic Literature: A Critical Reader*. Westport, CT: Praeger.

Sapiens, P. [T. P. Wiseman]. 2002. "At Figulus: J. K. Rowling and the Ancient World." *Classical Outlook* 79.3.93–96.

Saxby, Henry Maurice. 1997. *Books in the Life of a Child: Bridges to Literature and Learning.* South Yarra, Victoria: MacMillan Australia.

Saxton, Benjamin. 2013. "J. R. R. Tolkien, Sub-Creation, and Theories of Authorship." *Mythlore* 31.3/4.47–59.

Schachter, A. 1990. "Policy, Cult, and the Placing of Greek Sanctuaries." In *Le Sanctuaire Grec: Huit exposés suivis de discussions.* Eds. A. Schachter and J. Bingen. Geneva: Fondation Hardt. 1–57.

Schakel, Peter J., ed. 1977. *The Longing for a Form: Essays on the Fiction of C. S. Lewis.* Kent, OH: Kent State University Press.

Schakel, Peter J. 1984. *Reason and Imagination in C. S. Lewis: A Study of* Till We Have Faces. Grand Rapids, MI: Wm. B. Eerdmans.

Schakel, Peter J. 2010. "*Till We Have Faces*." In *The Cambridge Companion to C. S. Lewis.* Eds. R. MacSwain and M. Ward. Cambridge, UK: Cambridge University Press. 281–293.

Schlam, C. 1970. "Platonica in the *Metamorphoses* of Apuleius." *Transactions of the American Philological Association* 101.477–487.

Schlam, C. 1992. *The* Metamorphoses *of Apuleius: On Making an Ass of Oneself.* Chapel Hill, NC: University of North Carolina Press.

Schlobin, Roger C. 2000. "The Monsters Are Talismans and Transgressions: Tolkien and *Sir Gawain and the Green Knight*." In *J. R. R. Tolkien and His Literary Resonances.* Eds. G. Clark and D. Timmons. Westport, CT, and London: Greenwood Press. 71–82.

Schlobin, Roger C., ed. 1982. *The Aesthetics of Fantasy Literature and Art.* Notre Dame, IN: University of Notre Dame Press.

Schmeling, Gareth L., ed. 1996. *The Novel in the Ancient World.* Vol. 159. London: Brill.

Scholes, Robert E. 2003. "Exploring the Great Divide: High and Low, Right and Left." *Narrative* 11.3.245–269.

Scholes, Robert E. 2006. *Paradoxy of Modernism.* New Haven, CT: Yale University Press.

Schulten, Adolf. 1952. "Pompaelo." In *Paulys Realencyclopädie der Classischen Altertumswissenschaft.* Stuttgart: Metzler.

Schweitzer, Darrell. 2001. "Lovecraft and Lord Dunsany." In *Discovering H. P. Lovecraft.* Ed. D. Schweitzer. Holicong, PA: Wildside Press. 72–87.

Scodel, Joshua. 2010. "Imitation and Mimesis." In *The Classical Tradition.* Eds. A. Grafton, G. W. Most, and S. Settis. Cambridge, UK: Harvard University Press. 472–475.

Scullion, Val, and Marion Treby. 2013. "Repressive Politics and Satire in E. T. A. Hoffmann's Fairy-tales, 'Little Zaches Acclaimed as Zinnober' and 'Master Flea.'" *Journal of Politics and Law* 6.3.133–145.

Seaford, R. 2003. "Tragic Tyranny." In *Popular Tyranny: Sovereignty and Its Discontents in Ancient Greece.* Ed. K. A. Morgan. Austin, TX: University of Texas Press. 95–115.

Senior, W. A. 2000. "Loss Eternal in J. R. R. Tolkien's Middle-earth." In *J. R. R. Tolkien and His Literary Resonances*. Eds. G. Clark and D. Timmons. Westport, CT, and London: Greenwood Press. 173–182.

Senior, W. A. 2012. "Quest Fantasies." In *The Cambridge Companion to Fantasy Literature*. Eds. E. James and F. Mendlesohn. Cambridge, UK: Cambridge University Press. 190–199.

Shay, J. 1994. *Achilles in Vietnam. Combat Trauma and the Undoing of Character.* New York, NY: Simon & Schuster.

Shelfer, Lochlan. 2011. "Crime and Punishment in the *Aeneid*: The Danaids and the Legal Context of Turnus' Death." *Classical Journal* 106.3.295–319.

Shippey, Tom. 2000. "Orcs, Wraiths, Wights: Tolkien's Images of Evil." In *J. R. R. Tolkien and His Literary Resonances*. Eds. G. Clark and D. Timmons. Westport, CT and London: Greenwood Press. 183–198.

Shippey, Tom. 2002. *J. R. R. Tolkien: Author of the Century*. Boston, MA: Mariner Books.

Shippey, Tom. 2003. *The Road to Middle-earth: How J. R. R. Tolkien Created a New Mythology*. Revised and expanded edition. Boston. MA: Houghton Mifflin.

Shorey, P., trans. 1969. *Plato: Plato in Twelve Volumes, Vols. 5 & 6*. Cambridge, MA: Harvard University Press.

Silver, Carole G. 1999. *Strange and Secret Peoples: Fairies and Victorian Consciousness*. New York, NY and Oxford, UK: Oxford University Press.

Simon, Erika. 1983. *Festivals of Attica: An Archaeological Commentary*. Madison, WI: University of Wisconsin Press.

Simonis, Annette. 2014. "Voyages mythiques et passages aux Enfers dans la littérature fantastique contemporaine: *Le Seigneur des Anneaux* et *À la croisée des mondes*." In *L'Antiquité dans l'imaginaire contemporain: Fantasy, science-fiction, fantastique*. Eds. M. Bost-Fiévet and S. Provini. Paris: Classiques Garnier. 241–252.

Simonson, Martin. 2008. *The Lord of the Rings and the Western Narrative Tradition*. Zurich and Jena: Walking Tree Publishers.

Skulnick, Rebecca, and Jesse Goodman. 2003. "The Civic Leadership of *Harry Potter*: Agency, Ritual, and Schooling." In *Harry Potter's World: Multidisciplinary Perspectives*. Ed. E. E. Heilman. New York, NY and London: RoutledgeFalmer. 261–277.

Slusser, Geroge, and Eric S. Rabkin. 1993. "Wars Old and New: The Changing Nature of Fictional Combat." In *Fights of Fancy: Armed Conflict in Science Fiction and Fantasy*. Eds. G. Slusser and E. S. Rabkin. Athens, GA: University of Georgia Press. 1–11.

Sly, Debbie. 2000. "Weaving Nets of Gloom: 'Darkness Profound' in Tolkien and Milton." In *J. R. R. Tolkien and His Literary Resonances*. Eds. G. Clark and D. Timmons. Westport, CT, and London: Greenwood Press. 109–119.

Small, Christopher. 1973. *Mary Shelley's Frankenstein: Tracing the Myth*. Pittsburgh, PA: University of Pittsburgh Press.

Smith, Alden. 2005. *The Primacy of Vision in Virgil's* Aeneid. Austin, TX: University of Texas.

Smith, Peter. 1980. *On the Hymn to Zeus in Aeschylus'* Agamemnon. American Classical Studies Vol. 5. Ann Arbor, MI: Edwards Brothers.

Smith, Steven. 2009. "Lucian's *True Story* and the Ethics of Empire." In *A Lucian for Our Times*. Ed. A. Bartley. Newcastle upon Tyne: Cambridge Scholars Publishing. 79–92.

Smuda, Susanne. 1997. *H. P. Lovecrafts Mythologie. "Bricolage" und Intertextualität—Erzählstrategien und ihre Wirkung.* Bielefeld: Aisthesis.

Solomon, J. 2013. "Film and Television." In *The Virgil Encyclopedia*. Eds. R. Thomas and J. Ziolokowski. Hoboken, NJ: Wiley. 484–485.

Sommerstein, Alan H. 1980. *Aeschylus:* Eumenides. Cambridge, UK, and New York, NY: Cambridge University Press.

Sourvinou-Inwood, Christiane. 1988. *Studies in Girls' Transitions: Aspects of the* Arkteia *and Age Representation in Attic Iconography.* Athens: Kardamitsa.

Spencer, Richard. 2015. *Harry Potter and the Classical World: Greek and Roman Allusions in J. K. Rowling's Modern Epic.* Jefferson, NC: McFarland & Company.

Starr, Nathan Comfort. 1968. *C. S. Lewis's* Till We Have Faces: *Introduction and Commentary.* New York, NY: Seabury Press.

Stein, Ruth M. 1968. "The Changing Styles in Dragons—from Fáfnir to Smaug." *Elementary English* 45.2.179–183 and 189.

Stevens, Benjamin Eldon. 2014. "The Sensory Media." In *Antiquity*, vol. 1 of *A Cultural History of the Senses*. Ed. J. Toner. London and New York, NY: Bloomsbury Academic. 209–226.

Stevens, Benjamin Eldon. 2015a. "Virgil in Jules Verne's *Journey to the Center of the Earth*." In *Classical Traditions in Science Fiction*. Eds. B. M. Rogers and B. E. Stevens. Oxford, UK: Oxford University Press. 75–104.

Stevens, Benjamin Eldon. 2015b. "Plato's Republic in the Age of Ultron?" *Public Books*. 5 May 2015. At http://www.publicbooks.org/fiction/platos-republic-in-the-age-of-ultron. Accessed 3 January 2016.

Struck, Peter T. 2004. *Birth of the Symbol: Ancient Readers at the Limits of Their Texts.* Princeton, NJ: Princeton University Press.

Styers, Randall. 2004. *Making Magic: Religion, Magic, and Science in the Modern World.* Oxford, UK: Oxford University Press.

Suarez, Michael. 2003. "Swift's Satire and Parody." In *The Cambridge Companion to Jonathan Swift*. Ed. Christopher Fox. Cambridge, UK: Cambridge University Press. 112–127.

Sullivan, C. W. 1996. "High Fantasy." In *International Companion Encyclopedia of Children's Literature*. Ed. P. Hunt. London: Routledge. 300–310.

Sullivan, C. W. 2000. "Tolkien the Bard: His Tale Grew in the Telling." In *J. R. R. Tolkien and His Literary Resonances: Views of Middle Earth*. Eds. G. Clark and D. Timmons. Westport, CT: Greenwood Press. 11–20.

Surtees, Virginia. 1971. *The Paintings and Drawings of Dante Gabriel Rossetti (1828–1882): A Catalogue Raisonné*. Oxford, UK: Clarendon Press.

Suvin, Darko. 1979. *Metamorphoses of Science Fiction: On the Poetics and History of a Literary Genre*. New Haven, CT: Yale University Press.

Swift, Jonathan. 2008. *Gulliver's Travels*. Ed. C. Rawson. Oxford, UK: Oxford University Press.

Syson, Antonia. 2013. *Fama and Fiction in Vergil's Aeneid*. Columbus, OH: The Ohio State University Press.

Takacs, Stacy. 2009. "Monsters, Monsters Everywhere: Spooky TV and the Politics of Fear in Post-9/11 America." *Science Fiction Studies* 36.1.1–20.

Talairach-Vielmas, Laurence. 2014. *Fairy Tales, Natural History and Victorian Culture*. New York, NY: Palgrave Macmillan.

Tarrant, R., ed. 2012. *Virgil: Aeneid Book XII*. Cambridge, UK: Cambridge University Press.

Taub, Deborah J., and Heather L. Servaty-Seib. 2009. "Controversial Content: Is *Harry Potter* Harmful to Children?" In *Critical Perspectives on Harry Potter*. Second edition. Ed. E. E. Heilman. New York, NY: Routledge. 13–32.

Teverson, Andrew. 2013. *Fairy Tale*. London and New York, NY: The New Critical Idiom, Routledge.

Thomas, Richard. 2001. *Virgil and the Augustan Reception*. Cambridge, UK: Cambridge University

Thompson, Raymond H. 1982. "Modern Fantasy and Medieval Romance." In *The Aesthetics of Fantasy Literature and Art*. Ed. R. C. Schlobin. Notre Dame, IN: University of Notre Dame Press. 211–225.

Tierney, Richard L. 2001. "The Derleth Mythos." In *Discovering H. P. Lovecraft*. Ed. D. Schweitzer. Holicong. 52–54.

Tierney, Richard L. 2011. "The Derleth Mythos." In *Dissecting Cthulhu: Essays on the Cthulhu Mythos*. Ed. S. T. Joshi. Lakeland, FL: Miskatonic River Press. 10–12.

Timmerman, John H. 1978. "Fantasy Literature's Evocative Power," *Christian Century* 17.533–537.

Timmerman, John H. 1983. *Other Worlds: The Fantasy Genre*. Bowling Green, OH: Bowling Green University Popular Press.

Todorov, Tzvetan. 1970. *Introduction à la littérature fantastique*. Paris: Éditions du Seuil.

Todorov, Tzvetan. 1973. *The Fantastic: A Structural Approach to a Literary Genre*. Trans. Richard Howard. Cleveland, OH: Press of Case Western Reserve University.

Todorov, Tzvetan. 1975. *The Fantastic: A Structural Approach to a Literary Genre*. Intro. Robert Scholes. Trans. R. Howard. Ithaca, NY, and New York, NY: Cornell University Press.

Tolkien, J. R. R. 1965. *Tree and Leaf*. Cambridge, MA: Houghton Mifflin.

Tolkien, J. R. R. 1966. *The Tolkien Reader*. New York, NY: Ballantine Books.

Tolkien, J. R. R. 1980 [1936]. Beowulf: *The Monsters and the Critics*. London: Arden Library.

Tolkien, J. R. R. 1984. *The Monsters and the Critics and Other Essays*. Ed. C. Tolkien. Boston, MA: Houghton Mifflin.

Tolkien, J. R. R. 1988. *The Annotated Hobbit: The Hobbit, or, There and Back Again*. Introduction and notes by D. A. Anderson. Boston, MA, and New York, NY: Houghton Mifflin

Tolkien, J. R. R. 1994. *Poems and Stories*. Boston, MA: Houghton Mifflin.

Tolkien, J. R. R. 2001 [1977]. *The Silmarillion*. Ed. C. Tolkien. Boston, MA, and New York, NY: Houghton Mifflin.

Tolkien, J. R. R. 2012a [1954–1955]. *The Lord of the Rings*. Boston, MA, and New York, NY: Mariner Books.

Tolkien, J. R. R. 2012b [1937]. *The Hobbit*. Reissue edition. Boston, MA, and New York, NY: Mariner Books.

Too, Y. L. 2001. "Legal Instruction in Classical Athens." In *Education in Greek and Roman Antiquity*. Ed. Y. L. Too. Leiden: Brill. 111–132.

Travers, P. L. 1943. *Mary Poppins Opens the Door*. London: Peter Davies.

Travers, P. L. 1982. *Mary Poppins in Cherry Tree Lane*. London: Collins.

Travers, P. L. 1984 [1934]. *Mary Poppins*. Harmondsworth, UK: Puffin.

Tucker, Martin 1957. "The Face of Love." *Chicago Review* 11:92–94.

van Mal-Maeder, D. 1997. "Lector Intende: Laeteberis. The Enigma of the Last Book of Apuleius' *Metamorphoses*." In *Groningen Colloquia on the Novel VII*. Eds. H. Hofmann and M. Zimmerman. Groningen: Forsten. 87–118.

van Straten, Folkert. 1990. "Votives and Votaries in Greek Sanctuaries." In *Le Sanctuaire Grec: Huit exposés suivis de discussions*. Eds. A. Schachter and J. Bingen. Geneva: Fondation Hardt. 247–284.

Vickers, Brian, ed. 1974–1981. *Shakespeare: The Critical Heritage*. 6 vols. London: Routledge & Kegan Paul.

Vonnegut, Kurt. 1974. *Wampeters, Foma, and Grandfallons (Opinions)*. New York, NY: Dell.

Wall, Barbara. 1991. *The Narrator's Voice: The Dilemma of Children's Literature*. London: Macmillan.

Walter, Jochen. 2012. "Zur Rolle des Lateinischen in der Phantastik. Harry Potter, Aventurien und Lovecraft." In *Fremde Welten. Wege und Räume der Fantastik im 21. Jahrhundert*. Eds. L. Schmeink and H.-H. Müller. Berlin: De Gruyter. 103–121.

Ward, M. 2008. *Planet Narnia: The Seven Heavens and the Imagination of C. S. Lewis*. Oxford, UK: Oxford University Press.

Warner, Marina. 2008. *Phantasmagoria: Spirit Visions, Metaphors, and Media into the Twenty-first Century*. Oxford, UK: Oxford University Press.

Watkins, Calvert. 1995. *How to Kill a Dragon: Aspects of Indo-European Poetics*. Oxford, UK: Oxford University Press.

Watson, Ben. 2002. "Fantasy and Judgment: Adorno, Burroughs, Tolkien." *Historical Materialism* 10.4.213–238.

Weiner, Jesse. 2015. "Lucretius, Lucan, and Mary Shelley's *Frankenstein.*" In *Classical Traditions in Science Fiction.* Eds. B. M. Rogers and B. E. Stevens. Oxford, UK: Oxford University Press. 46–74.

Wellek, Rene. 1963. *Concepts of Criticism.* Ed. S. G. Nicholas. New Haven, CT: Yale University Press.

West, M. L. 1974. *Studies in Greek Elegy and Iambus.* Berlin and New York, NY: De Gruyter.

West, M. L. 1989. *Iambi et Elegi Graeci.* Oxford, UK: Oxford University Press.

West, M. L. 1990. "The Bough and the Gate." In *Oxford Readings in Vergil's* Aeneid. Ed. S. J. Harrison. Oxford, UK: Clarendon Press. 224–238.

West, M. L. 1997. *The East Face of Helicon: West Asiatic Elements in Greek Poetry and Myth.* Oxford, UK: Clarendon Press.

Westfahl, G., G. Slusser, and E. S. Rabkin, eds. 1996. *Foods of the Gods: Eating and the Eaten in Fantasy and Science Fiction.* Athens, GA: University of Georgia Press.

Wetzel, George T. 1980. "The Cthulhu Mythos. A Study." In *H. P. Lovecraft. Four Decades of Criticism.* Ed. S. T. Joshi. Athens, OH: Ohio University Press. 79–95.

Wetzel, George T. 2001. "Genesis of the Cthulhu Mythos." In *Discovering H. P. Lovecraft.* Ed. D. Schweitzer. Holicong, PA: Wildside Press. 54–62.

White, Michael. 2001. *Tolkien: A Biography.* London: Little, Brown.

Whited, L. A., ed. 2002. *The Ivory Tower and Harry Potter: Perspectives on a Literary Phenomenon.* Columbia, MO, and London: University of Missouri Press.

Whittington, L. 2010. "Vergil's Nisus and Euryalus and the Language of Self-Sacrifice in *Paradise Lost.*" *Modern Philology* 107.4.588–606.

Wildman, Stephen, and John Christian. 1998. *Edward Burne-Jones: Victorian Artist-Dreamer.* New York, NY: The Metropolitan Museum of Art.

Williams, Mary Frances. 2003. "Lawgivers and the Rule of the Law in the *Aeneid.*" *Studies in Latin Literature and Roman History* 11.208–243.

Williams, R. D. 1967. "The Purpose of the *Aeneid.*" *Antichthon* 1.29–41.

Wimsatt, W., and M. C. Beardsley. 1946. "The Intentional Fallacy." *Sewanee Review* 54.468–488.

Winkle, J. 2013. "Necessary Roughness: Plato's *Phaedrus* and Apuleius' *Metamorphoses.*" *Ancient Narrative* 11.1–39.

Winkler, J. 1985. *Auctor and Actor: A Narratological Reading of Apuleius's* The Golden Ass. Berkeley, CA: University of California Press.

Winkler, M. 2007. *From Homer's Iliad to Hollywood Epic.* Malden, MA, and Oxford, UK: Wiley-Blackwell.

Wippermann, Katharina. 2009. "The Cupid and Psyche Series for 1 Palace Green." In *Edward Burne-Jones: The Earthly Paradise.* English edition. Ed.

Staatsgalerie Stuttgart, Kunstmuseum Bern. Catalogue: Christofer Conrad and Annabel Zettel. Trans. P. Aston and B. Saunders. Ostfildern, Germany: Hatje Cantz. 84–95.

Wise, Jennifer. 1998. *Dionysus Writes: The Invention of Theatre in Ancient Greece.* Ithaca, NY: Cornell University Press.

Wittgenstein, Ludwig. 1958. *Philosophical Investigations.* Translated by G. E. M. Anscombe. Third edition. Upper Saddle River, NJ: Prentice Hall.

Wolfe, Gary K. 2012. "Fantasy from Dryden to Dunsany." In *The Cambridge Companion to Fantasy Literature.* Eds. E. James and F. Mendlesohn. Cambridge, UK: Cambridge University Press. 7–20.

Woolf, Virginia. 1928. *Mr. Bennett and Mrs. Brown.* London: Leonard and Virginia Woolf at the Hogarth Press.

Wootton, David. 1999. *The Illustrators: The British Art of Illustration, 1800–1999.* London: Chris Beetles.

Wright, John C. 2005. *Orphans of Chaos.* New York, NY: Tor Fantasy.

Wynne Jones, Diana. 1977 [1975]. *The Eight Days of Luke.* Harmondsworth, UK: Puffin Books.

Wynne Jones, Diana. 2007. *The Game.* London: HarperCollins.

Zahorski, Kenneth J., and Robert H. Boyer. 1982. "The Secondary Worlds of High Fantasy." In *The Aesthetics of Fantasy Literature and Art.* Ed. R. C. Schlobin. Notre Dame, IN: University of Notre Dame Press. 56–81.

Zaleski, P., and C. Zaleski. 2015. *The Fellowship: The Literary Lives of the Inklings.* New York, NY: Farrar, Straus and Giroux.

Zeeman, Nicolette. 1996. "The Schools Give a License to Poets." In *Criticism and Dissent in the Middle Ages.* Ed. R. Copeland. Cambridge, UK: Cambridge University Press. 151–180.

Zeitlin, F. 1978. "The Dynamics of Misogyny: Myth and Mythmaking in the *Oresteia*." *Arethusa* 11.149–81. Revised as Chap. 3. in Zeitlin, F. 1995. *Playing the Other.* Chicago, IL: University of Chicago Press. 87–119.

Zipes, Jack. 2012. *Fairy Tales and the Art of Subversion.* London and New York, NY: Routledge.

Index